The Arena Concert

Music, Media and Mass Entertainment

Edited by

**ROBERT EDGAR,
KIRSTY FAIRCLOUGH-ISAACS,
BENJAMIN HALLIGAN
NICOLA SPELMAN**

Bloomsb
An imprint of Bloc

B L O O M S B U R Y
NEW YORK · LONDON · OXFORD · NEW DELHI · SYDNEY

Bloomsbury Academic

An imprint of Bloomsbury Publishing Inc

1385 Broadway	50 Bedford Square
New York	London
NY 10018	WC1B 3DP
USA	UK

www.bloomsbury.com

BLOOMSBURY and the Diana logo are trademarks of Bloomsbury Publishing Plc

First published 2015

Library of Congress Cataloging-in-Publication Data
The arena concert : music, media and mass entertainment / edited by Robert Edgar,
Kirsty Fairclough-Isaacs, Benjamin Halligan and Nicola Spelman.
pages cm
Includes bibliographical references and index.
ISBN 978-1-62892-554-8 (hardback : alk. paper) –
ISBN 978-1-62892-555-5 (pbk. : alk. paper)   1. Rock concerts–Social aspects.
I. Edgar-Hunt, Robert.   II. Fairclough-Isaacs, Kirsty.   III. Halligan, Benjamin.
IV. Spelman, Nicola.
ML3918.R63A74   2015
781.64078–dc23
2015022932

ISBN: HB: 978-1-6289-2554-8
PB: 978-1-6289-2555-5
ePUB: 978-1-6289-2557-9
ePDF: 978-1-6289-2556-2

Typeset by Newgen Knowledge Works (P) Ltd., Chennai, India
Printed and bound in the United States of America

CONTENTS

ILLUSTRATIONS

Figures

Tables

ACKNOWLEDGEMENTS

Our thanks to our colleagues and students at the universities of Salford and York St. John. And thanks to those who have offered advice and support across the preparation of this book: Tom Attah, Paul Butler, Mark Duffett, Michael Goddard, Sunil Manghani, Laura Niebling, Matt Osborne (at Real World Studios), Gerald Scarfe, Carla Schriever, Jon Stewart and Julia Tulloh. Thanks to George McKay for inviting contributors to this volume to his AHRC-funded symposium 'Carnivalising Pop: Music Festival Cultures' (13 June 2014, University of Salford) to road test their chapters in development. Jon Stewart would like to thank Bryan Leitch for his generosity of spirit.

Thanks to Ally Jane Grossan, and her team at Bloomsbury, especially for her wisdom in picking out the arenas idea from the increasingly quixotic projects pitched over lunch in Spinningfield's Neighbour restaurant in Manchester, in April 2013.

Kirsty would like to thank Gordon and Evan for their love and support. Rob would like to thank Jenny, Fred and Stewart for financing his office, Agatha for sitting on the manuscript and Meredith for being a shining light. Ben would like to thank Ellie for her support and patience, especially during a Girls Aloud gig. Nicola would like to thank Stan, Jake and Mia for their love and good humour.

In fond memory of Sheila Whiteley (1941–2015).

CONTRIBUTORS

Mark Duffett is Senior Lecturer in Media and Cultural Studies at the University of Chester. His research interest is primarily in fandom and the dynamics of popular music audiences. Mark is the author of *Understanding Fandom* (Bloomsbury, 2013), has recently edited two special editions of the journal *Popular Music and Society* and is currently writing a book on Elvis Presley for Equinox Press. Mark also contributed a co-written chapter on the public image of Phil Spector to *The Music Documentary: Acid Rock to Electropop* (ed. Edgar, Fairclough-Isaacs, Halligan; Routledge, 2013).

Robert Edgar is Senior Lecturer in the Faculty of Arts at York St John University, where he teaches creative writing and film and television. He has research interests in postmodernism and cinema, popular music, theories of comedy, screenwriting and directing. Publications include *Screenwriting* (AVA, 2009) and *Directing Fiction* (AVA, 2010) and most recently the second edition of *The Language of Film* (Bloomsbury, 2015). Recent research projects include work on Hitchcock and Herrmann, contemporary television and *Top Gear*. Robert was a co-editor of *The Music Documentary: Acid Rock to Electropop* (Routledge, 2013).

Kirsty Fairclough-Isaacs is Senior Lecturer in Media and Performance and Associate Director (International) in the School of Arts and Media at the University of Salford. Kirsty researches in the fields of celebrity, popular culture and gender and is a member of the editorial board of the journal *Celebrity Studies* (Taylor & Francis). Kirsty was a co-editor of *The Music Documentary: Acid Rock to Electropop* (Routledge, 2013) and is the author of the forthcoming *Beyoncé, Feminism and Celebrity Culture* (I. B. Tauris, 2016).

Neil Fox is Course Coordinator for Film Studies at Falmouth University. His research interests include film education and music documentaries, and he writes for *Clash* and *The Big Picture* in the UK and *Bright Wall/Dark Room* in the United States, among other publications. Neil has written and produced award-winning short films and directed and curated for international film festivals. His most recent short film, *It's Natural to Be Afraid*, played at over thirty-five festivals, winning seven awards, including prizes given by Paul Greengrass, William H. Macy and Elijah Wood.

Benjamin Halligan is the Director of Postgraduate Research Studies for the College of Arts and Social Sciences, University of Salford. Publications include *Michael Reeves* (Manchester University Press, 2003) and *Desires for Reality: Radicalism and Revolution in Western European Film* (Berghahn Books, 2015). Co-edited collections include *Mark E. Smith and The Fall: Art, Music and Politics* (Ashgate, 2010), *Reverberations: The Philosophy, Aesthetics and Politics of Noise* (Continuum, 2012), *Resonances: Noise and Contemporary Music* (Bloomsbury, 2013) and *The Music Documentary: Acid Rock to Electropop* (Routledge, 2013).

Erich Hertz is Associate Professor and chair of the English Department at Siena College in New York. He is the author of several essays on Adorno, Benjamin, Surrealism and the ways that critical and aesthetic theory provide insights into thinking about topics ranging from music documentaries to turntabalism. He is the co-editor of the *Write in Tune: Contemporary Music and Fiction* (Bloomsbury, 2014) and recent chapters have appeared in *Reverberations: The Philosophy, Aesthetics and Politics of Noise* (ed. Goddard, Halligan, Hegarty; Continuum, 2012) and *The Music Documentary: Acid Rock to Electropop* (ed. Edgar, Fairclough-Isaacs, Halligan; Routledge, 2013).

Kevin Holm-Hudson, Associate Professor of Music Theory, is Coordinator of the Division of Music Theory and Composition at the University of Kentucky. He is the author of *Genesis and The Lamb Lies Down on Broadway* (Ashgate, 2008) and editor of *Progressive Rock Reconsidered* (Routledge, 2002). His articles on popular music have appeared in a number of publications including *Popular Music and Society, Music Theory Online, Genre,* and *American Music.* His research interests include progressive rock, musical signification, the work of Lithuanian composer-painter M. K. Ciurlionis, and – more recently – the music of Karlheinz Stockhausen.

Kimi Kärki hold a PhD in Cultural History from the University of Turku and works as a Coordinator in the International Institute for Popular Culture (IIPC). Kimi has mostly published on the history of popular music, especially live music in spectacular environments, and is co-editor of *Peter Gabriel: From Genesis to Growing Up* (Ashgate, 2012).

Robert Kronenburg, PhD RIBA, is an architect and holds the Roscoe Chair of Architecture at Liverpool School of Architecture, University of Liverpool. His research engages with innovative forms of architectural design, film and popular music. His books include *Live Architecture: Venues, Stages and Arenas for Popular Music* (Routledge, 2012) and *Architecture in Motion: The History of Portable Building* (Routledge, 2013). Robert is a past Fulbright Fellow and has been a Visiting Fellow at St Johns College, Oxford University. He curated the major exhibition *Portable Architecture* at the Royal Institute of British Architects and was curatorial advisor for Vitra Design Museum's exhibition *Living in Motion*. Robert was recently awarded a British Academy/Leverhulme Trust Senior Research Fellowship for work on the project *The Architectural History of Popular Music Performance*. Weblinks: Live Architecture (https://www. liv.ac.uk/architecture/research/live/), Portable Architecture (https://www. liv.ac.uk/architecture/research/portable/), Blog (http://robkronenburg. wordpress.com).

Sunil Manghani is Reader in Critical and Cultural Theory and deputy director of Doctoral Research at Winchester School of Art, University of Southampton. He teaches and writes on various aspects of critical theory, visual arts and image studies. He is the author of *Image Studies: Theory and Practice* (Routledge, 2013), *Image Critique and the Fall of the Berlin Wall* (Intellect, 2008) and editor of *Images: A Reader* (Sage, 2006), and *Images: Critical and Primary Sources* (Bloomsbury, 2013). Manghani also contributed a chapter on Kylie Minogue to *The Music Documentary: Acid Rock to Electropop* (ed. Edgar, Fairclough-Isaacs, Halligan; Routledge, 2013).

Jos Mulder is Lecturer in Sound at Murdoch University, Perth. His research is situated on the crossroads of music performance, sound technology, culture and society, and with a focus on the use of electronic amplification at concerts. Before embarking on an academic career, Jos worked as a live sound engineer for fifteen years, after studying music and sound engineering at the Royal Conservatory, The Hague in The Netherlands, his country of origin.

Alice O'Grady is Associate Professor in Applied Performance in the School of Performance and Cultural Industries, University of Leeds. With a background in education, Alice's expertise lies in using performance as a means of promoting social agency and engagement. Her research adopts autoethnographic methodologies to explore modes of participation, play and performance, especially within the contexts of popular music festivals and underground club culture. She is a member of the editorial team of *Dancecult: Journal of Electronic Dance Music Culture*.

Jeffrey Roessner is Dean of Arts and Humanities and Professor of English at Mercyhurst University, where he leads classes in contemporary literature and creative writing. His interests include cultural studies, music and historical fiction. He is co-editor of *Write in Tune: Contemporary Music in Fiction* (Bloomsbury, 2014), and has published on Peter Ackroyd, Angela Carter, Jeanette Winterson, The Beatles, rock mockumentaries, the post-confessional lyricism of R. E. M., and protest music in the wake of 9/11, among other topics. Along with his academic writing, Jeffrey has authored a book on songwriting: *Creative Guitar: Writing and Playing Rock Songs with Originality*.

Peter Smith is Emeritus Professor at the University of Sunderland. He has published over 250 papers, and spoken at conferences throughout the world. Peter has supervised, and examined, over 100 doctoral candidates, is a Fellow of the British Computer Society, a Chartered Engineer and a Fellow of the Higher Education Academy. His publications cover topics in science, engineering and education, and in recent years he has started to write about popular music, which is a great personal interest. Peter's *The PhD Viva* was published by Palgrave Macmillan in 2014. Peter has attended over 2,000 concerts, contributed a chapter to *The Rolling Stones: Sociological Perspectives* (Lexington Books, 2013) and writes a daily blog on his concert experiences (http://vintagerock.wordpress.com/).

Nicola Spelman is Senior Lecturer in Music at the University of Salford where she teaches composition, musicology and professional practice. She is Course Leader for the BA Music programme Popular Music and Recording, and her research interests surround issues of representation within popular music. Nicola's publications include *Popular Music & the Myths of Madness* (Ashgate, 2012) and *Resonances: Noise and Contemporary Music* (Bloomsbury, 2013; co-edited with Michael Goddard and Benjamin Halligan).

Jon Stewart is Senior Academic Lecturer and Course Leader of the Event Management and Music Business degrees at the British and Irish Modern Music Institute (BIMM) in Brighton. During his time as founder, guitarist and co-songwriter for the gold and platinum album selling Britpop band Sleeper (1993–1998) Jon played at arena and stadium venues in the UK (including Wembley Arena and the LG Arena, Birmingham), the United States (Mercer Arena Seattle, Bronco Bowl Dallas, Universal Amphitheatre, Los Angeles) and across Europe and Japan.

Lukasz Swiatek is a PhD candidate in the Department of Media and Communications, in the Faculty of Arts and Social Sciences, University of Sydney. His doctoral research examines awards and prizes from the perspective of media and communications, focusing on the Nobel Prizes in particular. Lukasz has taught on a range of undergraduate and postgraduate courses, covering media globalization, public relations and international and global studies. In 2015, Lukasz was appointed Faculty Postgraduate Teaching Fellow.

Emma Webster received her PhD from the University of Glasgow. Her thesis, 'Promoting Live Music: a Behind-the-Scenes Ethnography', was the first account of what live music promoters do, and the contexts within which they work. The research focused on the live music scenes of Glasgow, Bristol and Sheffield, and involved participant observation at venues such as arenas, clubs, festivals and pubs, and extensive interviews with live music workers and audiences. Prior to her return to academia, Emma worked for eight years in the music industries in a variety of roles and across a variety of genres (including opera, 'world music', musical theatre, acid techno and digital distribution). Emma is a co-founder of the Live Music Exchange, an online hub for anyone interested in live music research (www.livemusicexchange.org).

INTRODUCTION

'A Stately Pleasure-Dome'?

*Robert Edgar, Kirsty Fairclough-Isaacs,
Benjamin Halligan and Nicola Spelman*

The popularity of the arena concert, especially since the turn of the millennium, evidences a radical reshaping of the landscape of popular music, and the meeting of a demand for the actual presence of the global superstar in the global suburbs. In both instances, the old models of music dissemination and ownership are seemingly no longer enough for the music industry: the consumer wants to possess the song in a variety of material and immaterial ways (from revived vinyl to cloud archives accessible across a variety of digital platforms and devices) and wants to encounter the singer (i.e. wants celebrity and access). The concert no longer seems to operate in relation to the promotion of music (costly tours as a way of shifting records for the touring group), but becomes the prime generator of revenue in itself. Thus the music, which is now effectively free, becomes little more than a flyer for the impending, and at times impossibly expensive to attend, arena concert. Global concert promoters have taken on the role once reserved for artist's managers. And arena concerts seem to wield supernatural powers in the consumer landscape: the dead are raised to perform again (via holograms or video walls the size of houses), the deity-like superstar makes an actual appearance, long since disbanded groups are reformed to play again and time travel (at least back to the stars and music of yesteryear, now back on stage) becomes a possibility.

This development is one that prompts a reversal of a noted anecdote about the way in which music bends, and possibly breaks, in order to reach a wider audience (or, rather, expand its market share). If Bob Dylan's infamous 'electrification' of folk music resulted in an irate gig-goer publicly denouncing his former idol with the cry of 'Judas!' in Manchester's Free Trade Hall in 1966 (see Kershaw 2005), then the arena concert raises the accusation of 'Messiah!' It is difficult not to sympathize with those who baulk at the, at times, undeserved grandeur and unchecked hubris of the arena performer, taking to the stage in front of the massed tens of thousands, and those who express bemusement or anger at the way a couple of good-to-middling arena tickets for a global act can now amount to the same price as a reasonable second-hand car.[1] An additional edge of concern can be detected too, in the liberal commentariat, and critical writing: a distaste for the entire enterprise, which seems to blend a Messianic aspiration to the Sermon on the Mount with visions of totalitarian uniformity, in the name of a WASP-y whiteness and maleness of arena artists. There is too much branding, too much hubbub, too much waiting around, rubbish strewn everywhere and not enough spontaneity: that short step from 'mass entertainment' to 'mass produced', as emblematic of a trans-Atlantic monoculture (which is then routed through the Global South), is nowhere more apparent. A mass directive of 'be entertained' seems to be in operation (for Žižek: 'today's superego injunction to enjoy'; 2009, 188), obscuring the vulgar imposition of a dominant culture upon another; 'thus', for Negri, 'Pink Floyd alights in Piazza San Marco [15 July 1989], and anyone against this idea is accused of being against modernity and against the masses having fun' (2013, 182). And the event itself – for many (and for Mulder and O'Grady, in this volume) – can, in fact, be a misery. The sprawling and rustic experiences of music and mass entertainment, from festivals at Woodstock to Glastonbury, Burning Man to the Primavera Sound and beyond, seem to champion and accommodate individuality rather than impose a battery-hen style regimentation on the gig-goer. The danger of the former was limited to bad drug trips, of the latter to bad travel trips (panic attacks in crowded public transport, lost or stolen property, hours of waiting to exit a car park). If the former have been theorized as temporary autonomous zones, the latter seem more like state-sanctioned bread-and-circuses: the state's own pleasure-dome, to paraphrase Coleridge. But the festival tradition now, following the lead of its Baby Boomer demographic, has gone through a process of, to use Zweig's term, 'embourgeoisement'. In the British experience, expect to find wine tasting and cheese-making, picnic areas and organic food boutiques, theatre and ballet companies, television celebrities, supermodels and politicians (as accommodated in upmarket yurts) and the 'spoken word' (stand-up comedians and poets, television chefs and cultural commentators and academics in conversation).[2] And don't expect to find, at least at the time of writing, much in the way of female performers (see Vincent 2014 and Pollard 2015).

The arena audience, like the stadium audience of its immediate prehistory, seems positively working class in comparison, and is slotted into place in the arena rather than being free to explore the grounds of the festival. The arena concert seems to be a largely consumer environment rather than a cultural environment. And a distaste for such mass entertainment in the arena context, on the basis of class, could be said to go some way to account for the lack of critical attention paid to the arena concert. It is a lack that has been detrimental to academic fields associated with Popular Music. One is tempted to note that even Lenin, in exile, visited theatres in the Parisian suburbs to experience the working class audience, and was rewarded for his excursions by encounters with the dynamism of that audience; see Krupskaya (1970, 177). The writing about arena concerts from our contributors has invariably drawn on fields that remain a minority concern in Popular Music, most notably Celebrity Studies, New Media, Theology and Film Studies, in order to assemble critical frameworks with which to analyse the arena concert, and renew and revise engagements with extant tropes of theorization around feminism, post-feminism, semiotics, cultural capital, performance, aura, ethnography, phenomenology and fandoms. In many cases, a confrontation with the arena concert has revealed methodological lacunae, prompting such interdisciplinary excursions on the part of our contributing authors as they seek to account for a new age of Gesamtkunstwerk, and the intersections of music, media and mass entertainment. And the co-editors, with Stewart's invaluable work, have been prompted to 'drill down' even further, to hear from designers and musicians involved in arena concerts, and to hear from attendees too, reflecting on decades of gig-going, or experiencing the arena phenomenon for the first time. Empirical research into arena attendance currently remains outside the academy and in the realms of promotion and marketing, where it seems to inform Byzantine interconnections between certain credit cards and 'privilege tickets' presales, primary and secondary ticketing monopolies, legalized spamming and legal actions against touting, hotel package deals and cuts of car-parking fees, and a 'soft' surveillance via social media (allowing the ticket purchaser to find out which of his or her social media contacts are also booked to attend, and where they will be seated, in return for allowing data mining by unknown parties).

What has emerged from our research is arresting: the reconfiguring of the musical landscape, and concomitant with that new forms and genres of media (the arena concert film, and the centrality of the social media 'capture' of the star as validating individual fandom, for example), as orientated around the reappearance (i.e. the actual materialization) of the star. In this way, liveness is placed at the centre of this new musical landscape: we are to renew our acquaintance with the music by being actually present as it is performed. Indeed, this is seemingly the only way to be truly acquainted with the music: post-CD, it is no longer enough to find oneself listening to a certain singer (perhaps as selected and automatically played via an iTunes algorithm) and happening to like it. How does one then spend money, buying that liking? Only, really, through the concert ticket. And if the singer is one of a global standing, only the arena will accommodate him or her and their troupe and entourage. And if the singer is one of an historical standing, the arena exerts a global centrifugal force, pulling the icons into your orbit, to perform for you (and your parents or grandparents, or children or grandchildren).

Authenticity and intimacy are concerns that occur time and again in the current volume. And with this preferential option for liveness comes a return of ideas of musical pilgrimage (to the nearest capital cities, or even abroad, to see unique performances, as a trip to New York to, say, Birdland in the 1950s, or CBGBs in the 1970s, once functioned) or mass ethnomusicology (as if everyone with a Facebook or Tumblr account comes to ape Alan Lomax's field recordings). Aura (to use Benjamin's term; 1936) is restored: the importance of 'being there', of being in the presence of a one-off happening, as tied-up with a sense of selfhood and self-worth ('I can't miss this!'), of family (cross-generational concert attendance, the big gig as birthday treat and centrepiece of a holiday), of personal history (seeing the loved bands of one's youth) and of a validation, public and private, of one's taste and fandom. The essential contexts for these developments are the copyright wars of the late 1990s, and the eventual subsuming of file-sharing sites such as Napster, and the reorganization of music consumption for a post-'Top 40' age, and one in which consumable items became marginalized, and the financial crisis of 2007–2008, with resultant danger to all forms of charging pastimes. The latter would seem to have impacted on key classes (and, indeed, ticket prices for arena concerts only seemed to rise again once the crisis had been declared over) and even, during times of austerity, nation states. As Svenonius notes, in relation to 'the diminishing meaning of the group', the digital era has robbed the artist of the opportunities of considered presentation: 'groups are stripped of their packaging, robbed of identity, and reduced to being a few squeals leaking from an iPod' (Svenonius 2012, 237).[3] These things however return in the arena context: album cover design has been subsumed into video projection design, and a media archaeology suddenly comes into play: 'old' footage of stars is incorporated into (even duetting with) the star now, performing on stage. Kärki notes this of Roger Waters. And Kylie Minogue integrated footage from her 1980s pop videos into her stage show for the 2014 Kiss Me Once tour. We get the performer, then and now, and together, and inclusively, we look back at earlier incarnations of the performer. We have grown older together, and with this music as the central core of reminiscence, and the measure of the differences that time passing has caused for performer and audience member. (Or, for the younger audience member, who post-dates such footage: a wallow in retro, or the mythical '1980s'.)

At the same time, while the design of the arena concert seems to be about closing the space between performer and audience member on the grounds of intimacy there is still, paradoxically, a need to maintain a distance, on the grounds of celebrity. Ultimately, intimacy is denied by the social standing of the performer/s and thus closing the space is about providing the perception that we are getting closer to the artist. The confessional qualities that are used by some performers, as Halligan notes, create the illusion of a personal connection with a deified star while the space will always maintain that distance.[4] For early tours of Pink Floyd's *The Wall*, as Karki argues, the group declined to play along with the creation of such a perception, with audience reactions that ranged from puzzled to alienated.

The matter of intimacy and of being there is one that seems to have prompted a U-turn in relation to the development of arena technology across the 1990s. Cunningham's history of 'the rock concert industry' of that decade is one that tracks the progression of video screens (portability, size, higher density resolution images, tighter pixel formations and so on) to the point where they are able to offer an expanded view of the concert, and so cater for ever-bigger audiences in a satisfactory way. Cunningham notes, at the outset, that gig-goers were not that keen on the arena experience per se, unlike band promoters (1999, 16). A decade and a half later, such screens with live feeds are seen as detracting from the authenticity of experience, tempting the wandering eye to the mediatized and so second hand rather than actual event, and so these screens are increasingly marginalized – pushed further away from the performance areas themselves. The nature of concert performance then comes to be remade: how to perform for such an enormous crowd, how to get close to them, even how to play and what it means for an individual to find him or herself at the centre of that night's entertainment for so very many people. (The latter is a concern in Stewart's interview chapter 'Hello Cleveland . . . !', as balanced by Edgar's collaborative 'Rocking Around Watford': the view from the audience perspective.) The struggles across the 1990s for technological innovation have been, of course, forgotten, and their victories since long taken for granted. In terms of conceptualizing the arena concert now, the Prog Rock and Glam periods suddenly re-emerge as of more use: a taste for show, an attempt to be 'larger than life', the live concert as narrative and event and the performer (as with David Bowie/Ziggy Stardust) as so much more than 'just' a performer. Recent studies of both genres have incorporated concerns with spectacle as a major consideration: the 'theatricalization of rock' for Auslander (2006b), in respect to Bowie, and 'performance and visuality' for Hegarty and Halliwell (2011). But, this time around, technology enables rather than (as with the challengingly ambitious Genesis tour of *The Lamb Lies Down on Broadway* of 1974–1975; see Holm-Hudson 2008) hinders and frustrates.

The pressures are such that the arena concert seems to function as a trauma for a group: it possesses the potential to throw their abilities into such sharp relief as to engender self-doubt. The performance needs to be good enough not only to meet and match expectations (the 'Mach Scau' directive that Roessner examines, and achieving that 'eventness' that O'Grady notes), but to withstand the forensic scrutiny that is technologically enabled in the arena environment, and its afterlife in digital film releases and fan-made videos. Perhaps the trauma is the matter of a direct exposure to one's own iconographic status, in which the actual person, rather than icon, will always be found wanting: an encountering of one's own myth. Perhaps it is a matter of self-blame: the expectations that The Beatles seem to have heard in the screaming around Shea Stadium could only ever have been frustrated by their performance. And the enormity of the making of such mass entertainment, as understood and shouldered by the worthy group, is such that it requires a technological circumnavigation of the very laws of physics: light travels faster than sound (as many who attended arena concerts in the early 2000s would have experienced, in the disorientation of seeing before hearing), requiring a PA system capable of transmitting to all places at the same time. To deliver a bad show can be career-ending, especially when that fan-made footage cannot be 'deleted' from the internet.

The arena concert presents itself as a new pole of aspiration for mass entertainment, and at the epicentre of technological developments and new trends in digital and social media. And, while long established groups such as The Rolling Stones and Fleetwood Mac have shifted effortlessly into the arena context, which has itself allowed for the idea of a never-ending world tour, some stand-up comedians seem to have expressed nervousness at the phenomenon. Perhaps the space is simply too big? Perhaps it is only the arena that is now the true index of success, trailing all other venues (from pub backrooms to opera houses) in its wake? In 2014 this seemed to have emerged as a constant preoccupation: Simon Amstell noted that the very premise of his material precluded arena concerts ('I was at a silent retreat in Thailand, and . . . '); Stewart Lee noted that his coming superstardom would be predicated on growing the intelligent element of his audience, not naturally given over to laughing out loud, as inevitably then resulting in arenas full of silent audience members; and David O'Doherty fantasized about his imminent global superstardom for which arenas would be insufficient, so that he will need to deploy a loudspeaker from a hot air balloon to broadcast his observational comedy over each city in turn.[5] The problem seems to be that, as Edgar observes, the arena effectively auto-validates the performer: their presence on the arena stage indicates an a priori fame, so that the arena and performer are mutually indexical. Previously, stepping out into the stadium or arena had to be earned, and even then (as Roessner and Duffett find in the case of The Beatles in 1965) is not without danger. This new, postmodern ontology is one that seems to ignore, if necessary, traditions of senses of artistic worth: worth is bluntly recalibrated to cash value. For Hewison, writing about the monetization of 'creative Britain', this tension is embodied in Damien Hirst's 2007 work *For The Love of God*, with which 'the audacity of the piece lay not just in the glittering power of the object . . . but in the game that was being played with the concept of value' (2014, 151). *For The Love of God*, a platinum cast of an eighteenth-century skull, entirely covered in diamonds (with only the teeth of the unwitting donor remaining) was eventually apparently sold for US$74.3 million/£50 million. The experience of seeing this skull was the experience of getting to see it, and the process of seeing it, and then to have seen it and being able to state as much.[6] Could it be, as Benjamin wrote of the Parisian World Exhibitions of the 1800s, merely 'the enthronement of the commodity and the glitter of distraction around it'? (Benjamin 1999, 165). The ghost's stare of the skull of *For The Love of God* defied the viewer, aligning one's eyes with the skull's empty eye sockets, to declare this an inflated price-tag, in respect to the item's status as a bona fide objet d'art. What, exactly, are we admiring?

Tellingly, the blingy skull rematerialized in the arena context, shortly after: Minogue, for her X tour of 2008–2009, sang 'Like a Drug' while perched on a giant variant of *For The Love of God*, which appeared out of the dark and flew out across the stage, between mobile video walls on which were projected 3D body-mapping images, in the grass-green pixel-light colour of a stock exchange LED display. The skull hovered over the dancers for the next song, 'Slow', for which it was eventually recast as a spooky disco ball.

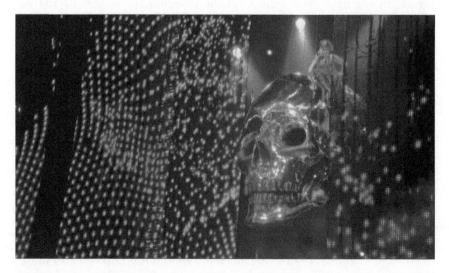

FIGURE 0.1 Kylie Minogue via Damien Hirst, for the X tour, as lit by Bryan Leitch; from *Kylie X 2008* (William Baker/Marcus Viner 2008).

Hirst's skull, akin to 'an alchemical object: a death's-head sublimed (as alchemists traditionally put it) out of base organic matter and into the stuff of wealth and grandeur' is understood in terms of hubris by Brian Dillon (2012, 29), in respect to misplaced hopes of transcending mortality, and living on forever. As Kylie and her team know, only their works will endure beyond death. But these are works that are now, in the arena context (and with its concomitant new genre of media, as Edgar argues: the arena concert film), imbued with a superabundance of life: everyone in the arena, in that moment, attuned to the astonishing stroboscopic EDM/Trance outro of 'Slow' (which closes with Kylie dancer-less and alone on the stage). And with the life and being there of this moment flooding out simultaneously across social media platforms (via images, texts, videos, Tweets): X as the central transmitter to the world outside the arena walls. Such 'being there' becomes, as Hertz argues, a way that the individual organizes, and curates, the experience and the memories of the arena concert.

The ambition of the arena event, which strikes home in moments such as 'Slow' (as experienced live), actually recalls another, and earlier, Hirst piece, *A Thousand Years* (1990), in which maggots take the role of carats. Here, in a large glass case with crackling insect-o-cuter, a severed cow's head in a pool of blood is set upon by flies and maggots. Lifecycles play out before our eyes in this grim aquarium: flies are born, hatch, gorge, fuck and are fried. Hirst's work embodies, rather than represents, life. The liveness of the arena concert is of a magnitude that seems propelled to push beyond the straight liveness of a finite stretch of performance (in Auslander's term; 2008). Rather, arena liveness seems to need to be the arc of life itself. Halligan notes the tendency for singers to address life-issues from the stage (especially illnesses), to make declarations that teeter on full-blown existential crises and to make the concert not just a rendering of the album du jour but of the entirety of their oeuvre. In terms of narrative and drama, meeting a myriad expectations, justifying the cost of attendance, filling the cathedral-sized space above the singer and the football pitches-sized space in front of the singer, what else will do? Such questions seem to have been in the air during the 1970s, and with the upscaling of popular music events in the wake of Woodstock in 1969 and similar festivals. Glam Rock and Prog Rock both sought to bring theatricality into play in response, as apparent in our chapters from Holm-Hudson and Kärki. This move was often dismissed at the time as hubristic and excessive, identified with the consolidation of a rock star aristocracy or Public School amateur dramatics (as with Genesis), and then understood as the central matter against which punk (and its performed authenticity) reacted. If this history is extended in the sense of the reaction against, to take in emergent rap and hip-hop cultures in the United States, and the appropriation and remaking/squatting of urban spaces (the warehouse, the disused factory, the basement), or British reggae and dub cultures in the 1970s and the use of sound systems in public spaces, then the arena concert seems to be on the horizon in terms of these new formations of mass music consumption. This is that process of transformation described by Kronenburg as 'from shed to venue'. The arena concert does not offer a picaresque experience, of walking around the site of a musical happening, but an enveloping, communal experience across a vast space, as arranged around a central performance, and so includes such elements of post-punk cultures in its prehistory too. And arenas are occasionally given over to electronic dance events, with a DJ area or platform, and the full use of the sound and lighting capabilities of the venue. A further series of parallels suggest themselves: between the opera house and conservatoire. However, the current volume does not aim to assemble a history of the arena concert but, rather, to engage with it as a contemporary phenomenon.

Such communalism is the very essence of the arena concert, despite an experience that (as O'Grady argues) seems to actively work against, and frustrate, or at least limit or curtail, communal potential. X, unlike *For The Love of God*, requires collective possession. The arena event is for and of all, not just a small consortium of anonymous buyers (as with Hirst's skull) and not (or, at least, rarely or only occasionally) a few select individuals (as with the oligarch or bloodied-hands dictator with funds to hire the global superstar for a private function).[7] This sense of collective possession seems to now be driving the development of technologies associated with the arena concert experience, as with Coldplay's 'Xylobands', as discussed here by Stewart, which cast everyone in the light show, or as with the filming of a Beastie Boys concert, as discussed here by Fox, in which everyone comes to be a film-maker. And with possession comes a sense of being part of that event: of being there, and so being part of the grand narrative of a certain band, and finding one's place in a gigography, and reaching back to touch the hand of those who had seen this band decades ago. The mythology is available for the new intake. Led Zeppelin's 2007 concert at the London O2 Arena (the Ahmet Ertegun Tribute Concert), as discussed by Smith, enticingly began with a choice vintage news report, played on the above-stage video screen, about a coming 1973 gig in Florida's Tampa Stadium.[8] Thus those there in 2007 were invited to feel a spiritual kinship to those who had once been there, in 1973. And such collective possession overcomes ontological problems associated with the 'show' rather than 'performance' aspect of arena concerts: mediation via live-feed and crash-edited video screens, and faked singing (i.e. lip-syncing), which would otherwise diminish a sense of liveness, are often no hindrance to buying-into the event. In some respects, then, the role of the singer can at times be regarded as aligning more to that of the DJ: a curation of work, rabble-rousing, sequenced music, shouted commands, 'fronting' rather than performing – in short, channelling and reflecting the audience.

The crowd seems to will the event to happen. This can be heard, and physically felt, in those electric seconds when the arena is plunged into darkness, but before the performer appears, in the roar of tens of thousands all around you.

Defining the Arena Concert

In terms of formulating a definition, our first consideration was to differentiate between the arena concert and the stadium concert. The temptation is to claim that the arena looks to mounting a show as a pole of aspiration, and the stadium looks to the performance. So the arena concert *may* be a matter of theatricality and preparation while the stadium concert *could* be more typically a matter of authenticity and spontaneity. However, such a clear divide is one that is beset by current examples with one foot in each camp, or the tour that freely moves between the two (albeit, as with X, with some theatrical down-scaling for stadia). This divide may, however, emerge as a more clearly appropriate demarcation in the years to come. For the moment, we offer a three-point definition, drawn up in collaboration with the contributors to this volume:

1. Enclosure

Our definition of the arena looks primarily to architecture: an enclosed space (i.e. under a roof) that can hold a few tens of thousands of people, and not an open space (in the manner of an outdoor festival) or a temporarily re-purposed open-air stadium (although the historical origins of the arena concert seem to begin in this way).

This enclosure is essential to our definition since it allows for the enveloping of the audience in the bubble of the 'total art' of the arena concert – an enveloping, or even surrounding, that is underpinned and facilitated by technology, and social media and participation. This then is not merely a 'big gig', somewhere in the distance, which an audience member can walk towards or away from, as they choose. The experience of the arena gig is often one of immobilization: to stay in your seat.

2. Enhancement

The stadium concert is one that is usually given over to a performance of live music to a mass audience. An arena concert seems to meet an assumed need to deliver much more than (or something somewhat different from, or an addition to) 'just' a performance of live music. The arena concert moves towards a 'show'.

The stadium concert has an established historical precedent and form, centred on the idea of a performance of live music. The arena concert remains in flux and development as it continues to strive to deliver that 'much more', via an ever further enhanced show. This looks to choreography, cabaret, design, theatricality, fashion, confetti, glitter and new media (even if these things are not unique to the arena concert itself). The arena concert may be placed in a continuum with historical moments in pop history that have favoured the 'show' over the 'performance': the idea of a social 'event' over a notable musical performance (Beatlemania), multimedia environments for live music (Warhol's Exploding Plastic Inevitable, and liquid lightshows), the theatrical aspects or 'excesses' of Prog Rock, the showmanship of Glam and even the nightclub-calibrated technologies (lighting, videos) associated with electronic dance music.

For the arena show, the music may be only one facet. Indeed, music may even be partly or wholly mimed rather than performed live. (This is not to say, however, that the arena concert need be, or often is, anything more than a relatively straight performance.)

3. Space

The arena concert therefore works to overcome distance, and disconnection between the audience and distant performers, by working to fill that vast enclosed space with the show. Stadium concerts have certainly incorporated such strategies, but typically privilege the sense of a performance area and the performance of music. Praxes of intimacy, and/or bombast, can be identified as dominant aesthetic/design strategies in terms of conceptualizing and putting on an arena concert.

Notes

1   Indeed, pop culture in the immediate wake of 1968 assembled its own morality tales concerning individuals who were granted their dreams of, or sold their souls for, stardom and the price exacted in the wretchedness that followed. This 'welcome to the machine' strand of ennui can be found on albums by Pink Floyd (*Wish You Were Here*, 1974 and *The Wall*, 1979) and Roxy Music (*Country Life*, 1974), is anticipated in the film *Privilege* (Peter Watkins, 1967) and then becomes full-blown for *Ciao! Manhattan* (John Palmer and David Weisman, 1972), *Stardust* (Michael Apted, 1974), *Tommy* (Ken Russell, 1975) and *The Man Who Fell to Earth* (Nicholas Roeg, 1976), and with encores in *Superstar: The Karen Carpenter Story* and *Velvet Goldmine* (Todd Haynes, 1988 and 1998 respectively). Such a theme of decadence and going-to-seed on the part of former stars was a preoccupation of the 1970s paparazzi too; see Burgess, Angeli and Dousset (1980).

2 For Summer 2014: 'Let's Rock Leeds', in addition to VIP 'unrestricted views'
   of the stage, offered a '[c]overed and heated marquee beautifully decorated
   with flowers and candles' and 'posh toilets' that were 'regularly serviced with
   attendants!' Green Man offered 'yoga, massage & spa'. The Big Feastival occurs
   on the organic farm of Blur's Alex James, with sponsorship from Renault cars.
   Camp Bestival featured a lactation area ('Breastival mother and baby chill-out'),
   'airstreams' and 'gypsy caravans' and Festival No 6's adverts even included
   the line 'You are cordially invited .. . .' A more satisfactory line of development
   has been traced between countercultural festival cultures/psychedelia and rave
   cultures (see Halligan on the 'Second Summer of Love' 2013b, 47–51), and
   squatting and the establishment and use of 'temporary autonomous zones'
   (although the resultant urban renewal around squatting and culture has
   dampened the appetite for legal/police action to reclaim such areas; see Aguilera
   2013, 222–225). For a full and definitive engagement with the radical history
   and contemporary cultures of music festivals, see McKay (2015).
3 The current vinyl revival, in part fetishistic, in part curating/inheriting the
   analogue formats that once represented, almost entirely, 'popular music', can
   be understood as an element of backlash against this immateriality.
4 The co-editors have resisted the temptation to pay the sizeable additional
   fees for a pre-show 'meet and greet' ticket for an arena concert, but feel it
   is unlikely that such a meeting would extend to levels of actual intimacy, as
   associated with extended conversations, shared personal concerns, swapping
   telephone numbers and so on.
5 These routines were featured in the following tours: To Be Free (Amstell),
   A Room with a Stew (Lee) and David O'Doherty Has Checked Everything
   (O'Doherty). On the other hand, comedian Peter Kay, in the Manchester Arena
   for The Tour That Doesn't Tour Tour (2010–2011), offered an ironic embrace
   of arena concert aesthetics: LED screens, glitter cannons, rising stages and the
   like.
6 For this co-author of the Introduction, this then was queuing in the Turbine
   Hall of the London Tate Modern for the Damien Hirst retrospective of 2012,
   being ushered into a small, darkened room with seemingly black velvet
   wallpaper (as if now trapped in the case in which a diamond ring is kept rather
   than entering an inner sanctum), the respectful silence that seemed to descend
   on those in the room and the jarring feeling of being in the abstract non-
   presence of money. It was, as Martin Amis had understood in relation to neo-
   liberalism and artlessness, deregulation and self-determination, an encounter
   with money's promise and crassness, its power and crudity, its self-governance:
   'It's money's fault' (Amis 1984, 45). The £50 million bought an item of 8,601
   diamonds, weighing in at a total of 1,106.18 carats.
7 This list of shame includes at least one artist discussed in the current volume,
   Beyoncé; see McBain (2013).
8 The news report can be seen in the concert film *Celebration Day* (Dick
   Carruthers, 2012). The opening song, after this report, was 'Good Times, Bad
   Times', which now seemed to nostalgically address the decades of the lifespan
   of the group (and its best of times, and the worse of times) for all present:
   'In the days of my youth / I was told what it means to be a man, / Now I've
   reached that age / I've tried to do all those things the best I can.'

PART ONE

Prehistories

CHAPTER ONE

From 'Mach Schau' to Mock Show: The Beatles, Shea Stadium and Rock Spectacle

Jeffrey Roessner

As The Beatles nervously helicoptered over Shea stadium before their concert on 15 August 1965, the opening date of their second US tour, they were stunned by the enormous crowd awaiting them and equally dazzled by the thousands of flashing camera bulbs. They were originally scheduled to arrive dramatically at the show itself by copter – something they had done for at least one previous outdoor performance – but safety concerns meant that they instead landed at the nearby World's Fair building and then were shuttled via Wells Fargo armoured car to the stadium. The literal approach to the show fairly well captures the extreme contrasts of their lives at this point. Touring was not tourism, as the band suffered a fairly merciless captivity on the road, trapped in the claustrophobic spaces of hotel rooms, cars and airplanes, and everywhere besieged by hysterical, clawing fans. But those suffocating spaces only represent half of the extremes they endured. Starting with large venues on the 1964 world tour, they would be propelled suddenly from their cramped quarters into the middle of a howling vortex, a vast expanse of space and volume that was the rock stadium show.

As in so many areas of rock music, The Beatles pioneered the massive stadium show, establishing a pattern hewed to by virtually every major band that came after. At this point in popular music history, the details all had to be sorted out, from handling the volume of ticket sales to establishing a sound system (inadequate though it was for the Shea concert) and attending to serious crowd control. In terms of numbers, Shea was a pop music concert of firsts and bests: largest audience (55,600), largest overall take ($304,000), largest fee for a band ($160,000) (Lewisohn 1992, 199). The concert was even filmed – a prescient move that resulted in the first concert film by a rock band. But amid all of these record-setting details and the sense of culmination the concert represents, it also has a sense of finality. Despite the exuberance generated by the mass of screaming fans, this stadium show embodied the contradictions exposed by The Beatles' success. Even as they heralded a new age of monumental live rock performance, they were nearly finished with it.

In retrospect, The Beatles' touring career seems remarkably compressed, and thus stunningly intense. Their first proper international tour began with dates in Sweden in October 1963, and they arrived in America to begin the famed invasion on 9 February 1964 – a visit that included their legendary first appearance on the Ed Sullivan Show and concerts at Washington Coliseum and Carnegie Hall. Their final performance occurred at Candlestick Park in San Francisco on 29 August 1966, marking the end of a career as international performing artists that lasted just under three years. No other band before or since has created such a formidable legacy in such a short span on the touring stage. In this chronology, the first Shea stadium show stands at the exact mid-point of their three official US tours, which began in August of 1964 and ended in August of 1966. This timeline appears too neatly balanced, however, and it obscures the show's significance. The concert didn't so much mark a new, sustainable level of success for the group as it was a dazzling climax followed by a fairly abrupt denouement.

The audacious plan to stage the Shea concert was conceived by New York impresario Sid Bernstein. Months before The Beatles' first visit to the United States, Bernstein had angled to book the band into Carnegie Hall, a bravura move that paid off handsomely as their success crested with the 'I Want to Hold Your Hand' single. In 1965, Bernstein had an even bigger coup in mind: a stadium show several times larger in magnitude than any that had been seen before by fans of pop music. It would be a triumphant moment for The Beatles and for New York – if he could sell the tickets. The idea for the show must have struck Beatles' manager Brian Epstein as at least a bit of a gamble, given that Bernstein sealed the deal by agreeing to buy any unsold tickets (see Schwensen 2014, 41). Fiercely protective of 'the boys' and ever-mindful of their image, Epstein had been reluctant to have The Beatles play in less than sold-out venues. By the 1965 tour, their momentum had mitigated the risks, though Epstein would not book them consistently into such enormous spaces for another year.

At the show itself, despite the enormous efforts to plan and stage an event of such magnitude, The Beatles apparently never considered deviating from the norm for their performances at the time. After multiple warm-up acts, they played a short set comprised of just twelve numbers.

TABLE 1.1 Songs performed at Shea

Song	US Release Date	UK Release Date
'Twist and Shout'	2 Mar. 1964	22 Mar. 1963
'She's a Woman'	23 Nov. 1964	27 Nov. 1964
'I Feel Fine'	23 Nov. 1964	27 Nov. 1964
'Dizzy Miss Lizzy'	13 Aug. 1965	6 Aug. 1965
'Ticket to Ride'	9 Apr. 1965	9 Apr. 1965
'Everybody's Trying to Be My Baby'	15 Dec. 1964	4 Dec. 1964
'Can't Buy Me Love'	16 Mar. 1964	20 Mar. 1964
'Baby's in Black'	15 Dec. 1964	4 Dec. 1964
'Act Naturally'	16 Sept. 1965	6 Aug. 1965
'A Hard Day's Night'	26 June 1964	10 July 1964
'Help!'	19 July 1965	23 July 1965
'I'm Down'	19 July 1965	23 July 1965

The song choice here represents chestnuts of their repertoire ('Twist and Shout' and 'Dizzy Miss Lizzy'), recent singles ('Ticket to Ride' and 'Help!') and, as always, vocal spotlights for George ('Everybody's Trying to Be My Baby') and Ringo ('Act Naturally'). The entire affair lasted all of thirty-seven minutes – which seems ridiculously short by contemporary standards, but which was routine for them (Schwensen 2014, 181).

Despite its brevity, the set-list was neither dated nor musically constraining. Nine of the songs had been released within the previous year, with five of them alone from 1965. The only surprises here for the fans would have been 'Dizzy Miss Lizzy', which had just come out on the US *Help!* album, and 'Act Naturally', which had not been released in the United States until a month later.[1] So as of the late summer of '65, although they had shown remarkable ingenuity as songwriters and were beginning to emerge as studio craftsmen, The Beatles hadn't yet fully exceeded their capacity to play their material live. The first stop upon arrival in the United States was the Ed Sullivan show, where they taped performances of six songs, all part of the Shea set-list, with one notable exception: McCartney did a solo presentation of 'Yesterday', backed with pre-recorded strings. The song was a considerable step forward musically, with its string quartet setting and its sophisticated harmonic approach, and they wouldn't include it in their concert set-list until the following year. Otherwise, on tour in '65, The Beatles essentially still played what they recorded.

In terms of The Beatles' lives as performers, then, the first Shea concert was perfectly timed – the audience still thrilled by the striking originality of the band, the songs still fresh and The Beatles themselves not yet so completely jaded, disillusioned with the sound and their performance, that they couldn't be awed by the experience. Reflecting on the show some thirty years later for *The Beatles Anthology*, assistant Neil Aspinall notes, the amazement still apparent in his voice, 'That was a good experience. That was the first really big open air – "Wow, look at this".' Even the normally cynical Lennon would later remark, 'at Shea stadium, I saw the top of the mountain' (quoted in Anon 2008). The film of the concert wonderfully captures the awe-inspiring sight of the mostly young, mostly female crowd: the camera pans across the pre-concert bowl of empty seats, then in a series of cuts shows them steadily filling with fans who wind up to fever pitch, loosing an unflagging torrent of screams.

Given the responses to the show from The Beatles and the fans, it's not surprising that the concert has attained mythical status, and for many good reasons. Not that many people in America had been able to see them because they undertook only three full-length tours of the country. Moreover, the crowd of 55,600 at Shea set a record that, remarkably, stood for almost eight years, until Led Zeppelin broke it in Tampa, Florida, on 5 May 1973 (see Lewis 2006, 208). But particularly in the contemporary Internet age, aggrandizement and simple misinformation about the concert abound. A host of websites, for example, repeat the claim that Shea was the first rock concert held in a US sports stadium.[2] In fact, it wasn't The Beatles' first show in an American sports stadium, let alone the first rock concert held in one. Both as part of a bill and as headliner, Elvis Presley had routinely played outdoor venues, including stadiums, in the 1950s. He had played open-air baseball fields as early as 1955, and he later performed at, among others, the Cotton Bowl (11 October 1956); Memorial Stadium in Spokane, Washington (30 August 1957); Empire Stadium in Vancouver, Canada (31 August 1957); Sick's Stadium in Seattle, Washington (1 September 1957); Multnomah Stadium in Portland, Oregon (2 September 1957); and Honolulu Stadium in Hawaii (10 December 1957) (Guralnick and Jorgensen 1999, 86, 109, 110). The Cotton Bowl is generally credited as being the largest of these shows, with an attendance of 26,500 – marking a record that stood until 1965, when The Beatles played Shea for the first time (Schwensen 2014, 41).[3] As for open-air sports stadium shows by The Beatles, they played four on the 1964 North American tour.[4]

Nonetheless, the mythology continues to outstrip the facts – in part no doubt because of the slippery definition of a 'large' stadium. For example, despite listing these shows at the end of his book *Ticket to Ride*, Larry Kane – a reporter who travelled with the band on their

TABLE 1.2 Open-air sports stadium dates on the 1964 tour

Venue	Location	Date	Attendance
Empire Stadium	Vancouver, Canada	22 Aug. 1964	20,621
Forest Hills Tennis Stadium	New York, NY	28 & 29 Aug. 1964	16,000 (each)
Gator Bowl	Jacksonville, FL	11 Sept. 1964	23,000
Municipal Stadium	Kansas City	17 Sept. 1964	20,214

1964 and 1965 US tours – suggests that Brian Epstein had 'determined in 1964 that The Beatles would not play large outdoor stadiums' for fear that they wouldn't sell them out (Kane 2003, 178). But some of these earlier stadium shows were quite big: at capacity, the Gator Bowl could seat 32,000 fans, while the Municipal Stadium in Kansas City would hold 40,957.[5]

Still, The Beatles' first Shea concert certainly outdid all their other shows in terms of attendance. On their previous North American tour, three stops had breached the 20,000 mark (Empire Stadium, the Gator Bowl and Municipal Stadium in Kansas City), but more typically, on tour in North America The Beatles played before crowds that averaged roughly between 12,000 and 18,000 fans – not so different from the numbers than Elvis racked up in the 1950s (see Guralnick and Jorgensen, 1999). So at Shea The Beatles played to an audience over three times larger than usual.

If Shea was the apex, the fulfilment of all the grand ambitions of Epstein and The Beatles, it was also, however, the start of their demise as a touring band. From his very early days managing the band, Epstein confidently averred that the band would be bigger than Elvis (Lewisohn 2014, 499). All along, The Beatles were also keenly aware of the lack of success of British artists in America: the biggest home-grown heroes, such as Cliff Richard and The Shadows, hadn't made a dent in the pop music charts across the Atlantic. After the triumph of the Shea concert, though, The Beatles had unequivocal proof that, numerically at least, they were bigger than the King of rock 'n' roll, and they had indeed conquered America. The contradictions embedded in that very success, however, pulled them apart as a touring unit.

One way to understand the splintering of The Beatles as a live ensemble involves the story of distance. In Liverpool and particularly at the Cavern, The Beatles recognized few boundaries between themselves and the audience. They openly ate, drank and smoked on stage, and the female Cavern dwellers in particular regarded them as their own: the fans passed song requests to the band on stage, visited them in the tiny space that passed for a dressing room and, for that matter, could easily ride the bus with them to their early gigs. The band drew much-needed energy from these crowds, even the unruly, sometimes violent clientele of the Reeperbahn clubs in Hamburg. But as much as they cultivated such intimacy, The Beatles also developed a sense of style, of showmanship, that distanced them from the audience. In Hamburg, they were famously instructed to 'Mach Shau', or make a show, in order to incite the audience and pull customers into the club to buy alcohol (quoted in Lewisohn 2014, 359). Fulfilling the duty of bar bands everywhere, they invented an energetic, at times provocative stage act that succeeded wildly, with band members stomping on the stage, yelling at the crowd, even jumping into the dancing beer-hall fray (see Stark 2005, 94). Lennon in particular became known for his outrageous antics, which included shouting 'Heil Hitler' to the German audiences, doing his spastic and 'cripple' routines and mocking other members during performance. But the frontline of the band as a whole – John, Paul and George – all developed a comic sensibility and repartee that captivated the fans.

The Beatles' attractiveness rested on a tension between these two conflicting drives: intimacy and distance. The fevered pitch of Beatlemania in fact grew out of a particular kind of distance: the exotic. When The Beatles arrived in Hamburg on their first trip, they fascinated the Germans because of their foreignness. Not only did they import rock 'n' roll music, but their stage manner and look immediately transfixed the audience. Describing her first reaction to the band, Astrid Kirchherr confirms the appeal: 'I was shivering all over the place . . . There was so much joy in their faces, the energy in their eyes' (quoted in Stark 2005, 95). The Beatles themselves had the opposite response: for their part, they were struck by the appearance and attitude of the Germans. The band absorbed the dark, European look of their new friends, culminating, of course, in their adopting the famous hairstyle, with bangs brushed forward. The relationships here had a peculiar symmetry. For the Germans, the British band – in all its naïve parochialism – represented an unfamiliar otherness, just as for The Beatles, the Germans held an exotic charm, which they mimicked in their own way. Indeed, when The Beatles returned to Liverpool from their first trip to Hamburg, some fans thought they were going to see a German group because they were billed as 'Direct from Hamburg' (Bramwell 2005, 2). That distinction of foreignness and the distance from the everyday heightened their appeal and created an aura that would be vigorously promoted in America.

As the band grew ever-more staggeringly successful and lost its basis in local culture, more boundaries were erected – at first in the name of professionalism, but ultimately for the sake of safety, both for themselves and for the audiences. As Epstein began his tenure as manager, officially in

January 1962, he instituted a number of changes in the band's appearance and the venues they played, all to bolster their appeal as proper entertainment. He banned smoking, drinking and eating on stage as a first measure. But he also radically transformed their stage act itself: 'Out too went the group's hit and miss presentation, to be replaced by one or two precise, pre-arranged, tight sets of never more than sixty minutes at a time' (Lewisohn 1986, 88). The transformation from the sprawling, Preludin-fuelled sessions of four or six hours that they had played in Hamburg could hardly have been more striking. Most famously, of course, Epstein had them trade their leather gear for suits and ties.

Epstein's professionalization marked The Beatles' shift from bar band or lunchtime diversion to a proper concert act – a step they knew they had to take if their career was to move forward. But it also established a formula that would ultimately trap them. For its effect, the exotic depends upon foreignness, strangeness and, most important, distance – and that distance is central to understanding the phenomenal success of stadium shows. If proximity suggests commonality and identification (the band is like us and they belong to us), then distance exponentially increases the magnetic force of fame. The Beatles began by desperately making a show to attract crowds to them: as their success exploded, they responded by withdrawing from the fans – literally increasing the space between themselves and their audiences by shortening the length and variety of their set-lists and decreasing the number of performances in general. By the time of their international tours, as Mark Lewisohn notes, the 'The Beatles were playing the huge open-air stadiums in order to satisfy as many fans as possible in the least possible time, with the least possible effort, while maximizing their income' (Lewisohn 1986, 196). This move had multiple consequences, but it certainly increased the frenzy and underscored their status as distant idols.

The 'show' they worked so hard to make appealing turned them into pure spectacle, and the point for the fans became witnessing it. For his part, Lennon at the time seemed fine with whatever the crowd wanted: 'We played for four or five years being completely heard and it was good fun. And it's just as good fun to play being not heard and being more popular. They pay the money, if they want to scream – scream' (Beatles 2000, 187). But the screaming did grind the band down. Ringo later observed, 'I never felt people came to *hear* our show – I felt they came to *see* us' (Beatles 2000, 186). This emphasis on sight recalls the work of French theorist Guy Debord in *The Society of the Spectacle*: noting that 'the spectacle is the *chief product* of present-day society', Debord suggests that because 'the spectacles' job is to cause a world that is no longer directly perceptible to be *seen* via different specialized mediations, it is inevitable that it should elevate the human sense of sight to the special place once occupied by touch' (Debord 1995, 16, 17). Although Debord goes on to offer an incredibly reductive dismissal of spectators as passive consumers, he astutely describes the faux intimacy evoked by, for example, seeing a band, which is almost as good as touching them.[6]

Even with his emphasis on the primacy of sight, though, Debord only considers the spectators' desire to look: at the Shea concert, the fans harboured twin fantasies of both seeing and being seen. One tells a story of what feels like an intimate exchange in the midst of tens-of-thousands: during the show, Lennon 'turned to us and waved back to us exactly the same way we were waving. So we knew that he saw us . . . *He saw us! Oh my God!*' (quoted in Schwensen 2014, 168). The fan revels in the desire for an intimate connection, shown in Lennon's mirroring wave (again, they're just like us): the concert holds out the tantalizing potential for such encounters since, after all, you can see the performer. But the venue itself – with its layout, barricades, police presence – establishes the *cordon* that cannot successfully be crossed, try and try as you might to breach it.

The spectacular nature of the stadium show thus envelops everyone – fans, musicians, members of the press – into an event that exceeds its ostensible purpose as a music concert. Repeatedly in Schwensen's oral

FIGURE 1.1 The stage for the Shea Stadium performance, as shown in *The Beatles Anthology*

history of the Shea concert, attendees note their pride at simply having been there: 'After a while I didn't even care that we couldn't hear them sing. We were just so glad we were at a *happening*' (quoted in Schwensen 2014, 148). Given the media-saturation surrounding the show – in both print and film – the concert might be considered what Douglas Kellner terms a 'megaspectacle': a mediated event, such as the O. J. Simpson trial of 1994–1995 or the attacks of 11 September 2001 that becomes so large and so pervasive a marker of cultural meaning that the event stands as a singular point in history (Kellner 2003, 93). The momentous nature of the Shea concert certainly wasn't lost on The Beatles, who can be seen on film looking around in astonishment at what they had wrought. And the very fact that the show was filmed and ultimately broadcast on television indicates the significance it was accorded, even at the time.

Despite their pervasiveness, megaspectacles do not have a singular, unconflicted meaning. But one possible effect of such spectacles is to diminish the individual agency of the performers, as they become the target of projected fantasies. As George Harrison commented, 'That is the main problem with fame – that people forget how to act normally. They are not in awe of you, but in awe of the thing that they think you've become. It's a concept that they have of stardom and notoriety' (Beatles 2000, 185). This 'concept' as Harrison describes it is an insightful definition of spectacle itself, which forms a layer of mediation, a level of distance that both entices with possible intimacy yet guarantees its absence. The results for The Beatles and their fans were alternately liberating, frightening and alienating. Barbara Ehrenreich persuasively argues that the seeming 'hysterical' reaction by young rock music fans was in fact a release of repressed physical energy – a disruptive, sometimes sexually charged joy in movement (Ehrenreich 2006, 207).[7] But the shows could also be dangerous. Aside from literal threats of violence to the band, both The Beatles and the fans themselves risked injury at the concerts. The Beatles famously arrived at Shea in an armoured car, and their performance took place at second base: with no seats on the field itself, the fans were a secure distance away, a space that was literally policed as the fans climbed barricades and dashed for the stage, only to be intercepted by the security forces.

At this point in their career, The Beatles could have embraced their role in the spectacle and carried on with tours in massive venues, relatively poor sound and – perhaps – increasingly grand, theatrical performances. Most bands that followed took that route. Mick Jagger and Keith Richards of The Rolling Stones were in the audience for the Shea concert, though they left early because of the poor sound and the out-of-control crowd (Schwensen 2014, 135). But the 'glimmer twins' could have been taking notes for their future; as their career gathered force and history, the Stones adopted tactics that allowed them to regularly perform in massive stadiums while producing an illusion of intimacy. They employed grand stage sets, for example, complete with enormous inflatable figures, and provided massive video screens, so that the increasingly distant crowd could actually see the band. The inflatables and screens convey a pseudo-intimacy with the audience, but at the same time underscore the mediated nature of the performance. The fans are sometimes so distant from the band that for many, the music remains out of sync with the live video.

Other than embracing the spectacle, with its inherent contradictions, what other way forward is there for the large rock show? During their peak fame, The Beatles did experiment with another response as they resisted and undercut the spectacle they created. If their stage antics began as a way to 'Mach Schau', to gather and focus a crowd, these same tactics ultimately became essential tools for remaining sane within the hurricane vortex of fame. Lennon's baiting of the crowd began in Hamburg, but it continued right through their ascent to world fame. At times the shows bordered on outright provocation, as Lennon would tell the crowd to 'Shurrup' and even shout obscenities at the fans while Paul and George sang (see Lewisohn 1986, 184). The shows also included elements of self-deprecation and mockery, as when Lennon misremembers the titles of American albums, falls into his spastic routine or – at Shea – imitates McCartney's hand gestures during the introduction of 'Ticket to Ride'. Viewed in the context of the large stadium shows, provocation may be an attempt to reassert intimate human potential or meaning in the face of an overwhelming event. Celebrities have a paradoxical relation to this new cult of power: after exerting enormous resources in pursuit of success, they then express ambivalence and even aggression at the audience's lack of understanding. It's as if they achieve wild success in order to be understood, but then find they're still misunderstood, or adored for the wrong reasons. The temptation then is to assault the audience or play down to expectations – and the music is often what's sacrificed for the 'show'. Perhaps not coincidentally, the performers who responded this way to success form a list of the tragically deceased, including Jimi Hendrix, Jim Morrison and Kurt Cobain.

The Beatles, of course, opted out: they neither embraced their role in the spectacle nor steeled themselves to endure it with mockery. Why did they stop touring? The answer has typically been that they were fed up with Beatlemania – the claustrophobic touring, the hysterical fans and, especially, their poor performances and their inability to reproduce their increasingly complex material live. Although the first Shea stadium show included recent singles and little dated material, the 1966 tour offered a very different story: they played twenty-three shows in 1966, in England, Germany, Japan, the Philippines and the United States – and, incredibly, all featured material from the same twelve-song set-list (Lewisohn 1986, 201).[8]

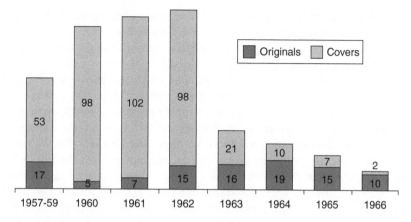

FIGURE 1.2 Songs in The Beatles' repertoire by year.

Although they did gamely attempt a few more harmonically and musically challenging numbers such as 'Yesterday', 'Nowhere Man' and 'Paperback Writer', they still relied heavily on staples of older set-lists ('Baby's in Black', 'I Wanna Be Your Man', 'Long Tall Sally' and 'Rock and Roll Music'). For a band that had already released *Rubber Soul* and, by the time they arrived in the United States in August, the acid-drenched sonic masterpiece *Revolver*, such repetition must have been especially mind-numbing: they clearly thought so, given that they didn't trouble themselves rehearsing for their tours (Lewisohn 1986, 184). If the point was to be *seen*, then why bother with the music?

But another reason to cease touring suggests itself: the band had to quit the road in order to preserve its radical social (and political) potential. The stadium shows not only predictably undermined their human connection with the audience, but also simply robbed them of their ability to communicate in a meaningful way. It's telling that when Lennon and Harrison did finally return to live performance, in the early 1970s, each attempted to use the power of the spectacle for political and social ends. Primed for such a move through the performance art of his bed-ins with Yoko Ono, Lennon supported various causes in several one-off performances in the United States, including the John Sinclair Freedom Rally (supporting Sinclair, who was in jail for selling marijuana), the Rally for Attica State Prison (providing relief for families of prison riot victims) and the One-to-One concerts (benefitting the Willowbrook State School) (Wiener 1990, 187, 192, 248). At these shows, he often played his overtly political material from the era – including 'Attica State', 'John Sinclair' and 'The Luck of the Irish', as well as 'Give Peace a Chance'. Lennon also was planning an anti-Nixon tour for 1972, before the efforts by President Richard Nixon and the FBI derailed his plans (see Wiener 1999, 110). As for Harrison, he returned to the stage in a grand gesture with a star-infused concert focusing on humanitarian aid for refugees of Bangladesh. For these two Beatles, at least at that point, it wasn't enough to entertain or accept their objectification for the money; both strongly felt the need to use their fame as a source of political and social good.[9]

In terms of The Beatles as a band, they of course did have one final performance after the 1966 San Francisco concert. After the failed plans to return to the stage and get back to their performing roots, their final gig took place on a rooftop, completely out of view of the fans – as though, in this last quasi-public moment, they averred that only the music mattered. This last public moment was an attempt to give the fans what they desperately wanted – a live show – without being trapped again inside the oppressive concert space. Initially, they had planned for the *Get Back* sessions to culminate with a performance, to take place perhaps either at a Roman amphitheatre or a stage in the Sahara desert (see Lewisohn 1986, 202). Even near their end they considered creating an even bigger spectacle of themselves. Indeed, one of the titles proposed for their final album was Everest: despite the ironic nod to a cigarette brand, the title suggested that – though Lennon had seen the mountaintop at Shea – there was always a higher mountain to climb. Tellingly, they opted to stay at sea level and chose the unaffected title *Abbey Road*, in honour of the street that housed their recording studio. This final aesthetic choice, then, honours their creative musical home rather than the spectacle they created, which, perpetually renewed, carries on long after the possibility of any live reunion.

Notes

1 'Act Naturally' was released in the United States on 16 September 1965, as the B-side of the 'Yesterday' single.

2 For example, the website maccafan.net breathlessly notes, 'This was the first time in the history of music that a stadium was used for a rock concert!' The site livescience.com reports in its matter-of-fact tone, 'On Aug. 15, 1965, The Beatles became the first rock band to perform at an American sports stadium with their show at Shea Stadium in Queens, New York.'

3 Guralnick and Jorgensen, however, call the two largest Elvis stadium gigs a draw, as they list the attendance at the Cotton Bowl and Empire Stadium at 26,500 each (86, 110). To further complicate the question, a Vancouver DJ named Red Robinson claimed to have seen receipts showing that 25,898 fans paid admission to the Empire Stadium performance ('One Night with You and Elvis Fled'). In any case, I can find no record of a larger popular music concert with a single headliner between Elvis' shows and The Beatles' Shea Stadium concert on 15 Aug 1965.

4 Attendance at the first three shows for the below table is sourced from Lewisohn (1992, 169, 171); attendance at Municipal Stadium from Kane (2003, 242). Note that in his attendance table, Kane reports 32,000 as the

attendance for the Gator Bowl (2003, 242); however, Lewisohn reports that 9,000 ticket holders were unable to attend due to Hurricane Dora (1992, 171).

5 Neither the Gator Bowl nor Municipal Stadium had capacity crowds, the lower-than-expected attendance in Florida, at least, explained by a recent hurricane that kept some 9,000 from getting to the show (Lewisohn 1992, 171).

6 In *Media Spectacle*, Douglas Kellner updates and complicates Debord's analysis: he offers an alternative to the totalizing notion of spectacle, recuperates a sense of agency for fans and emphasizes the 'plurality and heterogeneity of contending spectacles' as sites for working through conflicts over cultural values (Kellner 2003, 11).

7 Ehrenreich's contention that the music itself liberated this energy is more problematic – given that so many fans say they couldn't even hear it.

8 The source for these numbers in Figure 1.2 is Mark Lewisohn's *The Beatles Live!*, which offers lists of songs the band performed, by year, during the first half of their career. The song totals for the early years will always be approximations, of course, given the less-than-reliable documentation and the sheer number of performances.

9 Lennon in particular was punished for attempting to step outside his fab role as a spectacular Beatle with harsh reviews and political surveillance (see Wiener 1990, 229). He would later get castigated for his near-complete withdrawal into personal life in the mid-1970s – a retreat that can be read as partly his refusal to be co-opted by the spectacle, and partly the victory of spectacle in neutering his radical potential.

CHAPTER TWO

Beyond Beatlemania: The Shea Stadium Concert as Discursive Construct

Mark Duffett

My analysis here indicates, however, that something very much like imagined memory (remembered imaginings, perhaps) underpinned the audience's experience at Shea Stadium, since the audience was drawing on its memory of its own imaginings of the Beatles even while in their physical presence. The spectators' memories of the concert, therefore, would be memories (perhaps imagined) of remembered imaginings.

PHILIP AUSLANDER (2006A, 264–265; EMPHASIS MINE)

On 15 Aug 1965, the Beatles played to a crowd of over 55,000 of their fans at the Shea Stadium in New York City. Five decades later, the concert is remembered less than for how it sounded than the fact that it was drowned out by the crowd's deafening din (Millard 2012, 25). Interpreting fan responses, Phil Auslander drew on a concept that I suggested (Duffett 2003b) called 'imagined memories'. In my own formulation, an imagined memory is the product of a fan's desire to have been part of a past popular music event that has since become an object of nostalgia. Auslander inverted the idea to suggest that fans could project their wish to be part of a future music event, then later participate in it with a *screen* of desire between themselves and their artist. Auslander's claim suggests that fan interest is a form of *ontological blindness* – not admitting that the living people are there – but it is perhaps more appropriate to reflect on fans' estimations of their heroes as totems. Auslander's perception is a product of the mythic construction of Shea, and the way that it verifies wider perceptions about popular music fandom as public hysteria. In actuality the Beatles encounter with fans at the Shea Stadium took three forms: the first, a triumphant concert in 1965, the second, a lesser known concert in 1966 and the third, something quite different: a legacy, a kind of 'discursive Shea' that prioritized the first concert and marginalized the second. This chapter examines how the last of these – the discursive construct that referenced the Beatles at Shea Stadium – drew on stereotypes of pop fandom and perpetuated them in discourses about the group.

The Shea event came to symbolize the way that popular music fandom had entered the public sphere as a collective and 'excessive' emotional phenomenon. Discussions about Shea were framed by assumptions that young, mostly female 'Beatlemaniacs' did not care about music, but instead 'worshipped' band members as hero figures. Stories of concert chaos eventually enabled the Beatles to secure their place in the emergent rock revolution and position themselves as a more serious, 'adult' and 'music-orientated' band. Yet they have also perpetuated and become a cornerstone of stereotypical perceptions of music fandom in the public sphere. My aim in beginning to analyse the discursive Shea Stadium is to rescue the event from its own history. What follows will proceed in three parts. The first introduces one mechanism from Durkheim's notion of totemic religion in order to begin understanding the Beatles as celebrities. By this I do not mean to suggest that the Beatles were religious figures, although I accept that George Harrison's eventual advocacy of spirituality complicates that claim. Instead I suggest that we can understand the collective adulation of the Beatles in relation to the successful mobilization of a shared, symbolic economy: a secular process of human chemistry based on unacknowledged assumptions that are held in the heads of all individual fans and common throughout the fan base. The second section explores the way that those who later talked about the 1965 Shea event – including the Beatles themselves – levered popular notions of fandom to create a common perception in the popular imagination of a defective audience and maturing rock act. The third section considers the fans' own perspectives on Shea and explores how audience members spoke *through* the discursive resources available to them.

Totemic Beatles

The Beatles were not the first band to receive deafening audience responses. Some historians have forgotten that Elvis Presley had already generated deafening crowd responses. His guitarist Scotty Moore recalled: 'The only way I can explain it is if you dive into a swimming pool, the phasing underwater – the rush of the water. Well, the crowd would get so loud that your ears would close up.'[1] Elvis received thunders of approval well before the Beatles hit America. In terms of sheer audience size, though, Shea was more than double Elvis's own record at the time. His largest public event had been playing to 25,000 people at the Dallas Cotton Bowl. Over and above any specific kind of behaviour from fans, it was precisely the measurement of audience 'acceptance' *in quantitative terms* that defined the approach of the mass culture era.

It is relevant here to introduce the paradigm through which fandom was generally seen by non-fans in the 1960s, the mass culture critique. This set of ideas, which was propagated by elitist critics of various political persuasions, suggested that music audiences were manipulated by commercial culture. [2] At worst, the critique suggested that pop fans were empty-headed and infantile, naïve young people ensnared into a life of consumption, distraction and, worst of all, unthinking 'worship'. As part of his tirade against 'The Menace of Beatlism', Paul Johnson, in 1964, lamented the way that young people had been captivated: 'The huge faces, bloated with cheap confectionary and smeared with chain-store makeup, the open, sagging mouths and glazed eyes, the hands mindlessly drumming in time to the music, the broken stiletto heels' (Johnson 2006, 53). Rather than directly attacking the music, in this particular instance Johnson's critique takes issue with the 'enslavement' of its audience to vulgar commercial taste. He and his fellow mass culture critics dismissed pop fans as moronic and manipulated, borderline insane and lacking in intelligence. Johnson's Beatles devotees are, at least, however, *listening*. When Shea was discussed, it was in contrast criticized as an occasion where an *overly excited* audience spoiled any possibility of appreciating the music.

Popular music culture can be seen from a number of alternative perspectives. One way of understanding it is through the lens of totemism. In his 1912 book *The Elementary Forms of Religious Life*, Emile Durkheim argued that tribal religions in Australia worshipped totems: people (or objects) that marked the dividing line between the sacred and profane. Durkheim's work aimed to demystify totemism. He explained that totems are venerated as contagious agents of the sacred, but that their holy power essentially arises from their social position as objects of attention. For Durkheim, the totem therefore mediates between the collective congregation (the tribe of believers) and each individual follower. When a valued totem offers a follower some attention, he or she is excited by an emotional state that Durkheim calls 'effervescence': a thrilling, 'electric' jolt of excitement. Durkheim argued that this mechanism is the generative seed, not just of religions, but of other social institutions. Society organizes itself when the tribe develops shared values that prevent any dissolution of the totem's affective power.

The idea of fans as religious followers sometimes finds its way into framings of the Shea Stadium show (see Carlin 2009, 110). Such interpretations reference aspects of Durkheim's model, but also suggest mass culture thinking by interpreting fans as subservient and manipulated. While there have been a number of books written comparing music fandom to religion (see, for example, Till 2010), there are multiple dangers in making superficial comparisons based on apparent similarity and metaphor (see Duffett 2003a). Applying Durkheim's model wholesale to popular music is therefore a mistake. Although fans *are* very interested in getting closer to pop and rock stars, such heroes are, after all, not contagiously sacred. Instead, we can say that Durkheim aimed to demystify tribal religion by exposing its social mechanisms. Equally, the phenomenon of effervescence – which is, essentially, a process of human chemistry – can be seized upon as a kind of template, a working hypothesis with which to begin considering fandom. To recognize a totemic phenomenon we have to make sure that individual fans understand themselves as part of a collective social body (the fan base), pay attention *to* their hero and are demonstrably thrilled at the thought of receiving attention *from* him or her.

It is important to see the arrival of the Beatles in America as part of a much longer build-up. The archetypal form of collective, excited fan response to the Beatles was described by the media as Beatlemania. *The Cambridge Companion to the Beatles* dates the phenomenon's origin to October 1963, when 15 million UK television viewers saw the band on Val Parnell's 'Saturday Night at the London Palladium' (Womack 2009, xx). For American fans, Beatlemania was the advertisement that sold the Beatles. The band's success did not happen in a media blackout, but rather in the context of their existing popularity with European audiences. Well before the band set foot on US soil, two independent labels released Beatles singles but neither sold enough units to chart. When the band scored two number 1s in the UK, a major picked up 'I Wanna Hold Your Hand':

> Capitol's promotional plan for the Beatles in the United States was built around their previous success, their looks, and the frenzy of the fans rather than the merits of the music. Beatlemania was portrayed as a sort of disease, and the symptoms were often expressed in terms of record sales. (Millard 2012, 18)

Emphasis on sales as an indication of the band's vast fan base, and on looks as a reason for why they were a centre of attention, suggests an approach to marketing that was cognizant of totemic concerns, yet it was an approach that also negotiated the mass culture critique. In any neo-Durkheimian schema, fan interest in music reflects a desire for intimacy with one's hero; however, assuming a divergence between 'pure music' on the one hand and marketing on the other implies mass culture thinking.

The use of Beatlemania as an insanity – a mania – and 'a sort of disease' shows that record companies could capitalize on mass culture notions of fandom as shared madness. Capitol levered the Beatles' previous success to produce a marketing campaign that was both distinctly totemic *and* drew on mass cultural notions of fandom as a contagious phenomenon. Millard explained how Capitol spent more money promoting the first single than any others in its company history and how it later synergized merchandising and promotion – including the distribution of 'mop top' wigs – to take advantage of the Beatles' live tours. In the light of Capitol's efforts, the Beatles achieved a number 1 single before they had set foot in America (Millard 2012, 20). In other words, the Beatles were already immensely popular on record *before* they toured the United States as a live act. Their rapturous first appearance on 'The Ed Sullivan Show' in February 1964 capitalized on this, conveying a studio audience's excited response to millions of domestic television viewers. In a totemic sense, Beatlemania was not simply a consequence or afterthought of the Beatles' music. Instead this phenomenon was precisely the frame and context within which reception of their music happened.

Promoter Sid Bernstein established his reputation with the band's manager Brian Epstein late in 1963 when he secured a contract for two planned post-'Ed Sullivan' live shows in New York's Carnegie Hall. Over a year elapsed, however, between the Beatles 'Ed Sullivan' debut and Shea. Just like 'The Ed Sullivan Show', the concert was organized specifically to present the Beatles as a centre of mass attention. The first Shea Stadium event effectively came in the middle (not at the end) of the Beatle's three-year run of touring America. When Epstein raised concerns about whether his act could fill the stadium, Bernstein promised $10 for every empty seat (Millard 2012, 37). The Shea concert was therefore arranged through a hedge-bet on its own mass audience and designed to showcase the Beatles as a totemic phenomenon: 'It was, to that point, the biggest, most spectacular show in the entire arc of American popular culture' (Carlin 2009, 110). Shea has been described as 'a quintessential scene of Beatlemania' (Berman 2008, 169) and the associated audience responses have come to symbolize the event's very giganticism.

Shea's place in popular memory was secured when it was recorded for a television documentary, *The Beatles at Shea Stadium* (M. Clay Adams, 1966). Created in cooperation with Ed Sullivan's production company, the show was broadcast by the BBC in the UK on 1 March 1966, and in the United States on 10 January 1967, where it was also given a colour theatrical release. As much as the concert that it was based on, the documentary helped Shea become a benchmark in live music history. Crowd shots added to the drama as the comedian Murray the K introduced the event by saying, 'Welcome to what will probably be the biggest ever concert in the history of pop music . . . Scream as much as you want, but whatever you do, take care of yourselves, don't get hurt, and go home safely.' He then introduced various support acts that the audience seemed to neither know about nor care about. They were rapidly drowned out with 'anticipatory screams' (Berman 2008, 167). The Shea TV documentary therefore presented fan screaming as something that seemed *constantly there*, ready to decay only in relation to the recorded sound mix, not in response to any specific performance. By showing the audience making noise after the Beatles arrived but before they played, it also emphasized that fans were responding not to the music but rather to the presence of their heroes. Adding some narration, Paul McCartney explained, 'I think it makes us less nervous playing to a big crowd than a little crowd, because if you play to a little crowd, they are going to hear what you're playing.' In one shot, Ringo is seen smoking languidly backstage, despite the screams. In another on stage, John Lennon plays the keyboard with his elbow. On the Shea documentary soundtrack fan screaming was organized as a continuous accompaniment, as if to make the argument that the audience was always apparent as a sonic presence. In fact in January 1966 the documentary soundtrack was changed using 'a bit of audio dubbing by the group to improve upon their live stage performance' (Berman 2008, 170). The session at CTS studios in London resulted in some significant differences to the original concert. Two months ahead of BBC1's black and white broadcast, the Beatles re-recorded 'I Feel Fine' and 'Help!' and overdubbed other tracks.[3] The audio for 'Twist and Shout' was replaced with Capitol's 1965 Hollywood Bowl recording, while the original non-live studio version of 'Act Natural' replaced the film's live version and had crowd noises layered upon it (Winn 2009, 4). In other words, the Shea documentary located fan responses as continuous *noise* yet at least some of it was artificially constructed.

After the concert: The discursive Shea

The Shea Stadium concert was the start rather than the end of the Shea legend (Berman 2008, 176). Indeed, Shea has long since passed into myth. It has become enshrined, alongside other classic moments (such as playing at the Cavern), in the virtual environment of *The Beatles: Rock Band* (MTV Games/Electronic Arts 2009) (Millard 2012, 184). In context, however, Shea was part of a much wider historic shift where audiences discovered new levels of totemic excitement. A BBC archive page for the series 'The Seven Ages of Rock' reflects the general wisdom about Shea as a moment of music history:

> They had specially designed amps made by Vox to boost the sound and 2000 security staff were drafted in to look after the 55,000 people who had bought tickets for the event. It turned out that the amps weren't loud

enough (because of the screaming of the fans) and they were forced into using the house amplification system normally used for baseball games. As a result neither the audience nor more crucially the Beatles could hear what they were playing. The crowd control didn't work either, at several points during the show the frenzied crowd broke through the security and charged towards the stage. It was both a ground-breaking and record-breaking performance but one that would be remembered for what went wrong rather than what went right.[4]

This *relatively* objective portrayal suggests that the 1965 Shea concert was *both* a commercial triumph and a sonic disaster. It therefore links poor sound quality with commercial compromise and begins to read Shea as a kind of shock for the performers. In some accounts, the Beatles had a distinctly disconcerting experience. The commentary on one Beatles fan site claimed that, 'The Beatles were overwhelmed by the experience. Not being able to hear each other or even themselves, they just played through a list of songs nervously, not knowing what kind of sound was being produced.'[5] What is interesting, however, is that there is no clear evidence that the Beatles themselves singled out Shea in particular as an experience more negative than their other engagements. According to Paul McCartney, 'Once you know you've filled a place that size, it's magic; just walls of people. Half the fun was being involved in this gigantic event ourselves.'[6] On the original documentary, Ringo also assented: 'It's the fans that make you. Without them, you're nothing. We love the fans as much as they love us.' John said, 'I was looking for the ones [banners] with "John" on, waving to them, you see. I noticed them.' He added, 'I'm just sorry for people that can't see us live. Sometimes you haven't missed anything, because you wouldn't have heard us, but sometimes you might have enjoyed it.' André Millard explained that 'the band always seemed to be enjoying themselves . . . they were having fun, just as George said, "We had fun, you know, we really had fun"' (Millard 2012, 126). However, although the Beatles evidently had fun and *said* as much, in the documentary the band and audience were also portrayed as if the din between them was utterly unproductive. On each side, they appear to have given up caring.

In both 1965 and 1966 Shea-related coverage in the *New York Times* was influenced by a mass culture perspective. Its stories are indicative of a wider social attitude that, I suggest, both reflected and somewhat influenced the group themselves. Journalist Maureen Cleave (1966) portrayed the band members as world-weary, more concerned with money than fame and interested in masculine camaraderie more than female companionship. She added, 'If the Beatles ever decided to become social climbers, they would give the whole thing away by talking about it.' Nevertheless, they had an emergent interest in the avant-garde: 'Paul's mind is in ferment . . . he is fascinated by the work of Karlheinz Stockhausen and Luciano Berio' (Cleave 1966, 121).

Though the Fab Four had acquired considerable fame, wealth and knowledge, as chirpy Liverpudlian 'long hairs' they could never quite attain the status associated with elite society. Meanwhile, their concert fans were portrayed as swarming animals collectively trying to outwit older, male police officers (Schumach 1965c, 11; Schumach 1965a, 82; Clarke 1966, 80). The noise that the crowd made at Shea was interpreted as wild (uncivilized), hysterical (emotionally excessive) and evoking pandemonium (as something chaotic or demonic).[7] Yet, as the *Times* also noted, there were significant issues with the Beatles' claim on stratospheric popularity. In August 1965 a *Times'* writer noted that in Rome airport 150 policemen and just four 'docile' fans had turned out to meet the group (Shelton 1965, 40). The newspaper also said that 70,000 people had been to see the New York Philharmonic Orchestra play a classical music concerto in Central Park, that the Sullivan documentary took over a year to sell to TV networks and that the Beatles' 1966 Shea event did not secure maximum box office returns (Schonberg 1965, X11). The group's popularity was, it seemed, at least a little over-hyped. This view stands in stark contrast to some of the more heroic versions of Beatles history.

The group did not finish its full tour of duty immediately after the first Shea show. Its live touring ended a year later at Candlestick Park in San Francisco. Why did the Beatles give up touring? The reasons are more complex than one might expect. Five elements were seemingly involved: an ongoing feeling of discomfort about fame, the rise of 'Beatle bashing', the waning of Beatlemania, a more complex approach to recorded music and – finally – claims that the band could not actually be heard. I will examine each of these in turn.

Some of the Beatles were always somewhat at odds with their own mass popularity and uncomfortable with touring. As early as 1963 Paul McCartney told fans that the band preferred studio to live work (Julien 2009, 3). George Harrison was disillusioned with fame well before the 1965 stadium visit (see Harrison 2002, 33). Paul McCartney was eventually put off touring by the shabby staging of their stint at Cincinnati and St. Louis in 1966. John Lennon then said to Hunter Davies, 'I can't imagine any reason which would make us do any sort of tour again' (Julien 2009, 2). Later, he revised his opinion to say that he simply wanted more control over when he played live (Badman 2001, 77). His thinking may well have been shaped by the rising incidents of 'Beatles bashing' that increased dramatically in 1966. Ironically, John's ill-judged comment that the Beatles were 'bigger than Jesus' actually ruined the band's totemic appeal for vast sections of the American public. With characteristic cynicism in 1978 Lennon said, 'If I hadn't said that the Beatles were "bigger than Jesus" and upset the very Christian Ku Klux Klan, well, Lord, I might still be up there with all the other performing fleas!' (Jackson 2005, 126).

It was simply not a case, then, that Shea alone made the Fab Four turn their backs on the live performance. Indeed, by late 1966 – after a third tour in as many years – Beatlemania had begun to show signs of *waning*. When only 500 fans gathered at their New York hotel before their second performance at Shea, compared to 100,000 the year before, *Time* magazine ran an article called 'Is Beatlemania Dead?' The 45,000 strong 1966 concert crowd was 10,000 below the stadium's limit. If Sid Bernstein had repeated his capacity crowd guarantee, he would have lost $100,000.

The Beatles music also got more complex. Interviewed by Andy Gray for *New Musical Express*, soon after the final tour, Paul McCartney offered a composite response:

> One reason we don't want to tour anymore is that when we're on stage nobody can hear us or listen to us. And another reason is that our stage act hasn't improved one bit since we started touring four years ago. The days when three guitarists and a drummer could stand up and sing and do nothing else on stage must be over. *Stage performance as an art is going out, anyway. I think the Rolling Stones had a shock when they didn't do a bomb on their last tour. I think Mick was worried.* Many of our tracks nowadays have big backings. We couldn't produce the sound on stage without an orchestra . . . *We feel that only through recordings do people listen to us,* so that is the most important form of communication.[8] (emphasis mine)

McCartney's complex explanation in part refers to the complexity of the Beatles' recent music. Indeed, the more elaborate studio album *Revolver* had been released just *before* the band played its final live date (Julien 2009, 1). The interview also came in the wake of the Rolling Stones' fifth US tour in rapid secession. The group had recently prompted a 'middling turnout' at the 15,000 capacity Forest Hills tennis stadium (Shelton 1966, 11). McCartney's response was to suggest that savvy audiences were deserting the over-sold 'art' of live performance. In this unstable commercial environment, the Beatles conveniently complained that their skills as musicians simply could not be heard. Although there was no obvious evidence of them singling out Shea or its sound system specifically for negative comment, George had begun to separate two different kinds of fan on the Shea documentary:

> It depends entirely on the person, on the individual. I think most fans want to see us, and, say, 60% will want to hear us as well as see us. But the ones who just want to see us are the ones influenced by each other and are the types that if one person screams or shouts, then the one next to them will just follow suit.

The discourse of fandom as public hysteria was so strong that it was a resource that could be used by both critics and by the band itself. When the 1966 US tour turned out to be a strain, Harrison unofficially quit the

Beatles on the plane ride home. Ringo then said to Hunter Davies: 'It was wrecking our playing . . . The noise of the people just drowned anything' (reproduced in Julien 2009, 1). From this perspective, the Beatles' fan base was understood as a kind of monstrous entity threatening to engulf its object. For Millard, 'Beatlemania was bigger than the Beatles, drowning out [appreciation of] the [live] music and eventually overshadowing [attention to] the musicians themselves' (2012, 22).

In discussions of the Beatles' end of touring, historians have marginalized other reasons to focus, almost solely in some cases, on Beatlemania. According to the *Cambridge Companion*:

Concerts in the US were staged in mega-venues, the audience enormous and so fired-up that any artistic connection was impossible. Their performances, quite simply, could not be heard, obliterated by the mass hysteria of 'Beatlemania.' For the Beatles, touring became increasingly excruciating. (Womack 2009, 42)

In this context, Shea epitomized the curse of pop success. Some sources imply that gig itself was the reason that the Beatles stopped touring. According to John Lennon's biographer Jacqueline Edmondson:

In 1963, the Beatles toured the United Kingdom and had their first hit, 'Please Please Me.' Soon Beatlemania swept the country with throngs of screaming fans mobbing the boys at every venue . . . The queen appointed the Beatles as Members of the Order of the British Empire in 1965. By this time, Lennon had become disillusioned with fame and feared they had sold out to the establishment. The Beatles gave their last concert at the Shea Stadium in 1966, with the exception of an impromptu rooftop concert at their recording studio at 3 Savile Row in London, they performed only in the studio as they continued to record songs and release albums. (Edmondson 2010, xii)

Edmondson's account suggests that Lennon was disillusioned with fame by the time in October 1965 that he was awarded his Order of the British Empire ('OBE') honour, a few months after the first Shea Stadium event. From Edmondson's perspective, he had given up some time before late in 1965. She wrongly claims that the second Shea Stadium show – at least she does not specify the first – was the Beatles' 'last concert', completely forgetting about their performance at Candlestick Park. It is as if *any* mention of Shea (and here is now only one, mythic Shea) is enough to explain everything: it helps us understand the transformation of the Beatles into a more rebellious, 'adult' rock act by being seen as the epitome of commercial compromise.

The way in which the Beatles seemed to reject their live audience in 1966 was part of their process of rejecting their own image as pop idols. In their career, the group moved from a rock'n'roll outfit, to a pop act, then to a rock band. The first stage was associated with Hamburg and black leather; the second with mop tops and Shea; and the third with long hair, drugs and India. During one interview Paul McCartney later explained, 'We began to lose respect for the live act, and everyone started to become a bit disgruntled' (Miles 1998, 294). Elsewhere he elaborated, 'It was all gone, all that [mop top] boy shit, all that screaming, we didn't want any more, plus we'd now got turned on to pot and thought of ourselves as artists rather than performers' (Northcutt 2006, 136). *Sgt. Pepper* then redefined Beatles' fan base as *either* art appreciators *or* 'screaming Beatlemaniacs – who buy records, but make real contact and real music impossible' (Northcutt 2006, 131). By rejecting a supposedly uncultured faction of their own audience, the Beatles offered their remaining fans new opportunities to acquire and display cultural capital. They propagated a notion of 'real contact' and 'real music' that could only be understood in the context of artistic contemplation.

Back in 1964 a headline in the *Cincinati Enquirer* had exclaimed, 'Teenagers Revel In Madness: Young Fans Drop Veneer Of Civilisation For Beatles'.[9] In contrast, George Martin defined the band's new career phase by saying that *Sgt. Pepper* was a 'watershed which changed the recording art from something that merely made amusing sounds into something which will stand the test of time as a valid art form: sculpture in music, if you like' (Frith 1982, 4). His claim is important because it suggests that before *Sgt. Pepper*, the Beatles were making nothing of any lasting aesthetic worth. Suddenly, the band found a way to give their music credibility by emphasizing its relation to the fine arts. Martin's comparison of *Sgt. Pepper* to sculpture resonated with the words of theatre critic Kenneth Tynan, who famously said that the album was 'a decisive moment in the history of Western civilization' (Northcutt 2006, 130). Tynan's approval implied that the Beatles had now become artists who transcended the relatively 'uncivilized' world of stadium pop. From the perspective of the art discourse, the pre-*Pepper* audience was positioned as commercially exploited: blindly screaming over nothing of real value – or worse, perhaps because of its own inane demands, preventing the creation of anything of artistic value.

Beatles fans: Shea as totemic event

If the Ed Sullivan documentary, the *New York Times* and Beatles themselves all presented a closely associated understanding of live touring in general and Shea in particular, what was missing from their discussion was the voice of fans who had enjoyed the Shea concert live. Although the industry factored a totemic concern into music marketing, there was no explicit *discursive* conception of it in circulation. The mass culture critique was, for a long time, the *only* available framework through which fan excitement could be understood. Consequently, audience members at Shea have all tended to explain their perspectives within the possibilities defined by it.

Fans' accounts of their own behaviour at Shea have revealed various things. Most devotees stressed the fact that they also wanted to be in proximity to the Beatles as desired objects. One fan that attended the show recalled, 'Who could hear the music, but their mere presence was M-A-G-I-C' (Pryke 2005, 129). This notion of 'being in the presence of the Beatles' had multiple dimensions. For some, Shea was a moment of history in the making and the thing was simply to be there. One fan, JoAnne McCormack, wrote a set list of the songs to capture the occasion (Berman 2008, 170). According to another, Debbie Levitt:

> I went with my sister and I said, 'How could you not be into it? Open your eyes, this is history! They're here!' . . . It didn't matter what they were singing. Just to be enveloped in it, to be part of it, to take it all in. (Berman 2008, 173)

Millard (2012, 200) has argued that Beatlemania marked the coming of age of the baby-boomer generation. As the Fab Four conquered the American market, their fans got to participate in a moment of history: 'Attending a concert was the ultimate act of fandom that placed you in the epicenter of an overwhelming decade' (Millard 2012, 200). Simply attending the event increased one's experience base and stock of cultural capital within the Beatles fan community. For Barbara Boggiano, 'Being part of the Beatles club, I found out who went, who didn't go – we had a weekly meeting, outside our lockers, just to catch up on things' (Berman 2008, 175). Proximity to the band was a kind of crucial currency between such fans, and was indeed a currency *in general* as the Beatles were so popular at that moment. Fans who literally met the band – and thus received attention from them – became celebrities themselves. One said, 'Everybody was talking to us, and the newspapers came over. It was the *Journal-American*, the *Daily News*, and my aunt had heard us interviewed on the radio' (Berman 2008, 162).

For those that could not get so close, being able to at least *look at* the Beatles was an end in itself. It showed a certain level of proximity and for many this was more important than hearing music that they already knew from singles. According to Kathy Albinder, 'Most people you want to see at a concert, you want to listen to what they're doing, but we really didn't care about what they were singing, 'cause we knew all the songs, it was just seeing them' (Berman 2008, 171). Debbie Levitt similarly explained: 'For me it was more visual than a listening experience. I had seen them before that but here it's in the big arena, it's summertime, its everything you want a summer experience to be' (Berman 2008,168). Ilona Gabriel recalled, 'It was hard to get a view of the stage, 'cause everyone stands up, but you could tell everything was going on. We'd just focus on who our favourite Beatle was. We'd be nudging each other, 'Did you see that, did you see the way he moved?'' (Berman 2008, 170). Indeed, Millard (2012, 25) noted that many fans that came to Shea brought along still or 8 mm movie cameras. Such girls actively fulfilled their structural position by pursuing 'transformative' activities: they socialized, wrote set lists, scored points with each other, shot their own movies. In pursuits of totemic goals (being there, seeing the band and capturing the experience in films and photos) they did much more than the mass culture paradigm might predict.

Other fans have conceptually separated themselves from the crowd, claiming that they could not stand the din and just wanted to listen to the music. A second strand of responses therefore operated within the concerns of the mass culture critique. Linda Cooper (in Berman 2008, 172) said, 'I remember sitting and just being angry, like 'Shut up! I want to hear!'' Recalling his then-future wife's attendance at Shea, Paul McCartney explained in the 1995 *Beatles Anthology*: 'Linda [Eastman] was also there – but as she was a real music fan she was quite (annoyed) with everyone screaming. I think she enjoyed the experience, but she genuinely wanted to hear the show.' Through implication, McCartney's interpretation distinguishes 'real' fans (like Linda) who 'genuinely wanted to hear the [music] show' from 'false' fans ('everybody screaming'). By drawing attention to an annoyed, if relatively silent contingent, this interpretation breaks Shea's audience down into different factions and yet sets up some questionable distinctions. For instance, how could those who were annoyed at the screaming enjoy the show as an experience?[10] Did the fans who screamed not also want to hear the show? Is it possible that the screams could have enhanced, or perhaps even been a constituent of, the music as an experience? Rather than seeing the Beatles' music as something *beyond* the group's totemic status and their audience's response to it, we might argue that it had already functioned as *a vehicle for intimacy* that had enhanced their totemic role. From that perspective, their pop was not some kind of sealed-off art object that could only be approached through deep contemplation. Instead it was one link in a multi-part process that generated the band's immense appeal. It excited a live audience, who in turn acted as a *commercial* affirmation that was rebroadcast for all to see. This was a scenario which many wished to deny or destroy – arguing about unruly crowds, bad sound, abandoned music – so that the Beatles could later be resurrected as an art rock band. The irony is that their artistic journey was made more visible precisely because of Beatlemania.

In mythic formulations, Shea combined commercial triumph with sonic catastrophe and represented the beginning of the end for the Beatles as the 'performing fleas' of the pop circus. Offering a kind of reversal of the Faustian formula, this reading suggests that Lennon and his friends turned their backs on a vast live audience at the height of their popularity in order to create better music in relative isolation. The facts of history, however, are not quite so conclusive. There were two Shea events. The Beatles continued to tour after the first Shea concert and their live audience began to wane. The in-concert television documentary, however, fuelled a version of events that said Shea was the beginning of the end: the band supposedly giving up, sonically engulfed by throngs of their own admirers. That reading caricatured concert-goers as morons who did nothing but scream. The way that Shea has been historicized has therefore been shaped by mass cultural formulations. What was awkward was not just that the Beatles could not be heard: it was a commercial context within which music and what Lennon called 'bloody tribal rites' (Northcutt 2006: 136) *had necessarily become same thing.* Indeed, in popular coverage the noisy *behaviour* of fans *en masse* was beginning to eclipse the attention *given to* their heroes, displacing the Beatles as the centre of spectacle. A *New York Times* headline describing the 1965 Shea concert quipped, 'Fans Put on Show to *Rival* Beatles' (Schumach 1965a, 82; emphasis mine). The group's solution to the problem was to present their recordings as sonic art at the expense of live performance – a move that both changed wider perceptions of youth culture and, ironically, enhanced the Beatles own totemic appeal. The music industry's rapidly evolving solution to the wider problem of fan 'hysteria' was in turn neither to numerically decrease nor pacify the audience. Instead it raised the level of live amplification, quashing debates about sound quality and associated commercial compromise while maintaining the 'special quality' of mass spectacles. Shea stadium itself was later to play host to, among others, Grand Funk Railroad (see Waksman 2007), the Who, and Simon and Garfunkle. Despite Mick Jagger's shock at the audience noise at the Beatles' first show, the Stones also played six sold-out Shea shows in October 1989 (Antos 2007, 75). The Beatles 1965 concert has been perceived as a kind of high water mark for the mass audience, when in fact it was only a beginning.

Soon after the Beatles finished touring in 1966, John Lennon complained that his popularity had made his role as a musician redundant, saying, 'I reckon we could send out four wax work dummies of ourselves and that would satisfy the crowds. Beatles concerts are nothing to do with music any more. They're just bloody tribal rites' (Northcutt 2006, 136). His words return us to Auslander's notion of fans blinded by their 'remembered imaginings.' The Beatles had not exactly been eclipsed by their fantasy image. The excitedly screaming fans in the Shea Stadium audience *did* know that the real John, Paul, George and Ringo stood before them. Indeed, the Beatles' presence was actually a *necessary ontological premise* for the fans' deafening counter-performance. It is not so much that Beatles fans were blinded by their fantasies (remembered or otherwise). Instead, their fans knew from mediated traces of them that the band had a tremendous appeal and vast following. As stars of immense standing, their mere presence was enough to trigger performed solicitations of intimacy (screams) that were, collectively, louder than the music. Fans would not have screamed at wax dummies unless the context was somehow associated with an expectation of seeing the 'real' Beatles. At last, they were in relative proximity to their heroes and simply could not believe their own luck. The moment of opportunity to attract the attention of such socially proven figures had finally arrived. In the context of a competitive environment full of distraction for the group, fans' audible excitement was an involuntary means to attract their interest. As well as screaming, many fans at Shea dressed to attract the bands' attention. As JoAnne McCormack said, 'we figured we had to look good' (in Berman 2008, 166). It was not just that audience was going to see the Beatles. As stars the band members were, in an important sense, also *giving* audience, even if they did not, as musicians or artists, eventually come to enjoy it.

Notes

1 See http://www.scottymoore.net/interview_by_Dave_Schwensen.html (accessed November 2014).
2 See Duffett (2014b) for further discussion.
3 See http://www.beatlesbible.com/1966/01/05/recording-overdubs-for-the-beatles-at-shea-stadium/ (accessed November 2014).
4 See http://www.bbc.co.uk/music/sevenages/events/stadium-rock/beatles-at-shea-stadium/ (accessed November 2014).
5 Taken from 'The Beatles at Shea Stadium – Aug. 15/23,1965' posted on The Fifth Beatle Movie Discussion Forum: http://fifthbeatle.proboards.com/thread/536/beatles-shea-stadium-aug-1965#ixzz2yL06tutF (accessed November 2014).
6 See http://www.thebeatles.com/film/beatles-shea-stadium (accessed November 2014).
7 See *New York Times* stories by Montgomery (1966, 40), Schumach (1965c, 11 and 1965b, 29) and Clarke (1966, 80).
8 The interview was published in May 1967 in the American magazine *Hit Parader*. See http://www.beatlesinterviews.org/db1967.05HP.beatles.html (accessed November 2014).
9 See http://www.beatlesbible.com/1964/08/27/live-cincinnati-gardens/ (accessed November 2014).
10 Goddard, Halligan and Spelman (2013) have discussed Beatlemania as a kind of joyous and unrestrained 'case of noise meeting noise' (3).

CHAPTER THREE

Through a Lens Darkly: The Changing Performer-Audience Dynamic as Documented by Four Progressive Rock Concert Films

Kevin Holm-Hudson

Edward Macan's seminal musicological survey of progressive rock, *Rocking the Classics*, notes that between approximately 1968 and 1975, the market for English progressive rock shifted from a primarily British university-bohemian demographic in smaller clubs to a primarily middle class American demographic in arenas and stadiums (Macan 1997, 153–154). During this same period, concert film documentaries became a popular means of bringing the concert experience to fans in locations that a given artist might not visit on tour, also sometimes affording fans a glimpse into the private backstage or recording-studio world of their favourite performers.[1] Changes in the filming techniques used in these movies also tell us something about changes in progressive rock's reception during this period.

In this chapter, I examine the evolving portrayal of the progressive rock concert ritual using four films: Nicholas Ferguson's film of Emerson, Lake and Palmer's *Pictures at an Exhibition* (released in the United States as *Rock and Roll Your Eyes with Emerson, Lake and Palmer*) (1972 UK; 1973 US); Peter Neal's *Yessongs* (1975); Adrian Maben's *Pink Floyd at Pompeii* (1973), recorded in October 1971; and the widely circulated pro-shot bootleg of Pink Floyd's performance of *The Wall* at the Nassau

Coliseum in Uniondale, New York on 27 February 1980. All but the last named of these films saw theatrical release in Great Britain and the United States in the mid- to late 1970s; two of these (*Pink Floyd at Pompeii* and *Pictures at an Exhibition*) saw re-release in forms of various lengths.[2] In the case of Neal's *Yessongs* and Ferguson's *Pictures*, there was a 'lag time' between filming and release; Yes, for example, was playing stadiums by 1975, not the mid-size theatre that was the setting for their concert film (and subsequent live album of the same name).

Each of these films highlights a different facet of prog's reception during the period 1970–1980. In *Pictures at an Exhibition*, frequent use of colour-filter 'negative' effects situate prog as an outgrowth of psychedelia. The unaltered concert footage, and that of *Yessongs*, shows prog in its early 'club' phase; the emphasis is more on music than the special effects (which are decidedly low budget). Pink Floyd's *Pompeii* was filmed without an audience, and is thus more artist-centric, the performers deeply focused on their music making; again, though, there are camera tricks and multiple-exposure sequences that would not have been out of place in a psychedelic film of the late 1960s/early 1970s. Finally, the documentation of *The Wall* shows late prog's (mostly American) arena context; its focus on larger-than-life spectacle was to become routine in arena concerts by the 1990s (see, for example, the special-effect excesses of U2's ZooTV tour). At the same time, the live production of *The Wall* offered its own critique of the arena show experience.

Historically, these four films capture different stages in the evolution of the live concert performance into arena spectacle. The historical placement of progressive rock's emergence and flourishing neatly corresponds to the changes in rock concert presentation dynamics.

It is important to note that, even in the earliest of the progressive rock films reviewed in this chapter, audience shots are minimal and brief. This is in stark contrast to rock festival films such as *Monterey Pop* (D. A. Pennebaker 1968) or *Woodstock* (Michael Wadleigh 1970), in which the audience members seem to be as important a subject as the performers. Even in other films devoted to a single artist or group, such as Pennebaker's concert film of David Bowie, *Ziggy Stardust and the Spiders from Mars* (1973), select audience members' reactions to the performance they are witnessing become a prominent part of the narrative. By contrast, progressive rock films are largely given over to individual performer shots, sometimes in aggressive faceless close-up on the performer's hands as they perform. This kind of camera technique foregrounds the 'faceless virtuosity' of progressive rock musicians, as it excises expression and emotion by keeping facial gestures out of the frame. Even the kind of group shots that distinguish a film like Martin Scorsese's concert film of The Band, *The Last Waltz* (1978), which help to convey band chemistry and camaraderie, are largely absent. Progressive rock comes across as a most insular type of stage performance.

Pictures at an Exhibition

Pictures at an Exhibition was filmed at the Lyceum Theatre in London, a 2,100-seat venue built in 1834, on 9 December 1970, towards the end of Emerson, Lake and Palmer's first European tour. Macan notes that this is a 'fascinating documentary of ELP's formative period, when a distinctive progressive rock style had largely but not completely parted company from late-sixties psychedelia' (Macan 2006, 138). That a feature film of a full performance was made barely three months after their public debut shows how meteoric their rise of the top of the rock pantheon was. At the same time, the film captures something of progressive rock's performance roots. Macan makes the following observations about progressive rock's early audiences:

> During this period [between 1966 and approximately 1971], progressive rock was still the music of a regionally distinct subculture that was essentially homogenous in terms of its members' ages and class origins. Like the musicians, the audience was young (under thirty); it was centred above all in southeastern England; its socioeconomic background was solidly middle-class; and it shared the musicians' general educational backgrounds, and thus their familiarity with the art, literature, and music of high culture. The only major difference between audience and performers at the time involved gender: while the audience seems to have had a roughly equal female-male ratio, the performers were overwhelmingly male. (Macan 1997, 151–152)

Macan goes on to assert that 'for these audiences listening to records and listening to live music was not usually an accompaniment for dancing or other activities; it was the primary activity' (Macan 1997, 152); indeed, shots of the audience in this film (during 'Take a Pebble' and 'The Sage', especially) reveals about an equal proportion of men and women, sitting quietly and paying rapt attention in the manner of listening to a classical recital.

For the performers, too, the emphasis at this stage of ELP's career seems to be on the music making, Keith Emerson's familiar theatrics at the organ notwithstanding. The band makes do with a minimal stage set-up compared with later tours, and there is little in the manner of special lighting effects. Almost all of the footage frames band members individually, which emphasizes their singularity (even as a 'super group') – there are very few 'wide' group shots. While the camera does capture some interaction among band members (mostly between Emerson and Drummer Carl Palmer), still only one person at a time is generally shown in the frame. Some shots focus on hands or torso close-ups, leaving the performer's facial expressions out of the frame (Emerson's string sweeps on 'Take a Pebble'; Greg Lake's bass playing on 'The Barbarian'), having the effect of foregrounding technical virtuosity over expressiveness.

Before beginning their performance of Mussorgsky's classical suite, Keith Emerson remarks that 'the pictures on display are some of Mussorgsky's and some of our own'. Some of the most controversial 'pictures' in the film, giving it its American title, are the post-production 'special effects' added to the concert footage, introduced in a cumulative or 'escalating' fashion as the film proceeds. The first colour effects – colour-filtered 'negative' images of the performers – occur during Lake's acoustic guitar interlude on 'Take a Pebble'. In 'The Old Castle', rotating geometric shapes are superimposed in multiple exposure upon the colour-filtered footage, a clear throwback to the kind of lightshow projections used at places like the Avalon Ballroom in San Francisco and the UFO Club in London. Finally, and most intrusively, a quick-cut collage of Marvel Comics figures is added during 'The Curse of Baba Yaga', all but overwhelming and even replacing the concert footage at times. Macan comments: 'I'm sure the effects were meant to capture the zeitgeist of the time, specifically the experience of a late-sixties light show (and, in all likelihood, the acid trip experience too), but the effects soon become annoying, and finally (by the Marvel Comics episode), simply silly' (Macan 2006, 137). In general, these colour effects are reserved for extended instrumental passages; thus, when the band 'stretches out' instrumentally, the director may be said to take the opportunity to 'stretch out' as well, taking interpretive liberties with the raw footage. (The colour effects are allowed to continue through most of the final verse of 'Take a Pebble'; however, reverting to normal only once Lake has sung 'the colours have all died', in a nice correspondence of image to text.)

Yessongs

Director Peter Neal had previously made several documentaries chronicling the British rock scene: *Experience* with the Jimi Hendrix Experience (1968), the BBC Omnibus documentary *Be Glad for the Song Has No Ending* with the Incredible String Band (1970), and the rock festival feature film *Glastonbury Fayre* (1972). *Yessongs* documented the band's performances at London's Rainbow Theatre, a venue that held about 2,800, on 15 and 16 December 1972, on 16 mm film. The staging is admittedly Spartan – a disco ball provides most of the lighting effects, and Rick Wakeman's keyboards are arrayed in front of a large mirror, providing the illusion that his rig has twice as many keyboards. (The angle of the mirror also allows the audience to watch his hands, a gesture recalling Liszt's profile placement of the piano in solo recitals.)

There is more of a light show to *Yessongs* than ELP evidently had at their disposal for *Pictures* – rhythmically flashing blue lights help to emphasize Alan White's kick drum on 'Your Move', and different coloured lights are used to correspond to different sections of a song. Like *Pictures*, there are also flashbacks to psychedelia. Stock footage of microscopic pond life and opening Venus fly traps is used during the 'nature' sections of 'Close to the Edge' (like the special effects in *Pictures*, this was a directorial choice – such footage was not projected during the band's performances). During Wakeman's keyboard solo spot, the camera work is often trained on close-ups of Wakeman's glittery cape or shots of Wakeman's mirrored reflection, not Wakeman directly; this technique has the effect of obscuring Wakeman's physical presence on stage, as the distinction between the real Wakeman and his reflected doppelgänger is blurred.

The camera work on *Yessongs* is more dynamic than on *Pictures*; shots often move from one band member to another, and there are more pair and group shots. This creates a perception of band 'chemistry', as opposed to a performance by the ensemble of individuals on *Pictures*.

Compared to the ELP performance of a couple of years before, the presence of the audience is also *heard* more – applauding in recognition at the beginning of a song, clapping along and so on. A quick shot of the audience after 'And You And I' reveals again a fairly equal mix of men and women, seated in rows as one would for a classical or jazz concert (see Figure 3.1). Several audience members are shown enthusiastically clapping to the music at the beginning of the gospel-tinged introduction to 'Yours is No Disgrace'.

FIGURE 3.1 Mixed-gender audience sitting politely and attentively as they watch Yes; *Yessongs* (Peter Neal, 1975).

Live at Pompeii

Pink Floyd had already done soundtracks for several 'art films' before *Live at Pompeii* (Peter Sykes' *The Committee* 1968; Barbet Schroeder's *More* 1969; Michelangelo Antonioni's *Zabriskie Point* 1970), so the unusual settings and effects in *Live at Pompeii* can be regarded as an attempt to make a concert movie with 'art film' sensibilities. *Pompeii* is also unique among the movies in this study in having interview and studio sequences, which purport to show the aesthetic views and 'day in the life' of the reclusive techno-artistes.

As critics have widely observed, Pink Floyd were regarded as a 'faceless' band (after their debut album they were not even pictured on their albums until 1971's *Meddle*); Kimi Kärki has suggested that at a Pink Floyd performance,

> the star of the show is the audio-visual spectacle itself, not the performers of the music. This technological mask is what defines the group and, paradoxically, while covering and surrounding them with modern phantasmagorica, gives them their special place in the field of rock performance. (Kärki 2005, 27)

Pink Floyd accordingly found a sympathetic director in Adrian Maben. Maben has referred to his film as an 'anti-Woodstock', the absence of an audience allowing him to break away from 'the clichéd concert film convention of focusing on audience reactions to ordinary stage performances' (Reising 2005, 16). As a result, this concert film focuses instead on the band's engagement with its technology. The interviews are dominated with philosophical discussions about the way the band uses technology in the service of making music, and the opening titles depict the seeming ritual of setting up their gear in an empty Roman amphitheatre. The extended instrumental jam in the opening segment of 'Echoes' is devoted to a long 'orbiting' truck shot around the band's equipment, a camera technique reprised in a tighter orbit around the band itself during the 'Celestial Voices' conclusion to 'A Saucerful of Secrets'. These 'orbiting' shots harmonize with the circular layout of the performance space as well as Pink Floyd's association with 'space music'.[3] Truck or pan shots are also a pervasive motive in the film's interview and studio footage; several studio scenes truck past unused keyboards, subjecting them to our gaze.

Six days were scheduled for filming at Pompeii; unfortunately, three days were lost in unsuccessful efforts to get sufficient electricity to the amphitheatre. Because the power supply at the site was insufficient, a cable had to be run from the town centre of Pompeii to the amphitheatre.[4] 'Echoes', 'A Saucerful of Secrets' and 'One of These Days' were filmed at the amphitheatre; 'Careful with That Axe, Eugene', 'Set the Controls for the Heart of the Sun' and 'Mademoiselle Nobs' were filmed afterwards at a studio in Paris, with additional lighting on hand to suggest the band was performing at night. Additionally, some of the multi-camera footage for 'One of These Days' had been lost, with the result that drummer Nick Mason dominates the footage for that song. Like ELP's *Pictures*, the performance footage is centred largely on individual band members or close-ups of hands playing instruments, rather than group shots that show interaction among band members. Group interaction is instead shown in the casual dining footage, that is, when not at 'work' as recording artists.

The size (or even presence) of the audience was seemingly irrelevant – as it was remarked in a 1972 press conference in Canada, 'If the band is together personally, and the sound is together; then we do a good show' (quoted in Kärki 2005, 33). Of course, those seeing the film become the audience for this event – a 'long-distance' audience witnessing the spectacle through yet another layer of mediating technology. The fact that one is not actually seeing the band 'in the flesh', but instead witnessing a simulacrum (here projected on a large flat screen in a darkened theatre), is a theme taken up in the staged tour for *The Wall* eight years later. By this time, the performance context and audience for progressive rock had been vastly transformed.

The Wall – Recorded 27 February 1980, Nassau Coliseum

By the end of the 1970s, concerts had become big business. Multi-artist festivals, which reached their peak with the Summer Jam at Watkins Glen in 1973 (which featured the Band and the Grateful Dead and attracted an audience of an estimated 600,000 people), eventually gave way to concerts in arenas featuring single artists, sometimes with one opening artist.

Playing for larger audiences also resulted in changes in such aspects of staging as costume, lighting and special effects. This can be seen in the attire of the Who, for example, comparing their outfits for the 1967 Monterey Pop Festival and the 1970 Isle of Wight Festival. By 1970 the Who were playing for much larger crowds: Pete Townshend's white jump suit ensured audiences could see his body from far away (especially when playing at night, as The Who did at both Woodstock and the Isle of Wight); Roger Daltrey's fringed jacket made him look larger-than-life as he spun and swung his microphone. For Pink Floyd, the tendency was to head towards ever more elaborate visual and sonic effects in a display of state-of-the-art technology.

Ironically, such spectacles only distanced the band from their fans even more. As Roger Waters later recalled, 'In the Old Days, pre-*Dark Side of the Moon,* Pink Floyd played to audiences which, by virtue of their size, allowed an intimacy of connection that was magical. However, success overtook us and by 1977 we were playing in football stadiums. The magic was crushed beneath the weight of numbers. We were becoming addicted to the trappings of popularity.'[5] Indeed, in this unreleased concert film the distance between performers and audience is memorably shown in the opening notes of 'In The Flesh?', which are filmed from an extremely *wide* shot – the opposite end of the 15,000-seat arena.[6]

The live performances of *The Wall* incorporated elements of past tours – the floating pig from the *Animals* tour (the In the Flesh Tour) and the crashing airplane from the *Dark Side of the Moon* Tour – but they also involved the choreographed construction of a massive wall, measuring some 210 feet wide and 35 feet high, between the band and the audience. The wall was made of approximately 450 bricks made of fire-proof cardboard, each weighing 19 pounds (Huck 1997, 119). Approximately 340 of these bricks were added to complete the wall in about 45 minutes, so that the last brick would be added at the end of 'Goodbye Cruel World', the last song in the first half of the show.

Janet Huck reveals how the wall was designed to be free-standing and also capable of controlled collapse:

> [Special effects assistant Graham Fleming] came up with ten metal columns which were planted inside the bricks to keep them from tumbling down prematurely. A master control board monitors the up and down movement of the columns so they don't stick out the top of the wall and give the secret away. The columns are topped off with levers which can knock the individual bricks either back or forth: When the wall has to crumble, the operator drops the column supports row by row and flips the levers, sending the bricks crashing down. For safety, the top rows are knocked back on the stage, giant metal cages protecting the equipment and musicians . . . The lower rows, which are less likely to bounce into the audience, are knocked to the front of the stage. 'If we didn't control the collapse of the wall, we'd wipe out the first twenty rows,' said Fleming. (Huck 1997, 120)

Constructing the wall in the proper span of time required two months of rehearsal before the tour; in the first rehearsal, assembling the wall took two hours (Huck 1997, 120). To cover situations where the wall builders fell behind schedule, the band had devised 'expandable riffs' in several sections (Huck 1997, 121).

The band had experimented with elements of spectacle before – including an inflatable octopus that was deployed at the 'Garden Party at the Crystal Palace

Bowl' in London on 15 May 1971 – but the scale of the effects for this show was unprecedented. Such theatrical excess, Macan observes, 'is both peculiarly American (in that the parallels with Disneyland, etc., are obvious) and very much a product of the early 1970s, when general economic prosperity made spectacle on this scale a viable proposition' (Macan 1997, 157). So daunting were the logistics that the initial 'tour' consisted of only three cities – Los Angeles (seven shows), New York (five shows) and London (six shows).

The 27 February 1980 performance at Nassau Coliseum was shot on videotape because 'the initial plan for the 1982 Alan Parker film *Pink Floyd – The Wall* was to feature live concert footage from the tour, interspersed with the terrifying, yet breathtaking animation of Gerald Scarfe and a few extra bridging scenes featuring Waters himself as the main character . . . a rock star facing increasing isolation due to the many "bricks" he has built in "The Wall" around him' (Macek 2012). The tour was accordingly extended to two additional cities – Dortmund (eight shows) and London (another five shows) – for filming purposes in 1981, but ultimately it was decided not to incorporate any concert footage into the film of *The Wall*. Unfortunately, because the Nassau Coliseum show was shot on videotape, the result was too dark and murky, a quality unfortunately made worse by additional generations of bootleg duplication.

To cover the extra instrumentation necessary for live performance, the band was augmented by Andy Bown (bass), Snowy White (guitar), Willie Wilson (drums) and Peter Woods (keyboards) – in essence, an additional band. The additional personnel enabled an innovative critique of performance authenticity.

The opening title of *The Wall* (and the concert) bears a question mark ('In the Flesh?'); upon its reprise in the second half of the show, when the 'concert' is revealed to be a Fascist rally, the question mark is missing, making the title an assertion. It is in this reprise that the musicians are revealed to be a 'surrogate band' standing in for the rock star Pink. In the live show, Bown, White, Wilson and Woods thus become the 'surrogate band' alluded to on 'In the Flesh'. The deception is played out in the opening 'In the Flesh?'; Pink Floyd themselves are nowhere to be seen in the opening number, and instead the audience is treated to the 'surrogate band' wearing rubber life masks of the Pink Floyd band members.[7] It was assumed that, due to the scale of the spectacle and the distance from performers to audience, no one would be able to determine the difference.

The authenticity critique posited by the presence of the 'surrogate band' carried over to other aspects of the show as well. For example, before the show began the audience was greeted with a 'radio personality' who welcomed the audience and laid out the familiar ground rules for enjoying the show:

Good evening, ladies and gentlemen. Welcome to Nassau Coliseum. My name is Gary Yudman, and we're going to have a fine show this evening. We ask you to please enjoy the show from your seats, so that security doesn't hassle you . . . then everything will be all right. The band is setting up and will be ready to go pretty soon. Halfway through the show, there will be a twenty-minute intermission, which will give you a chance to buy some T-shirts. Now, because of the nature of this show, we ask you that, please, no flash cameras be used. If they are, unfortunately they will be confiscated. And please, if your car is blocking an emergency exit, put it in a place where it will do no one any harm. Right, I think the band is about ready to go . . . No, not quite yet. Also, something very important: The band has requested that you refrain from using anything like fireworks. They would like you to be able to hear the words and listen to the music that they have created. If there are disturbing distractions in the Coliseum, it will only bother and disturb the many people who have come here to watch and hear the fantastic show that you are about to witness. So please, no fireworks. Believe me, there will be enough explosions in your mind. Well, I think the band is about ready to go . . . No, not quite yet.

The apparent stalling tactics used ('I think the band is about ready to go . . . No, not quite yet . . . ') made it seem as if these remarks were extemporaneous; however, before the Fascist rally and the reprise of 'In The Flesh' the audience is given the same speech, this time read by a party thug with his voice slowed down (using a harmonizer) to a menacing growl. It is at this point that the deception is revealed – the 'announcements' were as carefully scripted as the rest of the show.

The sheer size of this event means that there are no close-up 'audience shots' in this film, any more than one would expect to see of close-up audience shots at the Super Bowl (unless the audience member is famous, of course). The camera work instead tries to capture the wide-angle enormity of the event itself.

Conclusion

It is indicative of the rapidly changing dynamic of how progressive rock concerts were staged in the early 1970s that the three commercially released films reviewed here depicted bands whose shows had become very different by the time the films saw release. *Pictures at an Exhibition* saw US release just before ELP began its massive 'Welcome Back, My Friends' tour, which by now involved thirty-six tonnes of equipment, hauled in four semi-trailers (Macan 2006, 316–317); by the time *Yessongs* was released, Rick Wakeman had left Yes and the band was about to embark on the *Relayer* tour with new keyboardist Patrick Moraz, after a year-long hiatus that saw each individual band member releasing solo albums;

at the time of *Live in Pompeii*'s release, Pink Floyd was playing arena-sized venues and had released the iconic *Dark Side of the Moon* album. All three of these films, then, had become time capsules of a moment in progressive rock's maturing even as they were released. As for the unreleased concert film of *The Wall*, by 1982, when Parker's cinematic re-imagining of Waters' story was released, it could be said that the 'rock concert film' was a thing of the past; music fans now wanted their MTV (and the short, easily digestible music video format therein), and so feature-length concert films were soon to be niche-marketed to fans on video rather than showing in movie houses. The old guard of progressive rock, too, was a thing of the past – although King Crimson, Genesis and Yes carried on into the 1980s with markedly different (and, for the most part, more pop-friendly) musical styles.

Yet, these films – as anachronistic as they must have seemed after their delayed releases (and subsequent half-life as midnight 'rock features' in campus-town cinemas) – collectively document the changes in progressive rock performance as shows moved from regional events in small clubs and mid-size theatres to large-scale arena events – a change of performance context that Macan argues cut off progressive rock from the cultural roots that nourished it.

Notes

1　D. A. Pennebaker's documentary *Don't Look Back* (1967), chronicling Bob Dylan's early-1965 British tour, was the template for this sort of movie. More than simply an amalgamation of concert footage, the film also contained scenes of press releases, backstage wranglings and hotel room ennui.

2　Emerson, Lake and Palmer's *Rock and Roll Your Eyes* is a full-length film (91 minutes) that includes performances of 'The Barbarian', 'Take a Pebble', 'Pictures at an Exhibition' and 'Knife Edge', whereas *Pictures at an Exhibition*, at least in its video release, features only the titular suite. *Live at Pompeii* has a somewhat more complicated history, existing in a shortened form that only uses the performance footage (62 minutes), the version for theatrical release that includes interviews and footage of the band recording *Dark Side of the Moon* (85 minutes) and a 'director's cut' that includes, among other things, a sci-fi 'space' opening sequence with an electronic soundtrack (92 minutes).

3　The association of Pink Floyd with 'space music' dates back at least as far as 1968's 'Set the Controls for the Heart of the Sun', though one could cite 1967's 'Interstellar Overdrive' and 'Astronomy Domine' as well. The band's music was used as a soundtrack for the BBC's coverage of the moon landing in 1969.

4　See 'Adrian Maben – Live at Pompeii – Interview with Brain Damage': http://www.brain-damage.co.uk/other-related-interviews/adrian-maben-live-at-pompeii-2003-with-brain-d.html (accessed August 2014).

5　Quoted in the accompanying CD booklet for Roger Waters, *The Solo Years, Volume 1: The Flickering Flame* (released 2002).

6 Though still commercially unreleased, the full-length video may be viewed on
  YouTube at http://www.youtube.com/watch?v=p_anNGjld7w (accessed August
  2014).
7 These life masks are depicted on the cover of *Is There Anybody Out There?*
  (2000), the audio CD of *The Wall* live shows.

CHAPTER FOUR:

Evolutions of *The Wall*: 1979–2013

Kimi Kärki

Everyone said that a show like this could never be toured.
– STAGE DESIGNER MARK FISHER (QUOTED IN MORETON 2010)

Introduction

Roger Waters (1943–) is known as a founding member in the British rock group Pink Floyd, of which he was a member from 1965 to 1985.[1] After the original singer and guitarist Syd Barrett left the group in obscure circumstances, around 1968, Waters quickly became the prime motor of the band, supplying the majority of songs and lyrics. The double album *The Wall* (1979) is arguably, along with *The Dark Side of the Moon* (1973), the best known of Pink Floyd's album, and was largely written by Waters – to the point the album could be reasonably considered to be a solo record.[2] Thus it is no surprise that, after departing the group, Waters has continued to rely on this musical work as an integral part of oeuvre, and live shows. After the original live shows of 1980–1981, *The Wall* was then performed once, in 1990, and toured again in 2010–2013. While the first outing was with Pink Floyd (released in 2000 as *Is There Anybody Out There? The Wall Live 1980–1981*), the second and third time *The Wall* was presented as a solo Roger Waters event (and *The Wall – Live in Berlin* was released in 1990, but Waters's 2000 *In the Flesh – Live* also contained several songs from *The Wall*). In addition, the film *Pink Floyd – The Wall* (Alan Parker/Gerald Scarfe 1982) can also be considered as a 'legitimate' public version of the original concept album, as can the promo video for the single 'Another Brick in The Wall (Part Two)' (1979), directed by Scarfe. 'Illegitimate' releases, via bootlegs of various media, have also remained in circulation.

The theatrical elements of the performance have been redesigned and developed for crowds of three different decades. How has this effected the production and performance of *The Wall*? This chapter engages with this concern, and contends that the cultural and historical contexts of each of these shifts of performance have actually shaped the productions very significantly, as they have been developed. In this extended timeline, *The Wall* suggests itself as an extremely instructive case study for consideration of live arena music: the wall itself becomes akin to a blank canvas, ready to be painted on again and again. And, although significant changes took place across these productions – Waters's exit from Pink Floyd, and advances in staging technology, as well as enormous changes in the political, social and cultural contexts across three decades (especially around the fall of the Berlin Wall) – the artistic or thematic continuities seem to have held. Waters's themes of alienation, displacement and disruption have remained acutely relevant. And the overarching and unifying theme of *The Wall*, which can be said to be the struggle for communication, seems to have spoken to audiences of the 1970s, 1980s, 1990s and 2010s.

The idea of *The Wall* was born out of frustration. By July 1978, during the last North American leg of the Pink Floyd *Animals In the Flesh* tour, in support of the *Animals* album (1977), Waters grew increasingly frustrated with playing live. The idea of building a wall between the band and the audience had already occurred to him, during a 1975 North American tour: Waters did not enjoy the screaming mass audiences which had, after the commercial success of *The Dark Side of the Moon*, replaced their earlier, and more introspective, fan base (see Schaffner 1992, 219–220; Povey and Russell 1997, 141, 161). Building from this impulse, the foundational concept of *The Wall* came to concern all kinds of walls: every disappointment in one's life was 'another brick in the wall', as the lyrics had it.[3] And Waters wanted this wall, both real and metaphorical, to now be erected during a live show. To realize this idea, architectural designers Mark Fisher and Jonathan Park were to be invited to design one of the most ambitious rock shows that had yet been seen and certainly, for the end of the 1970s, entirely groundbreaking in terms of spectacle.[4]

The album *The Wall* is partly an autobiographical psychodrama, as focused on Waters's childhood memories, but melded with a commentary on popular music stardom. This latter concern is presented in scenes of a dystopian British near-future of fascism, during which the rock star protagonist experiences encroaching madness. From the outset of the creative process Waters planned *The Wall* to be an album (for 1979), a stage show (for 1980–1981) and a movie (then released in 1982) (see Jones 1996, 122; Sedgwick 2000a, 7).[5] In this way *The Wall* was, to use Herkman's term (2012, 10–20) an 'intermedial' product family, with simultaneously planned different stagings of the same narrative. *The Wall* is 'intermedial' in the sense that it exists across different forms: its existence can only really be found or understood as existing between the forms, or as a concept that spreads across different forms.

FIGURE 4.1 The teacher puppet; production drawing for the film of *Pink Floyd – The Wall* (Alan Parker/Gerald Scarfe, 1982). © Stufish Entertainment Architects.

Motifs are generated and then impinge on each variant. One of the designs shared by the stagings and the film was a gigantic puppet of the character of The Teacher (seen here as a production drawing for the film set). Rather than just create an inflatable effigy, Fisher and Park designed a complex and motorized creature, with means to enable disconcertingly 'natural' movement.

Multiple architectural challenges were involved in the staging of *The Wall*, relating to both engineering and the safety of the musicians and audiences. But a fundamental difficulty concerned how to build, and then tear down, a wall of 450 cardboard bricks, and indeed how to fabricate these bricks so that they could be easily transported from one show to the next. The solution was to have designed fully customized and hollow cardboard bricks, assembled from four parts which, after the shows, could be dismantled and transported. And this was one of only a number of challenges, not least as most of the components used in the shows were actually prototypes. After a long test run, with the whole set being assembled and dismantled and moved a couple of times between Culver City and Los Angeles Arena, Fisher and Park noticed that any mechanical design would inevitably be prone to errors under the uniquely 'anarchic and unexpected conditions' of a rock tour, where everything needed to function while the crew was bombarded by noise and flashing lights (Lyall 1992, 22).

In part, *The Wall* is a 'rock opera' about fascism. And rock music, as staged in stadiums and arenas (as with Pink Floyd in the 1970s), seemed to contain the potential to provoke the audience into hysterical or even violent responses. For Waters, the content met and matched the form: a satire, where the rock concert was re-imagined as a fascist gathering. Scarfe's contribution to *The Wall* seemed to work to abstract images of fascism, especially in the visual motif of marching hammers.[6] So, instead of a feeling of, or striving for, a musical connection with the audience, Waters felt he was violating them: dropping bombs from the stage all around the audience, as it were, with the massive levels of sound capable to being held in an arena (see Sedgwick 2000b, 5). References were made to the Second World War in this way – the use of the falling aeroplane (moving on a wire from the back of the arena to the stage) for the opening number of the concert, 'In the Flesh?', and the song 'Vera' about the famous British wartime entertainer Vera Lynn ('Remember that she said / that we would meet again / some sunny day.'). For *The Wall* Waters wanted to shatter any extant operating assumption of the band and the audience communicating during a live concert, as he told the *Music Express* in 1980: 'There is an idea, or there has been an idea for many years abroad, that it's a very uplifting and wonderful experience, that there is a great contact between the audience and the performers on the stage. I don't think that's true' (quoted in Fitch 2001, 266). And such a confession, on Waters's part, leads us to the core of *The Wall*: it is a spectacularly public narrative about non-communication and mental isolation and, as such, a paradox.

The plotline evolves to be a story about traumatic childhood experiences, which cause the protagonist, Pink, to lose his mind. From the outset, Pink's life revolves around an abyss of loss and isolation: born during the war, losing his father (who is only present in family photographs) and brought up by an overtly protective mother. He chooses to build a mental and metaphorical wall between himself and the rest of the world. As enclosed by this wall, he can live in an alienated solitude, as hopefully freed from life's endless blows. Every new incident that causes Pink pain is transformed into yet 'another brick in the wall', and so redeemed. As this metaphorical wall comes closer and closer to completion, each brick further closing Pink off from the rest of the world, he becomes mad and totally isolated. However, once the wall is complete Pink begins to realize the destructive effects of total mental isolation, and now wants to break free from this self-imposed prison. In the so-called Trial scene, Pink's problems are resolved: the trial, which would seem to occur in his mind, results in the judgement that he should start communication again. Or as Waters put it for the *New Musical Express* in 1980: 'And in the end, the judgment on himself is to de-isolate himself, which, in fact, is a very good thing. The wall is then torn down' (quoted in Fitch 2001, 273).

The Wall as intermedial spectacle

My focus is on the large-scale arena or stadium show, of the kind where there is an understood need to create huge media spectacles, and stage constructions, not least to make the concert appealing, even for those positioned at the far back of the venue.[7] Auslander has even claimed, looking to a more contemporary timeframe, that this need to fortify and exaggerate stage events with media technologies has resulted in an audiovisual experience in which 'liveness' is marginalized: massive video walls and screens display a variety of visual representations of the stage, and even then mostly mixed with pre-recorded streams of film. This constant visual feed captures the attention of the spectators, even to the extent that they can then ignore the actual live performers playing under or to the side of the screens (Auslander 2008, 25–26, 42). Pink Floyd, in their capitalization on just such a tension (an aesthetic that required such technology in order to emphasize the staging of the spectacle), seemed to present, within the live realization of this concept, a critique of this tension. The band, dwarfed by such a spectacle, was rendered as effectively invisible. Furthermore, perhaps this overblown production could be said to be a stubborn reaction to the challenges mounted to popular music by the punk movement of this time, and its do-it-yourself aesthetic, and the earlier critical attacks on Pink Floyd's performances as boring or possessing just '[t]oo much overpowering technology and too much dull pain' (Farren 1977). Not only were the visuals pre-prepared but also many of the aural elements of *The Wall* were pre-recorded and sequenced. The resultant interaction between the live and the pre-recorded was provocatively problematized by Wurtzler:

The apparent collapsing of distinctions between live and recorded, and the difficulty of theorizing a subject effect for the popular music concert, result from the simultaneous presence of two, by definition, mutually exclusive categories: the live and the recorded. Even though the live concert struggles to reinstate a notion of the fully present original event in popular music, the co-presence of the live and the recorded contribute to a potential crisis in our notions of a real that exists prior to representation. (Wurtzler 1992, 94)

This crisis is a wider crisis of contemporary media culture, where it becomes increasingly difficult to distinguish the real from the simulated, and the live from the scripted. For Guy Debord, in his seminal 1967 work *The Society of the Spectacle*, the notion of 'spectacle' has traditionally worked in opposition to the experience of immediate reality. On everyday levels, the populace are treated to a technological, mediated, materialized and dominantly superficial and 'visual' ideology. Deceptively, the nature of spectacle is seemingly positive, indisputable and obviously tautological: 'Everything that appears is good, whatever is good will appear' (Debord 1995, 12).[8] Debord later nuanced his original thesis by positing that the nature of spectacle has changed as a consequence of a battle between a unified, 'totalitarian' model (as with the Third Reich, or the Soviet Union) and the more flexible and internationalized, 'Americanized' model. A new 'integrated' and global spectacle, which represents the synthesis of these two opposing models, has then become dominant in the contemporary media landscape (Debord 1990, 8–13; Pyhtilä 2005, 140–152). Spectacular forms of entertainment, as with the arena concert or the opening ceremony of the Olympic Games for example, are at the very core of this kind of integrated and intermedial culture. These are the 'mega events' (as defined by Close et al. 2007, 25–26) or, rather, 'media events', with elements of mixed media forms, and a potential wider availability beyond the immediate sphere of the event via recording or broadcasting.[9] *The Wall*, as a variety of media manifestations, and all incorporated into the sense of one evolving opus, makes for a pioneering 'product family' for just this kind of theorizing: a spectacle evolving in tandem with, and as a critique parallel of, the society of the spectacle.

A more inclusive conceptual understanding, which is useful when approaching arena rock, comes in Kellner's notion of the 'media spectacle'. Kellner partially rejects the 'monolithic' and 'all-embracing' spectacle, as formulated by Debord and the Situationists, and claims that an analysis of particular phenomena within the spectacle allows for a much more complex and nuanced reading of the culture in which we find ourselves (2010, 76–80). Kellner here synthesizes ideas of Debord with the notion of a 'media event': the 'media spectacle' incorporates 'media events', or becomes the sum of their parts. This is the same critical impulse that allowed Jean

Baudrillard to consider the idea of actual warfare as overridden by a media/ state imperative to create 'live' war imagery for broadcast, in his provocative 1991 writings collected as *The Gulf War Did Not Take Place*.

The relationship then between 'media spectacle' and intermediality is one that is methodologically helpful in mounting a culturally sensitive reading of spectacles, especially for the multi-platform distribution models of the digital age. Intermediality concerns the relationships and continuities between different forms of media, their entanglements and mutations, evolutions and extinctions, and incorporates an understanding of the constant state of change of media technologies.[10] *The Wall*, in its spectacular nature, seems to yearn for an extinction: the wall is built across the arena stage, as if to block communication, because Waters disliked being on that stage so intensely in relation to the ways in which it diminished communication. The Wall is an articulation or dramatization of this matter, as well as an attempted anaesthetization of these negative feelings.

The Wall live

The original Pink Floyd tour set, which was only seen in a few indoor arenas from 1980 to 1981, used space in a revolutionary way in relation to staging an aesthetics of, or for, rock. Gerald Scarfe's grotesque animations, including the 'fucking flowers', and marching hammers, were projected onto the wall itself, via three 35 mm film projectors, which were all synchronized as well as possible in the days before digital sequencing. In addition, the show featured a living room attached to the wall, a 'fascistic' version of the famous flying pig (now painted black and decorated with Scarfe's crossed hammers symbol), as first seen on Pink Floyd *Animals* album cover (1977), and huge puppets, both inflatable and mechanical, individually operated by cranes. The concert ended with the trial scene, after which the wall was torn down to the accompaniment of loud and disturbing rumbles, emanating from sub-woofers hidden beneath the stage.

The beginning of the show, which journalist Hugh Fielder described in *Sounds* as unexpected and intentionally confusing, seemed to be devised to achieve a Brechtian 'alienation effect'. At first, a 'house announcer' warmed up the audience, followed by the band starting amid flashes of light, and sounds of thunder. An 'aeroplane' (a model of a few feet in length, accompanied by a Stuka-like sound of diving bomber emanating from the PA) then flew through the hall, on a wire, and crashed into the wall with a loud explosion. But the band playing was not, in fact, Pink Floyd. Rather, 'it was four clones performing like an Americanized version of the band. After a couple of minutes, the real Pink Floyd emerged. This had a disquieting effect on the audience' (Fielder quoted in Fitch 2001, 265).[11]

This surrogate band wore masks resembling the facial features of each Pink Floyd member (masks which are also seen on the cover of the live album *Is There Anybody Out There?*). This idea of hiding behind a real or metaphorical mask tallied with the narrative of *The Wall* and this sense of being at one remove, as it were, seems to have extended to the wider experience of the project. Keyboard player Rick Wright remembered he didn't enjoy playing the shows, since the band was indeed playing while hidden for almost half of the show – a substantially contrarian state of affairs in respect to arena rock stardom. Wright recalled how the roadies would run all around, building the wall and tearing down the set components once used, and that chasm between their actions and his inactivity and non-presence resulted in an experience that was jarringly impersonal (Sutcliffe 1995, 75). In the 1990 incarnation of *The Wall*, the audience members were given 'worm' masks, as per the song 'Waiting for the Worms', and already familiar from the film version. In this way the audience became a literally 'faceless' mass, as if infected with the original concerns of alienation and hiding.

Anthropologist Victor Turner theorizes masks as a facet of a cultural obsession with the notion of play. The mask conveys the idea of an otherness within. Once masked, the resultant performance is distanced. The mask is a sign of role – masked performers play the game of otherness, being 'more', or something else, than normal (Turner 1982, 40).[12] On one level, the masks seem to look to this role-playing, but on another, and thinking more about Pink Floyd in this context, we can say that the band was also effectively masked by their state-of-the-art technology. The show's growth left them in secondary role: as an absent centre. Drummer and percussionist Nick Mason felt this state of affairs to be *The Wall*'s central and fascinating thesis: that everyone can be replaced.

> I'm sure someone will do it, even if we don't, that is, to design a show like a play in which you can use different actors to perform a 'thing.' I don't see anything wrong in that, but we haven't yet managed to make that jump. (Quoted in Fitch 2001, 278)

Indeed, Waters was soon to make that leap. He left the band in 1985, and re-staged *The Wall* without his old band mates.[13]

When *The Wall* was resurrected in Berlin, on 21 July 1990, it was a Waters solo project. The Berlin concert was charity orientated: arranged to fund, and raise awareness of, the World Memorial Fund for Disaster Relief. But Berlin was not the original location of choice. According to set designer Jonathan Park, 'we investigated the idea of doing it in the Sahara Desert or in extraordinary places – Monument Valley in America [for example] – somewhere where we could make a big statement'.[14] Other possibilities considered were the Grand Canyon, and Wall Street in New York. But in the immediate aftermath of the fall of the Berlin Wall, Berlin presented itself as the self-evident, and supremely iconographic, location for the event.

The show was upscaled to suit the ten-hectare site on the derelict Potsdamer Platz, a part of the 'No Man's Land' between East and West Germany that is often regarded by Berliners as the symbolic heart of the former city (pre-Cold War) of Berlin. The ten-metre high cardboard wall of the original show was now replaced by a 25 metre high polystyrene and scaffolding structure, which was 168 metres wide. This was constructed from 132,087 kilos of steel scaffolding and 2,500 polystyrene bricks, and required four lifts, and an additional four backstage lifts, and two huge construction site cranes. The stage itself was 30 metres across, and was designed to accommodate not only the band, which was assembled specially for the performance by Waters, but also an 80-piece orchestra, a 150 person choir, the Marching Band of the Combined Soviet Forces and a variety of limousines and military vehicles that featured in the show. Waters, keen to ensure that the absence of the other Pink Floyd members was not felt, brought in a variety of stars: The Scorpions, Bryan Adams, The Band, Sinead O'Connor, Joni Mitchell, Van Morrison, Cindy Lauper, Ute Lemper, Paul Carrack and Marianne Faithful. Michael Kamen conducted the choir and orchestra, and approximately 600 people helped with the various theatrical elements of the show and the actual building of the wall. Ticket sales were halted after 250,000 people had been admitted but at least another 100,000 gained entry after that. According to some sources there were 500,000 people present in the area, and the television broadcast was seen by an estimated 300 million people (Rowley 1991, 25–27).

The Teacher puppet was this time controlled by massive construction cranes, as seen here in the production drawing. It is notable that Scarfe's original level of grotesque satire is pushed even further for this later staging of *The Wall*.

FIGURE 4.2 Production drawings for *The Wall Live in Berlin* (1990). © Stufish Entertainment Architects.

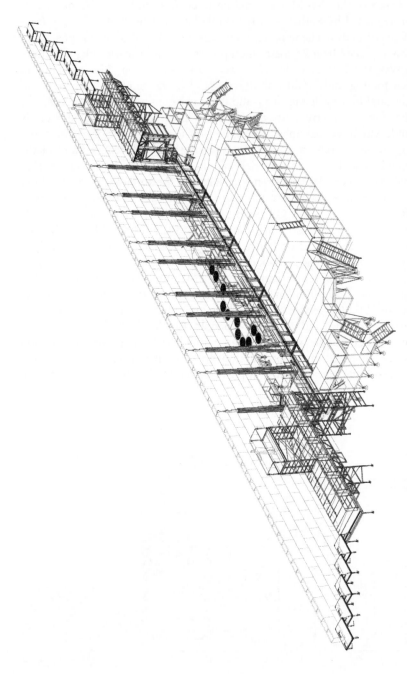

FIGURE 4.3 The production model for the latest incarnation of *The Wall* (2010–2013) is an immensely complex affair, zoomable to the smallest technical details of the design. © Stufish Entertainment Architects.

And, more generally, the show was bleaker than the first tour. The projected images, of the original Scarfe animations, were intentionally blurred by photocopying them repeatedly, and then they were mixed with graffiti images from the Western side of the actual Berlin Wall. The show contained all of the totalitarian elements of the original narrative, but now seemingly historically materialized: actual military helicopters and anti-aircraft lights (used in a similar way to their deployment in Nuremberg, by Albert Speer, for Third Reich rallies and the 1936 Olympic Games). Waters performed in a full uniform, playing 'Pink', as a demagogue rock-Fuehrer.

The next re-design of the whole show was done twenty years later in conjunction with Stufish Entertainment Architects (The Mark Fisher Studio) for TAIT, a Pennsylvania-based set production company. This would be for a Waters solo tour: *The Wall Live*, from 2010.

In a statement on his website, Waters outlined the need to use *The Wall* to engage with a contemporary audience:

> I recently came across this quote of mine from 22 years ago: 'What it comes down to for me is this: Will the technologies of communication in our culture, serve to enlighten us and help us to understand one another better, or will they deceive us and keep us apart?' . . . I believe this is still a supremely relevant question and [that] the jury is out. There is a lot of commercial clutter on the [Inter]net, and a lot of propaganda, but I have a sense that just beneath the surface[,] understanding is gaining ground. We just have to keep blogging, keep twittering, keep communicating, keep sharing ideas.[15]

Making good on this imperative to communicate, and make meaning outside the paradigms of the mainstream news media, Waters even requested, via Facebook, stories and images concerning families and friends lost in wars. These were integrated into *The Wall Live*.

This new production was indeed a technological tour de force. I saw the concert at Hartwall Arena, Helsinki, in April 2011. The essential change was that the audiovisual material had been much developed and expanded in comparison to the old Scarfe films, and even to material familiar from Potsdamer Platz show, although these earlier streams of audiovisual material still found a place in this new show. Sublime three-dimensional effects were presented across the full width of the wall, this time perfectly synchronized with the music. Once the wall had been completely built, halfway through the show and at the point of the intermission, it was covered with the photographs of men, women and children who had lost their lives in different conflict zones, from Anzio in the 1940s to Iraq and Afghanistan of the 2000s. Waters's intention was clearly presented: the original narrative foundation, which concerned the formative and alienating effects of loss during the Second World War for the protagonist, had remained entirely topical during a time of the so-called 'War on Terror'.

But the autobiographical elements remained as well. This time Waters sang the song 'Mother' as a duet with his (as he said) 'miserable and fucked up' younger self, of thirty years prior, as projected above Waters. The footage was from the Earls Court 1980 performance. Evolution had been both technological and emotional. And the memories of those people lost, seen in the submitted images, had met and merged with the memories of the singular loss that, decades before, had been an artistic inspiration for Waters as he first conceived *The Wall*: a requiem mounted by its world-wide audience.

Conclusion

Across the later incarnations of *The Wall*, and indeed as a part of the evolution of the work itself, Waters seems to have become more at ease with his role as an arena performer. Those new waves of technology, incorporated into the show, have functioned both as tools for new kinds of communication while, simultaneously, having been seen as objects for critique. The promise of safety and isolation, as enclosed behind a wall, seems even more enticing in respect of the 'noise' of useless information streaming across digital media platforms, and the mantras of the brands we all need to consume. Thus Debordian ideas about the experience of contemporary society, which find a resonation in *The Wall*, have become more and more topical.

The Situationists opposed the idea of a society given over to, or mesmerized by, the spectacular. The cultural and historical processes which gave rise to contemporary media spectacles need a careful and distinctive historical contextualization: even if I have chosen to compare the three versions of a same live show in different decades in this discussion, I am not seeking to claim that they are all essentially the same event revisited. In the three versions of the live show we see a different wall each time, as always recontextualized by its surroundings. But we seem to run into a vortex of intermedial paradoxes or ontological crises. If spectacle is supposed to show and incorporate everything to a maximal effect, why then does the band disappear behind a wall? Capitalist spectacle is understood to make the citizen passive, and mistake the visual surface of the spectacle for a deeper reality. But *The Wall* induces critical thought and even revolt. I oppose the rigid Debordian model of 'the society of the spectacle' primarily because the 'integrated spectacle' is not just a primary forms of global capitalism; it also contains the seeds of its own destruction within it. The spectacle cannot, ultimately, sustain the belief of those who would believe in it: this God will always fail. Spectacle is susceptible rather than absolute. Spectacle can be analysed, measured, experienced and even abandoned through the act of consuming the critical message found within, as in a work like *The Wall*. The same media technology that blurs reality with unreality, by making everything spectacular, also offers tools for cultural criticism: the imminence of deconstruction within the construction of the spectacular. *The Wall* prompts such a revision, or nuancing, of Debord. Let us call *The Wall* a meta-level spectacle then: one that is, paradoxically, intended by its dramaturg to call into question its very own nature. The origins of this auto-critique are clear: the creation of the spectacular arena experience by one who professed hatred of the experience of being at the centre of spectacular arena concerts. That the conception seems to have been strong enough to elicit audience reactions across the decades validates Waters's methods. And that this conception has worked on ever bigger levels, reaching to the arena scale (and indeed pioneering such an upscaling in this respect), suggests that the intellectual impulse of popular music is not exclusively confined to the intimate, to communication and even to the presence of the band. The impact of *The Wall* comes in its size. Once the wall is torn down, the audience is offered a highly spectacular work that is intrinsically against the spectacles found outside the arena, and in society at large.

Notes

1   My heartfelt thanks to Professor Bruce Johnson for the language refinement, and Dr Benjamin Halligan for the detailed comments, during the completion of this chapter.
2   According to the Recording Industry Association of America, *The Wall* has certified sales of at least 23 million copies, making it the fourth biggest selling album of all time (see https://www.riaa.com/goldandplatinum.php?content_selector=top-100-albums).
3   On the idea of the 'concept album' see Macan (1997, 11, 40–46, 68) and Rose (1998, 14–16).
4   For more on Fisher's career, see Holding (2000).
5   And Waters co-directed, along with Sean Evans, the 2014 documentary *Roger Waters: The Wall*.
6   For different accounts of *The Wall*'s take on fascism, see Schaffner (1992, 224–226), Jones (1996, 122–123) and (Fitch 1997, 316–320).
7   On such massive stage constructions, see Goodwin (1990, 269), Kärki (2005, 36–39), Kärki (2010, 226, 239–240) and Kärki (2014).
8   On the concept of 'the society of the spectacle' see Debord (1995, 12–15, 17–18), Baugh (2005, 3–7) and Pyhtilä (2005, 137–139).
9   For the evolution of the concept of 'mega events' see Dayan and Katz (1996, 1–24), Couldry (2003, 55–74) and Couldry and Hepp (2010, 3–13). For further discussion, see Kärki (2011, 43–45) and Kärki (2014, 62–63).
10   On the relation of intermediality and audiovisual aesthetics, see Richardson and Gorbman (2013, 23).
11   This can be seen on the bootleg film of one of the concerts: *The Wall Live* (1980).
12   See also Helbo (1987, 118–119).
13   After leaving the band Waters entered a protracted legal battle with the other members, on the basis that Pink Floyd should be terminated. Waters was to

eventually lose the case, and has reunited with his old band mates only very infrequently since.

14 Quoted in the documentary *Pink Floyd: Behind the Wall* (Bob Smeaton 2000).

15 See http://rogerwaters.com/why.php

PART TWO

Arena Concerts Now

CHAPTER FIVE

From Shed to Venue: The Arena Concert Event Space

Robert Kronenburg

Introduction: The arena as a distinct building typology

Imagine approaching a building whose perimeter walls soar above you, grand and impressive. Inside, you enter a dramatic open space with continuous raked seating for the thousands of spectators who look across a flat, wooden floor upon which the event they have come to see takes place. Above you a lightweight roof spans this wide open space and contains the activities within, focusing the audience's attention so that they become not only spectators, but almost a part of the show, engaging in it with their voices, movement and actions. The spectacle is made possible by numerous behind the scenes stagehands creating an event that includes music, noise, giant sets and performers, and yet it is not a play or an opera. This building is the Colosseum in Rome, built nearly 2,000 years ago between AD 70 and 82, an entertainment facility that enabled 50,000 spectators to view hugely ambitious spectacles including the recreation of land and sea battles. This structure, and the lesser examples built across the Roman Empire, can be seen as the direct ancestor of the contemporary arena building, including all its key features: a superstructure that can be erected in any suitable location; dedicated to the viewing of spectacle and contests by large numbers of people; able to accommodate multiple entertainment types; and enclosed for protection from the elements but also to contain and intensify the event.[1] This example, drawn from such an early phase of history, defines the arena as a distinct building typology – an architectural archetype.

The Colosseum is like the modern-day arena in another important way – its purpose was to be primarily a place for contests and games (gladiatorial exhibitions and competitions) rather than performance. The architectural form of the contemporary arena arises from its original design brief as a container for large sports events, its progenitor being the open-air stadium with its all encompassing seating, raked stands and multiple points of entry for both the viewed and the viewers. Most stadiums, even today, are open-air structures, partly because of the requirements of the sports they support but mostly because a big (and therefore costly) problem in creating large spaces like this is in the creation of lightweight wide span roofs. A roof with intermediate columns would interfere with audience sight lines, a problem that is exacerbated when covering a field of play, which, cannot be obstructed at all.

The size of the enclosed sports arenas that emerged in the twentieth century was set as a consequence of these structural restrictions, the building layout and capacity determined by the technical and economic limits of building large open span roof structures. Early modern-day arenas, such as the Antwerp Sportspaleis, Belgium (1933), a cycling venue, and the third Madison Square Garden, New York (the first MSG that can be classed as an arena, 1925–1968), built for boxing, were usually primarily dedicated to one sport.[2] However, it soon became recognized that the spatial arrangement of arenas had benefits in terms of flexibility (Kronenburg 2007). The large flat floor area (for the sports activity) could be used for different events, sporting and otherwise, and its location in the centre of the space meant that the distance from activities in this area to the furthermost seats in the arena could match that in an auditorium or concert hall even though there might also be considerably more people in the audience. The fully enclosed space allowed set-up and use independent of the weather, and, if blacked-out, full control over artificial lighting, providing staging opportunities not available in open-air venues. All this encouraged entrepreneurial operators to seek alternative ways to use the building – for exhibitions, meetings, conference events and popular entertainments. If the acoustics and internal environment in terms of air quality, temperature and character were lacking because of the shed-like qualities of the building, the ability to host multiple different events combined with a quick turnaround still made the development of new buildings commercially viable. Even in the late 1970s when it began to be technically possible to enclose stadium-sized structures, arenas were still designed and built, primarily as sports, family entertainment, exhibition and conference centres.[3]

Arenas in the United States: Sports versus entertainment

If The Beatles' first performance at Shea Stadium on 15 August 1965 heralded the dramatically expanding possibilities for popular music concerts, it also clearly identified the problems to be faced in creating successful performances for such large audiences. It was not only the lack of volume from the onstage equipment (though comparatively large 100 watt amplifiers had been specially provided by Vox for the tour) and the quality of sound through the stadium public address system, but the distance between audience and performer, and the lack of staging and stage lighting. The arena provided a suitable compromise between the mega-audiences of the stadium (55,000 at The Beatles show) and the much smaller scale concert halls and theatres (usually up to c. 3,000). More sophisticated and more powerful amplification was quickly developed by manufacturers, and people like Bill Hanley, who had been chief sound engineer at the Newport Jazz and Folk Festivals from 1957 and the ground-breaking Woodstock Music and Art Fair in 1969.[4] Lighting also improved, using theatrical sources and equipment, but also taking inspiration from film and fine art. Though still a compromise compared to a smaller auditorium, the enclosed spaces that arenas afforded were not only easier to fill with sound than a stadium – they also potentially provided a better environment in which to create a more complete 'show'.

One of the first arena venues to be designed with both sport and popular music shows as part of the brief was the Spectrum, Philadelphia, United States, which opened in September 1967. Designed by respected architects Skidmore Owings and Merrill, the 18,000 capacity arena was initially home to both a basketball team (Philadelphia 76ers) and an ice hockey team (Philadelphia Flyers); however, its flexibility as a venue for a wide range of other popular entertainment events was also important. The facility was named by Lou Scheinfeld, former President of the Spectrum, ostensibly as an acronym: SP for sports and South Philadelphia, E for entertainment, C for circus, T for theatricals, R for recreation and UM for 'um, what a nice building' – although another story is that 'spectrum' sounded similar to other words like spectacular and splendid and its reference to a variety of colours and types fitted with the developers' vision (Rys 2009). The first ever event held in the arena was the Quaker City Jazz Festival, held in the round, which sold out – the second was a boxing match.

Promoter for rock concerts at the Spectrum was Larry Magid, co-founder of Electric Factory Concerts, who recalls: 'What happened with the concerts was that we started looking at the Spectrum as really just a big club. What if we didn't have seats on the floor? We said, we'll call them dance concerts.

We'll keep the ticket prices low and try to build exciting shows, rather than waiting for the headliners or the Johnny Cashes or the Ray Charleses of the world, which was the standard. Let's break out of this mold, and let's go into the Spectrum with rock shows' (Rys 2009). For four decades the Spectrum provided the venue for virtually every major rock act that toured the United States, some returning many times.[5] Magid recalls: 'A lot of it becomes a blur, because there were so many. Dylan coming back and playing with The Band, that was a big deal. The Rolling Stones in '69. Elvis in '71. We did a show with Led Zeppelin . . . Springsteen's first show there – he opened for Chicago and got booed' (Rys 2009). One of the first rock shows at the Spectrum was on Friday, 1 November 1968; the fourth from last date on British power rock trio Cream's farewell tour. The stage was set in the centre of the arena and slowly revolved. Yes also used a rotating, in the round stage for their 1979 tour; however, most music acts performed from a fixed stage positioned at one end of the arena.[6] The Spectrum's last event was a Pearl Jam concert on 31 October 2009, its sport and concert functions now taken over by the larger, 20,000 capacity Wachovia Center (now Wells Fargo Arena), which opened in 1996.

The Spectrum was an immensely popular venue, inspiring great nostalgia among those who saw their favourite acts there. Some talk of its intimacy (compared to its replacement); of the freedom to approach the stage (at least in the 1970s); and of the sense of event that the big concerts had.[7] The sound had all the qualities of an arena show in one of these 'first-generation' buildings – for good or ill. A report by W. Mandel on Led Zeppelin's show on 13 June 1972 describes the technical conundrum: 'To fill a hall the size of the Spectrum (which last night held 16,847 persons), huge amplification systems are needed. Every little instrument, even the hi-hat on the drum kit, must have a microphone placed next to it. What happens then is that a little sound, such as a tambourine being shaken, becomes a mighty apocalyptic noise, louder than if the sky were to fall. Everything, in other words, gets bigger and louder and seemingly more important.' And then there is the recognition of what the performers have to do to reach their immense audience: 'The histrionics of the band members, the awesome pretension of their loudness and stage antics, made it clear that several elements go into 'superstar' concerts.' Mandel had identified that the arena concert adds up to something more than a music experience; is more than the sound and the sight of musicians – it becomes an event in which the venue becomes an integral component: 'the ambience of the hall and the people in it is important. With about 17,000 people on hand, rock-festival-like hassles are inevitable. That sense of hearing the concert, "in spite of" the surroundings make everything seem that much more delicious.'[8]

However, despite being used for popular music concerts from the 1960s on, very little had been done by arena designers to improve the inherent problems that these very large internal spaces provided for a live music event. Despite the 'delicious' experience, poor sound, sight, comfort and other 'hassles' were perceived as 'inevitable'. They came with the territory – the higher quality of sound, vision and comfort expected as the norm in other entertainment industries was absent in the big rock show. The major reason for this was that buildings built up until the late 1990s were still primarily sports 'sheds', behind which all other functions were secondary.

Arena development in the UK

Like North America, large sports stadia have a long history in the UK for sports such as football (soccer), rugby football and cricket, but unlike the United States, there is no comparable indoor spectator sport (such as basketball and ice hockey) with frequent league games of such popularity that they would necessitate each large city to have an indoor sporting arena with permanent seating for an audience of thousands. However, some arenas were built to fulfil the requirements of a special sporting event, with the permanent building identified as 'legacy'. For example, the Empire Pool was built in Wembley, London, in 1934 as a swimming pool used for the British Empire games of that year. The reinforced concrete building designed by engineer Owen Williams spanned 72 metres across both the pool and the raked seating on either side for 4,000. This was an innovative structure for the 1930s, providing the building with the long-lasting flexibility of a column-free space. The pool was last used for the 1948 'austerity' London Olympic Games for which no new buildings were constructed; however, the building retained its original name until 1978, when it became the Wembley Arena. The 12,500 arena has also hosted many other indoor sports including tennis, boxing, martial arts, ice hockey and badminton (including the 2012 Olympic Games events), and during the 1960s and 1970s, the Skol six-day cycle race was held there taking place on a temporary 166 metre long velodrome.

In the mid-1960s the arena was the venue for the *New Musical Express* awards events with the Beatles, The Rolling Stones and the Beach Boys, among many others, playing live in shows that were filmed and then broadcast on television. For these events a stage was set on the floor towards one end of the arena with the audience on the floor in front, and in surrounding raked seating; a semi-in-the-round performance, although those behind the stage must have had both a poor view and sound. The Beatles played in the arena three times and it was the venue for their last live scheduled show on 1 May 1966.[9]

Such well-publicized events provided an identity for the venue as the largest capacity music arena in London, and although its primary role remained in hosting family entertainment and sports such as tennis, wrestling, ice-skating and the horse of the year show – throughout the

1970s, 1980s and 1090s top music acts filled the former swimming pool with big audiences despite its typical echoing shed-like environment.

In 2006, the old Wembley Arena building benefited from a major £35million refurbishment as part of an urban redevelopment plan led by Brent Council that included building a new Wembley Stadium, shopping and commercial centres and over 11,000 homes. Architects Tooley and Foster relocated the main stage to the opposite end of the building with a new main entrance and service yard. Concourses containing merchandizing and catering kiosks were introduced, and the building's roofs, walls, windows and doors were renewed. Wembley Arena was relegated to second largest venue of its type in London due to the opening of the O2 Greenwich Arena in 2007 (20,000 capacity); however, with the improved facilities it has continued to be successful. In April 2014, AEG signed a 15-year contract to run the facility and announced it would now be know as the SSE Arena, its new operators showing confidence in its long-term viability. The 2006 regeneration at Wembley is a familiar pattern in arena development – part of a trend in new building and refurbishment that has taken place across the British Isles in the last fifteen years.

The commercial model for arena development in the UK was significantly influenced by the Manchester Arena (for many years known as the MEN, the Manchester Evening News Arena). The building was commissioned as an athletics venue as part of the city's unsuccessful bid for the 2000 Olympics, and was one of the first new arenas to be built. Built in 1993–1995 over the top of Victoria Railway Station close to the city centre, it was the first enclosed arena in Europe to follow the US model of having seating arranged on multiple tiers all around the viewing area, a vast open space made possible by a 105-metre-long steel truss to support the roof. The building's sporting roots were at least partly fulfilled in 2002 when it was used to host the Commonwealth Games, and other sporting events have a regular place in its events programme including basketball, boxing, ice hockey and gymnastics. When it was built, it was anticipated the arena would also hold exhibitions, conferences and family entertainments such as ice shows; however, its largest source of visitors has been as a touring popular music venue. Between 2003 and 2007 more tickets were sold at the Manchester arena than for any other comparable venue around the world, and even in 2013, it sold the second most number of tickets for concerts and shows (1.9 million) behind the O2 Greenwich Arena, London (2.12 million) and above the Barclays Center, Brooklyn, New York (992,000) (see Pollstar 2013).

The arena could not be described as a memorable building, nor does it add to the urban character of the city (Hartwell, Hyde, Pevsner 2004).[10] It was not designed for staging concerts and the audience experience has routinely been described as poor with dreadful echoing acoustics, and an empty shed-like character.[11] However, it has some key advantages for promoters. Its location is excellent, close to a major city centre that is itself the centre of a large conurbation, with both good public transport links (Manchester Victoria train station is under the same roof as the arena) and substantial on-site and local car parking. Its size is right, able to hold a very large audience at its maximum capacity (standing in-the-round shows). Finally, it is flexible, allowing many different show configurations; side-stage for an 11,000 audience and end-stage for up to 15,800 fully seated or 19,350 with standing. With major acts seeking bigger audiences to make touring their large, expensive shows viable, the Manchester Arena with its large, adaptable space and good position at the centre of a large, interested audience catchment has proven to be an inevitable port of call. Though not originally designed for music concerts, the Manchester Arena was pivotal in showing how a large-scale arena could not only be profitable for this form of entertainment, but how it could also be an important element in generating income and recognition for the city in which it is located. Manchester became a name that promoters recognized as the building was nominated for the International Venue of the Year in the Pollstar awards every year between 2003 and 2009 after winning it in 2002.[12]

The new arena building typology

Facilities like Manchester Arena provided an important new opportunity in the development of popular music entertainment, and yet these ex-sports and exhibition halls clearly had many shortcomings. Compared to traditional theatres and concert halls, for most of the audience the experience was compromised with poor sight lines, much longer distance to the stage and dreadful acoustics. Servicing facilities for audiences such as catering, toilets, air quality and temperature, and accessibility were unsatisfactory. Other factors such as speedy and convenient loading for large, complex sets, acoustic separation from neighbours to avoid time curfews and planning restrictions were also becoming more important. Building owners and developers began to recognize the viability and potential of dedicated new facilities, created around an enhanced commercial model that spawned a spate of new arena building and refurbishments of older exhibition and sports centres in the UK and beyond. As well as Wembley Arena and the O2 Greenwich there is the Metro Radio Arena, Newcastle (1995, 10,500 capacity), Belfast Odyssey Arena (2000, 14,000 capacity), Liverpool Echo Arena (2008, 12,000 capacity), O2 Arena Dublin (rebuilt 2008, 14,500 capacity), LG Arena, Birmingham (refurbished 2009, 16,000 capacity), Leeds First Direct Arena (2013, 13,500 capacity), SSE Hydro, Glasgow (2013, 13,000 capacity), Motorpoint Arena, Sheffield (refurbished 2013, 13,000 capacity). Each of these projects has its own specific local context; however, they share a similarity in brief that can be summarized in three key ambitions: to provide an improved customer experience that will draw audiences regularly and increase the arena's appeal as a destination venue; to provide an improved operating experience that encourages repeat bookings by promoters and major artists; to provide a focus for development opportunity and urban regeneration in the cities in which they are sited.

All these ambitions connect with the commercial importance of creating a new brand. The management companies of arenas that were once named for their location or function now seek out sponsor partners anxious to connect directly with the thousands who attend events in the building, but also to take advantage of the publicity associated with the promotion of the artists who perform there (e.g. Empire Pool, then named Wembley Arena, now SSE Arena). Branding also has building design implications. The quality of the environment and the experience needs to be high to reinforce the brand – frequently, new buildings or ones that undergo rebuilding are able to attract a new sponsor as the project comes to completion, or the introduction of a new sponsor is directly connected with a subsequent investment in freshening the image and facilities.[13] Competition between venues has stimulated the creation of new or improved facilities across the sector so a stream of new and refurbished arenas, utilizing designs that are enhancements of older specifications, have appeared in a relatively short amount of time, effectively creating a new building typology for large-scale performance spaces.

One example is the Dublin Arena (the O2 Arena prior to September 2014, now the Dublin 3 Arena). The building was originally a Victorian railway goods terminus situated on the banks of the River Liffey in Dublin's docklands that was crudely converted into The Point concert venue by local developer Harry Crosbie and promoters Apollo Leisure in 1988. Though it had a long history of memorable performances the 8,550 capacity building was notoriously uncomfortable with poor sound, sightlines, primitive catering and toilets. By 2007, the Dublin Docklands North Lotts Area in which the building was sited was undergoing regeneration, and the new Dublin light railway (LUAS) improved audience transportation with a stop right outside the venue. Apollo Leisure had also changed, becoming Live Nation, the world's largest music promoter, and its Dublin venue was now just one of the 120 it owns or operates internationally. The competition had also intensified, notably with the Odyssey Centre in Belfast, and so the decision was made by Crosbie and Live Nation to remake the venue into a new arena with much increased capacity, new facilities and a new image (Kronenburg 2012).

Perhaps uniquely for a contemporary arena, the building has an elegant nineteenth-century façade on three sides, which helped form a ready-made focus for its new image. Much improved bar and restaurant facilities were placed in this listed part of the building that faces the river, creating a destination element for the site. The historic façade became an architectural symbol both for the building's reinvention but also for the regeneration of the area – a new and fashionable place to visit regardless of whether or not there is a performance. The rest of the building was new – a vast steel frame spanning 50 metres, which had a high load rigging capacity of 50 tonnes. Roofs on the new arenas must be column free so sightlines are not impaired, but they must also have a high load capacity to support flown equipment needed for a variety of shows, but also because of tougher regulations regarding sound protection for neighbours. These thick skin roof and wall layered constructions substantially reduce sound transmission, thereby mitigating (if not removing) curfews for performances. If carefully designed, they also improve the internal acoustics. The ideal acoustic environment for amplified sound is a neutral one so that the desired experience can be created at the desk and reproduced by sophisticated sound systems with speakers set around the performance space. If the natural live acoustic environment of the space can be minimized then the opportunity is there for more of the audience to experience good sound, though this is not always provided by touring sound systems.

The new arena in Dublin is designed for flexibility. The floor plan was turned through 90 degrees with the stage now along the long side of the building and directly behind it, a new internal loading area through which articulated lorries can drive was created, with internal parking for six in total. A flat floor area, coupled with retractable seating, allows for speedy changes with a variety of layouts ranging from 9,500 fully seated to 14,500 utilizing the maximum standing area. Even with this increased capacity, turning the plan around has meant that the furthest seat from the stage is 60 metres; 20 metres closer than it was for The Point. The arena space is not in the round, as with the sports-derived arenas, but it is dramatic – a single fan-shaped raked seating area behind which a continuous concourse provides bars, kiosks and access to toilets at two levels. This space to 'mill around and enjoy the buzz of the show' is praised by fans but also aids crowd access and escape in an emergency. There was great nostalgia for the old building; however, the new building receives unremitting praise from audiences for views of the stage, speedy entrance and exit, plentiful concessions and easily accessed toilets.[14]

The architects for the Dublin arena were Populous (at that time HOKSVE), a global practice, well experienced in sports and entertainment facility design, and it is significant that their most recent UK arena building, First Direct Arena in Leeds, although a completely new facility, follows the same plan shape and seating layout. This shape provides a compact spatial layout allowing greater control of the performance systems (visual and acoustic) but also the environment in terms of air quality and temperature. Also, there is no lost seating to the rear of the stage area for the majority of shows, which are not in the round performances. These new, dedicated

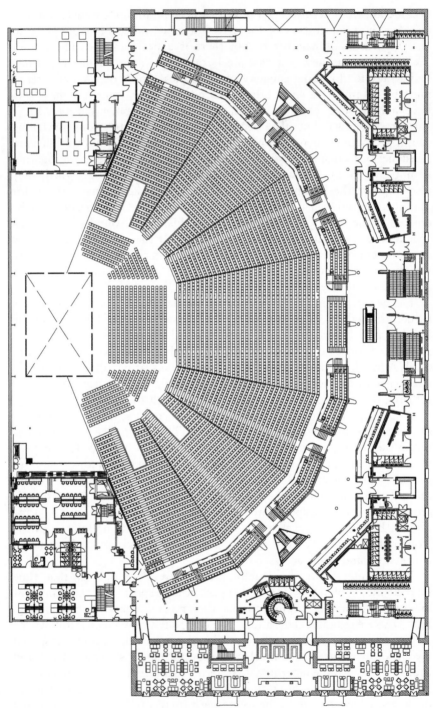

FIGURE 5.1 3 Arena (formerly the Dublin Arena), with its concert-style, fan-shaped seating layout. Floor plan © Populous.

music performance buildings indicate a move back to the auditorium layout (though much, much larger) as the optimum arena performance space, made possible by modern building structures that can span the required volumes while still providing acoustic containment. The focus on easy and quick turnaround means that the buildings are in use more often, that less staff are needed to operate them, though paradoxically there is now an increase in the size and quality of back-stage areas to provide better facilities for performers and crew, and to cater to the increased trend towards multiple night runs. Perhaps the greatest changes are still to happen in front of house facilities. The O2 Greenwich (also a Populous conversion of the Richard Rogers Partnership designed Millennium Dome) has led the way in this regard. The venue becomes a centrepiece for the facility but not the only reason for visiting it. Bars, restaurants, shops, VIP and membership lounges, and other entertainment facilities providing cinemas, bowling, casinos and shopping provide an entire leisure experience (Barrow 2010).[15]

Conclusion

It is certain that the demand for new popular music performance-focused arenas is still developing outside the UK. Populous have recently designed new buildings in Australia and the United States. The most ambitious project is the Philippine Arena, at Ciudad de Victoria, Manila, a 50,000 capacity indoor venue, which opened in July 2014 – it is now the largest in the world. Designed to accommodate church services, sports events and popular music concerts, the plan form expands the fan shape into a giant one-sided bowl. The 170-metre span column free performance space can be divided with visual and acoustic curtains so that just the lower tier can operate for smaller audiences. These new buildings' function and layout reinforce the mature architectural typology that now exists for arena design.

In the UK there are, however, some doubts that the increasing number of venues can be commercially sustainable in the long term – SMG, operator of both the Manchester and Leeds Arenas and twelve other venues across Europe, found that audience numbers were down in 2012 as the buildings struggled to match the number of events held the previous year (Insider Media 2013). Live Nation (who merged with Ticketmaster in 2010) saw profits drop in 2014 due to falls in concert attendance (Armental 2014). Other issues and uncertainty to how this business will develop, such as the role of ticket resellers and the added costs of attending a show that does not support the venue or the artist. Nevertheless, the two key factors in the design of the new arenas (that is also present in the older buildings that have been refurbished to extend their viability) are that of flexibility – the capacity to cope with many different types of event and therefore change in the entertainment industry, and the addition of multiple attractions to visit arenas alongside the central event – e.g. restaurants, clubs, shopping, cinemas (Kronenburg 2014b). However, despite the business uncertainties and the changes in how venues operate, the fundamental existence of live performance as a draw for large audiences cannot be in doubt – it is something that has taken place across two millennia, with built examples to prove it; from the Roman Colosseum to the Philippine Arena. It also cannot be doubted that arena architecture has added a new and dramatic element to urban life, it has expanded the limits of popular music performance, and added a catalytic component to aid in the regeneration of cities.

Notes

1   It is believed the Colosseum featured a lightweight, retractable roof called a 'velarium'. It utilized tensile technology constructed from ropes and canvas to span the 189-metre wide arena, with an opening in the centre for illumination and ventilation (Kronenburg 2014a).
2   Other large entertainment and performance buildings were designed from the nineteenth century such as the Royal Albert Hall, London (1871), and the Alexandra Palace, London (1873, rebuilt 1875). Today, both these buildings fulfil multi-functional roles with a similar brief to arenas; however, the character of the spaces they contain differs significantly from the arena setting and is therefore not examined here.
3   Large span lightweight roofs have become possible primarily through innovations in tensile structures of different types. The Tokyo Dome (baseball, 1985, 70,000 capacity, know as the Big Egg) is an air-supported structure in which the roof is supported by a small difference in air pressure between outside and inside. Wembley Stadium (football, 2007, 90,000 capacity) has a 315-metre lattice arch from which tensile cables support a retracting roof. Both stadiums regularly stage popular music concerts.
4   He was also engineer at Bill Graham's Fillmore East Venue in New York between 1968 and 1971.
5   For example The Grateful Dead played the Spectrum fifty-three times and recorded three live albums there. British progressive rock group Yes played there thirty-two times.
6   The concert by Yes was released as *Live in Philadelphia* in 1979.
7   There are several well-supported fan appreciation website for the Spectrum. See: www.rememberthespectrum.com and www.facebook.com/pages/The-Philadelphia-Spectrum-Concert-Appreciation-Group
8   Press report reproduced at http://www.ledzeppelin.com/node/618/244 (accessed April 2015).
9   Not counting the Abbey Road rooftop performance in 1969.
10 It is described in Pevsner as a 'huge soulless sports and entertainment complex' (Hartwell, Hyde, Pevsner 2004).
11 ' . . . the MEN [is just] a concrete shell of a place with poor acoustics if [*sic*] your not right up near the stage' Larry.Cool commenting on Taylor (2010) as a reader's response.

12 See the Pollstar Awards Archive: http://www.pollstarpro.com/PCIA-Static/ (accessed 26 February 2015).
13 For example, as part of its five year deal with Phones 4u, the managers of the Manchester Arena, SMG Europe agreed a comprehensive refurbishment of its interior and exterior (see Ferguson 2013).
14 This blog entry, from 2010, is typical: 'It was long overdue for the Capital to have an excellent, large capacity venue. [*Sic*] Its great that they took The Point, which was an acoustically awful old barn and made it into something world class. The sound is really good whether you are standing up front or sitting at the back. Also, the access to the bars and toilets and handling of queues at them is great. The Luas to it has only sweetened the deal.' Available at: http://www.yelp.co.uk/biz/3arena-dublin (accessed November 2014).
15 John Barrow, Senior Principle and project architect for the O2 Greenwich, Populous; conversation with the author, 7 June 2010. The Populous blog describes the requirements that new arena operators are requesting; see http://populous.com/posts/the-changing-nature-of-arenas/ (accessed November 2014).

CHAPTER SIX

Constructing the Cosmopolitan Arena Concert

Lukasz Swiatek

Introduction

Arena concerts that care about the world have been flourishing in recent times. These music events provide large-scale, immersive, socially conscious entertainment. They engage on-site and external audiences, who consume the all-enveloping shows and the humanitarian messages they convey.

Three elements characterize the cosmopolitan arena concert: focus, assemblage and reach. First, its focus extends beyond the local. It embodies a cosmopolitan ethos: an outward-looking spirit of openness that attempts to connect with the other (Kendall, Skrbis and Woodward 2009). The concert features universal messages that are conscious of, and value, publics around the world. It usually takes the form of a tribute or benefit concert, supporting social causes and advocating particular messages. Second, it brings together audiences, performers and hosts from a range of backgrounds. The arena encloses them in the all-embracing music event. Third, it reaches wider audiences – in the home nation and other countries – through terrestrial and online broadcasts, or later distribution. Hence, while the concert is anchored in a particular locality, it spills out beyond the arena's confines. Space is as important as place for the concert.

However, this type of music event is problematic, like cosmopolitanism itself. The concept has been criticized as illusory: a utopian idea with 'a nice, high-minded ring to it' (Himmelfarb 2002, 77). Although the concert strives to embrace and value the other, and assemble elements from around the world, its idealistic approach also faces limitations. It often features elite cosmopolitans: a specific group of individuals who have greater resources and skills than others. It can privilege global sounds over local ones and global space over local place, marginalizing local publics. It champions causes lacking universal support, and must sometimes engage in compromises that challenge its values. Consequently, although they aim for inclusiveness, cosmopolitan arena concerts can be exclusionary.

The Nobel Peace Prize Concert illustrates these difficulties. Launched in 1994, the concert takes place each December at the Oslo Spektrum Arena in Norway. Its producers describe it as an 'international musical celebration' of the Peace Prize laureate(s), their work and peace in general; it airs annually in over 100 countries, reaching approximately 577 million households, and features popular international artists, as well as Norwegian talent (IMG Media 2013, 4). The concert's problematic cosmopolitan construction is analysed in this chapter through photographs and videos, as well as other communication resources (such as documents), available on the official website. This evidence is supplemented by online reports from producers and an interview with Geir Lundestad, the former Permanent Secretary of the Norwegian Nobel Committee, Director of the Norwegian Nobel Institute and the Chairman of Nobel Peace Prize Research & Information Ltd., which produces the concert.[1]

Cosmopolitan arena concerts merit greater academic attention, as they are flourishing around the world. Understanding these concerts' dynamics and problems helps us better understand a significant component of the international arena concert landscape. The chapter begins with an overview of the concerts, discussing their characteristics in relation to the notion of cosmopolitanism. Next, it examines the Nobel Peace Prize Concert and its construction. The problems that these musical events face are then analysed with reference to the concert.

The concerts' characteristics

The cosmopolitan arena concert has a socially conscious ethos. Cosmopolitanism derives from an ancient Greek term meaning 'citizen of the world'. It is marked by an open, receptive attitude towards the other; as Kendall, Skrbis and Woodward (2009, 1) explain, it is:

> an ethical stance, in which the individual tries to go beyond the strong psychological and evolutionary pressures to privilege those nearest to him or her . . . and endeavours to see the value of the other, and to work towards the possibility of connection and dialogue with the other.

In looking outward, cosmopolitanism attempts to see differences as opportunities for connection. This is also true of this type of arena concert, which aims to connect audiences on- and off-site.

Although cosmopolitan musicians have drawn on, and juxtaposed, musical elements from different local and international sources throughout history (Turino 2000, 135), cosmopolitan arena concerts have a scale and international reach that makes them distinctive to other cosmopolitan music events. Their proliferation is partly the result of ongoing advances in global media and communications, which allow the concerts to be staged in ways that let worldwide audiences consume them. They are also partly the result of the growth of transnational civil societies: groups of individuals and organizations that are not involved in state apparatuses or government institutions; they include NGOs, social movements, advocacy groups and protest networks (Kaldor 2011). For these actors, the concerts and other media are vital for issue-advocacy: raising public awareness of, and generating support for action on, particular issues.

The arena concerts can generate enormous exposure for the issues that they communicate. As Lahusen (2001) notes, social movements often use such 'mega-events' to raise awareness for their causes. The immersive, all-encompassing nature of the arena concert helps them to achieve maximum impact in communicating their messages. The arena enhances the grandness of the spectacle, amplifying its dynamism in 'demanding movement, action, change, and exchange on the part of human actors who are at center stage' (MacAloon 1984, 244). Issue-advocacy is enhanced by the cosmopolitan arena concert's three central characteristics: assemblage, reach and focus. As the introduction outlined, the concert assembles individuals from around the world, reaches wider audiences and focuses on others as part of its cosmopolitan ethos.

The concerts also typically take the form of benefits or tributes. Benefit concerts provide channels for publics to respond to important social issues or critical events, such as catastrophes, while tribute concerts honour individuals, usually the dead. Watts and Porter (2013, 57) note that these concert types influence audiences, as there is a 'powerful pedagogical and political function in tributes and benefits'. Lull (2007, 167) also highlights that benefit concerts have been known to provoke 'extraordinary outpouring[s]' from individuals, as well as increase publics' awareness of major issues.

Recent examples of cosmopolitan arena concerts that have taken the form of tributes include: Unity – A Concert For Stephen Lawrence (held at the O2 Arena in London, on 29 September 2013), Lennon Remembered (at the Echo Arena in Liverpool, on 9 December 2010) and the Ahmet Ertegun Tribute Concert (at the O2 Arena in London, on 10 December 2007). Examples of benefit-focused concerts include: Amnesty International USA's Bringing Human Rights Home Concert (at the Barclays Center in New

York, on 5 February 2014), Peace One Day's Global Truce 2012 concert (at Wembley Arena, on 21 September 2012) and Islamic Relief's Concert for Peace in Darfur (at Wembley Arena, on 21 October 2007).

The above-listed concerts – cosmopolitan in their focus, reach and assemblage – have engaged audiences on-site and abroad, experientially and ideationally. As musical events that are geared towards others and are broadcast to the nations or regions in which they take place, or to the world, the concerts help to foster a 'mediatised solidarity' among publics. As Dant (2012) explains, drawing on the ideas of Durkheim, television programmes (and other media) help keep societies intact by connecting social subgroups and allowing them to share common values. This mediated solidarity 'supplements the continuing interactional relationships in both the traditional space of the community and the modern space of the impersonal city' (Dant, 51). The concerts can thus unite disparate audiences around particular causes through representations of shared social values, in encouraging individuals to be open and receptive to others.

The Nobel Peace Prize Concert and its construction

The annual Nobel Peace Prize Concert, which is mainly a tribute (with elements of a benefit concert), provides an excellent case study for illustrating the characteristics of cosmopolitan arena concerts. The event takes place each year on 11 December, the day after the anniversary of Alfred Nobel's death, at the Oslo Spektrum Arena in Oslo, Norway. Opened in 1990, the multipurpose, enclosed venue is used for a variety of events, ranging in size from large-scale televised concerts and award ceremonies to smaller music shows and trade fairs. According to its owners, the arena is annually visited by 400,000 people and plays host to around 100 events; of these, 80 per cent are concerts and shows, 17 per cent are trade fairs, corporate events or conferences and 3 per cent are sporting events.[2]

In staging the Nobel Peace Prize Concert, the entire arena is used to create an immersive space that enfolds the audience totally in the show. This envelopment aids in fully communicating the concert's peace- and conflict-related messages and creating an enclosure for celebration. Consequently, the musical event is able to mobilize both seriousness and festivity, in conveying sombre humanitarian issues, on the one hand, and encouraging participation in feting the laureates and their achievements, on the other.

This use of space is achieved through a range of staging elements that create a sense of grandeur and intimacy. The music event, whose length has varied over the years between four hours (Lofthus 2000) and ninety minutes (Berglund 2013), takes place in an amphitheatre-style structure in the Oslo Spektrum; the audience sits in a semicircle around the stage: on ground level and in rising tiers. The customized stage, designed by Peter Bingeman (Bright Group 2014), is divided into three oval segments; two smaller stages flank a larger, central stage that features a recessed orchestra pit.[3] The three-stage design helps ensure that the live televised concert runs seamlessly, with artists alternating between stages (Total Production International 2013). Three moveable, circular screens hang above the stages; projections – of both abstract light patterns and the faces of previous Nobel laureates – are beamed onto them at various times during the concert. Lighting fixtures line all three stages, along with background projections that provide colourful, abstract backdrops; the lighting and visuals are designed to provide each musical act with a unique 'look'. Large – approximately 2 metre – three-dimensional letters of the word 'Nobel' are placed equidistantly across the stages; the letters are illuminated in different colours to match the lighting colour palette for each musical act. The screenshot below illustrates these staging elements.

Although these large-scale features make the concert impactful and compelling, they are also designed, along with other elements, to create an atmosphere of intimacy, thereby enhancing the immersive nature of the space. The musicians' alternation between the three stages means that all sides of the audience – left, right and centre – are able to engage more closely with the artists. The Nobel laureate, along with members of the Norwegian Royal family and the Norwegian Nobel Committee, which selects the honouree, sit among the audience in the middle of one of the

FIGURE 6.1 The concert's stage design.

tiered sets of seats. The lighting elements also embrace the audience, as one production report notes:

> The entire arena became Collier's [the Lighting Director's] canvas and lighting not only added sparkle and beauty to the acts on stage, but also reached out into the audience, making them an integral part of the show, blurring the line between performer and observer to give a rare sense of intimacy in such a large stadium [sic]. (Total Production International 2013)

Lofthus (2000, 31) also notes that the concert had previously been organized as an 'exclusive gathering' that featured classical contemporary music and that took place in various locations, including Oslo's 'prestigious' National Theatre.

As a cosmopolitan construct, the concert draws together international performers from around the world. In 2014, for example, they included: America's Steven Tyler, Queen Latifah and Girls of the World; Pakistan's Ustad Rahat Fateh Ali Khan; Norway's Gabrielle; the United Kingdom's Laura Mvula and the Bolly Flex Dancers; India's Amjad Ali Khan; and Sweden's Seinabo Sey. The hosts – usually a man and a woman – are film and television personalities, typically from the United States and Britain; past pairings have included Claire Danes and Aaron Eckhart (in 2013), Gerard Butler and Sarah Jessica Parker (in 2012) and Rosario Dawson and Helen Mirren (in 2011). In 2014, only one person – Queen Latifah – hosted the event. During the concert, images and footage of individuals (especially Nobel laureates), as well as scenes relating to peace and conflict, are projected onto the screens in the arena and shown in the broadcast; the footage and images also help to draw the world into the concert. For example, in 2013, before a speech given by two representatives of the Prize-winning institution – the Organisation for the Prohibition of Chemical Weapons (OPCW) – James Blunt performed his song 'No Bravery', about the Kosovo War; during the performance, a minute-and-forty-five-second sequence of historical footage of war and the use of chemical weapons was presented.

The concert is also designed to be as universally appealing as possible. The global lingua franca of English is used, rather than the native language (Norwegian). The universal language of music helps to tell the story of the Nobel Peace Prize and those of the laureates; as Geir Ludestad explained, one of the central goals of the concert is to tell these stories by 'reach[ing] new countries and new groups through music'. This universal approach is also adopted by performers. The singer Rosanne Cash (2010) recounts that, when preparing for the 2003 concert, she was asked by another performer to change the line 'imagine no religion' in John Lennon's song 'Imagine' to avoid offending audiences. Similarly, Larsson (2011) comments that Yusuf

Islam (formerly Cat Stevens) dedicated his song 'Peace Train' to Muhammad Yunus – the pioneer of microcredit and 2006 Peace Prize laureate – explaining that poverty was a major obstacle to peace; however, the song has also been understood to be a narrative about the journey to the kingdom of God. All of these elements help the concert achieve a more universal appeal, in reaching audiences around the globe while drawing together different elements of the world into the arena: a space designed to immerse audiences totally in seriousness and grandeur, as well as festivity and intimacy.

A problematic musical construct

Cosmopolitan arena concerts face a range of challenges and tensions, as the Nobel Peace Prize Concert demonstrates. This type of musical event is problematic, just as cosmopolitanism is problematic. Franceschet (2009) notes that many see cosmopolitanism as being too idealistic; the notion of broad openness to others might sound promising, but ultimately can be a flawed and utopian position. Kendall, Skrbis and Woodward (2009, 16) observe that, among the many difficulties inherent in the notion, cosmopolitanism is often associated with global elites, especially business elites. The individuals who belong to this class have superior intellectual and social skills, more knowledge and are rich in the three C's: concepts, competence and connections (Kanter 1995). They are also 'invariably from first-world countries or the privileged classes whose identification is largely with Western ideals' (Kendall, Skrbis and Woodward 2009, 16). The Nobel Peace Prize Concert certainly features a broad array of such cosmopolitan individuals. Among them are: the hosts, who are members of television's and cinema's elites; the performers, who are rich in music skills, knowledge and connections; and the laureates on whom the concert focuses, many of whom are elite leaders: presidents (such as Barack Obama and Ellen Johnson Sirleaf), vice-presidents (like Al Gore Jr.), diplomats (such as Martti Ahtisaari) and heads of international organizations (like Mohamed ElBaradei). Although these elite cosmopolitans' fame helps to enhance the communication of the concert's core messages to worldwide audiences, they often do not help in generating a universal and populist image for the concert. This tension is compounded by the fact that the choice of laureate(s) for the Peace Prize is often controversial and, as a result, the concert celebrates individuals or groups and causes that lack universal support.

This problem links directly to another key challenge: the holding of a concert by, and reflecting the spirit of, an elite-level institution. Described by many – including Black (2002), Dardo (2004) and Goodrich and Walker (2010) – as the 'most prestigious' prizes on earth, the entire Nobel 'family' is a distinguished, eminent institution. Van den Dungen (2001, 518) notes that the Nobel enterprise is 'synonymous with excellence' and represents 'an amalgam of achievement, prestige, and respectability'. Although the concert is a celebration – of peace, peace work and the laureate(s) – it is obliged to maintain the solemnity and dignity of the Nobel brand. The issues relating to peace and conflict communicated through the Prize are also serious and likewise entail a degree of gravitas. The concert conveys this honour, solemnity and prestige through various elements, such as a trumpet fanfare played when the Nobel laureates take their seats, and a speech given by the laureates during the concert. These sombre aspects help to subdue the arena's audience members, who are 'frozen in their seats' (Richards 2010) for most of the show.

These exclusive elements also manifest themselves in the concert's overall branding. The official website's colour scheme features black, white, red and gold (Nobel Peace Prize Concert 2014). This colour scheme also permeates the concert's print and online advertising campaign designs (IMG Media 2013). Black and white, as McCulloch (2010) notes, convey sophistication, elegance and even grandeur, enhanced by the gold. This branding was designed in 2011 by the advertising agency *UP There, Everywhere. The agency was commissioned by the organizers to create a more contemporary identity for the concert that would appeal to a greater number of audiences, especially younger ones. The organizers were worried that the concert's identity matched that of a classical music concert. Although the final design is described as having 'a much more human feel', conveying passion and energy, the brand identity 'had to maintain the [concert's] noble heritage'; many of the design elements, such as the classical components of the title's typography and the incorporation of a stylized Nobel medal, reflect this prestigious heritage.[4] These design elements can be seen in the screenshot (below) of the concert's website.

FIGURE 6.2 The concert's homepage.

Another challenge that such concerts face is that they decouple sound from scene and embrace global space, rather than a particular place. As Connell and Gibson (2003, 90) note, specific locations or scenes give rise to particular kinds of sounds; music, they explain, 'is made in specific geographical, socio-economic and political contexts, and lyrics and styles are always likely to reflect the positions of writers and composers within these contexts'. The Nobel Peace Prize Concert, however, de-links sound from scene. The majority of the musical performers selected annually for the concert is international; Scandinavian artists are few. This can potentially alienate local, Norwegian audiences. This problem also figures in the show's worldwide broadcast; as Geir Lundestad noted: 'We always insist on a Norwegian contribution [to the show], although this is frequently edited out in the international versions.' Integrating all of the various international sounds can be highly challenging. Odd Arvid Stromstad (in Richards 2010), the concert's executive producer since its inception, has commented that this is a 'difficult' production component: 'It's like bringing different parts of the world together on one stage and [forcing] it to work together.' The stage design is also neutral; it does not feature any Norwegian cultural elements. The concert, its official website and many of the promotional materials are in English, as well as descriptions of content on social media (such as YouTube and Facebook). This highlights the fact that the concert embraces global space, rather than a particular place.

Additionally, the concert is challenged by problems relating to consistency or integrity: problems that are typical for such large-scale musical events that aim to be all-encompassing, ethical and humanitarian. Richards (2010) notes that the concert has been controversial in Norway, where critics have argued that it 'trivializes the gravity of the award'. In the past, Lundestad (in Lofthus 2000, 24) has had to defend the event's populist orientation, commenting: '[W]e need to make some compromises to reach out to the general public. We could, of course, have wished for a greater sense of connection between the music and our message, but then it becomes limited to a smaller group of people'. In this respect, the concert has been criticized by commentators such as Heffermehl (2010, 92) as an 'American-style rock show' that is contributing to the Peace Prize being 'ruinously corrupted by commercial thinking' (162). Such concerns are often shared by the performing artists. Melissa Etheridge (2010, 3), for example, was 'sceptical' about the concert and its motives before performing in it in 2007; she critically summarizes her concerns thus: 'Let's bring peace to the world, shall we? And now, a word from our sponsor.'

The artists themselves are often the subject of criticisms, too. For example, commentators (such as Martin and Steuter 2010) found it ironic that the pro-war American musician Toby Keith sang at the 2009 concert, honouring Barack Obama. Norwegian publics were also 'furious' that the singer Morrissey performed in 2013 after making controversial comments about the 2011 Anders Breivik massacre (Trendell 2013). Watts and Porter (2013, 57) note that criticisms of artists are habitual for large benefit concerts in particular: 'Artists producing and participating in mega events have been accused of simplifying or even depoliticizing issues – not to mention making bad music – in their efforts to appeal to the compassion of a large audience of potential donors.' The producers face significant challenges in selecting suitable artists. Lundestad explained that it is difficult to find appropriate artists, as they are often less philanthropically minded, as opposed to the film-star hosts, who 'seem to be more socially aware and committed to various causes'. He added: 'Contrary to what many think, it's not true that we can simply call up a famous name and they will say yes. They will normally say no, because the concert is at an awkward time of the year for them: close to Christmas. They have finished their tours; they want to go home and relax, and have a break around Christmas.' The organizers also face financial challenges. The show's producers pay the artists' expenses, but do not remunerate them for their performances. These expenses can often be very high, and come in addition to the concert's other costs. A funding shortfall in 2013 meant that the concert was shortened to just 90 minutes (Berglund 2013).

Conclusion

The Nobel Peace Prize Concert is just one, but prominent, example of a musical event phenomenon that continues to grow around the world. Cosmopolitan arena concerts aim to be affective and socially beneficial enterprises, designed as immersive shows. They are large-scale, all-encompassing music events that value others and embrace differences, draw disparate publics together and reach beyond their immediate localities. The concerts often take the form of tributes or benefits, and are organized by civil society groups, with profits usually being directed towards charitable causes.

However, such concerts face multiple challenges linked, fundamentally, to their cosmopolitan nature. This reflects in the concerts' elite elements, especially in their focus on elite cosmopolitans. The concerts also decouple musical styles from particular scenes, and privilege global sounds in a 'neutral' scene, both of which marginalize local publics. Additionally, they face difficulties in maintaining consistency, in ensuring that they do not alienate or offend publics and in remaining true to their key messages, which often lack universal support. The challenge of selecting appropriate musical artists is compounded by the financial difficulties that organizers face in staging the concerts. As a result of these multiple tensions, the concerts can be exclusionary, either excluding publics (such as locals) directly, or giving the appearance of exclusiveness or both.

The organizers of such concerts need to be aware of these types of problems. Although it may be impossible to eliminate these tensions entirely, the production dynamics should aim to minimize them as much as possible. Concerts that entail solemn or distinguished components – such as the Nobel Peace Prize Concert – should be constructed carefully in order to avoid conveying the impression of elitism and to maximize inclusivity. This chapter has examined only one concert; other insights and recommendations could be drawn from analyses of other concerts. The focus here on production could be enhanced by analyses of reception; further research could examine how audiences respond to cosmopolitan arena concerts and the extent to which such concerts are achieving their goals and helping to raise awareness of, and support for, particular causes.

Notes

1 The interview with Lundestad, under whose tenure the concert was established, was conducted for PhD research, with ethics approval granted by the University of Sydney's Human Research Ethics Committee. Lundestad retired at the end of 2014.

2 See http://www.oslospektrum.no/about-us.131980.en.html.

3 See http://brightgroupnordic.com/case/nobel-peace-prize-concert/. As of 2014, a new stage design is being used. However, it does not figure in this discussion as, at the time of writing, only a pre-show artist's design is available on the official website (see http://www.nobelpeaceprizeconcert.org/), which is also lacking photographs and videos from the 2014 concert.

4 See http://www.upthereeverywhere.com/?portfolio=nobel-peace-prize-concert

CHAPTER SEVEN

'Roll Up and Shine': A Case Study of Stereophonics at Glasgow's SECC Arena

Emma Webster

'You have to put as much effort into putting somebody on to 120 people as to putting them on to 2,000 people, almost. It's a bigger gamble, financially, but probably less work . . . The bigger the act, it's probably less work' (S. Basford, pers. comm., 6 July 2009). So Sheffield-based promoter, Stuart Basford, concluded when considering his role within large-scale live music events, and whose somewhat surprising analysis will form the basis of this chapter. While promoters stand to lose or gain more at large shows than for smaller shows, both in terms of financial and reputational gain, their involvement at large shows such as arena concerts is often far from being anywhere like as hands-on. Hence the seemingly paradoxical statement that as the size and scale of the show increases, so too the promoter's active role *decreases*.

This chapter will examine this paradox within the context of arena shows in the UK and show how the diminished role of the promoter is a result of two factors. First, the necessary division of labour for such large shows means that the promoter uses secondary and tertiary intermediaries to mediate on his behalf (the male pronoun is used deliberately here, as discussed later). Indeed, Howard Becker's work on the production of culture shows that works of art – taken in this chapter to include arena concert shows – are not the products of 'individual makers', but are rather 'joint products of all the people who cooperate via an art world's characteristic conventions to bring works [. . .] into existence' (1982, 34–35). At the level of an arena show, 'all the people' necessarily operate on an industrial scale. Second, the diminished role of the promoter is also caused in part because of the nature of the UK's arena promotion sector – which will be shown to be what Simon Frith describes as 'a new sort of live music corporate oligopoly' (2010, 3) – in which a small number of players compete in a market with a relatively small number of venues and artists. Later in the chapter, this will also be used to show why, at the time of writing, ticket prices for arena shows in the UK are high and getting higher.

To understand the promoter's role in the arena show, I spent a day backstage at a Stereophonics gig at Glasgow's Scottish Exhibition and Conference Centre (SECC) on 2 March 2010. I interviewed some of the main players and watched the show from in front of and behind the stage. Drawing on this ethnographic research, this chapter will examine the multi-layered operation of an arena concert show such as the Stereophonics from the promoter's perspective. It will set out the role of the promoter, offer particular insights relating to the 'behind the scenes' activities at the Stereophonics show and finally consider what this means for the UK arena concert sector.

Simon Frith (2012) has posited that live music events require five elements – venue, artist, audience, appropriate technology and a promoter, or catalyst, to bring them all together. My doctoral research (2011) showed that live music promoters perform three distinct functions. First is planning the gig in the form of artistic direction (selecting the artist and the venue) and administrative organization (setting and confirming the date and time, and organizing contracts). The second is the publicity function, or marketing of the gig. The final function is organizing the production of the gig, which takes the form of artist liaison (including planning the running order and providing a rider if required); technical liaison (including hiring technicians, equipment and volunteers as required); and accounting (paying artist, venue and technical staff). These three functions – planning, publicity and production – define the promoter's role, and highlight how promoters are both administrative *and* creative. Promoters invest in the gig, economically and socially, but they also innovate, by selecting an appropriate performance space for the artist, choosing support acts, setting the running order, promoting to the 'right' audience and creating the 'right' environment for the show.

At an arena-level show, however, the various functions of the promoter's role, perhaps unsurprisingly, are divided between a number of people, either within the promoter's company, employed by the artist's management, or contracted out to an external organization. As agent Paul Charles explains: 'The truth is that the promoter is now rarely more than a figurehead. There are teams of people doing everything' (2004, 140). In this context, the promoter's role involves setting the ticket price, selling the tickets and brokering the various payments to the venue and to the artist. The role becomes financial rather than creative; they are less of an 'auteur' or catalyst and more a cog in the machine. The promoter may even employ someone else to undertake their accounting function, rendering their role at the gig itself a purely social one; they are there to 'chew the fat' with backstage crew such as the tour managers, as will be discussed later, and generally have a much reduced on-site role.

Planning the show

The promoter for the 2010 Stereophonics gig was Mark Mackie, a full-time professional 'commercial' promoter who puts on concerts to make money (see Frith et al. 2013, 15). Mackie has been working for nearly thirty years for Edinburgh-based Regular Music and is an 'independent' promoter who is not financially affiliated to either venue or artist (see Brennan and Webster 2011, 5). The planning of an industrial-scale arena show depends on Mackie working with a number of secondary intermediaries to work on behalf of the artist and the venue, including booking agents, artist managers and ticket agents. This is in contrast to smaller gigs, for which 'independent' promoters will often liaise directly with venues and artists.

The booking agent will tender for a tour – or part of a tour – to find the most appropriate promoter by evaluating promoters' bids. In the competitive oligopoly that is the UK's arena show market, what impacts on the agent's choice is the promoter's expertise in a particular genre of music or geographic area (Competition Commission 2010a, B4), reputation and market knowledge. While many tours these days are promoted by one company such as Live Nation, location does still matter to some extent in the UK market. For example, due to the need for local knowledge and local relationships, very few English promoters promote in Scotland; indeed, agents will often use a Scottish promoter for the Scottish part of an artist's tour, invariably DF Concerts or Regular Music. Other promoters such as the American-owned global corporation, Live Nation, promote all over the UK. Loyalty may also play a part in the agent's choice. As Metropolis promoter, Conal Dodds, explained, Coldplay's 2010 tour was promoted 50/50 between Live Nation and the band's historic promoters, Metropolis, partly as a result of loyalty built up between the promoter and the artist's management over time (C. Dodds, pers. comm., 29 March 2010).

The next part of the planning process is to select the date for the show. For a large rock band such as the Stereophonics, the tour is based around the release date of an album; the tour sells the album and the album sells the tour. In this case, once the Stereophonics' management, agent and Mark Mackie had pencilled in the tour dates to coincide with the release date of the album *Keep Calm and Carry On*, the venue was chosen and booked. However, it seems clear that once an artist reaches a certain point in their career, the choice of venue is almost a foregone conclusion. The only venue in town big enough to hold the artist's estimated fan base will be the arena, of which, with the exception of London and Birmingham, there is usually only one choice once the artist's route across the UK has been decided. At the time of writing, there were only eighteen members of the National Arena Association across the British Isles, including the SSE Hydro in Glasgow and the O_2 Arena in London, with a total indoor standing capacity of just over 220,000 for a population of 68.3 million people (ONS 2013; CSO 2013), as shown in Table 7.1.

TABLE 7.1 Arena capacity data

	Capacity (standing)
AECC Aberdeen	8,500
SSE Hydro	13,000
Motorpoint Arena Sheffield	13,600
Capital FM Arena Nottingham	10,000
Ricoh Arena Coventry	12,000
Alexandra Palace	10,400
Wembley Arena	12,500
Earls Court & Olympia (combined)	35,750
O_2 Arena	20,000
Brighton Centre	5,488
Royal Albert Hall	3,951
Bournemouth International Centre	4,012
NIA	14,200
LG Arena	15,700
Motorpoint Arena Cardiff	7,500
Echo Arena Liverpool	11,000
3Arena Dublin	14,000
Odyssey Arena Belfast	10,800
Total	222,401

Source: Capacity data was obtained from each venue's website on 20 October 2014.

The other vital element in the planning of a show is to decide on a ticket price, based on factors such as artist and agent's fee, venue hire and production costs, promotion costs, box office commission and anticipated profit margins. It is worth noting that for Stereophonics, the ticket price at Glasgow's SECC in 2010 was £30.65 (US$45.70), which had risen to £39.50 (+ £3.95 booking fee; US$58.90 +$5.90) for the 2013 gig at the newly built Glasgow Hydro, an increase of nearly 30 per cent in just three years. At Newcastle's Metro Arena, Stereophonics ticket prices have risen from £22.50 (US$33.60) in 2001 to £32.50 (US$48.50) in 2013, not including booking fees, a rise of 44 per cent in twelve years. At the time of writing, then, ticket prices do not appear to be heading anywhere but up, as will be discussed later.

Publicizing the show

Once the artist fee and ticket price have been agreed with the agent, the promoter must then commence with promoting the show and selling the tickets to the audience on behalf of the artist. As with the planning of an arena show, however, the promoter's direct role in publicizing such a large show is diminished, because it depends on the promoter working with a number of secondary intermediaries to work on behalf of the artist (and the venue), including distributors, ticket agents and PR companies. To distribute publicity material such as posters and flyers, for example, promoters such as Regular Music will use professional distributors in order to target particular areas or audiences. Smaller-scale promoters, on the other hand, may do such publicity distribution themselves, thus taking on the risk of poor publicity themselves rather than contracting out this aspect of the promoter's role.

While promoters have become increasingly reliant on the internet to advertise their shows, Mark Mackie describes his own company's website, RegularMusic.com, as 'just a list of shows'. For email communication, he instead relies on the databases of ticket agents and venues which contain millions of customer details and past attendance records, thereby again using secondary intermediaries to carry out the publicity aspect of the promoter's role. Artists are also able to access their fans directly via the internet and build a relationship with their fan base that bypasses such 'traditional' intermediaries as record labels or, indeed, promoters. Mark Mackie explains that:

> For good websites, the bands' are the best, because they're doing blogs, diaries, they're giving you free downloads. So if I'm a Stereophonics fan, I'll check their website once a week . . . [The band have] got a great relationship with their fans. When they're not working and touring,

every week . . . you get amazing stuff [which] builds up people's need or wish to visit and use the website. (pers. comm., 1 July 2008)

Hence promoters at the arena show level rely on artist-generated promotion in order to sell a show, perhaps almost as much as that which they themselves control or pay for.

The selling of tickets is also mediated on behalf of the promoter at the arena concert level. A promoter at a small-scale show may be able to sell or distribute tickets personally to the audience, but a promoter at an arena concert relies on ticket agents to sell the advance tickets on their behalf. This is because selling 9,000 tickets by hand on the day would be impossible, and also because it allows the promoter to know in advance whether he will be in profit or loss, and whether he needs to spend more on publicity for the show. At the time of the interview with Mark Mackie, Regular Music used Ticketmaster as its primary ticket agent, then swapped to See Tickets and, at the time of writing, appears to be back with Ticketmaster again, Regular Music citing the two companies as the 'only two credible ticket agents of any real scale in the UK market' (Competition Commission 2010b, 27). In the same report, Regular Music highlighted the importance of the ticket agent due to fact that customers are usually more *au fait* with 'business-to-consumer' ticket agents than with the more 'business-to-business' arena show promoters (see Webster 2011, 92).

Producing the show

The third and final element of the promoter's role is the production of the show itself. For smaller gigs, this can sometimes be a slightly chaotic affair in which the promoter may act as artist liaison, technical support *and* front of house, necessarily moving between front of stage and backstage and back again. The backstage operation at an arena show, on the other hand, is a highly industrialized and mechanized process, with a number of intermediaries who mediate between promoter, artist, audience and venue, and who set up and operate the appropriate technology. In order to illustrate the promoter's diminished role in the production of such a large-scale show, it is useful to refer to the 'behind the scenes' activities witnessed at the 2010 Stereophonics gig.

Originally designed as a conference centre, the largest venue within Glasgow's SECC complex is Hall 4, a cavernous metal shed-like structure which can hold up to 10,000 people. Arena shows are usually self-contained touring productions in which the artist tours with staging, lighting, sound and catering. For the Stereophonics tour in 2010, for example, seventy-seven crew members travelled with the four-piece band (Kara Anderson, pers. comm., 2 March 2010), and it required six trucks to move the equipment and crew around the UK. The venue is just a 'shell' into which the touring production, like a conjuror's trick, appears and disappears in the course of a day.

For this particular gig, once I had obtained the correct pass, I was waved past the security staff to reach the concrete, labyrinthine inner sanctum of the backstage area. Here there are a number of offices and dressing rooms, divided into the artist's (and support artist's) crew, such as the production manager and stage manager; those working for the venue, such as the event planner; and those working for the promoter, such as the promoter's rep and safety adviser. The crew rooms house the tour manager, the production manager and the stage manager, although the majority of the latter's time is spent within the arena before the show itself starts. In this backstage world, the tour manager is generally regarded as being the 'top of the tree' (below the artists themselves) and is the person ultimately responsible for the entire tour once it is on the road, in terms of looking after and managing the crew. One promoter admitted to me that his main responsibility at an event was to the tour manager, because the tour manager reports to the booking agent, who decides whether to use the same promoter again in the future.

I interviewed both the stage and production managers, both of whom were employed directly by the Stereophonics' management company. When interviewed, the stage manager, Derek McVay, explained that he is responsible for the load in and load out, in terms of all the logistics of the equipment coming into the gig: unloading the equipment; putting up the equipment (lighting, sound, lasers, special effects, video and cameras); running the local crew; and liaising with the venue (D. McVay, pers. comm., 2 March 2010). For the load out, the stage manager oversees breaking down all the equipment and putting it back in the trucks ready for the next date on the tour. The production manager, Neil McDonald, explained that he was responsible for everything from booking trucks and hotels to getting crew and equipment, and that his main point of contact for the day is the promoter's rep, the 'go-between' between himself and the venue (N. McDonald, pers. comm., 2 March 2010). The production manager had an assistant for the Stereophonics tour, one of only two women in the seventy-seven strong crew, the other of whom worked in catering. The responsibilities of the production assistant, Kara Anderson, included decorating the dressing room and preparing the band's clothes, as well as what she described as 'general motherly duties' such as sourcing painkillers for a band member with a headache (K. Anderson, pers. comm., 2 March 2010). This reflects firstly the male dominance of the backstage world of live music, and secondly, that when women *do* work backstage, it is often in such 'traditional' female (caring/domestic) roles.

It should also be noted that backstage staff work incredibly hard and endure extremely long hours, but also that part of the work of backstage is precisely to *disguise* the work of backstage. Live music for some is about escapism and the last thing an audience wants to see are the mechanics of the show and the people sweating backstage to make it happen. At the start of a tour, the production manager may work from 6.30 am till 2.00 am the next morning, and may walk between 8 and 15 miles on concrete per day (D. McVay, pers. comm., 2 March 2010). During the show itself, the stage manager and production manager work on the next show via phone and email. At one point during the Stereophonics show, I popped backstage to see what was happening. Sure enough, the stage and production managers were working away on their laptops to finalize arrangements for the next shows on the tour. Later, I saw them briefly leave the production office to check the show was running okay, before heading back to their office (once the show is up and running, their actual role while it is on is minimal unless there's an emergency).

When I arrived at the venue at 1.00 pm, the general mood seemed fairly relaxed, so relaxed that at one point during the afternoon, the promoter's rep and safety advisor nipped down to the pub for an hour or so. I should also point out how cold the venue was. The heating is not used in the main venue because the audience's body heat warms the room, meaning that I could see my breath; the frigidity in the vast space is intensified by the 'fog' that is pumped out all day in order that the lighting technicians can focus the lights and check the effects. The head of security, John Thompson, had warned me that at 4.00 pm when the band arrived, he would have to go to work (J. Thompson, pers. comm., 2 March 2010). Sure enough, his mobile phone rang just after 4.00 pm and the backstage area suddenly became hectic as the operation stepped up a gear as the band and support act began their sound check. At 6.30 pm, the doors to the venue opened and at 7.30 pm exactly the support act, Hip Parade, entered the stage and the show began.

The chapter will now address the role of the promoter at the arena show itself. The promoter's team at the Stereophonics gig consisted of the promoter's rep, contracted safety adviser and accountant. The promoter's rep (in this case, Graeme Roberts) is the person whose role is to 'run the day' on behalf of the promoter (G. Roberts, pers. comm., 2 March 2010). His role at the Stereophonics show was to liaise with the following parties: venue staff and the band's employees, the stage and production managers (to oversee the load in and the set-up of the show) and the tour manager (for the early stages of the settlement). For a 'normal' show, Roberts arrives at 5.00 am for a 6.00 am load in, and leaves at around half past midnight for a show finishing at 10.30 pm and a load out lasting around two to three hours. It is imperative that the load ins and outs are completed on time, as the promoter can be fined by the venue if either end of the show overruns, as had happened with Lady Gaga the previous night (G. Roberts, pers. comm., 2 March 2010).

When asked about his role at the gig itself, promoter Mark Mackie explained that it is to 'pull everything together that has been done for me'; although, as previously discussed, the promoter at an arena show also relies on intermediaries to do this on their behalf, most notably, the promoter's rep. It is significant that for the Stereophonics show in 2010, Mark Mackie did not show up until after the show had started – his rep, on the other hand, had been there from 5.00 am. As explained to me by a promoter's rep for DF Concerts, the promoter's role at the gig itself is therefore mainly financial: they are there to work on the settlement with the artist's representative and to agree the final promoter/artist 'split' (Graeme Smillie, pers. comm., 13 April 2014). While at a smaller show, such a settlement would most likely be made with cash, more and more there is a desire to move and handle as little cash as possible, and people are encouraged and willing to have balances transferred by BACS transfer after the show (Graeme Smillie, pers. comm., 13 April 2014).

However, as mentioned earlier, the promoter's role is not entirely financial. The other, equally important, function of the promoter at the arena event itself is social. Hence, as Mackie explains:

> There's a fairly social side to it as well, and it's sort of a respect thing. I mean, if you didn't go it'd be a bit odd. But a lot of the tour managers I know anyway, know quite well, so you say 'hello' and have a glass of wine with them halfway through the night or something, or just sit and chat to them, and, you know, just chew the fat and go, 'What's happening?' You know, 'How was your Dutch tour, and are you off to Norway next, and . . . ?' You show an interest, and build up knowledge as well, and relationships are formed that way (pers. comm., 1 July 2008).

In this way, promoters build loyalty and knowledge with important figures like tour managers, which enables them to continue to promote successfully over a sustained period.

Returning to what was happening front of stage, just before 10.15 pm, the band left the stage to whistles, cheers and applause, only to appear three minutes later for their planned and rehearsed three song encore. After the final song, 'Dakota' – probably the most well-known Stereophonics song and the band's first UK number one – lasers flashed, confetti bombs exploded, the audience went wild, the band left the stage at almost exactly 10.30 pm and then nearly 9,000 people tried to get home at the same time. (Usually this is the point when many of the crew members start work again but, on this occasion, the band were playing two consecutive shows and so the load out was postponed until the following day.)

Conclusion

In conclusion, returning to the Sheffield promoter's claim at the start of the chapter that for bigger shows, 'it's probably less work', it could be argued that this may indeed be the case in terms of man-hours per ticket sold. However, the financial risks are higher and the knowledge/experience required to be able to promote at the arena level is much greater (G. Smillie, pers. comm., 17 April 2014). There is also a higher risk of something going wrong at larger gigs, as it so tragically did in Canada in 2013 when Radiohead's stage collapsed, killing the band's drum technician; in an ongoing case, the promoter, Live Nation, has been charged for safety violations (Cooke 2013). In this way, the promoter's role at an arena show is perhaps not 'less work' in the way suggested by the promoter from Sheffield, but it *is* different from their role at smaller shows, being less hands-on/multi-tasking, and more clearly focused on the financial and social aspects necessary for career longevity.

Arena shows are more spectacular than ever before and as audience expectations increase as to what is possible – aided by the mediatization of arena shows via television and the internet – so too must arena tours continually outdo each other in terms of what they offer. As Regular Music's safety advisor, Davy White, explained to me, the Stereophonics show included playback video screens, a confetti cannon and lasers and a dazzling light show, in order to 'give the audience more of a show' (D. White, pers. comm., 2 March 2010). As can be seen with shows like Lady Gaga's and even the much less flamboyant Arctic Monkeys and Stereophonics, there is a continual increase in production values and hence production costs. This naturally impacts on promoters, in that the costs of buying an artist's tour (or show within a tour) inevitably get more expensive, exacerbated by the higher fees demanded by artists as global recorded music revenues continue to fall (Dredge 2014). High artist fees result in very high barriers to entry for less established promoters because the high fees make it impossible for them to breach the higher levels, meaning it is less and less likely for smaller-scale promoters to secure a toe-hold within the arena market. Consequently, only a small handful of commercial promoters nationwide are able to afford to promote at the arena show level.

Dave Laing has suggested that the UK's live music sector is a duopoly, formed of the American promotional super-giants, Live Nation and AEG Live.[1] However, the arena show sector is, in fact, an *oligopoly*, in that there are a small number of interconnected players. The following is a list of the major arena show promoters in the UK at the time of writing:

- Live Nation
- DF Concerts
- AEG Live
- Kilimanjaro
- 3A Entertainment
- SJM
- Metropolis

It should be noted that DF Concerts is majority-owned by Live Nation subsidiary Live Nation-Gaiety Holdings, in which SJM's Simon Moran also owns a share. Metropolis and SJM work together via booking website, gigsandtours.com, and Metropolis is also linked to both SJM and Live Nation via Maztec Ltd., the parent company for V Festivals (Walters and Raj 2004, 366). As can be seen, then, this particular oligopoly displays interdependency between the players, and potentially runs a high risk of collusion in ticket pricing. Promoters have to have a good sense of how much other promoters are paying for the tour, but also have to have a good understanding of what ticket prices are at venues across the tour. Such an oligopoly, with few promoters, few venues, few artists and high artist fees, declining revenue from recorded music sales, is a perfect storm for high ticket prices for fans. It is in promoters' and arenas' interests that the current situation continues, of course; more arenas and more promoters would mean increased competition which could then lower ticket prices and hence profit.

To finish, it is worth noting that the John Knight, Vice President of Leeds Arena operator, SMG-Europe, surmised that there is only room for one more arena to be built in the UK, most likely in Bristol.[2] After that, he believed that the market would be 'saturated'. However, perhaps the only way to break the oligopolistic stranglehold over the arena market is for local authorities (and/or promotional companies/venue operators) to invest in *more* venues, or for the government to regulate the arena market – and the broader live music sector – more stringently. In this way, promoters would be forced back into a more innovative and competitive role, thereby reducing the scarcity of such shows and bringing ticket prices down.

Notes

1 Dave Laing, 'Live Music in an Age of Austerity – Some Current Trends.' Paper presented at the Live Music Exchange London conference, City University London, 15 May 2013.

2 John Knight, 'Leeds Arena in the Context of the City and the Region.' Panel member at the Live Music Exchange Leeds conference, Leeds College of Music, Leeds, 4 May 2012.

CHAPTER EIGHT

Being There: Encounters with Space and the Affective Dimension of Arena Spectacle

Alice O'Grady

Music moves us; it makes us feel. It can set our hearts racing and make our skin tingle. It can stir up feelings hidden in our deepest recesses and bring them soaring to the surface with uncompromising intensity. Music can make us cry when we least expect it. Music makes us smile and urges us to dance. Music helps us fall in love; connects us to each other and provides a soundtrack to our lives that we can replay at will, transporting us effortlessly to particular moments in time that we wish to relive. Music forms part of our emotional DNA. Where we listen to it, and by which means, ultimately shapes our experience of it. Set and setting are paramount. With ubiquitous pocket technology, most people have access to vast libraries of recorded sound on their mobile phones and lock themselves into a private, headphone world as they go about their daily business. In contrast, and perhaps as antidote to this individualized and consciously isolating experience of music, is the arena concert where music is experienced with thousands of others as an event, and where the individual listener is dwarfed by the sheer size of the building in which the concert takes place. This is music for the masses, quite literally. Our relationship to the music is altered by these vast spaces, and one could argue, ultimately controlled by them and the precision planning that has gone into designing the optimal 'customer experience'. Living through an age where technological advancements alter our patterns of leisure consumption at an ever-increasing rate, understanding the connection between space, music and emotional engagement has never been more pressing. This 'experience economy' (as Pine and Gilmore term it) is booming and, as savvy consumers of leisure, our expectations are flourishing too. In this chapter I will consider the affective dimension of being present at a large-scale, indoor gig and ask to what extent does the embodied experience of the arena concert influence our engagement with the event? How does the arena's spatial arrangement shape the emotional meta-narratives that stay with us long after the music has ended?

Where others have studied the architecture of arenas and the technological developments and innovations designed to improve audience experience, here I examine the phenomenological, sensorial and emotional responses the arena concert provokes. I consider the primacy of 'being there' as a visceral means of accessing the cultural product. And I utilize existing auto-ethnographic methodologies developed within my own Electronic Dance Music research (see O'Grady 2013, 18–38) to investigate the embodied experience of the arena concert and how physical space impacts upon our felt responses. The narrative sections serve to illuminate how it feels to be present in the space of the arena: they describe my encounter with the materiality of a building and the emotional responses that emerged during an event, namely the Vampire Weekend concert that took place at Leeds Arena on 16 November 2013.[1] As first-hand accounts, these sections prioritize personal, physical, subjective experiences and utilize them as triggers for analysis and critique. As Di Benedetto points out, 'academic language is not always the best way to describe the subjective experience of perception' (2006, 126) and so, with this mind, I purposefully oscillate between two registers in order to capture the spirit of the event and my place within it.

What is outlined here is one person's account of a particular experience on a specific date, and at specific times. Reflections are made on what was felt on that night by someone who prefers to participate rather than spectate. My musical preference lies not with rock bands but with dance music. I prefer the collective space of the dance floor to the tyranny of raked seating and the pricing policies of venues that seek to separate rather than unify a crowd. My tendency is to immerse myself in musical experiences that are interactive, unpredictable, sociable and driven by grassroots ideologies rather than ones that revel in celebrity and align themselves with consumerism and capital gain. An arena concert is, by its very nature, the antithesis to the DIY ethic of the underground dance scene and so my reactions to the event are perhaps not difficult to guess. However, what I offer here is an analysis of my arena experience that unpacks the ways in which space, value and emotional response to music intersect and explores the commodification and control of the spectacular arena event.

Leeds Arena, operated by SMG Europe, opened on 4 September 2013. It was awarded the prestigious title of 'New Venue of the Year' at the Stadium Business Awards, in London, in June 2014. The 13,500 capacity venue cost £60 million (approximately $97.5 million) to build and is the landmark development in a city that is currently undergoing considerable development and investment in its leisure and tourism industry. The arena's partners include the online retail bank First Direct, the beer company Heineken, the soft drinks company Coca Cola and the confectionary company Cadbury as well as Leeds City Council, who had been striving to secure an arena for the city for many years in the hope that such a building would boost the local economy and improve the city's cultural offering. Up to this point, Leeds was losing out to nearby cities Sheffield and Manchester and, despite its musical heritage and cultural profile in other areas such as theatre, dance, opera and film, had no equivalent sized building in which to host major rock, pop and sporting events afforded by an arena.

The venue is currently known as the First Direct Arena and occupies a prominent place in the heart of the city centre. It dominates the skyline towards the north of the city and further building works are underway in its immediate vicinity to provide additional infrastructure and facilities for its visitors, including car parks, hotels, bars and restaurants. It is the first arena of its kind in the UK to have a fan-shaped orientation that promises every visitor 'a seat that faces the stage regardless of seat location'.[2] It was consciously designed for intimacy, the longest distance from the stage is 68 metres, as opposed to the standard 95–130 metres of the more traditionally shaped arena venues elsewhere. Standing outside the building, it is hard to imagine how the word 'intimate' could ever be applied to such a monolithic structure but perhaps this concept is relative when dealing with the collective experience of 13,000 or so people. John Rhodes, chief architect of the building, describes Leeds arena as 'a machine for delivering entertainment' (cited in Wainwright 2013). This terminology imagines the building in reference to manufacturing processes associated with corporate entertainment and gives an indication of the industrial scale of the experiences the building is designed to house.

The taxi drops us outside the huge, new building that, for the occasion, is lit up and pulsating with neon light that changes colour. It looks like an outsized Christmas decoration that has somehow been magnified and discarded in the middle of the city. The first thing that hits me is the smell of donuts – a sweet and sickly, cloying smell hangs in the air and as I look up at the multimillion pound behemoth in front of me, I'm reminded of garish fun fairs that used to rock up on the playing fields when we were kids and vanish after the Bank Holiday weekend without a trace. I doubt this is the effect the architects were going for.

The external appearance of Leeds Arena is undoubtedly bold. It is vivid green in colour and is reminiscent of a giant space ship. Voronoi tessellation is used on the exterior to break the building's bulk into smaller pieces, replicating the pattern of a honeycomb. The building adopts what Rhodes describes as 'dazzle camouflage' (cited in Wainwright 2013), a disguise that seeks to detract from its enormity in order to minimize its overwhelming presence within the urban landscape. Not only does the vast scale of the arena dazzle the observer but so too does the light show that plays on the side of the building when a concert is in full swing. As Oliver Wainwright explains in his 'Architecture and Design Blog' for *The Guardian*:

> It is a lot for the eye to digest by day, but by night the lurid exterior moves to a whole new level. With a combination of illuminated tracery, throbbing back-lit mesh and spotlights shining through the windows, the building is transformed into a psychedelic technicolour dreamboat. (Wainwright, 2013)

This is a building that performs for its audience and for the city at large. For the residents of Leeds, the arena performs civic confidence. It represents significant economic growth, investment and development in the city's future and has provided many jobs both within the construction industry and within leisure and tourism. It is quite literally a flashy building and announces itself as the headline act for a programme of artists that are known globally and who require a stage befitting their profile. An audience's expectations in attending an event at an arena such as this, are as much wrapped up with the building, and what it signifies, as they are with the musicians who perform within its walls.

Even though we are a little late, I was expecting crowds. There are none. The place feels deserted and I wonder how thousands of people could have been simply swallowed up by this building. Clutching our tickets, we follow behind three women in their early twenties and approach the doors. The entrances are manned by stewards in bright yellow jackets with appliquéd logos announcing their allegiance as members of the arena team. We duly hand over our tickets as the marshal barks at us to see if we have any of our own food or drink. Once in, there are countless other yellow jackets on hand asking us whether we know where we are going. We are ushered up some stairs with urgency. St John's ambulance volunteers are lingering around the stairwells. More yellow jackets hover, all of them looking grumpy. We are pointed in the direction of the toilets and the bar and, as entrance doors open and shut to allow members of the audience to nip in and out, I become aware of the huge power of noise that is contained within. Whenever the support band, Noah and the Whale, begin or finish a song a tremendous shout

goes up from the crowd and I begin to visualise for the first time the
huge number of people who are hiding behind that wall. My sense of
separation between here and there fills me with a kind of dread.

Studies in environmental psychology show how the particularities of
both indoor and outdoor space have significant impact not only on how we
feel, and our general sense of well-being (Ulrich 1984; Kaplan 1993; Hartig
and Staats 2006), but also on the way we behave (Sullivan et al. 2004).
We may not always be fully alert to the position of entrances and exits or
appreciative of the nuance of colour schemes, layout, ambient temperature
and so on, but the emotional or felt response to our surroundings is often
instant and registers at a subconscious level. As Pine and Gilmore have
suggested, our 'experience derives from the interaction between the staged
event and the individual's prior state of mind and being' – thus rendering no
two experiences the same (1999, 12). A late arrival to an event, a solitary
entry to a building designed for hoards of people or a hurried interaction
with busy or over-eager door staff are all factors that can influence the way
we encounter space and make a judgement about it, thereby framing how we
engage with the cultural event or experience for which we have paid. With
an absence of crowds, what I might describe as 'the staffing of experience'
is thrown into sharp relief. Noise, excitement, spontaneity, the thrill of
being enveloped by the swell of a crowd or the sense of participating in a
cultural event on a grand scale are lost, and the mechanisms of the tightly,
and perhaps over-managed customer experience, are revealed. The front of
house operations of any entertainment venue cannot be underestimated in
terms of how audiences are emotionally prepped for the main event they
have come to see. The emphasis on slick corporate identity and consumerism
that is apparent in an arena's bar and merchandise areas may well be
designed to facilitate the smooth shopping experience of spectators prior
to the concert beginning, but it also underlines the operational imperative
of financial returns (rather than creative gains) and the processing of
customers (as opposed to participants) which, in turn, commodifies the
spectator–performer relationship and the event itself.

Finally we're ready to go in. Our tickets are checked, the door opens and
we're in. The scale of the arena hits you the moment you enter the space.
It's bigger than a cathedral and noisier than any club I have ever been
too. It's like being inside a huge aircraft hanger with the grandest state
of the art sound system imaginable. The sound is all-encompassing. We
head upwards. The stairs are smooth, grey concrete. It reminds me of a
sports stadium. The place is dark and it's hard to see the letters printed
on each step. We're looking for Row J. There is an usher to make sure
we sit in our allocated spot but she's busy with someone else. We have
to find our own seats in the darkness and push along a row of people,

making sure we don't lose our footing in the gap between the chairs in front. Despite the cavernous space, up here in the 'not so cheap' cheap seats, there isn't much room. Finally we've made it. We sit and survey.

As Robert Kronenburg points out, 'the architecture of a venue can have a highly significant effect on the character, power, and relevance of the performance, adding layers of meaning and expression for both performer and audience' (2011, 137). A venue's design is perhaps the single most important mediator of experience and plays a fundamental role in how the musical event is not only received by an audience but also framed culturally, socially and, in some cases, politically. According to Kronenburg's 'building typology' (2011), Leeds arena is 'dedicated space' (specifically designed for purpose rather than adopted or adapted space) and represents the ultimate in the management of experience through built design. As he suggests, the architecture of live music performance space is so critical in terms of making the venue financially successful, that every last detail is minutely considered, controlled and manipulated. The size, shape, volume and proportion of the space are designed to deliver the best acoustics possible (2011, 139). Temperature, humidity, lighting and amplification are all controlled for audience and artists' comfort and pleasure. Front of house operations provide a wealth of facilities for audience members – bars, toilets, restaurants, information hubs, merchandise outlets, medical assistance, security – to ensure the price of each ticket not only proves value for money, but also to create the optimal conditions for audiences to part with their money readily and easily, as part of the overall arena package. In the über-designed, dedicated performance space nothing is left to chance, serendipity or fortune. Production values for each concert are high and the promise of a smooth customer experience is top of the agenda. For those who prefer the striations of less engineered musical events, this can produce a profound flattening of experience and even result in a deadening of the event's live qualities.

That there would be an 'intermission' had simply not occurred to me but, of course, it makes sense. We are an audience of 13,000 or so with cash in our pockets. Noah and the Whale play their last song and the lights come up. The atmosphere is broken and everyone resumes normal behaviour. This is everyone's cue to go and load up with drinks, chips, sweets, ice cream, t-shirts, merchandise. And so we file out too and go and queue for another drink. The queue is orderly. The bars are well stocked. The staff are trained. Everything is fit for purpose and functions smoothly. This is a musical experience that has been crafted and planned to the point where unpredictability and surprise is eradicated. I feel immediately drained of any excitement I may have felt to begin. It's like the musical equivalent of a trip to the supermarket.

As Kronenburg points out, 'the creation of dedicated places in which to experience music can be viewed as part of its commodification' (2012, 7). He suggests some argue these spaces are essentially designed to 'eliminate variability' (2011, 139) so that customer satisfaction can be more or less guaranteed. Certainly ticket prices are high and audience expectation naturally rises with the financial commitment. For artists the live event has become the latest weapon in the arsenal against the ubiquity of file sharing, downloads and easy access to music via Spotify and YouTube but, in return, audiences expect the live sound to be as close to the recorded version as possible, and they want a show. While acknowledging the positive aspects of technological perfectionism, the eradication of variability is a worrying turn towards bland certainty, sameness and cultural monotony. It is essential to question what is lost when one swaps unpredictability for homogeneity, particularly in the realm of the creative industries. With the eradication of variability there is no risk, no surprise, less opportunity for interactivity and alterity and, as French philosopher Jean-Luc Nancy reminds us, the event per se must surprise us 'or else it is not an event' (2000, 167). Often the illusion of surprise finds its place within the theatrical or spectacular elements that wrap the arena concert rather than within the musical performance itself. We are living through a time where there is both the thirst for the exciting, experiential qualities of live events and an expectation of neatly packaged, consistent, high-end production that never fails to deliver.

Our seats are about 10 rows from the back. We are high up. Very high. The view is incredible. You can see the whole stage perfectly and Noah and the Whale are framed with light and colour. What strikes me, though, is that I am sitting when thousands of people below me are dancing. Looking down I instantly envy the people who were in time to buy standing tickets. That is how I feel music should be experienced – in a moving crowd, physically responding to the music with my body. For now, I'm imprisoned in a chair, restricted to tapping my foot or drumming my fingers while I watch from a distance. Having said that the onslaught of sound is far-reaching and I can allow myself to feel cocooned by it. I may be sitting far away from the band but their sound is definitely reaching me. I sip my cider and try and adjust to being there.

How seats are organized at cultural events is not merely a question of practicalities and logistics. Seating arrangements are heavily coded signifiers of taste, expectation, cultural convention and, above all, operate as behaviour modifiers. Their configuration is a concrete and tangible representation of differing artistic traditions, values and ideals, relating specifically to notions of audienceship, spectatorship and what musicologist

Thomas Turino calls the 'politics of participation' (2008). Turning to theatre history for a moment, Kimberley Jannarone reminds us of the advent of the 'homogenized bourgeois audience' in the early 1920s which altered the audience/performer relationship from 'one which allowed for multiple kinds of spectatorial activity in exchange for a bare minimum of violence to one with a single rule: the audience will behave' (2009, 194). Prior to this, theatre audiences were decidedly unruly and thought nothing of moving, talking, heckling and even, on occasion, exchanging blows as the dramatic action unfolded on stage. Developments in theatre building design effectively enabled the 'physical regulation of spectators' (Jannarone 2009, 194). Designated seats placed spectators and kept them there. The introduction of electric light focused the spectators' attention on the stage and plunged them into darkness, augmenting the sense of isolation and individualism that prevented contact with other audience members. Now that dominance had been achieved over the audience, the stage capitalized on this victory by presenting ever bigger, better and more elaborate spectacles. Such 'policing', as it were, of the body resulted in a reprioritizing of the ocular (see also Halligan 2009). As Jannarone argues, 'this desire to overwhelm was manifest in both performance and theatre architecture' (2009, 194). Theatres were built whose intention was to create 'silent awe' among its audiences (Blackadder 2003, 10). In a similar way, the space of the arena overwhelms us with its magnitude, encourages us to marvel at the sheer mass of humanity it can contain and yet, with its strict adherence to seat allocation and crowd control, confines us into stillness and prevents us from connecting physically with the music and those around us.

> *My overwhelming view is that we need to experience Vampire Weekend from the standing area. Here we will get the true crowd experience. Here we will dance with and brush against other people, even people we don't know might speak to us! We head downstairs hoping to infiltrate the inner reaches of the arena. Security is tight and without a wristband we don't stand a chance. Despondent we head back upstairs and resume our place in Row J. I'm starting to resent Row J.*

With vertiginous seating arrangements at the top of the arena, significant physical movement is not only restricted but somewhat foolhardy to attempt – although, moved by the music, many do.

> *I begin to watch the crowd and see their attempts to circumnavigate the rules of this seating game. As the crowd get whipped up by the band, they start to stand rather than sit. A chain reaction occurs up here with more people standing to see over the heads of others. Other people as keen to get moving as me wander off to try and find somewhere to stand but get told to sit down by the ushers policing the aisles. People even try*

'sit down dancing', an awkward and unnatural jiggling of arms, in an attempt to break out of the imposed physical confinement.

With sections of the crowd denied any significant physical response to the music through dance, the dazzling visual shows and breathtaking spectacles of light do offer some kind of compensation for spectators. Lighting plays a major role in shaping our emotional responses and has become a key player, if not star performer, in the arena phenomenon. Artists such as Lady Gaga, Take That, Madonna and even Coldplay have become known for their theatrical pyrotechnics, laser displays, confetti explosions and other spectacular effects designed to excite the crowd and to augment the 'eventness' of the moment. With these awe-inspiring and dazzling displays of theatrical wizardry audiences are reminded of the specialness of this moment and their presence in the moment. However staged, choreographed and ultimately repeatable these effects may be, the crowd takes pleasure in an illusion of the unexpected and revels in the very 'liveness' of the here and now and an event that declares itself as such through its commitment to visual extravagance and excess.

At the allotted time of 8.45 everything changes. The scurrying roadies on stage stop scurrying, the auditorium plunges into darkness. The band run on and everything kicks off. The show has started and lead man Ezra Koenig begins to sing. The music is louder than Noah and the Whale, the lights more intense, the crowd below more wild. This is what they have come to see – Vampire Weekend! There is electricity in the air that seems surprising given the scale of the building.
The stage is set with a number of Greco Roman pillars suspended from the ceiling and another bunch of them rise up from the floor. On each pillar is a light that is capable of rotating and casting the most powerful beam across the stage and into the crowd. The lights oscillate quickly. One moment the drummer is lit, the next he is invisible. The stage is lit and then the crowd are illuminated. This to-ing and fro-ing is dizzying. The crowd cheers the band every time a new tune begins and another one ends but, curiously, they also cheer the light. The lights punctuate the music and add drama. They pinpoint the lead singer in an intense star shape that makes him appear God-like and cut through with bright white light. The lights are truly an incredibly significant part of the show and I began to wonder what the gig would be like without them.

The spectacular lighting effects that accompany most arena concerts are an integral part of a sensorial experience that can be both mesmerizing and overpowering. If Guy Debord's insurrectionary aim, in his critique of what he identified as modern societies given over to mounting overwhelming spectacles for its overwhelmed citizens, was to 'wake up the spectator who has been drugged by spectacular images' and to fight against spectacle as 'a permanent opium war' (1995, thesis 44), this arena concert experience is spectacle with a different pharmacological narrative. Here the visual spectacle unfolding is characterized not by opiate passivity but as amphetamine high, where the lights whip the crowd into a type of visually induced hysteria that rises into a crescendo along with the music, and leaves the crowd immediately wanting more. This is intense visual stimulation that, along with the driving music and the sensation of being part of a mammoth gathering of people, creates powerful emotional affect, causing people to shout, cheer, scream, wave flags, climb balustrades and strip off their shirts. The lighting display is spectacular. At times it illuminates the crowd. The crowd becomes spectacular and 'being there', physically and emotionally present in this particular space, in this moment in time, is the real commodity that is being sold.

With growing cultural interest in the concept of 'eventness' after Bakhtin, where time is open and the present is figured as a gateway or threshold (1984), the fundamental concept of 'being there' is highly prized both by participants and by promoters and is a thread that runs also through dance music and club culture discourse. In Kronenburg's words, 'musical performance [. . .] transforms the space, internal or external, into an identifiable "place" the boundary of which is limited by the aural and visual experience of being there' (2011, 137). Regardless of how easy it is to access live streaming, to witness major musical events second hand through the internet or view countless images of gigs and festivals online, being physically present carries with it significant cultural capital and can command the huge ticket prices that secures our presence at a particular cultural or musical event. Ironically, perhaps due to the improved and increased remote accessibility to such events, attitudes to the authenticity of 'being there' are undergoing a paradigm shift. We want to experience the event for ourselves, physically, but at the same time we want to record our presence and broadcast it so that others can observe our participation. Being present is important but only if others validate that presence by accessing a digital representation of it. As Connell and Gibson suggest (2003, 29), the ideology of authenticity in live music is paramount but, in a technology-saturated world, our own physical experiences of liveness are now authenticated by virtual, mediatized versions of these physical experiences.

From our vantage point up high, we can see the thousands of people that have come here for the gig below us. From here you get a sense of the spectacle we must make as a mass of bodies. What strikes me though is the multitude of lights from the mobile phones people have on. The darkness is pin-pricked with light, digital candles glinting, flicking off and on. Photographs are taken, statuses are updated with alarming frequency and it makes me feel as though some of the people around me are virtually somewhere else.

According to Prendergast the majority of mediatized performance, namely that which is reliant on technology for its delivery, fragments our audience experience from the collective to an individual one. She argues mediatized performance focuses our attention for us and tells us what to think and feel as closed interpretations, caring about our presence and involvement only in terms of numbers and profit margins. In contrast, live performance is predicated on a shared social presence where there can be active, attentive involvement in the performance and an open, playful interpretation of it (Prendergast 2010, 48). What this modelling does not account for, however, are those modes of performance that challenge any concrete distinctions between, or definitions of, live and mediatized forms. The arena concert is most certainly a live performance (it has live musicians performing in real time in front of spectators who are co-present) and yet it exists and is experienced also as a mediatized performance, not only through the eradication of variability that has already been discussed but also in the way it is viewed, recorded and disseminated by many through the screen of the mobile phone. The result is an audience whose priorities are split between being there and recording being there.

As the gig continues the lights become even more intense. I try experimenting with closing my eyes but I can still see the lights, even through shut eyelids. My shirt is vibrating with the bass. I feel bombarded by light and I'm beginning to long for the darkness of outdoors. Even though the music is good, I've seen enough. We leave before the gig is over.

Music, emotional response and our relationships with space, and the cultural values to which we subscribe, are complex and slippery, individual and contradictory, and so cannot always be comprehensively defined or accurately captured using neat theoretical frameworks. Music is beautifully personal and exquisitely elusive. How and why it moves us depends on a host of reasons, ranging from the physiological to the social, and beyond. What we can be certain about, however, is that the context in which we experience music will have a significant impact on our emotional responses to it. These responses may, of course, vary from person to person but spatial dynamics and the physical conditions under which we listen to music or attend a musical event are intimately connected. As a devotee of dance floor experiences where the freedom to move represents a type of collective and personal autonomy, the sit-down experience of the arena concert will always unsettle me. The management of bodies in space will always be political. How our musical experiences are controlled and shaped by huge corporations is not only a matter of concern for us as individual consumers but raises questions about changing attitudes to cultural value and the commodification of creative expression on an industrial scale.

Notes

1 Vampire Weekend, supported by Noah and the Whale, performed as part of a UK arena tour that included Birmingham, London, Glasgow, Leeds and Manchester. The tour followed their third studio album, *Modern Vampires of the City*, and was announced shortly after their appearance at the UK Glastonbury music festival in June 2013.
2 Details of the arena's layout is given on the official website under Frequently Asked Questions http://www.firstdirectarena.com/venue-information/frequently-asked-questions/ (accessed 11 September 2014).

PART THREE

Perspectives – Personal and Professional

CHAPTER NINE

'Hello Cleveland . . . !': The View from the Stage

Jon Stewart

This chapter considers the experience of arena concerts from the ethnographic perspective of performers and those who work with them onstage. The text is compiled from five semi-structured interviews with musicians and technicians who play and work in arenas around the world, conducted in 2014 and 2015. The chapter considers how arena spaces shape the possibilities of front of house audio, whether mediation via cameras and video screen technology impacts upon the 'liveness' of a performance and how it feels and sounds to perform on an arena stage compared to the experience of a theatre or club show.

Jon Stewart

Jon Stewart, the author, played arena concerts in Europe, Japan and the United States with platinum-selling Britpop band Sleeper the 1990s.

Jon Burton

Jon Burton is one of the UK's most prolific and experienced arena sound engineers. He has worked with Stereophonics, The Prodigy, Pulp, Bryan Ferry and many others.

Vinnie Lammi

Vinnie Lammi was drummer on the Spice Girls re-union tour 2007–2008, where he performed at arenas and stadiums around the world from the London O2 to Madison Square Garden.

Matt McGinn

Matt McGinn has been a full-time stage tech for Coldplay for fourteen years, a role that at one time also involved playing acoustic guitar on key tracks. He is the author of *Roadie: My Life On The Road With Coldplay* (2010).

Kieron Pepper

Kieron Pepper has performed at international arena and stadiums shows from Russia to South America with The Prodigy. He now plays with The Radiophonic Workshop.

Rachel Wood

Guitarist Rachel Wood has appeared at European venues such as the London O2 Arena and across the United States in Cirque Du Soleil.

> Jon Stewart: My first experiences of an arena gig, like most people, was as a fifteenyear-old fan at Wembley and NEC Birmingham. I was overwhelmed by the size of the space and number of people, but frustrated by the distance that separated me from the tiny speck that was Mark Knopfler or Bob Dylan on the horizon – and genuinely disappointed by the weak sound that bounced between us.

Jon Burton: Arenas have always been built as multi-purpose spaces. Most were originally constructed for sports such as ice hockey, while others were conference centres. All were designed with few considerations for acoustics, which still falls down the list of priorities. When they started putting on bands the unsuitability of arenas led to frequent complaints about the sound. It is only in the last few years that arena developers and owners have even begun to look at acoustics, and only recently that the public are getting used to shows sounding better as venues begin taming reverberation times. Even today most changes usually happen as the result of external noise problems that threaten an arena's ability to put on shows. Only rarely are they driven by aesthetic reasons. It's almost as if musical requirements are still the last thing to be considered.

My experience as an arena performer began with Britpop band Sleeper when we played the same venues I'd attended as a teenager – Wembley Arena and NEC Birmingham. My first thought while walking on stage was how very distant the back rows appeared. I imagined we would need to play at an unfeasible volume and throw ourselves around like circus performers in order to make any kind of impression on the sea of tiny expectant faces below. Then, while striding across an acre of space to pick up my guitar, I realised how long I'd been walking and how much room there was between us all. For musicians who spend time rehearsing in a box room at the back of an industrial estate and playing clubs and small theatre shows, where it's an achievement if you haven't tripped over the drum kit at some point during the set, an arena stage can seem sparse and intimidating. For those who suffer from performance anxiety, one of the most disconcerting aspects of this experience is how far away you seem from your fellow bandmates. You're not only nervous, you're also quite alone.

Vinnie Lammi: The first time you perform on a large stage it is a very strange sensation. You feel almost entirely detached from the people you're

FIGURE 9.1 Jon Stewart (left) with Sleeper.

supposedly interacting with. The Spice Girls stage was enormous and we definitely struggled for intimacy as musicians. The set up had two sections so the Musical Director (MD), percussionist and first guitarist were in another space altogether on a platform that I couldn't see. I had a television screen attached to my kit with a camera facing me. The MD had a screen and camera on his side. He was looking at me on his television and I was looking at him on mine.

Kieron Pepper: When you first get to play on a big stage you can feel the need to spread out and fill it up. Suddenly you've got distance between all the band members which causes two problems: you lose all sense of intimacy and any subtler elements of musical interaction between you can evaporate. The solution is to set up close together so the band can convene in the middle of the stage for the more intimate moments when you need to communicate.

Despite the stage space and unfeasible audience size there's often a pleasant surprise in the way things sound for arena performers. The stage monitors boast high-quality speakers, positioned and mixed by skilled technicians who provide each performer with a dedicated signal. These are not the beer-sodden bins early career club musicians might be accustomed to, where in acute circumstances band members are sometimes obliged to share the same mix in monitors that are either inaudible or feeding back.

Kieron Pepper: The advantages of playing an arena stage are that you'll have an excellent monitor engineer who will feed you exactly what you need. The onstage sound will be clearer and better than you're used to in any club, theatre or festival gig. The results can be spectacular.

Onstage sound is changing, however. Monitor speakers are less frequently seen at stage front today because the musicians commonly use in-ear systems. Even guitar and bass amplifiers are often dummy shells. The stage soundscape is now comprised of acoustic instruments, vocals and noise spilling behind the line arrays [columns of public address speakers hung in arena spaces]. It can be quiet enough for people to converse in comfort.

Vinnie Lammi: We used in-ear monitors throughout the Spice Girls tour so there were no monitors or amplifiers on the stage. Nothing at all. The first week of rehearsals felt extremely alien. The sensation is rather like playing along to an iPod and can be difficult to get used to. On the first day we all thought: 'We don't want this, we want real monitors!'

Like anything else, you acclimatize to it. Once I became used to in-ears I found it very tough to return to standard monitor speakers. You can get an individual mix of exactly what you want in the finest detail, less or more guitar, BBC Radio 4, whatever you like. Monitors simply don't offer that kind of clarity, plus I didn't come off stage with tinnitus. If an audience member were to come and stand next to me during a Spice Girls show it would be a bizarre sonic experience. They'd just be able to hear the vocals, the acoustic guitar, my snare drum and hi-hat; very different to the other side of the speaker arrays.

The downside with in-ears is the loss of contact with the audience. The muffling is extremely powerful and you feel entirely detached. On my very first Spice Girls gig I was anxious to do a really good job so had the in-ears in position before we all went on stage. After the gig I went back in the dressing room and unplugged them, only to hear the crew talking about how they were blown away by the crowd's noisy reception. I had missed all of that because of the in-ears. Next night I didn't put them in until we actually got on stage and I couldn't believe the screams. After that I wouldn't put them in until the last moment, and quickly whipped them out on the final beat of the encore. I didn't want to miss the vibe of the event. Of course between those moments, basically for the entire set, I was working to a muted sound. I didn't get that sensation of the audience going crazy after each song because I was following song cues and click tracks.

Matt McGinn: One thing I'm pleased about is that Coldplay still have a pretty full stage sound. Jonny [Bucklands]'s guitar is always really loud at gigs, big or small. Valve amps just sound better and are more exciting to use when they're cranked up, and Jonny might want to interact with them, get feedback or do other fun stuff. That said we do turn some of the amps the wrong way round so they face the back of the stage and don't bleed into the vocal microphones.

David Byrne propounds the theory that arena shows suit mid-tempo music because faster rhythms get confused as they bounce around the venue: 'basketball arenas and stadiums . . . tend to have terrible acoustics – only a narrow range of music works at all in such environments. Steady-state

FIGURE 9.2 Chris Martin with in-ear monitors; *Coldplay Live 2012* (Paul Dugdale, 2012).

music (music with a consistent volume, more or less unchanging textures, and fairly simple pulsing rhythms) works best.' (Byrne 2012, 24)

Matt McGinn: I see what he means. Broad strokes do seem to work better in big spaces, by and large. There's definitely something to be said for keeping it simple, and a lot of bands that do well at arena level get by with quite a straightforward line-up and musical arrangements that can reach out over the vastness – although the PA quality has now improved so much that no-one except Pink Floyd really need slow down to 'Shine On You Crazy Diamond' tempo anymore. The cathedral analogy in Byrne's book still holds, though. Mid-afternoon, post-soundcheck and pre-punters, that's exactly how an arena feels.

Jon Burton: Large venues need to sell seats, so they put on popular music, but in the early days of arenas only medium-paced anthems seemed to work in such spaces. Woeful acoustics and poor sound reinforcement rendered faster songs and busier arrangements blurred and incomprehensible. The reverberation is more controllable today. Acoustically absorbent seats and

FIGURE 9.3 Jon Burton with a line array, October 2011.

drapes that close down areas to make the audience space less reverberant can have significant benefits. Sound reinforcement has improved as PA systems became larger and more full-range. Until recently even the best were prone to dead spots, phasing and comb-filtering issues. Today large format V-DOSC line arrays, developed by physicists Dr. Christian Heil and Prof. Marcel Urban at French company L-Acoustics, can throw sound waves over long distances with little loss of pressure (see Cooper 2004). Such systems can accurately and predictably cover the top seats at the back of Wembley Arena while avoiding the roof and the troublesome reflections that would cause.

Matt McGinn: Arena technology has changed a lot in the time I've been with Coldplay. Digital sound desks, for example, are tiny compared to the flight decks the crew used to operate. V-DOSC was a relatively new thing when we first went into big rooms but the line array systems have just kept on improving. With the right gear, knowhow and a band that's playing well you can make a decent noise pretty much anywhere in an arena these days. It's not easy though. Every show requires military precision and a walk around the venue doing sums with a dB meter on the sound crew's part beforehand.

Kieron Pepper: You certainly notice the acoustic when sound checking in a deserted arena. Sometimes there can be a huge delay and you have music bouncing back at you from the far wall a quarter of a second late and entirely out of time. In the cold light of day when there's no-one in but the band and crew they're quite foreboding spaces and seem like a much bigger place to fill, especially when you see staff walking across back of the hall with boxes of t-shirts and they look like Lego people.

I think that ultimately, as a musician, I preferred medium-sized theatre shows. I always found it awkward to interact with the audience in an arena – partly because they don't feel like particularly musical places.

Rachel Wood: To be honest with you I don't like doing arena gigs because there's just too much space. You can't see the audience. They're way out there, and you've got no idea what's going on because you can't distinguish anyone's facial expression. It's not just the distance either. There's no atmosphere as it's usually quite cold. Plus people are less likely to be standing and jumping around and more likely to be sitting down and expressing less emotion. I don't like watching arena gigs either. I saw a terrible show with the Red Hot Chili Peppers. It didn't work because everything was too busy. The bass was clanging around and you seemed to be hearing something Flea was playing from a bar [of music] earlier.

I always felt the need to play differently and throw new, larger, shapes.

Rachel Wood: I didn't do that at first then I saw some video playback and realized that you have to do *huge* movements to make any kind of impression whatsoever. You have to make much more of an effort in an arena, otherwise no-one will see you. Most musicians have a bit of an arena make-over – maybe a different coloured guitar or a bigger costume. Ironically, costume is more important at a distance. I wear a big long coat because things like that help give you a bigger stage presence. If you were wearing a little t-shirt and jeans you'd just fade away.

> Musicians can't just take a club or theatre approach to arena shows – people need to see more happening on a large stage. And yet, although you're essentially constructing a new performance, the presentation still needs to be authentic and appropriate to the music.

Matt McGinn: Coldplay have become a very busy band on stage, throughout the whole show. Back in the day Jonny often stood in one place for much of the set but now he really gets about. I'm not sure how much of it they plan compared to what comes naturally but I imagine it's a fairly even blend of both.

> Coldplay, like other successful artists, work particularly diligently to involve the audience in their arena concerts.

Matt McGinn: Their level of gig fitness and commitment to the task continues to startle me on a daily basis, particularly during the parts of the show that involve long catwalks to the B-Stage in the middle of the arena space; or secret runs to the C-Stage, a hidden surprise platform way up in the Gods. These playing areas are so far away from the main PA speakers that the group experience a pretty off-putting acoustic delay. They really have to concentrate on what's coming down their in-ear monitors, not what they can hear in the hall. It would be impossible to play in time otherwise. I've tried it. It's like singing along to a tune coming from next door's stereo, but one line in advance.

> Coldplay's 'Xyloband' audience bracelets proved highly successful at incorporating large audiences in the spectacle of a show on their 2012 Mylo Xyloto world tour. They introduced a novel means of interaction-at-distance by combining remote-controlled radio receivers with light-emitting diodes that glowed in different colours and flashed in time with the beat of the song. This completely reinvented the familiar 'slow song, cigarette lighter aloft' stadium rock trope. The wrist bands can be seen in action in the band's video for 'Charlie Brown' (2012). A spokesperson commented: 'If fans are paying £50 for a ticket, they are entitled to a good show and a spectacle. It's no longer enough to jump around on stage, looking pretty.' (Moodie 2013)

Matt McGinn: It looked stunning from the stage. Arenas can be quite dark spaces towards the back – you can't always appreciate the size of them – so when everyone had a wrist band it really emphasized how enormous those places were. They also made the shows more intimate, funnily enough. Suddenly the gig became a party and you could see everyone's face light up. It did a great job of gluing the whole thing together.

FIGURE 9.4 The 'Xyloband'; stills from *Coldplay Live 2012*.

Kieron Pepper: If you can generate enough energy and warmth arenas can feel like a surprisingly intimate gig and Coldplay's Xylobands achieved that very effectively. It's all about communicating with people a couple of hundred yards away. Visuals are also really important in that respect.

> So with cameras and video screens now a common means of mediation between arena audiences and artists, what does it feel like to interact with such technology? Has it changed how you approach the practicalities of stage performance, for example?

Vinnie Lammi: The Spice Girls look like little dolls on stage for kids at the back of the arena, so it's vital that they get certain close-ups such as Victoria's [Beckham/'Posh Spice'] expression. You also need to see any vocalists wording their lyrics. That's really important. Interestingly the cameras began focusing more on the band as the Spice Girls tour continued. Apparently this included a lot of me because of the physicality of the drum kit.

It is important to look right-sized. You can't really go on a large stage with a three-piece kit. It has to look suitably grand. I used a bigger drum set and added lots of cymbals to build the kit up. I really went to town now that I think about it. In the end I had three crash cymbals, two splashes and two rides. It made me play differently too. There were more things to hit and you consciously want to play with the cymbals in particular as they look better from a distance, more flamboyant. It's very much like shooting a music video. You're thinking visually as well as musically, trying to imagine what it looks like performance-wise.

> Do the cameras endorse or detract from the 'liveness' of your performance?

Vinnie Lammi: With the Spice Girls most of the audience probably wouldn't be aware of or care about that. With a band like Coldplay you have a different crowd, music connoisseurs who want to see what's going on such as guitar chord shapes and drum fills. The musicians know these elements will be shown, and it authenticates their performance.

Kieron Pepper: People pay a lot of money to see arena shows so you need to maintain consistent entertainment value. If you can't see the band too well they need to provide other focal points, such as a light show and a detailed visual projection of the performance. You can't see the banter between two musicians or what someone's doing from way at the back without technology to mediate between the stage and the audience. Cameras capture moments that would otherwise be missed and make the gig feel more intimate.

When cameras are feeding live streams to giant screens it does make you approach a show very differently, however. You're now thinking about how you're interacting with the camera, as well as how you're interacting with the crowd. If you try *too* hard, for example, you risk looking contrived and stupid. You want the audience to know you're up on stage giving a performance that communicates some emotion, but cameras can also capture things when you're unawares or pick up too much detail.

Ultimately, what happens off the stage is out of your control. It becomes a matter of trust between you and the crew. You have to have confidence in the camera operator to create a common shared experience. You need a good team around you, people who understand what you're about and who can make sure that your message gets projected with some element of sonic and visual integrity.

Matt McGinn: Playing for the video screens is a skill that arena and stadium-level artists have had to get to grips with, and it has become an essential part of their performance. Keith Richards said The Rolling Stones initially worried about audiences watching the big TV all night, but soon realized how to interact with the cameras and make it part of the show. What's the use of Mick doing his thing if no-one past Row 20 can see the wiggle? Some bands will always work better in clubs and theatres though, where you can get close enough to smell them. Dr. Feelgood were perfect in the Southend Kursaal but would you have wanted to watch them play at Wembley?

> One thing I noticed when playing arenas was the total lack of interaction with audience members before and after the show. You have your own exit and entrance to the complex and are totally screened from the public areas in dressing rooms that can be located some distance from the front of house.

Rachel Wood: You're in an isolated production space with trucks, catering, backstage facilities and electrical equipment. There's no time to interact with the audience. When you do see people they're more scared to come and talk than at a club gig. You can bring guests backstage but that's not quite the same thing as a punter you don't know coming up after the show saying how much they enjoyed it. Then again sometimes the privacy can be quite useful too.

Matt McGinn: It's easy to forget where you are if all you see is a closed-off backstage world. I often go for a walk around the venue once the crowd comes in, to see the excitement on the faces as much as anything. It wakes you up and reminds you what you're there for. Coldplay work hard to try and bridge gaps and make connections, which I always like to see. It reminds me of how bands like The Jam behaved towards us when we were kids. They would often spend time with fans pre-show or invite us in for the sound check and it's good to see a little bit of that old spirit is still at large.

Kieron Pepper: An arena production tour is a travelling village where the crew, caterers and transport staff are all in an enclosed bubble and very much their own community. With The Prodigy I used to have time on my hands after sound check so would wander outside as people were queuing up, trying to get a sense of what was going on or a feeling for the city we were in. If you garner some interesting facts about what's happening locally you can pass them on to the band. That can open doors and spark ideas. We played Sydney when athlete Kathy Freeman was awarded Australian of the Year [having controversially brandished the Aboriginal flag during the Commonwealth games (see Rowe and Stephenson 2006, 202)] so Keith [Flint, singer and dancer] carried the same flag on stage and wore it like a cape. Everyone knew why, and it made a real connection with the audience. We had a similar experience when playing on the ceasefire line in Beirut. Concerts like that almost become a political event; partly because an important show will impact on people who aren't necessarily present in the audience via press reviews or word of mouth, and also because of the physical consequences for the surrounding area when it takes time for the traffic to clear. You can do a theatre tour and pass through a town without getting noticed, but an arena tour is a different animal.

Vinnie Lammi: Different arenas in the UK have their own qualities – some good, some bad. This was not the case when we toured the United States. All the arenas seemed identical in size and design: ice hockey stadiums with very wide perimeter corridors that had lots of big rooms running off them for catering and such. It felt like you could be anywhere. The only exception was Madison Square Garden.

Matt McGinn: North American arena tours can feel a bit like *Groundhog Day* after a few weeks. Not the people, just the shapes of the venues. They're sort of all the same but with just enough differences to mess with your head and keep you slightly confused. Hockey arenas, for example, can be quite slippery around the edge. This gets treacherous when you're in a new venue every other night, you come pelting down the stage stairs and forget the rink is in a different place to where it was yesterday.

How does sponsorship impinge on musical events? Is it more noticeable at arena shows?

Vinnie Lammi: The arena shows I played were entirely corporate affairs. You have to remember that [their manager] Simon Fuller set The Spice Girls up with sponsorship deals from Sony, Benetton, Asda, Pepsi and British Telecom (see Whiteley 2000, 222) and in those days everyone wanted to be associated with the band. It's not been quite so crazy on the reunion tour but it still had a distinctly corporate feel, particularly in the North American arenas which had eye-catching billboards plastered outside the venue and all kinds of products advertised as you walked through the foyer.

We flew Virgin Atlantic to the United States and they even put the name of the Spice Girls up on one of their planes.

Rachel Wood: It is definitely more prominent in the United States. At Cirque du Soleil they run a series of announcements on behalf of the sponsors before each show. The Katie Melua tour I appeared on was sponsored by a car manufacturer who had them parked conspicuously outside each gig.

Jon Burton: It is a thing of the age. I have seen Manchester Arena called the MEN ['Manchester Evening News Arena'], Nynex and now Phones4U . . . I find LED [light-emitting diode] advertising boards very annoying too, because arenas never really go dark now.

Every show involves a certain level of preparation for the performers, but when you get to the arena level I found that it became more intense and even more thorough. Do you approach arena concerts differently to smaller shows?

Rachel Wood: I always get nervous so it doesn't matter. The first arena gig I did, I was very nervous just because of the sheer number of people. We didn't get a sound check because it was the first gig of the tour, and we hadn't used in-ears before so that was terrifying.

Vinnie Lammi: Funnily enough I didn't get any more nervous playing with the Spice Girls in arenas than normal. Actually I get much more uncomfortable playing to 10 people in a pub than I do playing to 10,000 people. You can see their faces and see the whites of their eyes. The strange thing was that on the arena shows I was playing a lot harder and hitting the snare really very powerfully. Maybe it's an adrenaline thing that means you put everything into it but as a result I also developed a repetitive strain injury in my arm and needed massage and treatment from the physio after each set. It seemed to be quite physically stressful. If I had warmed up more it might have helped!

Matt McGinn: There's no extra pressure, because you're just as nervous as any other gig. They're all the same. You just want things to go well and for the audience to enjoy the show. Occasionally something will come along that is particularly scary. The London 2012 Paralympics closing ceremony was off the scale in that respect: loss of power to the stage, water cannons leaking all over the guitars, five hundred million viewers and no cups of tea allowed on the pitch. It was alright on the night though.

Jon Burton: Actually, production tours in arenas are easier for the crew in many ways because most of the venues are a similar shape and you just roll the equipment in to replicate the same show night after night. There's also room to move forklifts around and lift heavy equipment, so large prefabricated systems are often employed using multiple amplifiers in large racks with built-in power and speaker cabling. This cuts set up times dramatically. You can't do that on theatre shows as they date from a time before amplified sound and are just not geared up to modern production tours.

What happens when things go wrong in front of all those people?

Jon Burton: If it can go wrong it will. Beer in the mixing desk, fire alarms clearing the building, equipment failing. Once the safety curtain refused to open and we had to cancel.
Matt McGinn: Don't *ever* have a massage before the show as I did once and felt so relaxed that I sent Jonny out with no guitar lead. The main thing about arena shows is that, unlike stadiums, there's no weather to worry about. As Keith Richards says in his autobiography: 'There's another guy that joins the band on outdoor stages – God. Either he's benign or he can come at you with wind from the wrong direction and the sound is swept out of the park' (Richard and Fox 2010, 488).

It seems the size and multi-purpose design of arena spaces significantly shapes the possibilities for front of house audio. However, sound reinforcement technology has now advanced to the point it can ameliorate many deleterious consequences. Unsurprisingly, the experience of performing on an arena stage is entirely different to that of playing a club show. This is in part due to the onstage sound, which is also now commonly re-defined by in-ear monitoring technology, and by difficulties in connecting with a remote audience. While the aesthetics of arena rock continue to be defined and driven by an overwhelming commercial impetus, performers and technologists have adapted to the demands of such spaces by creatively enhancing their visual presence and experimenting with increasingly innovative technologies to deliver a more inclusive mass experience.

FIGURE 9.5 Jon Burton at the mixing desk (image courtesy of Soulsound/Davide Roveri Visuals).

CHAPTER TEN

Illuminating Arenas: Towards the 'Ultimate Multimedia Experience'

Jon Stewart and Benjamin Halligan

The growth and development of arena concerts suggest new possibilities for, and new relationships between, the performance of music and its visual representation. The size of an arena space offers various opportunities and challenges for visuals and lighting. Technical developments such as the incorporation of video and projection mapping have revolutionized the practice, while financial changes such as the importation of low-cost technology from China has increased the scope of these innovations. As a consequence such technologies are now seen even in relatively diminutive spaces, such as large-scale theatre shows. Interestingly, given the rapid pace of change in this aspect of arena concerts over the last decade, many of today's leading arena-level lighting designers began their careers in very different working environments such as pub function rooms, night clubs and small rock venues.

This chapter was compiled from semi-structured interviews with four of the leading industry practitioners in this field. Despite their wide varieties of experience, which range from the largest possible pop arena concerts to arena-level indie bands and arena-level dance acts, all three share many commonalities in their practice and outlook. While each is an intensely imaginative individual, dedicated to their art and passionate about their creative output, professional bonds and loyalties are also extremely strong in this area of the industry. Each practitioner was therefore highly appreciative of, and extremely respectful towards, the achievements of their peers and mentors – including the other interviewees. The authors would like to thank Bryan, Tom, Davy and Rob for their input.

Bryan Leitch

Bryan Leitch is a legendary UK lighting designer who has probably done more than any other to shape the visual experience of arena concert audiences. His long client list, built over twenty-five years in the industry, includes Justin Timberlake, Kanye West, Alicia Keys, Brian Adams, Britney Spears, Il Divo, Kylie Minogue, James Taylor, Beck, The Killers, Manic Street Preachers, Coldplay, Echo And The Bunnymen, Paulo Nutini, Kasabian, Elbow, Pulp and Joss Stone. Bryan was awarded the Enrico Caironi Knight of Illumination Award for Lifetime Achievement by The Society of Television & Lighting Design and The Association of Lighting Designers in 2012 in recognition of his inspiration and mentorship.

Tom Lesh

Tom Lesh runs Lushious Design, formerly Lushlounge Design, and has thirty years experience in show design, production design and lighting design for arena-level live music and entertainment. His clients have included Muse, The Chemical Brothers, Paul McCartney, Simply Red, David Gray, The Feeling, Texas, Primal Scream, Moloko, Gorillaz, Nero, Lily Allen, Reef, Ocean Colour Scene, Alison Moyet, Siouxsie and the Banshees, The Waterboys EMF and Public Image Ltd, among a host of others. Tom is now involved in the design and direction of a host of the UK's largest music festivals.

Davy Sherwin

Davy Sherwin runs Light Image Design and has over a decade of experience lighting arena shows for artists such as Snow Patrol, Foals, Tinie Tempah, Athlete, We Are Scientists, The Darkness and Travis. He won the Clay Paky Knight of Illumination Award for Best Arena Event in 2009 and 2012.

Rob Sinclair

Rob Sinclair, a lighting and production designer, has worked extensively and worldwide for twenty-five years. He specializes in the creative coordination of all visual aspects of a show into a cohesive whole, blending lighting, video, lasers and effects into a single statement. His 'unusual results first, tools later' approach ensures that the emotion of his work always overshadows the technology used to accomplish it. Recent credits include: Miley Cyrus, Adele, Pulp, Kylie Minogue, Florence and the Machine, Charli XCX, Peter Gabriel, Vampire Weekend, Lorde, Queen + Adam Lambert, Pet Shop Boys, M.I.A., Bloc Party, Marina and the Diamonds, Hurts, Keane, Birdy, Will Young, Flans, Kaiser Chiefs, Goldfrapp and The Human League.

> Our interviewees have commonalities and differences in their routes into professional practice. However they all share similar key formative experiences.

Bryan Leitch: I'm from a working class background but one of my earliest jobs was an extra with Central Casting. This allowed me to see how people made amazing things on screen out of wood, crap props and some lights. I was watching magicians who were also just blokes in flat caps and not arty types in any way. It was all very crude but I was absolutely enthralled by the fact that something they used to knock up as cheaply as possible to keep the costs down could be magically lit, or enhanced with some dust thrown around it, and it looked brilliant on film. We had no money in the early days [as a lighting designer and engineer] so I also used very basic improvised equipment and made it look cool. That's what got me noticed.

My first real break came at a Cutting Crew warm-up gig in The Mean Fiddler, Harlesden. I bought the album and made a real effort by learning and playing every single beat. Five days later I was on my first tour bus. From that I got Snap's support tour for MC Hammer which ended up with eight nights at Wembley Arena. I always try to help people. You know two things I've learned are that it pays to help others, and that nothing is ever bad because something good will always come on the other side of it.

Rob Sinclair: I really enjoyed playing around with the couple of lights that there were at school, for doing theatre stuff there, and when I left school I became a disastrously bad mobile DJ. I tired of that fairly quickly, but I had become interested in the lighting side. From there I decided that I wanted to do bigger and more serious things so I did a course at the City of Westminster College, called the Theatre Electrics Course (basically an electrician City and Guilds [qualification] with a theatre bit tacked on the end). And out of that I got a job sweeping floors and coiling cables for Vari-Lite, the only people who did moving lights at that point, in the early 1990s. I moved from there to loading trucks, to fixing lights in the warehouse, to gradually going out on the road with them, to starting to operate things. They sent me down to the Grosvenor House Hotel in Park Lane a lot to do endless parties and award ceremonies. Then I gradually worked my way from being a technician to operating other people's shows to getting a chance to design my own shows. A linear path, over a reasonably long time.

Davy Sherwin: I used to work in theatres when I was at school, then I took a stage management and lighting course in Glasgow and started doing Scottish Ballet and Scottish Opera while doing a bit of freelance for the local rock and roll lighting company. I just learned that as I went along. Snow Patrol was my break in lighting design. I did some small shows for them and all of a sudden they had a hit single, at which point I had to go and learn how to do it properly. In Glasgow I'd seen bands with really good lighting designers like Primal Scream, Blur and The Charlatans. These were formative gigs for me: watching the lighting thinking how I'd like to do that and seeing how it worked. It's about trying to get ideas but not copying. You need the inspiration but you also need to bring in your own originality and put your own twist on things.

Tom Lesh: My father took me to see the Electric Light Orchestra [ELO] at Wembley Arena when I was eleven years old, in 1976. I'd never been in an arena before, and there was this spaceship sat on stage when we entered the venue. The house lights went down, smoke started pouring out from under the spaceship, lights started flashing on it and the spaceship took off. Underneath was the band with lights and lasers, with smaller spaceships flying across the audience on wires! It blew me away completely, and I knew that I wanted to do something like that for a living. I didn't know what role at the time, but I found work as an actor in a theatre company once I had left school, where I unfortunately had a motorbike accident and broke my leg. As I was incapacitated the company put me in front of the simple lighting console in the theatre where we were based and I found my niche. I've been doing the same thing ever since!

In 1984 I landed a job with Entec Sound & Light (a Lighting and sound company), which was owned by Harold Pendleton, who originally owned the Marquee Club in London and started The Reading Festival. I worked for them for two or three years, and as part of your training you were sent to the Marquee Club as the house lighting guy. You would originally be sent down there for three months and if you managed to come out of there without some sort of alcohol or drug problem you were considered fit to go on the road. You were doing two bands a night, seven days a week, with one day off a month and you didn't know many of these bands' music – you just had to get on with it and light them. That's where I originally learnt how to light bands, and pre-empt what was happening on stage and in songs. You were doing it so much that it just became natural. I ended up being there for nine months.

In 1987 I was working for a band called The Mission, and I had just started designing for a new band called All About Eve. Peter Barnes [the 'guru of pop lighting' whose credits include Live 8, Beyoncé and the groundbreaking SpiceWorld tour; on which, see Cunningham 1999, 331–340] came to see those shows and offered me a job with his company Chameleon Lighting. The first act he asked me to design was Siouxsie and the Banshees, in 1988, I was 22–23 at that point and dealing with an act like that was a big deal – it was quite scary – but Pete mentored me through it. He designed the set and said, 'do what you like with the lights! I trust you'. We had nine backdrops hiding a twisted runway set, so we had to get rid of each of them in order to see the band – which took about 45 minutes. It was a post-punk concept show and was great grounding in how to deal with original and perceived difficult artists, and create an original show! We took it around the UK, across Europe and around the United States. John Lydon's Public Image Ltd was my next client after that.

Pete and I still work together on a couple of large-scale projects each year, which is one of the joys of this industry. Once you're in, it becomes a lifelong career, which seems to have been lost in the transient work market place now. However you don't seem to be getting many of my children's generation wanting to join this profession even though my eldest son is a tour chef for Eat to the Beat (one of the leading tour catering companies). When I started, we felt like pirates: we ran away to join the circus, and had the attitude that we could conquer small countries touring through them! It was exciting! There was no formal training; we learnt from our peers. If we weren't any good, we got our arses kicked, and you didn't get work. You had to prove yourself to your elders and your betters, and you worked your way from the bottom up to the top.

> Like a lot of post-punk groups, Siouxsie and the Banshees were bringing theatricality and a sense of their image, and a certain look and ambience, to music. I imagine that it would have been a matter of entirely sympathetic lighting . . . or was it a matter that the band were talking to you, and had specific ideas?

Tom Lesh: You helped create the ideas: that was part of the job. As lighting designers we toured with the show, far more than LDs do now. For people like Siouxsie . . . she would suggest something or I would throw out an idea, and she would play on it, or she would do something I would see, and say 'Why don't you try that on the next show?', and most times it would develop into a set piece in the show. Being the lighting designer and lighting director, I was the one person who watched the shows religiously every night, from start to finish. I would have my dimmer man sat on headsets, with a pen and paper, and give him notes, and then go back to the band and make further suggestions. So shows developed like that, and because you were touring with the band you had a rapport and your judgement was trusted, through working and socializing over long tours.

> Such an organic process still seems to be in operation in shaping arena show design: audaciously, Peter Gabriel's Back to Front tour of 2014 opened with the house lights up, and Gabriel appearing unannounced to play an unfinished song on piano. How did this come about?

Rob Sinclair: Peter and I had long, long meetings about the show over six months. The absolute certainty of it was that the main set would finish with [the album] So, live. And so we built the show backwards. What do we hold back, for the So section? He wanted to then put an acoustic section at the front of the show rather than in the middle. It was a great idea: that the show would start informally (him at the piano, then the band would come out), and then it would become heavier, and then we would go into the So section.

I made the suggestion that we left the house lights on and he was up for it – no-one else was, just he and I, and we decided that it would be a good idea. The tour manager and everyone else was arching their eyebrows, thinking that it wouldn't last. So we did the first twenty minutes of the show with the house lights on (and the house lights would then cut very suddenly, half way through the song 'Family Snapshot'). The stage was very stark, the video screens were hidden . . . so you just thought, 'I've come to see Peter Gabriel, and I'm expecting a theatrical something . . . and all I'm going to see is this guy playing the piano with the house lights up!' So it was this very uncomfortable thing for them. We took it on too long: we were very, very aware that this was quite awkward for the audience, putting them quite on edge. But the moment of release when the house lights went out was so wonderful that it was worth pushing our luck. I watched the show every night and, in spite of the fact that I knew it was going to happen, you couldn't not but be completely and instantly focused on the stage. It came so out of nowhere, it was so surprising, and it changed things so dramatically that it was well worth it.

The watch word with Peter has always been that things are handmade and high tech. A combination of man and machine: the preciseness of robots and lights and the vagaries of people pushing lights around.

> There are numerous specialist roles in lighting and video at the arena-level, orientated around lighting, stage design and projection design. Understanding these jobs and the differences or similarities between them is a key element of contemporary professional practice. The roles seem to be gradually coalescing, and indeed our interviewees perform all of them in one way or another.

Davy Sherwin: The walls between professional roles are definitely coming down and I'm very conscious of that. There's none of the old 'we're the video guys, you're the lights guys' in-group scenario where no-one would help anyone else out. Everything's about the show. We're all in the visual department: one big team working together to the brief from the band or their management.

Rob Sinclair: I have an appreciation of how realistic an idea is, an appreciation of what I'm asking people to do for me, and an appreciation of what is possible, and not being told that something completely possible is impossible. I really hate the term 'Creative Director'; I'm a very good lighting designer (I like to think!) and I'm quite a good creative director (under some circumstances!) Whereas I'm very happy working alongside a great director like William Baker [long-term collaborator of Kylie Minogue] or Diane Martel [Creative Director for the Miley Cyrus Bangerz tour].

Davy Sherwin: One area of change is in the growing influence of set designers. Lot of bands employ them but I'm not really a massive fan of putting theatre sets on stage. I like to keep it nice and clean and open; more rock and roll than Spinal Tap. I worked on one tour where there was a concept guy, a set designer, an American lighting designer, a British lighting designer and a couple of creative directors overseeing the whole thing. Whenever you get a lot of people involved it can be difficult to make everything marry up.

Bryan Leitch: I've been integrating projections with lights for some time now and I see no difference. It's all the same thing. It's just light projection; be it back projection, front projection, 3D projection with massively complex AI servers that map to anything you want. Whatever, it's still just a light source hitting something. You have to understand what light does passing through air and envisage light three dimensionally.

For example I used a lot of projection with James Taylor. I helped create footage and took all the photos for it myself. The current James Taylor tour [James Taylor and his All-Star Band, 2014–2016 tour] has 3D projection and a gigantic chandelier that is animated. We pass film through it and use incandescent lights as pixels. We shot a fair amount of footage locally in Sussex.

So someone who originally came from Sussex could be watching James Taylor somewhere exotic such as Sydney or Los Angeles and find themselves thinking 'Oh, that backdrop looks remarkably like Newhaven Harbour!'

Tom Lesh: I started in the business thirty years ago when things were very different, but in these last ten years we've seen a massive change in this industry. There's a move towards show designers and creative directors that aren't necessarily lighting or video people; they have come from a completely different background. There seems to have been a whole new role created where they deal with the artist and you've become a cog in the process. You're dealing with a Creative Director who sees the sort of picture that I would have seen fifteen to twenty years ago. So things have changed, in that respect, quite a lot.

A professionalization of the roles?

Tom Lesh: You have a Creative Director who may have no technical knowledge of how a show may go together. So she or he may see things in one sense, as a big picture. But it won't necessarily mean that they understand the 'on the ground' crew person's concept of the reality that the show may have to load-in, in twelve hours, and load-out fairly rapidly, move to another city, move to another country and keep rolling! You do have to think about how a touring show works, and that you don't break your crew, and that it can go up quickly, and have left enough time for other departments to be able to work, and how the whole thing comes together on a daily basis.

However the touring industry is a different beast now with artists placing more reliance on making money from live shows rather than album sales, and with the explosion in festivals and the building of new arenas and the Americanization of our culture, this growth and development is inevitable, though whether a show like U2's 360° tour [2009–2011] can be beaten in terms of size and scale, or whether it was too big as a production, remains to be seen!

Rob Sinclair: It some ways it's a bit of an arms race really; how many trucks are expected at an arena tour nowadays? What people's expectations are now, versus what their expectations were then. Miley Cyrus toured with something like 28 trucks [for the Bangerz tour]. The Keane [Under the Iron Sea] tour was probably about four. It's the dual thing of the audiences' expectations and the lowering of the costs of technology, which are making productions bigger and bigger – which doesn't mean that they're cleverer. People expect more maybe, and go to more shows, and pay a lot of money for tickets.

All our interviewees face design challenges and cope with them in their own way. Although each employs different working processes, the key aesthetic and technical interactions between the musical and visual elements of arena shows remain similar across a wide variety of performance styles and venue sizes.
Davy has lots of experience working with arena-level indie bands such as Foals and Snow Patrol, whereas Bryan has worked on vast arena shows with huge artists such as Kylie Minogue and Justin Timberlake. Surprisingly, even in such large spaces there are always compromises over the budget, the venue size and the sight lines.

Davy Sherwin: Before you start to do any design we have to decide whether the stage is at the end or in the round. If it's at the end you then have to work out how far around it you can sell tickets. Normally we go 270 degrees around which means you'll have people on the either side of the band but not behind them. You have to make sure that the people at the sides can see your video screens as well as the people in front because it might only be a few seats but in a large arena then it can mean 2,000 people not being able to see properly.

Then again everyone in the venue is seeing the show from a slightly different angle. They all get their own view and their own unique experience. Those at the side of the stage are extremely close to the band whereas those at the back of the hall are much further away physically although that means they can also see the full effect of the screens and lighting.

It's all got to be very cleverly orchestrated, especially when bands spend a lot of money on content. You need to be able to see the content but don't want it to be overpowering. At the end of the day there's still five musicians standing on stage with their instruments and it's all about them rather than what's going on in the background.

Bryan Leitch: The people down front who bought their tickets online in the first two seconds of them going on sale care very little about the lighting, they just want to get as close to the artist as they can so you don't need to worry about them. You really have to think about the size of the space: typically from fifty rows back to the people in the nosebleeds at the very far end of the hall.[1] That's the kind of aperture that I'm looking at, from fifty rows back to 300 rows back. You've got to give the people at the very back something they can take away, something they wouldn't have got from watching a video. You've got to give people fifty rows back some of that as well, but less of it because they're closer to the artist.

Tom's worked extensively with The Chemical Brothers. We're interested in the challenges that electronic dance music (EDM) arena events can engender. Where you have DJs, or musicians who are fairly immobile behind keyboards, it's quite difficult to present them in a way that you would with a band delivering performances, guitar solos and so on. So there seems to be a much bigger emphasis on the effect – the experience – of The Chemical Brothers in an arena. Part of the way in which this has been done is to move the light design and the lasers away from the stage and put it above, or even in, the audience.

Tom Lesh: When I was brought in to design their shows [the Further and We Are The Night tours], they wanted a show that encompassed lighting, visuals and lasers but working in such a way that the whole thing was symbiotic. They all worked together, rather than as different elements. And the band was quite insistent that they didn't want to be lit. You're given full reign to light audiences and make huge pictures with lighting and lasers. You're lighting the whole area rather than just the stage: you can take a lot more creative risk. The songs may run in the same order but they're adding musical elements live on stage, and you still have to follow the tracks. The audience connect with it: they're there to see this show, that is a big deal, and has been discussed on social media or through websites and forums, so you're presenting the show as to peoples' expectations and beyond – it's all about the 'big picture'! There isn't a presence on stage commanding the show: the audio and visual elements have to take on this role – Tom and Ed Chemical [Tom Rowlands and Ed Simons] were very aware that there had to be a big show around them as they were anything but rock stars. They were two nerdy ex-students with a passion for dance music. When I came onboard they'd only ever used projection and I really wanted to break away from anything they had done before and utilize LED screen technology.

We had one of the first semi-transparent Stealth Screens: a brand new concept in screens. Madonna had the first one, I used the second one with Muse, for the show design of their Black Holes and Revelations tour [2006–2008] and then the third one with The Chemical Brothers show design, for the We Are The Night tour [2008]. The screen was 50–60 per cent transparent, so you could shine lights through it, which was something completely different. With The Chemical Brothers I had a full lighting rig behind the screen that I pixel mapped to light around and through, and to follow the visuals onscreen. We did some very clever things that came from conversations between myself and the video content creators.

As far as the band was concerned, they made the music and we created the visual side of the live show: myself, a video director, a laser operator and a lighting operator. We used time codes to trigger the lighting cue stacks, to set up the lighting looks and trigger the videos from media servers, and with Midi notes triggering underlying background sequence lighting, but we still ran the show live in terms of hitting cues, flashing lights and overlaying video elements to the tracks which differed slightly each night.

> I've seen Aphex Twin live [Warehouse Project, Manchester 2007] and it was just a bobbing head above a laptop screen. Leftfield were on stage for their performance, circled around an occasional guest singer, but really didn't seem to be doing anything. The question of making a spectacle from dance music is something that The Chemical Brothers seem to have solved.

Tom Lesh: The Chemical Brothers speculated to accumulate. They understood that they had to have a big show around them. If they had a big show, promoters – especially at festivals – would pay the fees the band commanded, and know that they were getting a good product for their money.

We carried an LED video screen everywhere, along with the stage set and consoles, all freighted to wherever they had to go. We could make a show appear out of nowhere with our fold up semi-transparent screen, which could be installed in a 30 minute change-over, and produce a completely original show. It was a very satisfying experience, utilizing the available technology and making it happen with a mixture of locally sourced equipment and our touring package, when we didn't have the luxury of touring the entire production!

Some performers, on the other hand, understand their role in the manner of Atlas: the weight of the world (of the arena show) balanced on their shoulders alone. Rising to the challenge seems to take audacity and panache as much as stamina and charisma. Tom Chaplin, of Keane, met and matched the rising popularity of the band by seemingly throwing himself into just such a role for the Under the Iron Sea arena tour.

Rob Sinclair: We talked about this a lot in the early days. It's an enormous responsibility, especially when Keane were just a three-piece and Richard [Hughes] was stuck behind the drums and Tim [Rice-Oxley] was stuck behind the piano. So Tom was the only mobile member of the band, and there are 10–15,000 people at the O2, all of whom had paid money and had come to have a good evening, and he was responsible for orchestrating that and he was holding the next two hours of their evening into his hands. He felt that responsibility very greatly, took it very seriously and worked very hard to make sure that he could communicate with all of them. And when they all sang along and had a good time, he really thrived. And the Tom I first met, when they were new – he'd be slightly scared and hide behind his mic stand all the time. It was quite a transformation.

They gave me a great opportunity: a leg-up into design shows. They had great faith in me, for someone who had never designed an arena show before, to spend an awful lot of their money on the Under the Iron Sea show, and I'm forever grateful to them, and they remain friends.

With live music, even electronic dance music, there's always the risk that events won't go to plan. However at the arena-level the mistakes appear to occur during the extensive production rehearsals and in the set up rather than during the show itself. Nothing goes wrong on the night because there's just too much at stake. There's no room for error so it simply doesn't happen. In some respects it seems these aren't technically 'live' events in certain ways, because much of what the audience sees on the night is pre-programmed in advance. At the very largest scale pop shows everything is synchronized to a time code started that afternoon, sometimes hours before the doors are opened, and the performance is almost as much in the original design and engineering as it is on the evening itself.

Davy Sherwin: There's no room for improvised set changes, they're just not possible when you get to arena-level at the point where you have moving mechanics involved and programmed content. When you've spent weeks in rehearsals preparing, for instance, moving video screens or kabuki curtain drops, giant LED pods that can create different shapes for different songs, you just have to keep a structure to the band's set list. We always had a cut-off point in the day come 4.30 pm, at which point the set list was finalized because if you're going to get theatrical you've got to keep organized or it will go wrong and the show will suffer for it.

It seems that there has been something of a role reversal here. Previously Bryan, who is also an accomplished drummer, described how in his early days as a lighting engineer he would learn the beats of the music and 'play' the visuals alongside a band's performance – much as a percussionist might do. In that orthodox or traditional sense the lights were an added accompaniment to the music. However in complex contemporary arena shows the bands now play along to pre-shot video and pre-programmed lights. The musicians are still performing live but, in some respects, it is they who are accompanying the visuals.

Bryan Leitch: It's all triggered. On Justin Timberlake we started the time code running two hours before doors. It was all run from the keyboards. The band were all proper musicians and all playing live, but the MD [Musical Director] would press go on the keyboard in the afternoon of the show and the time code machine that the desks and Avos [Avolites consoles] were connected to would just start rolling and that was it. You couldn't stop it after that so we started the show on time every night. There was no other way. When you have so much money riding on an event like that you can't leave anything to chance.

You lose a sense of intimacy; a very important sense of being in a unique moment with an artist you want to see. This seemed to be the case with Katy Perry's 2014–2015 tour, as argued elsewhere in this book.

Tom Lesh: There seems to be a tendency to turn shows into theme park rides. Is it control freakery or just not trusting your personnel to run the show in the way you imagine and see it? It's one of the drawbacks in the demise of the touring lighting designer! Someone hits the 'Go' button, the time code starts and the whole thing happens. To me it makes the whole show experience far less personal: no mistakes, everything perfectly cued to sterility . . . the Disney-fication of live music!

Is it difficult being tied to time codes when the show doesn't run entirely as planned for some reason? Should things go seriously wrong, either in rehearsal or on the tour, do you suddenly find yourself regretting or being intimidated by the complexities of your working environment?

Davy Sherwin: We were very lucky. Snow Patrol's set only malfunctioned once but that was in Wembley Arena during our production rehearsals. We were there for a week just getting it all together and one day it went wrong. Of course that was the day that management were in to have a look . . . and it never went wrong again.

That's just part of the thing when you're dealing with moving parts, technical equipment and band members on stage – it's asking for trouble to be honest. The production rehearsals were actually an amazing experience. At night everyone disappeared and it was literally more or less just me and a couple of the lighting and video crew sitting in Wembley Arena experimenting with a huge lighting rig and video rig all night, fine tuning things in a big empty barn.

Bryan Leitch: Kylie's show [for the X tour] was very complex, and as a result very hard work and very long hours. We did four days without sleep and without leaving the building because of the technical problems. For the first show in Paris we were all very tired and when something went wrong with a massive hydraulic structure which lifted the entire back of set including dancers and everything which caused the whole thing to shift and rip the stage to pieces. At that minute we didn't have a stage, and didn't have a show. The guys from Brilliant Stages [set design and fabrication company based in Hitchin, Hertfordshire] flew over with the team who originally made the stage along with their tools and parts at 6am the next morning. We'd lost hours and hours and had to hold the doors, which isn't easy with 20,000 tickets, and some of the show had to be put on manually.

The next night we had a show in a giant arena in Belgium and the team came with us to make further repairs. We were still hours and hours behind schedule and at one point 15,000 punters were in the arena and we were working behind a huge black kabuki curtain still building the stage while the punters waited. They got a big local hero DJ in to entertain people as we set it all up, but we were aligning things 'left a bit . . . right a bit' blind from out front. The show eventually started at midnight and everybody stayed and the audience went nuts for it. I've been involved in some horrendous situations but can tell you in all the years I've been doing this we've never lost a show.

Most arena shows seem to be so perfectly planned that when things go wrong it's all beforehand – in the run up and production rehearsals. Very little seems to go wrong on the night itself. In that respect the performance happens before everyone's up on stage and the gig itself, ideally, becomes another run through.

Bryan Leitch: Nowadays there are massive amounts of preparation done in different parts of the world. I've currently got The Script rehearsing in Acton, London, while we're building the set elsewhere. There's a guy in Los Angeles creating some video content for us and another one in Europe doing more sections – it's like making a car where the parts have come from all over the place.

The most interesting area of collaboration during the preparation period is the relationship between the lighting designer with the artist. To some extent are they a 'technician', to another extent are they a co-author or creator of the event? One key skill is their ability to visualize concepts in a new and interesting way. The input varies from band to band, but all our interviewees were entirely included in this process.

Although all work on large scale arena shows remains dominated by commercial concerns and imperatives, that doesn't mean there's any less 'art' in the approach of the show-makers. Davy works closely with his clients to help them scale up their live presence from medium-sized indie bands into viable arena acts, and rightly takes great pride in the creativity and energy he brings to this role.

Davy Sherwin: The ball really starts rolling for me about four to five months before the actual tour starts. That's really the initial stages of preparation. The first thing is a meet with the band to find out what concept and vibe is taking shape. This is really a basic informal chat with band and management to find out how they want to head with it.

They would have the album finished and I get a copy of it, then there's usually about a month or so where they would be out on the road doing promo in either smaller gigs or TV and radio shows with audiences. Obviously all the new tracks are there for us all to listen to and we'll just work from that basis really.

Sometimes the band will bring their own visuals. The two world tours I did with Foals were quite similar in that they came to me at quite an early stage, just after they'd written the album, with maybe just one idea that I would base the whole concept around. For instance they might say we want some animation or a huge giant screen or an abstract idea. Usually that gets me up and running. The album artwork's another good one as a lot of times you can base your screen layouts or have your visuals on that. Luckily most bands I've worked with have come forward with ideas themselves and that kind of gets me started. I can go off and design the whole concept and show around that, which seems to be the way it works. Luckily most of the bands I work with have got their own ideas, which really helps the process.

The album two tours ago with Snow Patrol [*100 Million Suns*, of 2008[2]] had amazing album artwork based on origami stars, galaxies, suns and moons – all really nice colours. So that became our starting point for what became the encore staging. They played the last three songs on the record at the end of set, in one fifteen minute piece, and we came up with an animation that went with the music to turn into a 'Pink Floyd moment'. It was childlike – playful and simple – so that some of the animation would be projected on to screens in front of the guys. Then we'd do like a kabuki drop where the screen would drop out of the way to reveal the band, and there would be another screen behind them.

For each section we'd have like a different way of showing the videos with three different screen set ups. Most of the work for that tour was all about the last fifteen minute section. They spent a lot of money on the animators who worked on it for a long time as it was quite a complex piece. Obviously it all had to be synced in with the music, then we had to get the visuals in and out on the right times. We used moving LED screens behind the band which all had to move in time with the content as the visuals changed, and the screens also had to line up at the correct times or the image would be lost.

So that gave us our physical stage layout because we know we needed the three screens – and we had to decide how to start the show without giving away our three screen gag too early. So we gradually introduced the different elements and saved the ending until we really needed it. A lot things had to tie in between me, the guy who actually triggers the video, the band – remember the band have to be seen as well as us being able to show this amazing content. The people at the back of the 02 Arena still have to see the singer without ruining the mood of the video.

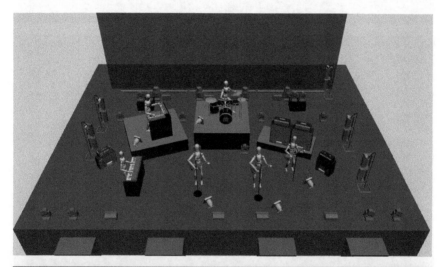

FIGURE 10.1 Computer-aided designs for the Foals stage (Davy Sherwin, Light Image Design).

Tom Lesh: When I decided I wanted to utilize video projection, into a show I was designing for Reef, in the late 1990s, I wanted to show the album artwork that was part of the album promotion campaign. This was a billboard that I now wanted to utilize as an integral part of the set, and control the lighting and video from the lighting console. The video technician and I developed probably one of the first media servers, to project images triggered from the lighting console. It gave me an understanding, at that time, that lighting and video should become synonymous – even with video as a lighting tool, acting as a lighting enhancement.

In arenas, video close-ups of a performer allow for an intimacy that would otherwise be impossible.

Tom Lesh: You need a good video director, working with the lighting designer, getting the colour temperatures and camera positions right etc, and making the artist look good – that takes sitting down, and talking about how you see your vision. For a long time, people didn't understand this, didn't embrace it and fought against it. Now people watch screens as much as they watch what is going on onstage so you have to embrace the fact that you need to make it look good on the big TVs either side of the stage! My teenage children can't remember a time before moving lights and video screens in a live production, as much as they've never known their home without a computer. Most people may go to a show once a year, but will watch *X Factor*-style shows and, as we have very little live music on television nowadays, expect a live show to look along those lines. (Of course, *X Factor* is itself a rip off of a live show.)

Bands have changed. You'll find a lot more middle class bands, who have aspirations and an idea of the way they want to look. They have had the privilege of music lessons, a good education and parental support in these aspirations! The demise of the working class attitude band went when the government stopped paying dole money [social security] to kids who had no jobs but a creative restlessness that they turned into music by teaching themselves how to play. The rough-and-ready lads bands are long gone! Creative teams are engaged a lot earlier in a band's careers. And the artists want to sell their product, though their careers tend to have much shorter timeframes as the concept of a record company nurturing and allowing an artist to grow through a number of albums has long since disappeared, along with the record companies.

Twenty years ago there was a hedonism around the bands that emerged from the period of Britpop, and before that: more about having a good time. Around that period you could still do a forty date UK tour. You would struggle to do that nowadays. A lot of upcoming artists get bumped into arenas very quickly, and I don't think that most are ready for that. For a lead singer to command 10,000 people – well, it takes a certain person to be able to get up and do that. There is a stagecraft sometimes missing, and one that only comes from doing a lot of shows and becoming comfortable with yourself, and your persona, on stage. It's not a question of training, it's a matter of actually getting out there and doing it, and being able to deal with whatever is thrown at you. It takes an awful lot of guts to get up there and do that, especially with female artists.

Is there something that's especially challenging then for a female artist – to be in an arena that can come to be such a close scrutiny of a band, and contain negative elements within the audience?

Tom Lesh: Personally I always thought that female artists were far better on the stage than the majority of male artists. Creatively you got an awful lot more out of them: they are willing to experiment more, they are willing to become a persona of their character a lot more, especially with stage costumes and props. Guys often just want to stand there and hang off the microphone, or look cool with a guitar. It's more difficult to find star quality in male artists than it is in a female artist.

> For the Moloko 'Statues' tour of 2003 the lighting seemed to be minimalist, sympathetic and tasteful, and that seemed to be the limit of what was going on then. I remember seeing Keane about four years later in the Manchester Arena (for the Under the Iron Sea tour), and the major development was the inclusion of giant video screens behind them: animations and a vertical strip of screen for each band member. Is that a fair comment about how these things were working in 2003?

Tom Lesh: Even though moving light and video technologies were prevalent in 2003 it was still an expensive proposition to take out a video package with a middle-earning band. Moloko were one of those bands: no real name in the UK, but did really well elsewhere, especially in Europe. I watched them go from clubs, in the Spring, to packing out festivals in the Summer. to headlining arenas by the Autumn. And it was all down to stage performance as there was no money for a large light or video show! [Singer] Róisín Murphy's performance was mesmerizing. She would do things off the cuff, I would spot it and it would be pulled into the show – developing and touring it over eighteen months. This was one of the most gratifying shows I've done: working with someone who had ideas, who would listen to ideas and who would make those things happen on the stage. She carried the show: it was all about her. So we didn't need video as long as we had a couple of follow spots on her. The show element wasn't as important as her persona.

There are performers that carry shows and there are a lot of shows that carry the performers nowadays. We lit her from the pit. I had a guy with a handheld spot who followed her from the pit [for 'Where Is The What If The What Is In Why?']: we were just playing with lighting very simply to create effects, with a white backdrop.

> And there is the song 'Forever More' when Róisín uses a bunch of roses – plucking the petals and showering herself with those petals.

Tom Lesh: Using those petals she is showering herself with as metaphorical tears! That started one night at a festival in Belgium. And that song was all about her relationship break-up with the bass player (which was the musical partnership of Moloko). They had been an item for ten years and were still trapped together in a cycle of touring, though very much apart. There were some flowers in the dressing room and one night she brought them on stage and showered herself with petals as she sang, and at a break in the song proceeded to destroy them with real vengeance. It looked so great that we brought that gag back every night. It's little things that work really well. That was a performer ad-libbing, and letting off steam over something personal in her life, in front of a vast audience. This ended up being one of the highlights of the show, whereas nowadays it's so much more polished and choreographed. Artists have gags but they're quite expensive gags – a hydraulic lift, a bridge coming out over the audience, armies of dancers. I think that these 'old school' simple tricks are missed. I learnt a lot of this from lighting designers in the 1970s and 1980s.

When I started as a lighting designer there were no moving lights readily available. Vari-lite had just brought out the first product for the glorious new world, and Genesis were the first band to use this remarkable technology that we now take for granted. For the rest of us – well, we just had to get creative to keep up with this emerging brave new world. You would send a crew guy along to change the colours on floor PARs [parabolic aluminium reflectors] and ACLs [aircraft landing lights] between the songs, have old PATT 252 [effects] projectors with rain, or cloud, or fire wheels, that would be swapped between songs, Optikinetics oil wheel projectors with rotating oil wheels and gobos to look like moving lights, with techs shaking backdrops to

FIGURE 10.2 Flay bouquet: Moloko perform 'Forever More', from *11,000 Clicks* (Dick Carruthers, 2004).

create ripple effects! We utilized what (and who) we could to create the show. There seemed to be more of a feeling of being part of the circus rather than a small cog in a large machine. We weren't trying to produce a television show live; we were producing rock 'n' roll shows and it was special!

> Rob Sinclair maintains that less is often more: an arresting example came in the use of the relatively unsophisticated technology of the 'kiss-cam' during the Bangerz tour: live footage of couples invited to 'make out' was projected behind Miley Cyrus as she sang the ballad 'Adore You'.

Rob Sinclair: That was entirely Miley's idea. None of us really appreciated how well that would work, and she was very insistent that that's what we needed to do, and we needed this cheesy wedding ring graphic on the screen [around the kissing couples], and it worked beautifully.

> It cast the audience in the show: no longer passive consumers but finding a role in the collective creation of the spectacle.

Rob Sinclair: Often we talk about getting some shots of the audience up there [on the video screens]: we need to see the audience having a great time but it never really works. You as an audience member are looking at an enormous screen and on that is either someone who is less attractive than you or more attractive than you. They're either having a better or a worse time than you. And none of those things you really want to see. If they're having a better time, you feel rather hard done by; if they're having a worse time, it brings the mood down. The kiss-cam was such a fabulous way of engaging the audience, and getting them to do charming yet slightly silly things: it worked beautifully. The audience egged each other on, and anything went!

> As things get bigger and budgets higher, the planning meetings and hours of preparation don't necessarily get any less informal . . . At the very top of the arena concert industry, Bryan juggles vast commercial interests and international celebrity personalities to try and make the most from the budget he is allocated for each tour. Even at that size his work is no less artful and creative.

Bryan Leitch: The Circus Starring Britney Spears [2009 tour] was staged in the round and when you move up into that league you have to think differently. There were so many trap doors and lifts to get people on and off stage. They spent millions building it, and I had to justify that cost by sitting down with the tour accountant.

Justin Timberlake saw my work with Coldplay and James Taylor. He flew me to Paris, I had a meeting with him and I drew the 'axe blade' FutureSex/LoveShow 2007 tour stage on a napkin in front of him. Justin's got an incredible memory, every word you say goes in, so you've got to stick to what you say. He asked me if I could remember what I'd drawn (I'd done it upside down so he could see it) and just took the napkin, then folded it up and put it in his pocket – saying that this better be what he saw when it was all done. Later I met him on a gigantic Warner Brothers studio soundstage. We were up on a huge platform so you could see down the stage and he walked in and got the napkin out, looked over the stage and said 'yep, that's it. . .'.

Justin's FutureSex/LoveShow stage cost even more than Britney's because there was so much to it. We had gigantic moving 3D projection screens and over 140 Vari-lites. There were so many people on stage we needed twelve follow spots positioned around the arena but they were massive and each one killed fifty seats, which was costing hundreds of seats per night. Then I had this eureka moment when I realized we could put 360 degree spot chairs above the stage in the lighting rig and just whizz the follow spot operators up there in a harness using a high-speed rope lift. So I redesigned it all and took it to the tour accountant. I told him I was going to hand back hundreds of tickets per show – but he's a real hard businessman so I had to prove to him it could work first. When I did he told me I could have all the lights I want because we were getting so many seats back every night!

Economies of scale on that kind of production make anything possible. I started thinking about the business side of it and got the stage barrier cut from some car guys who do fancy stuff and built the Justin Timberlake logo into it. There were four bars of special seating immediately in front of the stage some of which could be purchased in pairs as 'love seats' while others were sold to corporations. From that I got Alicia Keys and came up with this idea of a 180 degree video screen that parted and opened up and a grand piano came out from inside, and we had a walkway built right around it so

FIGURE 10.3 Bryan Leitch's 'axe blade' stage design; *Justin Timberlake: FutureSex/LoveShow, Live from Madison Square Garden* (Marty Callner, 2007).

all the people could appear to be dancing on the video screen. The video wings were 130 foot wide. I designed them because we were in giant arenas and slightly smaller arenas, so they could swing round to fit the space.

After that I got Britney where we just expanded on that same gag. The dressing rooms were above the stage, which had a massive black tube inside it so the performers could come up and down through the tube while no-one could see what was going on. Meanwhile we'd be resetting the stage, totally reinventing the space.

> To work on this scale takes an enormity of shared creative vision, and one that seems to need the ability to remain open to happenstance, inspiration, improvisation, even accidents. Rob Sinclair identifies the 'amazing chaos – out of which came the Miley Cyrus [Bangerz] show, which was extraordinary'. The rehearsal period lasted for six weeks. It's a show discussed elsewhere in this book but the immediate experience was not one of beholding a circus, but finding yourself somehow cast unwittingly in the circus.

Rob Sinclair: I was bought in by Es [Devlin, stage designer, whose credits included the closing ceremony of the London 2012 Olympics, and tours for Shakira, Kanye West and Lady Gaga, as well as work with the Royal Shakespeare Company and Sadler's Wells]. We had just done our second Pet Shop Boys show together: we had done the Pandemonium World Tour in 2009 and the Electric World Tour in 2013, both of which I'm very proud of. Es had been approached by Diane [Martel] as she didn't want to use any of the usual people in Los Angeles who would put pop shows together. She wanted to build her own team, and Es very kindly suggested me. I was slightly bemused by the whole thing – quite why this enormous American production was wanting this slightly strange Englishman to come and light it. It was a huge learning curve; by far the biggest thing I had done at that point. It was slightly chaotic, but very stylish, and very well thought-out. All of Diane's ideas and all of Diane's video content was spectacularly strange in the best possible way. And what I did, for Es's set, is help to present it as being a strange Pop Art thing, rather than just 'straight' pop. It was expensive, but looked completely different from any other concert that I've seen.

One of the real challenges was keeping everybody lit. The choreography changed endlessly over this fairly enormous [stage] space. We used to video every rehearsal and later go through it, to move all the lights around. And then the choreography would change the next day, and we'd do it all again. It was mechanically quite difficult. Diane was quite keen that the dancers were properly lit at all times: they were wearing these outrageous costumes so needed to be seen at all times.

> That sets up a contrast with the performance of 'Wrecking Ball', which is disconcertingly minimalist: in fact, just Miley and yourself.

Rob Sinclair: Diane didn't want to make any content for it: this song was something that had been performed so much, and there had been so much focus on it, with the [Terry Richardson] video, that they now wanted to present it as something different. So we decided that we would do it as a lighting only song: a big wall of lasers that went into a big wall of lights.

> Verses with blue light, choruses with a wash of white lights: a moment of communion with the audience which Miley can only achieve by taking a temporary step away from the 'amazing chaos'.

Rob Sinclair: Emotionally it worked really well. We as the (wrong word!) 'adults', who put the show together, were really happy, but we had some feedback from the target audience of the show: teenagers found it a bit strange after the relentlessness of the rest of the show. People's kids found it a bit odd for this big song, turning it into something different. But it was a nicely different moment. Because the video screens were off, and because it wasn't completely in your face chaos. I was very happy with it, Diane was happy with it. It was a very different moment.

> There was a similar 'diva' moment in the Kylie Minogue Kiss Me Once tour of 2014 in which, all alone and with a flick of her wrist, and as if possessed of supernatural powers, she seemed to summon a storm of light out of the darkness.

Rob Sinclair: That was the best lighting cue I've ever done, for the song 'On A Night Like This'. What I do is not immediate: it involves long, long nights

FIGURE 10.4 Miley Cyrus, lit by Rob Sinclair, performs 'Wrecking Ball'; *Bangerz* (Diane Martel and Russell Thomas, 2015).

of programming and working with lights but it also happens while you're in rehearsals – it's not something that you can put together months beforehand, although I do think about things months beforehand. From conversations with William Baker (his video content budget was getting strained and he'd spent quite a lot of money on all the video at the beginning of the show), Kylie wanted lasers. And William and I had this whole conversation about when did we not need video content. And we picked 'On a Night Like This' and 'Slow' as two good songs that we use lasers with, and the dancers could be having a break at that point, or getting changed. I did a storyboard for how that would

FIGURE 10.5 Kylie Minogue, lit by Rob Sinclair, performs 'On A Night Like This'; *Kylie: Kiss Me Once Tour Live at the SSE Hydro* (Wiliam Baker and Marcus Viner, 2015).

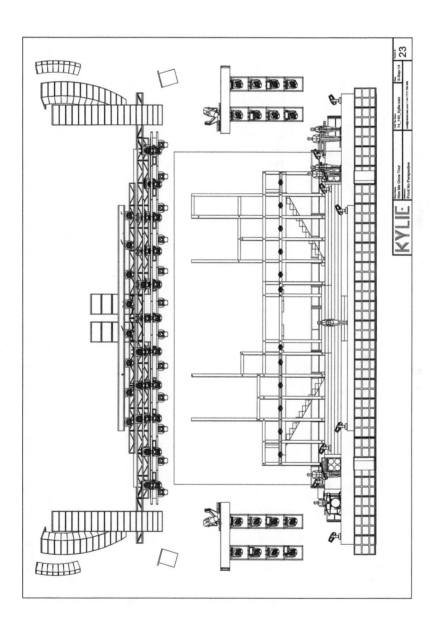

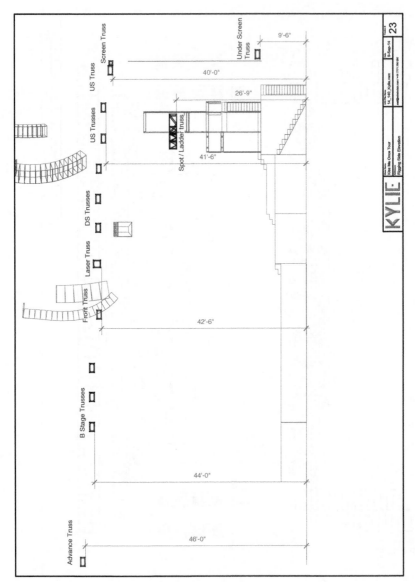

FIGURE 10.6 Samples from Rob Sinclair's lighting plots for the Kiss Me Once tour.

work: the important thing was the fact that we held off until the riff came in, rather than using lasers at the beginning of the song. And that gave this an immense moment of release. And it also turned out that because we needed to plunge the arena into relative darkness in order to make the lasers work, everyone could then dance without worrying about people looking at them which, with a slightly more mature audience, works well. One of the first reviews said that this moment turned us into the biggest disco in town. And Kylie started saying that – 'Welcome to the biggest disco in town!'

> It reminded me of the scene in King Lear, out on the heath in the mid-storm (' . . . all-shaking thunder, strike flat the thick rotundity o' th' world'): as if from out of nowhere this immense and engulfing hurricane of light.

Rob Sinclair: The simplest things are often the best. It's the element of surprise, of drama. And everyone love lasers; they're catnip to audiences, so if you present them correctly and give them room to breathe it can be very, very powerful. There was a similar moment in the song 'Drive' with Miley, which was a much slower song but again there was no video and we gave the lasers a real chance to exist on their own and have their moment. When I saw Katy Perry [for the Prismatic tour] they used lasers with everything else which I thought was less effective, although I did love everything about that show: it was beautifully executed and with detailed programming.

> For the arena visual industry, the future seems bright. 3D technology is advancing quickly and hardware is becoming increasingly affordable – even large theatres are now able to buy ambitious arena-style displays. Lots of interesting things are happening as a result but there are problems too, not least with the growth of digital news and social media, which means that when you've used an idea once you can't repeat it because everyone's seen it, whether or not they attended the show.

Davy Sherwin: The main thing is that the rental price of equipment has come down so much. There are so many huge screens out there, mainly from China, and a lot of hire companies now are buying into this equipment so it's become extremely good value as a result. Now even a band playing small theatres can afford an LED screen. Five or eight years ago that simply wouldn't have been an option. A lot of the lighting companies are now doing video too and making the screens nice and simple so that almost anyone can use them. Projectors were once the cheaper option but they weren't bright enough to cut through a lighting rig. Now, however, projectors are getting smaller and brighter too, so that's also a cost-effective way of showing content. A lot of bands that don't have a budget can take that route – although even bigger bands like Coldplay still use projection because it's such a beautiful way of showing content if you can get the brightness. There are now videos screens available in strips or circles, or squares and cubes. . . basically anything you can come up with or get an idea for you can physically make happen now quite easily.

You can also mix pre-recorded content with live cameras onstage . . .

Davy Sherwin: That's one of my trademarks, mixing live video in with existing content. We did that a lot on the last Snow Patrol tour. Rather than presenting one set of pre-recorded content on screen and a live shot of the singer on another, we consciously blended it all into one big image. There's a beautiful way of doing that now with low-profile cameras. We've put them on the guitar, on microphone stands, on a kick drum pedal or inside a drum head looking up through the transparent skin. You can do anything with them now, and you can buy them for £200. It's madness how cheap they are and how widely you can utilize them.

At live shows where lighting designers are taking a playful approach with visual effects it can mess with the audience's perspective and even their perception of what visuals are live or pre-recorded . . .

Davy Sherwin: That can get quite clever now. Audiences literally don't know what's pre-recorded content or what's actually happening live in front of them. Back in the old days with Metallica or Bruce Springsteen you'd have huge big screens with a giant colour image showing a close up of either the singer's face or a wide shot of the stage from front of house – often quite standard stuff. Today people are prepared to push boundaries almost to the extent where the singer is unrecognizable. It can be touch and go whether you get away with that or not because, for example with Snow Patrol, a lot of people are there to see Gary Lightbody singing and now you're making them into this distorted messed up image. So you have to keep in mind the more conservative audience at the back as well as trying to tick the art school boxes too. It's a fine line and you can't really do it all through a gig. You pick your moments when you can go abstract, and keep it nice and clean at other times.

It really is the ultimate multimedia experience, not least because of the lights as well. Let's not forget this is still an arena rock show. I treat the whole thing as one big image, it's not like there's cameras, content and lighting – everything is all at the same level so you're seeing the lights and video equally as one image. It's not one guy trying to be brighter than the other, or the lights distracting you away from the beautiful videos anymore.

There are big changes afoot and this is an exciting part of the industry to be involved in. It's great for people like us as there's a lot of work and good budgets. Back in the day it was the other way around – on my first tour I was paid by the merchandise money and very much the last one employed. In the next few years we'll definitely see 3D stuff such as projection mapping – a lot of which goes on in corporate world but it hasn't really broken into the live world in a big way as yet. There will be more crazy stuff with lasers as well as video content using lasers. Rather than just putting out old school 80s or 90s images they will be cleverly spitting out nice bits of content on to 3D moving shapes, so it's a pretty exciting time. I guess lights will become more of a secondary element. Moving lights have been moving lights for twenty years. They've got better and brighter and smaller but to the average guy in the audience they don't know that. It's another light that moves and flashes. It'll be led by 3D, lasers and explosions – clever stuff like that but done in an artistic way.

The Coldplay bracelets were a work of genius but then again they've done it now so no-one else can really use it. For any other band it would be obviously a Coldplay copy, the same as U2 with their big centre-opening screen that almost went on the scrap heap after they'd used it because no one wanted to buy it or use it again. Those things are in and out straight away, they're clever but you can only use them once.

Rob Sinclair: It's difficult to know what new technology will throw up. All I know is that I would like to continue to use the technology that is available to me in slightly unexpected and clever ways. There's a blurring of the edges between things being concerts or things being shows. How do you preserve that spontaneity of a group playing a concert while delivering these memorable visual moments that work so well on a grand scale? A band just shuffling on and playing as they would in a pub is not really acceptable in an arena anymore so you need to have some theatricality, and some showbiz, to it. . . but you try to do that in a more honest way than you would in a pure pop show.

Notes

1   A slang term to denote the seats so high up that it is as if problems affecting mountaineers, such as nosebleeds, may also trouble the fans seated in them.
2   See the film of the performance: *A Hundred Million Suns* (James Russell, 2008).

CHAPTER ELEVEN

A Personal History of UK Arena Concerts: Reflections on Gigs over the Past Forty Years

Peter Smith

Introduction

Rock concerts have always been an important part of my life. I find them fulfilling, and yet also, to turn to psychoanalyst Siegfried Zepf's term, 'inexpressible experiences' (2008). My story starts as a young man who sat in awe in Earls Court at Bob Dylan and Led Zeppelin concerts, struggling to hear poor quality sound, and watching grainy images on low-quality screens. My journey concludes in the luxurious O2 arena, where I paid more than I can afford to share in the sense of event and claim my share of cultural capitalism as I watched Barbra Streisand and the Rolling Stones. For each concert, I present my personal recollections and, where relevant, comment on the venue. I also include some factual details, such as ticket price, and the use of visuals, and discuss how these have developed and changed over the years. I use my concert experiences to illustrate how the development of the arena concert itself has been instrumental in establishing concert-going as a key part of modern culture, and reflect on the multifaceted nature of these events.

The Dark Ages

During the early 1970s I'd been lucky enough to see my heroes in small venues (of approximately a capacity of 2,000). I'd queued for 28 hours to score second row tickets for the Rolling Stones at Newcastle City Hall, been crushed a few feet away from Led Zeppelin in a dangerously crammed Sunderland Locarno ballroom, watched David Bowie, as Ziggy Stardust, play to a half-full Newcastle City Hall and cheered as Pete Townshend smashed his guitar into pieces in the Newcastle Odeon. There was an intimacy to those gigs: I could almost touch the band, their volume shook my entire body, and the power of the performance and the emotional rush of the crowd's reaction, were all exhilarating. I felt alive and refreshed, and would talk about the experiences for days afterwards.

But my heroes were starting to move away from me. The demand for rock concerts was growing, and bands needed to perform to larger crowds. Early arena rock used exhibition centres (Wembley Empire Pool, Earls Court), which were never designed for music performances. The sound was poor, visuals low-grade or non-existent, and we watched tiny figures on a small stage which seemed miles away – as if we were watching the performance at a cinema, or on the television. Feelings of intimacy and personal connection were lost, and the performers *became* distant. Yet some things were gained. There was a feeling of occasion, a 'gathering of the clans'. It was exciting to be in and to then bear witness to these historic events.

Scoring tickets for concerts in the 1970s often entailed queuing overnight outside a venue or record shop. It was all part of the experience; I found camaraderie in those queues, made lifelong friends and felt as if I had earned my seat at the concert. I was totally addicted to live music, and would go to any lengths to experience the buzz of seeing my heroes perform.

Early Arena Rock: Led Zeppelin, Earls Court, London, Saturday 24 May 1975

Ticket price: £2.50.
Seating position in the hall: Block 4, Row D seat 24, which was at the side and quite far back.
Size and nature of the crowd: 17,000, rock fans in t-shirts and jeans.
The visuals: rudimentary screen, early use of lasers.
No support act.
Tour concept: their 'laser-lit American show'.

This was the first event I attended which can be classified 'arena rock', setting a standard which others, including The Who and the Stones, would follow. Led Zeppelin initially booked three nights at Earls Court Arena, London (capacity 17,000). The venue had been used for concerts before, notably one by David Bowie, at which the sound was reportedly atrocious: 'one doubts whether more than half were able to even see what was going down on-stage, while the sound system veered from adequate to diabolical to totally inaudible' (Kent 1973). Due to what the promoter Mel Bush described at the time as an 'unprecedented demand in the history of rock music' two further dates were added, making the total attendance across five nights of c. 85,000.[1] There was no support act and Zeppelin played a long set, approximately three hours each night. This was the first chance for UK fans to see Zeppelin in three years.

Tickets went on sale to in-person applicants; I queued all night outside Virgin Records, Newcastle, with a group of mates. We were all heavily into rock music and seeing Zeppelin was a big thing. When the box office opened, we were disappointed to find the tickets gave restricted views, up at the back of the arena. This was often the case, with the best seats held at the venue itself, in London.

This was one of the first shows to use colour video screens. The sound wasn't great, drifting at times, but the massive PA ensured that everyone could hear the band. DJ Nicky Horne opened the proceedings with 'Welcome to Earls Court. For the next three hours you are going to hear some music that your mother wouldn't like'. Reviews were very positive. 'Led Zeppelin are THE biggest and, judging by the excellence of their performance at Earls Court last Sunday, one of, if not the most exciting live act in the world' (Makowski 1975). '[Sic] Earl's Court was more of an event than a week of great concerts' (Ross Halfin, quoted in Hoskyns 2012, 314).

I went to the concert with my friend John, a fellow lifelong rock fan, who recalls:

I thought the entire set was great with 'In My Time of Dying', 'Trampled Underfoot', the acoustic set and 'Stairway to Heaven' being the highlights. I am not a big drum solo fan and by then 'Whole Lotta Love' was sounding a bit overplayed, but minor quibbles on a fantastic experience. Jimmy wore the Dragon Suit. All I can say is this was greatest gig I have ever seen. A great venue, great visuals and sound, and a great time to see the greatest rock and roll band of all time. Like a lot of things, at the time it felt a bit special, but I now realize it was a historic event. Sometimes the sun, moon and stars are aligned, I feel very fortunate to have been present.[2]

Rocking a Cattleshed: The Who, Stafford Bingley Hall, 4 October 1975

Ticket price: £2.20.
Seating position in the hall: All standing, half way back.
Size and nature of the crowd: 8,000, rock fans in t-shirts and jeans.

The visuals: early use of lasers.

Support act: The Steve Gibbons Band.

Tour concept: 'The Greatest Rock and Roll Band in the World'.

Bingley Hall is a 10,000 capacity exhibition hall in the Staffordshire County Showground, which hosts a variety of events including antique fairs, dog shows and motor shows. It is in the centre of the UK, close to major motorways, and accessible from both the North and South. During the 1970s and 1980s, before the emergence of purpose-built arenas, it was a popular concert venue. Acts that performed there included The Who, Pink Floyd, David Bowie, ABBA and the Rolling Stones. This was the first concert to be held there.

The Who were out to prove themselves 'The Greatest Rock and Roll Band in the World'; there was little to choose between them, Zeppelin and the Stones. I attended the second of two nights. I drove down to the gig with a group of friends, all in our late teens. One friend was starting at Staffordshire Polytechnic that weekend, so the date of the gig fitted with Freshers' Week. We were hoping to stay in his room at the Hall of Residence, but arrived too late for that to be organized.

This was a set of Who classics, starting with 'Substitute', lots from *Tommy*, and closing with 'Won't Get Fooled Again'. The billing claimed 'the first stage act in the world to employ high-powered lasers' (quoted in Townshend 2012, 280): I was worried that they might hit me in the eye – 'if a beam stands still, it can blind someone' (lighting operator John Wolff, quoted in Neill and Kent 2007, 378). These were the Who's first performances in fourteen months, and they were simply on fire, with much mic swinging by Roger Daltrey and 'Townshend adopting his classic legs-apart stance and spiralling his right arm roughly across the strings of his Les Paul' (Charlesworth 1975). They played for two hours, with no encore. Pete didn't smash his guitar, although the crowd was willing him on to do so.

Thin White Duke: David Bowie, Empire Pool Wembley London, 8 May 1976

Ticket price: £3.75.

Seating position in the hall: South Upper Tier, Row K Seat 45.

Size and nature of the crowd: 10,000 Bowie fans, many wearing Ziggy gear.

The visuals: white light, stark contrast between black and white.

Support act: screening of *Un Chien Andalu* (Salvador Dalí, Luis Buñuel, 1929).

Tour concept: The Thin White Duke Tour.

This was the last of six shows at Wembley Empire Pool, Bowie's only UK gigs that year, and his first here since 1973. The Empire Pool (now Wembley Arena, and since rebuilt) was a cold, cavernous shed. After the bad experience of Earls Court, Bowie set out to ensure that this concert would work.

I drove down to London (some 250 miles) for the concert with three friends. We were all big Bowie fans, having last seen him at Newcastle City Hall during the Ziggy tour. One friend arranged for us to stay at his aunt's house in Walthamstow. The stage was bathed in white light. Bowie and the band wore black trousers and white shirts. I didn't quite get the concept at the time; it was too different from the rock'n'roll splendour and sass of Ziggy. The set included Bowie classics and tracks from *Station to Station*. Bowie was very much the 'white soul boy'. I remember feeling disappointed, but looking back it was actually clever – great theatre, a massive development from Ziggy and with hints of what was to come. Bowie was steeping himself in new influences, including Kraftwerk and the music of his new friend Iggy Pop.

Dave Thompson, who sent fan letters to Bowie, wrote: 'Would you believe I missed the film that opened [the event: *Un Chien Andalu*], because I ran out to hit the souvenir stalls while the crowds were otherwise occupied. But even from there you could hear a massive, collective "Bleaugh" go through the entire venue when the razor blade went through the eyeball' (Thompson 2002, 137).

A Pilgrimage: Bob Dylan, Earls Court, London, 17 June 1978

Ticket price: £6.50.
Seating position in the hall: Block 13, J134 (a poor view).
Size and nature of the crowd: 17,000, rock and music fans.
The visuals: I don't recall any.
Support act: None.
Tour concept: The Street Legal tour.

I returned to Earls Court to witness Bob Dylan play one of six sold-out shows. The concerts were a total success and demand was so high that a massive open-air show was added, at Blackbushe Aerodrome, which was attended by 250,000 fans. Dylan was reportedly paid £650,000 for the UK shows (see Southall 2012, 44).

Scoring tickets in 1978 was very different to today: no Internet. Demand to see Dylan, at his first UK shows since the 1969 Isle of Wight festival, was huge. Tickets were sold by in person application only (similar to Zeppelin) at box offices on a Sunday morning. I drove 100 miles and queued for more than twenty-four hours outside a Leeds record store to get mine. When the shop opened there was disappointment as they had a small number of upper tier tickets (approximately 1,000), satisfying only the first 250 people in the queue, since there was a limit of four tickets per person, and so leaving hundreds disappointed. I bought tickets for my girlfriend (now wife), myself and two friends who had turned up late in the queue.

Dylan was wonderful, playing a long set of his classics. The sound and the view weren't great from our seats; Dylan seemed a tiny figure and I remember being disappointed that I couldn't see him properly, or pick out any detail of his face. For some shows he wore a top hat: 'no leopard skin pillbox hat, but there's more than a hint of Marc Bolan in Dylan's choice of headgear' (Watts 2000, 22). His voice was strong; every time he played his mouth organ a great cheer came from the crowd. Reviews were positive, although Goldman dismissively compared it to a 'Las Vegas revue' (1978).

Modern Times

In recent years the emergence of the purpose-built concert arena has created new possibilities for concerts as corporate hospitality activities, far removed from the ramshackle events of the 1970s. The price of tickets has changed dramatically, moving from a few pounds in the 1970s to hundreds of pounds today. The methods for buying tickets for concerts also changed with the advent of the internet and online ticket brokers. There was no longer any need to queue for hours since tickets could be bought online, and often sold out in minutes. It all became more of a lottery, sometimes literally (e.g. Led Zeppelin at the O2), and online ticket touting, official and unofficial, started to mean that tickets go to the highest bidder.

Vegas comes to London: Barbra Streisand, O2 Arena, London, 18 July 2007

Ticket price: £100–£650.
Seating position in the hall: Cheap (£100!) upper tier seat.
Size and nature of the crowd: 15,000 Streisand fans and corporate liggers.
The visuals: screens.
Support act: None.
Tour concept: 'Streisand'.

This was my first visit to the O2 Arena, and one of the first concerts to be held there. It is a massive space (20,000 capacity), located in the centre of an entertainment complex. Named after its sponsor, it is the first American-style, multi-purpose arena in London, the second largest arena in Europe, and now the busiest concert arena in the world. The O2 was an ideal venue for the icon 'Streisand'. I'd wanted to see Barbra in concert for some time, having read of her reputation as the consummate live performer. Discussion around these concerts was as much about the price of tickets as the performance; but 'she has never been ashamed of her ability to make huge sums' (Edwards 1997, 12). Tickets ranged from £100 to £650. I paid £100 for an upper level seat and went alone. I couldn't afford to take anyone along, and none of my friends were fans.

The crowd gave Streisand a standing ovation before she sang a single note. Soon that powerful, emotion-full voice ran through the arena for classic Streisand hits such as 'The Way We Were' and 'Evergreen'. When she delved into the 'Great American Songbook' I felt the true artistry and soul in her performance. Some expensive seats remained unsold; during the interval I walked down to floor level and sat in an empty £650 seat. No one challenged me and I enjoyed the rest of the concert with an excellent view of Barbra seated on a stool, singing a moving version of Chaplin's 'Smile'.

Attending a Streisand concert is, for some, as much about the event, and being seen, as it is about the singer and her music. Comments from a Streisand fansite: 'I've been fortunate enough to see Barbra perform live in 3 different countries . . . there are just not enough adjectives to accurately describe her amazing talent . . . her performances are mesmerising.' 'How could I ever forget you once you had touched my soul . . . my Barbra. You may not know me, but you are always with me.' 'Her voice was a little shaky on a couple of notes as she nears the end of her tour, but Streisand at the O2 was just one memorable night! . . . everything I'd been waiting for since I was a lonely little sixteen year old, locked away in my bedroom . . . and slowly coming to terms with my sexuality became real—she totally delivered, and I haven't stopped smiling since.'[3]

Worshipping at the Shrine: Led Zeppelin, O2 Arena, London, 10 December 2007

Ticket price: £125.
Seating position in the hall: Block 407, Row E Seat 598.
Size and nature of the crowd: 20,000 die-hard Zeppelin fans, from all over the world.
The visuals: screens.
Support acts: several special guests.
One-off reunion: Ahmet Ertegün Tribute concert.

In 2007 Led Zeppelin reformed for a benefit concert in memory of music executive Ahmet Ertegün, who helped break the band in North America. This was their first concert since the death of John Bonham in 1980. Jason Bonham took his father's place at the drumstool.

Tickets were made available via lottery. One million people registered for the 20,000 available tickets. Jimmy Page commented: 'I knew it was going to sell out quickly, but the tidal wave of euphoria that preceded the gig – the anticipation – went beyond what I could possibly have imagined . . . we were going to do it properly and stand up and be counted' (quoted in Vogel 2012). I was determined to attend this concert and entered the lottery several times, hoping against the odds that I'd be lucky. I wasn't. The winners were emailed a passcode which enabled them to buy two tickets. I saw passcodes on sale on an internet auction site, and I decided to take the risk and bought two for US$100 each, which enabled me to buy four tickets. I bought two tickets in my name, and two in my wife's name, using different credit cards since the terms stated that you could only buy two tickets, and orders on the same card would be cancelled. Four of us: myself, my wife, and two of our children, went to the gig. We had to collect our tickets from the O2, along with photographic ID.

You could feel anticipation in the air. The show started with a short news report video of a 1970s US tour. Then the familiar opening riff of 'Good Times, Bad Times' echoed across the arena. The sound was patchy at first, and the atmosphere strange. The crowd was subdued, maybe they were awestruck – the fans couldn't believe what they were experiencing. But they came to as the evening progressed, with later songs receiving crazy receptions. Zeppelin were everything I could have hoped for. It was a great performance – Zeppelin reclaimed their legacy. Yet this was probably not the best time I had seen Zeppelin, but it was a momentous, unforgettable and emotional event, and 'the best Zeppelin gig since 1975' (singer Robert Plant quoted in Hoskyns 2012, 511).

Fan reviews from the official Zeppelin site: 'Best concert I've ever seen. Camped out overnight and got front row, totally worth it. I remember asking the people next to me if I was in heaven.'[4] 'It was hard for me to be critical of band I have anxiously waited 27 years to witness . . . Zep rocked the celebrity laced crowd from the opening number until the final note. [During] "Stairway to Heaven" a young girl cried tears of joy during the entire song . . . many cried tears of happiness during this emotional reunion, including me, three or four times . . . the greatest road trip adventure of my life.'[5]

Spectacle: Roger Waters, The Wall, Manchester Arena, 21 May 2011

Ticket price: £75.
Seating position in the hall: side tier.
Size and nature of the crowd: 20,000 Pink Floyd and adult rock fans.
The visuals: an amazing theatrical show.

Support act: None.
Tour concept: The Wall.

This must be the most impressive show I have ever seen, in terms of visuals and production. I wasn't a fan of *The Wall* album. In fact, despite my having seen the Floyd tours in the 1970s, I missed out on *The Wall* shows at Earls Court. I'd grown a little tired of their ever expanding stage shows, and I just didn't 'get' *The Wall* concept. I was also heavily into the punk/New Wave ethos at that time.

I went to this concert alone; as I get older it is more difficult to find people to come, or maybe I am just becoming more of a loner. The Wall itself was partially built as I arrived. I was surprised by the scale, detail and impact of the production. The story of The Wall tells of Roger Water's own isolation, drawing on themes of war, injustice, politics, oppression and inequality. Roger has updated the production to include current political and world issues, and technology enables a spectacle which simply wasn't possible thirty years ago.

The flying pig returned, much more impressive than the beast that flew over my head in 1977 at Wembley Empire Pool. There were inflatables of the teacher and mother. Roger dueted with himself using 1980 video from Earls Court. The wall was built throughout the first half of the show, transforming into a massive video screen, displaying images of fallen war heroes and from the storyline. By the intermission the wall was complete, and Roger and the band disappeared behind it. It stayed in place for most of the second half, with Roger performing in front and on top of it. The climax came with us all chanting – 'Break down the wall!' – and the wall collapsing in front of our eyes.

It's only (corporate) Rock'n'roll: The Rolling Stones, O2 Arena, London, 25 November 2012

Ticket price: £225 (up to £1,000).
Seating position in the hall: the back of the arena.
Size and nature of the crowd: 20,000 Stones fans, from all over the world.
The visuals: screens and the tongue stage concept.
Support act: None.
Tour concept: 50 and Counting.

A lot has been written about the expensive prices of tickets for these 50th anniversary gigs, with most seats costing in excess of £400. I wondered if there would be empty seats, but the venue was packed. The stage was modelled on the Stones' trademark lips and tongue, with a standing area (at £1,000 a ticket) in the centre of the tongue. I'd paid £250 for a cheap upper level seat and so I was on my own again.

The proceedings started with a video of stars congratulating the Stones on their 50th year, including Elton John, Iggy Pop and Johnny Depp. Next a troop of drummers in gorilla suits (matching the tour concept) paraded around the floor, filling the arena with sound and rhythm. Then the lights went down and Mick Jagger and the band took to the stage.

The first song was 'I Wanna Be Your Man', with Mick wearing a black and white jacket and matching trilby. We were back in the 1960s; the sound and musicianship was superb. I could hear every word clearly – crisp and loud. Screens showed images of the band in their youth. Mick was in a playful mood: 'How is it up in the cheap seats?' before adding 'Oh there aren't any, are there?' He took off his jacket, dressed in black for an amazing version of 'Paint It Black', and the whole arena sang along.

The band left the stage to a tremendous reception. They were quickly back, accompanied by a choir for 'You Can't Always Get What You Want', followed by 'Jumpin' Jack Flash' and the audience's voices almost drowning the band. You have to give it to them; they showed all their critics that they could still deliver. The self-styled 'Greatest Rock n Roll Band in the World' retained its crown.[6]

From the Stones fansite: 'There were so many great moments tonight. Mick said from his heart, and not reading from any scripts, how much he thanked us, the fans, for coming back, listening to their music, and buying their records. For fifty years . . . still . . . the greatest rock'n'roll band on this planet!'; 'The Rolling Stones were ON tonight. They were well prepared, they took the right amount of risks, they incorporated their guest stars well, and they did just about everything the loyal, or even casual, fan could expect for a 50th anniversary show . . . they expanded the boundaries of rock and roll by showing that a band with members at or close to 70 years old could put on a brilliant performance. Work the extra hours, put some possessions for sale, or make a trip to the pawn shop so you could make some show(s). If you thought seeing the Stones was life affirming before, you will see it in 2012 more than ever.'[7]

Conclusion

This chapter charts some of the changes in UK arena rock concerts over the last forty years. Zeppelin set the standard for others to follow. And yet there were few venues which could accommodate concerts of a capacity in excess of 10,000. Those which were at least partially suitable (Wembley Empire Pool, Earls Court) were in London and outside the capital world renowned acts (such as the Stones and the Who) would wind up playing in less than ideal venues (as with Stafford Bingley Hall). New technology was welcome, with the deployment of video screens, development of better sound systems and integration of various effects. And now purpose built venues (as with the London O2) have made arena concert going a pleasant, and quite usual, cultural pursuit. But the massive increases in ticket price has resulted in many music fans being unable to afford going to concerts, and fostered a concert-going elite. Perhaps this is the price to be paid for good sound and comfortable seating? These changes have also resulted in the rock concert becoming more mainstream; it is no longer part of some 'underground scene'. Maybe, as the 1960s hippies gained careers, families and mortgages, this was an inevitability?

For some bands, arena rock worked (and continues to work) well, and opening up new possibilities. Zeppelin, the Stones and the Who rose to the occasion: the power and depth of their music successfully filled the arenas. Others, and most notably Pink Floyd, used the arena concept to create elaborate shows which drew on and drew out themes within the songs, and created spectacles never before possible. But for some acts, as with Dylan, even when intimacy was lost, the fans accepted that loss as the price of necessary development. Today Dylan often returns to smaller venues. I recently saw him from the front row of Blackpool Opera House, and being so close added a new dimension to the experience, and helped me understand the man a little more. New technology has created new opportunities for everyone in relation to live music. If I miss a concert, I can see it on the Internet the next day, or even just hours after: a permanent record exists, and events can be relived again and again.

I still enjoy rock concerts, but in a very different way. No longer am I to be found sitting at the back of a cavernous shed, listening to tinny and drifting sound, and watching matchstick figures on a tiny stage in the distance. Instead I am in a comfortable seat, hearing crisp sound, watching the performance on high-tech screens and marvelling at intricate stage sets. But part of me still longs to be that young guy crushed against the barrier, trying to touch Plant, Jagger or Bowie. That was when I really felt alive.

Notes

1 Quotation from http://www.ledzeppelin.com/event/may-17–1975 (accessed January 2015).
2 Quotation from personal communication.
3 All quotations from http://barbra-archives.com/live/00s/europe_2007/london_o2.html (accessed November 2014).
4 Quotation from http://www.ledzeppelin.com/node/2065/562#comment-562 (accessed November 2014).
5 Quotation from http://www.ledzeppelin.com/node/2065/563#comment-563 (accessed January 2015).
6 For further discussion of their status, see Smith (2013, 201–222).
7 Quotation from http://www.iorr.org/tour12/london1.htm (accessed November 2014).

CHAPTER TWELVE

Rocking around Watford: Trying to Find What I Was Looking for

Robert Edgar, with Julia and Evan Shelton

Preface

The arena is a space in which amazing things can happen. The arena is a space transformed into an imagined environment where experiences form memories which in turn shape experience. It is easy to think that in attending the arena concert we form part of the history of a performer, a band or even a venue. This might be a desirable belief, depending on the individual's devotion to the act they have seen. However the experience and subsequent memory of the concert is individual and thus memory and the arena concert fits into the individual's own history, with the connection to the performer/s' only existing at a perceptual level. The conflation of the individual and the collective is understandable as the nature of the arena concert is one of participating in an event where we momentarily connect with thousands of others. In this chapter there are two voices, Julia and her son Evan, both recounting the memory of their first arena concert experience, and it is the broader experience that is of paramount importance.

In considering memory it is important to differentiate between individual memory, perceived individual memory and collective cultural memory. An historiographic approach, which embraces both time and space, fits the arena as a conceptual and a physical space.[1] The arena itself is timeless (in that it exists as a physical object, unmoving and totemic), and yet the event itself is transitory and thus fixed forever in a particular historical space; this leads inevitably to a sense of nostalgia. There is something in the corporate nature of the arena concert that allows for a sense of collective nostalgia; the performance is often part of a tour and has been shared with many thousands of others. Such is the enduring nature of a performance that the arena concert becomes part of the history of a band, and perhaps also of a venue; the individual attending the concert thus becomes part of a bigger collective history. This is where historiographic analysis is most useful, in viewing the arena as a significant historical building and one where legends have been created; the parallel with buildings of antiquity is valid and relevant. The corporate machine associated with popular music implies a sense of compliance, where the audience member's memory is subsumed into representations of the concert. There is clearly a sense of belonging and/or social status that can be associated with saying 'I was there', but this is very different to what is in essence the subsuming of an individual memory in the corporate and collective. The event is transitory and is fixed by the subsequent recordings (audio and visual), the television documentaries and even coloured by, achronologically, the albums that existed before the event. However this line of argument presupposes that nostalgia is the dominant response to the event. It is far more likely that we are nostalgic for the event that we didn't attend. What is important about the voices of the audience members is that their experiences exist beyond the event and alongside a corporate drive. The individual memory of the arena event is of something other than of witnessing a performance. In fact the performance is often secondary in importance to the lived experience of being at an arena concert. This is something that can be heard in Julia and Evan's accounts, which are reproduced below, and particularly in otherwise minor and even seemingly trivial details such as the feeling of shoes sticking to beer-soaked carpets, in addition to the feeling of being close to a performer of the stature required to play an arena.

The experience of the concert is remembered through more than memories and is grounded in the artefact that lives on after the event and still connects you to it; the artefact that legitimizes the experience as real. This fetishized object then takes on a status which is way beyond its primary function; the t-shirt is more than simply an article of clothing to be worn. It is, rather, an artefact that confirms presence at an event, and so it becomes iconic. This can be seen in the retro-nostalgia of t-shirts that sport advertisements or tour listings for concerts from decades ago, particularly for those groups with an iconographic status such as Pink Floyd, The Ramones and Led Zeppelin. The function of the residual artefact (such as the ticket) or the corporate artefact (such as the t-shirt, the limited edition single, the glossy programme, the key ring, the mug, the poster or set of badges) is such that there is universality in the object for any audience member. Thus there is knowledge of what is going to be available at the arena concert, in addition to seeing the band, and so what can then be brought back. In the same way that Edward Chaney refers to religious artefacts and the architectural delights of the Grand Tour as 'cultural memorials', the t-shirt and the ticket function as universal memorials with both general memories (all concerts have t-shirts) and individual memories (the t-shirt from the PopMart tour) attached. [2] This has been augmented by the advent and use of mobile technology and the ability to record and share the individual experience. These recordings themselves form part of a memory which stands outside the corporate but is still part of both individual and collective memory; the photo of the event is your own photo yet it is strikingly similar to all the others on Instagram.

Reading Julia and Evan's account of their first arena concert is a salutary reminder that attending any arena concert is a holistic experience. The temptation for the theorist is to focus on the event itself at the expense of that which precedes it. Julia's essay about first seeing U2 initially recalls the sense of lack that existed prior to attending the first concert, an absence that was not realized until that experience. Even then the experience of the concert is secondary to the experience of having to camp out to get hold of the tickets and the anticipation of getting to Glasgow and into the venue. In these terms the quest for the ticket is all; the band it allows you to see is secondary. The lament for the days of the printed ticket and the disdain with which the seasoned concert attendee now presents their mobile phone, displaying the downloaded e-ticket, at the venue door is not just a matter of an ageing audience being disgruntled with new technology. The simple printed slip of card represents something more than its function; it is the difference between being instantly transported to the great pyramid of Giza or sailing down the Nile and slowly approaching it (to draw on Chaney's terms of reference). The journey is paramount.

There is something in the individual memory of the arena event that is important in shaping a sense of self. In these terms, and for Julia, U2 serve a function as providing a sense of self but also a point of resistance, as the group then shifted in and out of style, and as she becomes interested in other genres of music. The desire for the band becomes hidden rather than disappearing. Yet there is something in the arena experience that remains and continues to be sought out and ultimately passed on to Evan, by going to see Arctic Monkeys. This is most fitting: a young band starting to play arenas at a young age playing to a young child starting his experience of attending arena concerts, and only time will tell if he feels the need to hide this early concert attendance if or when the band are no longer in vogue. The two pieces below, written independently of each other, recount similar emotions and this is where the universality of the arena experience exists: in the excitement of getting to the venue, the anticipation of the band, the feel of the venue and being near the performer. Julia's desire for Evan to understand the excitement of the event is palpable; the arena experience being passed down the generations. This is a very personal sharing of an experience which is open to thousands.

What is important in Julia and Evan's writing is the commentary on shaping not just memory but also a sense of self. Above all what is of paramount importance more than the pure joy of the arena experience?

Julia is a Teacher of English Literature and Law with postgaduate qualifications in Medieval History, Law and Teaching. A key part of her teaching practice is to encourage her students to write creatively and to always base their writing on subjects close to their hearts. She is a parent to Evan and enjoys taking him to see bands perform at arena gigs and summer festivals.

Evan Shelton is 12 and at school. He loves studying Classics, English and Physics and is learning to play the guitar and drums. It is possible that in the future he will be playing at an arena near you.

Introduction

I think it's fair to say that I didn't grow up in a musical household. Whenever people are interviewed they will tell you about how their mothers played them Miles Davies or Carole King or The Beatles and these were their formative musical experiences. I struggle to recollect any music in my house as a child and my parents certainly didn't go to see concerts together. There is one story of my mother going with her two friends to London to see Charles Aznavour, missing the last train home and then having to catch the milk train back to Watford in the morning. This was the most 'rock' thing that happened in my household in the 1970s.

For some reason London always felt a very long way from Watford: a huge, unattainable metropolis that we only visited a couple of times a year, and then only to shop or to go to the theatre. In actual fact, London was about twenty minutes by train from Watford Junction station, or a short drive up the M1. Irrespectively, we never went to any form of concert. I am aware of the seismic musical changes of that era only from documentaries: the immensity of Prog Rock; the excesses of disco; the back-to-basics freedom of punk; the development of New Wave, but none of this intruded on suburban Watford. We were geographically close to many of the most exciting musical venues on earth: the Hundred Club, Brixton Academy, Shepherd's Bush Empire, Wembley, but we were as good as a million miles away culturally.

From Birmingham to Watford

The first time I was aware of the arena concert was the video to 'The Reflex' by Duran Duran [released 1984]. In it, impossibly older and glamorous girls danced in the aisles while computer-imaged water poured from a video screen onto the audience and Duran Duran broke young girls' hearts. It was an impossible dream for me to ever be there: how could a skinny teen from Watford get to be in the presence of such greatness? I had no idea of how you would buy tickets or travel all the way to London to see your heroes perform. For me, my Duran Duran worship would have to be limited to sitting right next to the television during [the BBC's] 'Top of the Pops', ruining my eyesight, and playing the cassette tape of 'Rio' [released 1982] so many times that it ended up going mono.

In my mid-teens I put such adolescent pop idolatry behind me and became a 'serious' music fan. I transferred my Simon le Bon crush to the more politically worthy personage of Bono from U2. Many evenings I laid in the dark in my room listening to *The Joshua Tree* [1987] and being very self-consciously serious. If U2 still hadn't found what they were looking for then neither had I. U2 wore black and so did I. All my multi-coloured '80s tube skirts were put away and replaced by black, black and more black. For a few short weeks I considered the next big step of listening to The Cure and being a Goth but I had freckles and I didn't think you could be a freckly Goth. So I re-pledged my allegiance to U2 and continued my campaign of writing their lyrics on all my school exercise books.

Stealing It Back

Then, in 1988, *Rattle and Hum* was released. I still recollect the first listen to the album, in my bedroom, always in the dark. It was so profound. I can remember being confused by the opening to 'Helter Skelter' – 'this is the song that Charles Manson stole from the Beatles, we're stealing it back!' howled Bono. Quite who Charles Manson was and that 'Helter Skelter' was originally a Beatles track completely passed me by. It didn't matter that I didn't get any of the references: it was pompous and I loved it. Then I bought the video. I don't think I have ever been as jealous in my life. It was a sick spreading jealousy for all the people there, in the audience, watching U2. I still hadn't been to a single gig and I had no idea how you could get to be in the presence of that greatness. It became my main life ambition to see U2 play. Phil Joanou's direction on that video was hugely influential on my desire to see U2 play: the huge sweeping shots of the crowd, arms aloft, singing in ecstatic unity. The circling helicopter shots of stadia with the blinking lights and the cresting roar of the audience reaching upwards, it seemed to me, to heaven. The section I watched most obsessively was 'Bullet the Blue Sky', where the lights on stage were dim red until Bono crouched down and lit up [guitarist] The Edge with a blazing white spotlight, then kept swinging the beam between the guitar solo and the audience. There was something about that use of the spotlight that linked the audience to the band and I longed to be illuminated by that light. If I keep writing in quasi-religious tones that's because that's what U2 meant to me: they were something transcendental. In 1989 I went to university. Just as 'Madchester' and the Second Summer of Love was starting in the North [of England] I headed to a small, remote university on an isolated promontory sticking into the cold North Sea. In this corner of Scotland the likelihood that my musical education was going to take off was about as bleak as the weather. Looking back at my 18-year-old self I want to shake her and question that decision: why would any teenager choose to isolate themselves from any form of excitement and experience that effectively? I know the answer, though. Music was still a recorded medium for me: I had a developing collection of cassettes and even some new-fangled CDs in 1989 (Prince's *Sign o'the Times* [1987] and a 'best of' Simon and Garfunkel), but live music was still completely out with my existence: it simply didn't occur to me that had I gone to Manchester or Leeds I would have been able to see bands play, because I had never seen a live band it didn't occur to me to apply to a university where this state of affairs might change. However, on the first night at university I met the girl in the room next to me in Halls of Residence, Heather, and she was from Northern Ireland. The first question I asked was whether she was a U2 fan, and she was. That night we listened to 'Pride (In the Name of Love)' [1984] and swore that we would go to see our heroes when they went on tour. Suddenly, I was a grown up.

It took until 1992 for that promise to ourselves to come true. In the meantime I became an 'indie kid' and wandered St Andrews listening to The Pixies and The Stone Roses and sticking my nose up at local heroes, The Proclaimers. Deep down I still loved U2 but that love didn't match my Dr Martens [boots] and purple hooded tops, so I didn't mention it. But, somewhere inside, that jealousy for the people who had seen U2 still seethed. And then, one day, I was reading the *NME* [*New Musical Express*] and I saw that U2 tickets were going on sale in Glasgow later that week at the SECC (Scottish Exhibition and Conference Centre). I flew round to see my friend Heather and we decided that not only would we get tickets but that we would sleep out all night to get them. This was impossibly glamorous for me: not only to see this band but to be brave enough to sleep out all night on the mean freezing streets of Glasgow to get the tickets. This was true commitment.

In reality, we ended up laid on foam mats inside the hall of the SECC all night along with thousands of other fans. I recollect the sense of camaraderie in the room: we were U2 fans and we were united, or so it seemed to me. Across the hall people who were better prepared than us had brought ghetto blasters and we sang along to the hits somewhat self-consciously and cheered afterwards as a form of warm-up for the main event that would happen in this self-same hall a month-or-so afterwards. At some point we were given a plastic wristband which confirmed that we were in the queue and that we would definitely get the tickets that had seemed so desperately unattainable to me five years before. I can almost see myself writing out the £38 cheque for two tickets (an amount I could ill-afford) and then getting the ticket in my hand. I was going to see U2. In person.

FIGURE 12.1 The ticket as legacy and memory.

The gig itself was on 18 June 1992 so university term had ended and I had returned to Watford for the summer. I recollect being panicked that the train to Glasgow would be delayed and that I would miss my heroes but I arrived mid-afternoon into a surprisingly warm day. I was so excited that I couldn't eat. My entire sustenance for that day was Fanta and some Polo mints. As people who had queued all night we were stood in a separate pen near the front of the SECC and we positioned ourselves next to the walkway that jutted out into the crowd so the band would be within two metres of us when they went to play. What the gig was like is lost to me now; I just have fragments of recollection. I remember Bono being stood right in front of me to sing into a camera and him pouring champagne over the audience. Now I don't know whether some drops of champagne did touch me or not but, at the time, I claimed they had. After having spent a hot day travelling and then not eating enough I was faint and a bit sick and I remember fighting the security guards who were trying to pull me over the barrier to recover. There was no way I was giving up my plum vantage spot. Afterwards I was exhausted and stunned. I had seen U2 play. I had been this close to Bono and the others. I had the t-shirt. My diary entry for that evening is incoherent because I was simply overwhelmed. Without any personal frame of reference for what a great live concert might be like it all seemed incredible to me. The stage set was very different to the sparsity of the 'Rattle and Hum' video, with a jumble of TV screens heaped by the side of the stage flashing ironic statements. During 'Mysterious Ways' [1991] the roadies came out in bellydancer costumes and gyrated provocatively along the walkway which is, oddly, the image that has stayed with me the most clearly, probably due to the surreal nature of it. I hadn't realized the physicality of the live arena experience: the sweat, sore feet, ringing ears, elbows in the solar plexus or aching throat from singing your heart out. It might have hurt more than I had envisaged but I wanted more.

Since that day I have been to countless gigs, festivals and events. I've seen U2 play at Wembley three times, Murrayfield, Earl's Court and I'll see them at the O2 later this year. They aren't perhaps the coolest band to admit to loving, I suspect that if I was more disingenuous and hadn't grown up as a square in Watford I would have written about seeing The Flaming Lips at Sheffield City Hall or Pulp in Leeds before *Different Class* [1995] came out. The 1992 me, in her U2 t-shirt, was replaced by a far thinner, more sophisticated and much more musically educated me who saw pretty much everyone in the '90s. Virtually every weekend I would be on the train across the country to see Dinosaur Jr at Manchester University, Sleeper at the Leeds Town and Country Club or My Life Story at Dingwalls in Camden. That urge to be part of the crowd, to be one of the dedicated few, has never left me. There is something about that arena concert experience that is addictive to me. Often the evening promises so much more than the music actually delivers, but that doesn't stop the urge to go to see the next band play. I remember feeling wretched after spending £150 to take my sister to see Madonna at Earl's Court and spending the whole concert feeling dissatisfied because we weren't a crowd, we were merely an audience: there to witness Madonna's performance without being invited to participate in it. Then I remember seeing the Beastie Boys at Manchester Evening News Arena and hating the fact we were seated. You just shouldn't be sat down in the presence of the Beastie Boys. The worst one was probably Blur at Sheffield Motorpoint Arena in the late '90s when I was frustrated at the teenyboppers singing along to 'Parklife' [1994] and then found myself fancying a dad collecting his pre-teen daughter. Somehow, it marked a point where I had moved from being one of the crowd to being simply a member of the audience.

Arctic Monkeys Rock Stage: Evan Shelton

When I was 8, I went to see the Arctic Monkeys in Newcastle at the Metro Radio Arena. At that point I knew some of the Monkeys' songs from the album Humbug *[2009] – I only knew these from when Mum would play that album in the car. Anyway, I still loved these songs and knew them word by word. I particularly liked the song 'Cornerstone' so when Mum told me we were going I couldn't wait to hear it live.*

The arena seemed huge to me. The biggest place I'd been in to see music before was probably the Leeds Town Hall. The other scary thing about it was the sheer amount of people and how they were so huge – I felt quite claustrophobic even though I'm fine with small spaces. The demographic was mainly drunk students with a peppering of thirty to forty year olds sat down. The students were a bit angry at times from not being too sober. At one point, there was a bloody fight that I had to look away from. All of that sounded a bit extreme, I bet, but that happened a long way away and I felt safe with Mum by my side.

Inside, we were in seats because I was under 14. Although I'm not sure I would've liked to be in the 'Hell on Earth' down at the front. Everything around me stank of beer, which I realised was not a one-off as I went to more gigs, and my shoes were almost glued to the ground with stale alcohol. It seemed forever until the band would actually come on and the atmosphere got increasingly more static. Suddenly, it spiked as the Arctic Monkeys came on.

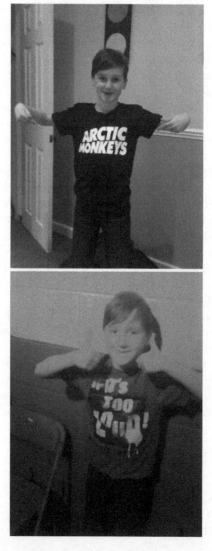

FIGURE 12.2 Before and after.

I could not believe it. I was in the same room as Alex Turner. I could only see the side of his head, and was a mile away from him, but I was still in the same room as Alex Turner. I cheered and whooped wildly as the band entered the stage. They went straight in with the first song and I realised just from a few seconds of hearing it just how different live music is from recorded music. Live music is just there. It can't just be tuned out and be the background for a light chat. It surrounds you and it is definitely not even – in any way – contained.

Another fundamental difference is how the songs they played were just so loud! The vibrations pulsated through my body. I could physically feel them travelling up from my feet. Even with the earplugs my Mum handed me, the noise was still the loudest thing I'd ever heard. I didn't know what the lyrics of the songs were unless they were on Humbug. *But I could still copy the choruses of them. There was a strange routine I used where if I knew the song I would stand up. This was fun but I felt quite awkward doing that because everyone else around me would be sat down. Towards the end of the gig, I was exhausted and then I found out the beauty of having a seat – being able to sit down.*

Walking out, I felt part of a family, especially with the band t-shirt I was wearing. I didn't feel afraid of the drunks for they just seemed to be enjoying the experience rather than being violent. Obviously not everything was perfect – there were still the odd cases of bad language being exchanged but I kept my head up high. I didn't mind the masses of people crowding round me so much and I didn't have to stick to my Mum all the time.

For ages I waited for them to play the aforementioned Cornerstone *but they just didn't play it. They didn't play my favourite song. Whilst that was deeply gutting, I heard a song called 'Don't Sit Down 'Cause I've Moved Your Chair', which became my new favourite song. I wanted to get it on disc so I bought the album it was on,* Suck it and See [2011]. *This led to my collection of the Monkeys' albums. Because of one gig, I became a proper fan of The Arctic Monkeys.*

Three years on, I went to see Jeff Wayne's The War of the Worlds [1978] *for my twelfth birthday. It was at the First Direct Arena in Leeds – it had a much bigger capacity than the Metro in Newcastle. It was a very different experience altogether: I didn't have my ear drums almost shattered, there were a lot more people, and that time the demographic was thirty- to fifty-year-olds, and some kids. But there was still the pre-show static atmosphere and feeling of family there, as well as the euphoria of being near huge stars, namely Jason Donovan!*

Conclusion

My son has grown up at festivals and been to gigs on school nights. His childhood has been far more musical than mine was. This was a definite and conscious decision: I wanted him to be substantially cooler than I had

FIGURE 12.3 Finding what you are looking for . . .

been at his age. But it's really easy to see concerts now: as long as you have an internet connection and patience you are likely to be able to see whoever you want to see, wherever you want. Your phone dings weekly with updates of who is on the road and how to get 'priority tickets'. And I'm sad for my son that he won't ever get that experience of sleeping out all night just to get tickets to see his heroes.

From here, I can look back on that freckly, gawky girl and see what a big deal it was to go to her first arena gig. And that experience was so much more than just the gig itself – that's the part I don't remember very clearly at all. It was the years of desire and yearning, and then the fulfilment. I found what I was looking for.

Notes

1   The histographic approach to memory is something developed and used in the journal *Memory Studies*. The development of memory studies is significant in recognizing and unpicking how history has been created and this can be through distortion and fabrication and narrativization. The creation of legend is paramount and in the arena there is a status attached to the group by virtue of the space, by their performance in charts, by their social standing and so on. The legend is not purely conferred by the concert or the venue but by a complex interrelationship of the physical space, the events that happen within and the legacy of the event that continues after.

2   On the concept of the cultural memorial, see Edward Chaney (2006).

PART FOUR

Arena Media

CHAPTER THIRTEEN

The Aesthetics of the Arena: Live and Recorded

Robert Edgar

Introduction

The physical space of the arena confers a sense of legitimacy on the performer/s which is both at one with and at odds with the nature of economic success. The intimate venue is the preserve of the few or rather the deceit of the many, as evidenced by the number of people who claim to have been present at the infamous Sex Pistols gig at the Manchester Free Trade Hall in 1976.[1] The arena thus provides a space for the majority to have access to the performer/s who can command this kind of space. This chapter explores the nature of aesthetic authenticity as the defining factor in the relationship between audience and performer/s which, while evident in the smaller venue, is legitimized by an appearance in the arena as a site of 'success' and mass appeal. Furthermore, this analysis identifies the recorded arena concert as an aesthetic entity in its own right, rather than being simply a recording of a 'legitimate' performance. In this sense, this chapter argues, the arena concert film cannot be understood in straightforward postmodern terms; it is not a copy without an original, it is the original.

The topography of the arena

The arena is a simple space to map out, and while there are differences between different arenas in terms of size and seating, such arenas remain fundamentally the same. The audience is largely distant from the performer/s, but sit or stand looking at one central staging area as often flanked by screens. And, while occasionally there may be a thrust or curtain stage, this is by no means the norm. This arrangement is no different to the smaller and more intimate venue; an equivalent staging area often exists with an audience facing forward in ranks. Often the real difference is in the repurposing of the arena venue, and its potential for rearrangements: transforming it from one thing to the next. This quantitative difference in physical space between the arena and the smaller venue of course allows for a different kind of access to the performer, and a different kind of access to the show. The smaller venue suggests intimacy, although access to the performer is still limited. In fact proximity, rather than access, is provided by the space – but there is a conceptual conflation of the two. While the pleasure inherent in proximity should not be underestimated there is, however, an inherent paradox in this. The smaller venue allows for proximity to the performer, but by virtue of seeing this performer in such a setting the performer is effectively of a different standing to the act that can command an arena.

An analysis of topography is not limited to discussion of physical space; this would be to negate a large part of the experience of the concert event. More difficult to identify is the semiotic space that the arena occupies and confers. By this I mean the process of signification that occurs from the recognition and unification of multiple signifiers. To borrow from Christian Metz, in developing an understanding of the channels of communication of the arena, it would prove useful to provide a list of signifiers that are allowed, in part by the architecture of the arena itself. Metz identifies: 1, The Visual Image; 2, Print and other Graphics; 3, Speech; 4, Music; 5, Noise (SFX) (see Metz 1974). Without question there are expectations held by an audience before they arrive at the venue, and these are the expectations that have to factor in shaping the experience. But that experience itself can be broken down into several strands, or 'channels of communication', that make up the arena event:

The Arena Concert Channels of Communication:

- The performer/s
- The ticket (real or virtual)/Wristband
- The entrance lobby/stairwells
- Video screens plus what then appears on the screens
- Specifics of staging
- Support bands
- Other visual FX
- Walk-in music
- Support and guest performer/s (playing with the main performer/s)

- Merchandise
- 'Unofficial channels' including audience costume, social media, etc.

The physical environment then provides the parameters of meaning and the individual channels of communication become unified within its walls. What is significant is that even at the base level of signification the band/performer is only one element of the communication in operation. But, in similar fashion to Metz's prioritization of the visual image in cinema, the band/performer, it must be argued, find themselves assuming just such a priority in these channels. (And they also have an extra-'textual' function in that they are known about prior to the concert.) Many of these facets of the performance could apply to live events in other venues but only acts of a certain stature will play an arena, and in these terms the space itself functions like a genre in framing certain expectations which are met, or not. The physical space of the arena thus acts like a cinemascope screen; we are free to look wherever we want but everything within our gaze is part of the performance. Part of the communicative dimension of the space is in its physical shape and size – a 'channel' not afforded to the recorded medium. However, in terms of a process of signification, the smaller venue may have many of these elements as well.

On the part of the audience there is inevitably knowledge of a band prior to seeing them on stage, and there will be an aesthetic on entering which frames the experience, and there will be walk-in music, etc. The difference between the general run of live popular music events as they have occurred and the relatively new phenomenon of the multimedia-heavy arena concert is the scale of that which happens on the stage. And yet, nominally, the performance is more about the music and the band than the show. This suggests that the simple process of signification in itself is not enough in terms of theorizing arena concerts. That process provides a framework to consider the elements of the concert but is not sufficiently wide-ranging, and so its results fall short of a definitive status, and engenders further questions of an aesthetic response to arena and the performer/s who work in them.

The mediated arena

Mediation as a concept is not as simple as the idea of the recording of an event. The mediation of an arena concert is undertaken by the business machine that surrounds performer/s. This evidences important questions about the economic pressure of the arena concert tour; a concert is inevitably part of a tour and has to be seen by many people. The recent tour of Jeff Wayne's 1978 *The War of the Worlds*, that landed at the Leeds First Direct Arena, was witnessed on one night (6 December 2014) by some 13,500 people, with the venue sold out. However this mass was only a fraction of those who would see the show on tour, which took in another seventeen venues in the UK alone. And this is, of course, only the most recent incarnation of a show which has previously been seen by countless thousands, with only minor variations in performance; your age dictates whether you see/didn't see Richard Burton or Liam Neeson, Justin Hayward or Jason Donovan. The subsequent recording of the live event is intended to meet the needs of those who went to the concert, those who couldn't get to the concert and those who would wish to revisit the performance. The event is at once a kinetic act which, while rehearsed and polished to the nth degree, is transient. The performance is also an advert for a DVD/download, as well as the t-shirt and the album, and all the previous albums.[2]

The nature of contemporary mediated performance has been theoretically undercut by the democratization of media – by the ability we have to record the event ourselves. The act of recording on a mobile phone is of a different order to the concert film; the pushing and shoving of a small venue allows for the aesthetic of the venue to be captured on the device, as countless YouTube bootlegs attest. This focus is something that cannot occur in the arena. If the vantage point or zoom setting is up close, then all that might be captured is an extreme high angle shot of Sting's knee or The Edge's digital delay pedal; to be at the back of a raked seating bank captures the reality of the arena venue but also the feeling that you are watching ants on the stage. What tends to be captured in this instance is the video screen: a video of a video of something that might be happening on stage. Watching through screens is part of the act of viewing, and the sight of the mobile phone is now quite normal in all venues. It is the universal presence of this mode of recording that further legitimizes the arena concert film as being of a different order.

The crucial facets of the arena concert film arise partly from the geography that defines the film, and partly the perceived experience that the film captures, but also from the fact that someone else has recorded this event – a professional, and not a fan lost in the audience. This dynamic is immediately apparent in the arena concert film *Who Put The 'M' in Manchester?* (Bucky Fukumoto, 2005), documenting Morrissey's 'homecoming' Manchester Arena concert of 2004, on the occasion of his birthday. The film opens with a close-up of a Morrissey tattoo, followed by a pan up the arm to the interview subject, an emotional fan, standing outside the entrance to the arena itself ('He's always meant the world to me . . . We came from California, we flew all the way here from San Diego, me and my girlfriend, and we're so happy to be here. We know that we just couldn't miss this day . . . Nothing can beat this day.'), and then to shots of the city and locale, and news report-like footage of fans queuing and finally to Establish Shots from the back of the arena as Morrissey enters. This smooth reportage, melding witnesses and event, the intimate with the enormous, provides legitimacy to the recording, as sanctioned and conferred by the band, by the venue and by the fact that someone deemed that event and that moment in time to be captured, and so employed a crew of professional film-makers to do so. This furthers the sense of a sociocultural value to what is in essence a product for sale, 'just' a commodity. This is the difficult irony inherent, then, in Peter Gabriel's talk of Steve Biko's fate as intrinsic to his concert and artistic formation and the wider agency of popular music, or Bono bemoaning the plight of the Global South, a trait now inseparable from his public persona. At the end of this process is sales and dissemination: both are simply paid for such proclamations. Thus worthy proclamation and tawdry promotion shade into one another.

There are then differing levels of mediation, from the 'unofficial' footage of the moment in which the audience member captures a performance 'as it happens', to the professional and 'official' reconstruction of the event for commercial release. But in whatever form it may take, mediation of the live concert occurs at a communicative level (the meaning imbued by the band being in that space) and through the nature of the recording (the spatio-temporal facet of the recording). The archived recording of the arena concert then functions as a separate artefact, to be enjoyed/utilized/cherished later – and, perhaps once uploaded onto the internet, forever. The professional recording and the fan-filmed video both function as ways of shaping memory rather than capturing a moment in time. The fan video is the personal memory, even when posted to a public forum like Vimeo or YouTube. This is 'as it was seen by me'. The official arena concert recording is effectively the public face of the band: 'as it is meant to be seen'. The authorized view of the band thus functions as (or, more accurately, aspires to) collective memory. It is the single source which is then hyped and advertised, is associated with an album, which appears on broadcast television, and which is timeless and repetitive – becoming, eventually, the only available document of that performer's moment in history. And even the performer begins to find that the official narrative is, somehow, incredible:

> Meanwhile, somehow alive, I am New York's 'hottest ticket', as a stinky and steamy July brings me to the [Madison Square] Garden's vast and lavish dressing rooms. I sit by a grand piano awaiting the evening's call-time . . . I am afforded all of the luxuries and attention and private bathrooms where Elvis Presley had soaked before me, and as I lower myself onto the very toilet that where Elvis had no doubt whistled away the call of nature, I wonder how all of this could possibly be, yet at the same time I am confused by its naturalness and its *right* to be. (Morrissey 2013, 192)

The arena stands as different to other forms of concert: the venue is, as it were, as big as the band (in size, if not always in name). And there is a particular cultural cache associated with venues such as Madison Square Garden. But these venues are few in number. For other sites of performance, particularly the open-air festival, the performance is limited by the available geography of the lay-out, and the available technology in the field (reference pretty much any headline act on the Glastonbury main stage, with its vast hinterland of massed audiences, for whom the video screens are the only access to the event). Other events such as Live Aid venues, in 1985, presented similar problems for bands. Such sites allow the artists to perform but they don't allow them the control over their performance that the arena affords. In these terms the festival field, the open air stadium or the small club venue function in the same way, where the performance is central. In creating a visual recording of the arena concert – now pretty much de rigueur for all arena world tours – this level of control is vital, and the opportunity to evidence the full nature of the show via showing such control is crucial. This suggests a conceptual relationship between the arena, as a venue, and the recording that happens therein. However this relationship is a problematic idea in respect of the concert film, and to suggest that the concert film is simply a recording of an event is to negate its existence as an aesthetic object distinct to the performance to which it is perceived to relate.

The arena concert instinct

In *The Art Instinct*, Denis Dutton outlined his view of evolutionary aesthetics. In part, this approach takes a view on art (and in this case the concept he develops is being applied to the arena concert as such a form of 'art') which stands as separate from the ideological or cultural analysis of music. Dutton identifies twelve potential functions of the object in respect of artistic status, which Torres (2010) lists as:

Direct pleasure
Skill and virtuosity
Style
Novelty and creativity
Criticism
Representation
Special Focus
Expressive Individuality
Emotional Saturation
Intellectual Challenge
Art traditions and Institutions
Imaginative Experience

The tradition of assessing, for instance, subcultures and music, is well established, and there have to be enough reminiscences, academic texts and documentaries on the importance of, say, punk rock and its contexts (i.e. its times and places). In terms of the present discussion, it can be said that what popular music allows for is an established analysis of music/image/performance as in unity – that is, with all the elements of style and performance and musicality as integrated. It is in this unity, and in the creation of the arena concert film, that it is possible to see direct connections with Dutton's perspective on the development of the aesthetic object.

There is something fundamentally specific about the arena and the function that environment serves. This specificity is in relation to the sense of a form of grandeur – in a comparable way in which there is 'gritty' legitimacy conferred on an artist exhibiting in a pop-up gallery, for a performer playing music in CBGBs in New York, King Tut's Wah-Wah Hut in Glasgow or even the Adelphi on DeGrey Street in Hull. The arena functions as a national gallery might; a sense of heightened status conferred by the exalted environment. And with this comes the placing of a set of artistic values on the performer/s. This is different from the cultural capital a band may or may not have and, paradoxically, may be inversely proportionate to their critical appeal (as with Justin Bieber's 2012 Believe tour for instance, in which the massed fans seemed to wrong-foot the dismissive critics). The very status, as 'artist' or 'artists' (indeed the very term: as opposed to 'band' or 'group' or 'singer'), is enhanced by the arena venue. This seems to be a fact not lost on Morrissey: the poster of his 2014 tour of North America pronounced him playing venues such as the Barclays Center with Sir Cliff Richard and the Los Angeles Sports Arena with Sir Tom Jones while Moz, sporting a pinstriped suit, leans casually on an alabaster statue. Morrissey is no longer toying with distinctions between different levels of aesthetic value (one thinks of his idiosyncratic engagements with 'low culture' across the 1990s): he is playing arenas, and this is, self-consciously, an 'event', and he is performing as a work of art.[3]

This is a performance that is understood to have no intrinsic value other than as artistic object, and in fact it may hold back the evolution of the form.[4] Dutton's consideration of the nature of the aesthetic object is one that looks to 'skill, style and a sense of accomplishment – [as those] values we admire in art. It is human intelligence and creativity that transforms appealing landscape scenes and plot outlines into works of painterly or literary art' (Dutton 2010, 136). And this is what Morrissey achieves in composite fashion. He himself precedes the event with a body of work (songs, performance and legend) and this becomes part of the arena performance. This is no different from Jack White at the Leeds First Direct Arena in November 2014: blues heritage and indie superhero here unify in a performance that is predicated on knowledge and understanding of both of these aspects from the audience. And the fact that this tour only took in four UK venues forces the audience to travel to stare in awe at this particular work of art (possibly in the same way that people travel to the Louvre and stare at the *Mona Lisa*, just to say they have); enjoying the performer's work may be secondary. However, this is to focus on the live performance and it is noteworthy that these performers often try to ban the recording of their performances, even on mobile devices (as with Prince's UK tour in 2014) – thus the (enforced) mystique of the transitory performance remains. Until, of course, the official recording is released for sale.

The arena concert film: Even better than the real thing

To view an arena concert film is not, of course, to view a concert. It is not even to view the recording of a concert. To risk a tautology: to view an arena concert film is to view an arena concert film. And to view one as 'original' and the other as a 'fake' is, in Jean Baudrillard's terms (1994), a fallacy; to read the recording of the arena concert as a simulation is to fail to recognize the separate and distinct function it serves. The arena concert film is not a facet of the hyperreal, in being an ontologically questionable copy of something authentic – a process of reproduction which positions the concert itself as the 'original'. Indeed, the notion of the original is not as straightforward as the existence of the one *Mona Lisa*: the arena concert film captures one concert of many in a tour, or assembles bits of each as blended into one. The sense of one point of origin begins to slip away, and so this line of argument is therefore of negligible use. The arena concert film is an object in its own right and the recording of the event highlights it as an artefact of a different order. The concert film functions in addition to and separate to the physical performance, and is a wholly different aesthetic object. In *The Critique of Pure Reason* (1781/1787), Kant observes:

> When we say that the intuition of external objects, and also the self-intuition of the subject, represent both, objects and subjects, in space and time, as they affect our senses, that is, as they appear – this is by no means equivalent to asserting that these objects are mere illusory appearances. For when we speak of things as phenomena, the objects, nay, even the properties which we ascribe to them, are looked upon as really given: only that, in so far as this or that property depends upon the mode of intuition of the subject, in the relation of the given object to the subject, the object as phenomenon is to be distinguished from the object as a thing in itself. (Kant 1993, 66)

In reductionist terms, a useful distinction here arises: the object as phenomenon (the live concert), and the object-in-itself (the live concert film). And the relationship between the two is muddied by a series of perceptions and values imparted by the concert-goer/film-watcher.[5] And these values, as I've argued here, predate the live event. Thus, in aesthetic terms, the arena concert film is predicated on sociocultural knowledge of the performer/s and the ritual of the arena performance, despite the subtle differences that might exist. The dependence of the arena concert film on a sense of a veracity of reportage is predicated on the perception of the performance.

There is a clear facet to the recognition of the concert film being of a wholly different order to the experience of the live concert itself. The camera allows access that an audience would have otherwise missed. In an age of digital recordings of concerts presented in 3D on IMAX screens, this access can best be described as forensic. The sensory overload associated with the live experience in the arena space is replaced by the clarity of the recording, and unimpeded vision. However, this wholly different order is about more than this; it is about a sense of authenticity as endowed by the recording itself. The film of the event is not a record of something which is understood to be authentic or legitimate. The arena is already a space where the performer is distant, and thus both removed and objectified. It is a space where the event is already lacking when compared to the concert film, and yet the space is the space of this event (it allows it, and it houses it), so both of these matters occur at the same time. The recording of the event is more than a record of something that happened and was witnessed by others. It is an aesthetic object in its own right, and one which serves a social function in which a unity of audience and performer are the essence. To refer to the arena concert film as an artefact would be to imply it is in existence as a result of a preceding concert or tour. This is true in a literal sense, that one object could not exist without the other, but this is a necessity of production rather than an influence on viewing. In a fiction film it is essential that actors are sought, scripts finished, locations dressed and so on. All of this work is hidden and it is better that an audience doesn't know about this so that the object stands in its own right. The same is true of the concert video; confusion between forms may exist where there is a use/creation of a sense of preparation for a performance, or direct interaction with the audience. These are constructions or selections and are established to give the illusion of a connection to a 'real' event when this is forever absent – it has to be as the arena concert film is of a different aesthetic order.

Dutton identifies the difference between nominal and expressive authenticity in respect of an audience's aesthetic appreciation of an event. The sense of nominal authenticity is conferred on a performance by the presence of the performer/group; this suggests an intention and that there is provenance to the work. In these terms the intention is to perform for an audience and the provenance is the visual evidence that an event took place, even though the film doesn't provide connection to that event. A sense of expressive authenticity is conferred by an individual witnessing that performance. Audiences, even on a large-scale arena world tour, are limited and access to the concert and thus the experience of the performance is also limited. The recording of the event therefore serves a second-level aesthetic function, in that the image of the performance and the audience witnessing that performance become one unified object, sutured together, and this in turn represents an expressive authenticity. This is to suggest that the earlier identification of the cinema screen in a semiotic sense (i.e. the use of semiotics in terms of the analysis of cinema) collapses in the wake of the aesthetic function of the recorded artefact. Or, put another way: a semiotic consideration provides a viable method of analysing how meaning is communicated, but it does not capture the experience of viewing a concert film. It is in the viewing of the concert film that expressive authenticity is conferred but the perception of it existing within the film means it remains as nominally authentic.

In Dutton's terms, evolutionary aesthetics allows for the consideration of different acts and the qualities they embody for an audience and it is these qualities that further confer a sense of authenticity for and of a recording. This is the case after the passage of time or after a group has disbanded or a performer has died. Bands such as Dire Straits (for *Alchemy: Dire Straits Live*, directed by Peter Sinclair and first released in 1984) or Queen (for the film of the 1986 performance *Queen at Wembley*, directed by Gavin Taylor and first released in 1990) have slipped in and out of public favour. The music may not necessarily be enjoyed, or even liked. But the close-ups of Mark Knopfler's virtuoso guitar playing, or Freddie Mercury's showmanship, are respected. In these terms the aesthetic authenticity of the whole remains intact.

The question of reception and aesthetic appreciation can be interrupted, or even overwhelmed, by a difference in temporal location. That is, years later we may find things funny when they were supposed to be deadly serious. Thus there is a fracturing of the authentic: we can see the mechanics of the performance, as if suddenly revealed in isolation, and this shatters the unity of the whole. Nowhere is this more evident than in *Peter Gabriel: Live in Athens* (Michael Chapman, 1987). There is pomposity in the performance which is accentuated by the production values, and an 'excessive' over-choreography; these risible qualities in the film transcend the performance of the songs. A live album version would stand as another aesthetic object and, blind to the 1987 performance, would probably work. As it is, the negotiation of the status of the arena has an effect which subsumes the music and negates its positive qualities. The film is, in theory, underscored by the aesthetic quality provided by Michael Chapman and the fact that the executive producer is Martin Scorsese. It is undeniable that there are high production values, and many people may enjoy the music, but together they lack the authenticity required of the artistic artefact. In this example there is a loss of authenticity in respect of a perceived live event, and more particularly a sense of fakery as a concert film: 'Forgery and other forms of fakery in the arts misrepresent the nature of the performance and so misrepresent achievement' (Dutton 2010, 187). The status of the authentic is never fully conferred on *Peter Gabriel: Live in Athens* where the performance loses its reference to the environment and to the audience. In fact the 'performance' seems wholly out of context for an arena venue – an irony when compared to the theatrics of Gabriel's earlier stage endeavours, particularly with Genesis. The result is that concert film creates its own signifiers which do not relate to the arena concert or the concert film; Tony Levin's coat has a lot to answer for. The presence of the audience in an arena concert film remains as a vital aspect for the film's viewing audience. The presence of the audience signifies a liveness and kineticism (in a perceived original) and ensures the perceived connection to the live event; *Live in Athens* focuses attention on the performers and while an audience are clearly there (we glimpse them and can hear some cheers) they fail to be referenced by the performers, or the performance, in the way we might expect from a live performance – and certainly not integrated in the way that we see in other arena concert films. This further fractures a sense of authenticity, and makes the live performance look fake, and this perception of forgery then extends to the film. While one would be tempted to look to Brecht's 'Alienation' technique, in terms of an aesthetic discourse that reveals its own workings (consciously or otherwise), and contrast this favourably with the sutured 'Spectacle' that Debord diagnoses (as discussed elsewhere in the current volume), a more useful comparison can be made with film critic and painter Manny Farber's 1962 dichotomy of 'white elephant art' and 'terminate art' (1998, 134–144). The former is self-consciously important, hubristic and bloated, and essentially redundant (and so, for Farber, fairly natural for Hollywood film-making of certain periods). The latter holds no direct claims to importance or artistic integrity but, having adopted a given vernacular at the outset, begins to subvert meaning, usurp expectations, derail narrative and so burrows into the substance of (and from there destabilizes) the expected discourse. For Farber, such 'termite' artistic strategies were often and intriguingly present in film noir and Hollywood B-movies. A termite art in the arena concert film would seem to need the film to be achieved on its own grounds: acknowledging, at the outset, a need to construct a language that is self-contained and exploratory of this new form of film, and not aggrandizing and 'cashing in on' the legitimacy that the arena space confers on the performer.

The standing of Jonathan Demme's *Stop Making Sense* (1984) is as a film, along with it being a film of a concert, as well being a film of the group Talking Heads, and it has equal levels of nominal and expressive authenticity. Here the status of the film as an object in its own right is more fully realized. The performer and the audience fuse into one and this renders the film as nominally authentic in its aesthetic function. The person witnessing the performance is the person at the cinema/at home who thus confers the expressive authentic aesthetic function. This is different from the simple semiotic reception of a series of signifiers. The function is the conferment of a sense of beauty which, in terms of pop/rock music, is essentially about witnessing something that stands in its own right.

Notes

1 Indeed, the contested nature of this specific has become the subject of a book in itself – *I Swear I Was There*; see Nolan (2006).
2 The original album, which has been reissued in various restored and high-performance formats, has also had foreign language, remixed and re-performed releases. In these respects, Wayne's continual live explorations of the album are comparable to Roger Waters's returns to *The Wall*, as discussed elsewhere in this volume. The original concept album was loosely based on H. G. Wells's 1898 science fiction novel *The War of the Worlds*.
3 See, for example, 'The National Front Disco' (from 1992's *Your Arsenal*), 'The Boy Racer' (from 1995's *Southpaw Grammar*) or 'Roy's Keen' (from 1997's *Maladjusted*). This notion of importance finds a place, rather crassly, in the concert film *Morrissey 25Live* (recorded at Hollywood High School, Los Angeles in 2013, and directed by James Russell). A microphone is passed around emotional audience members, mid-concert, who address Morrissey directly, in terms of the importance of his music for them. This is qualitatively different, in formal terms at least, from the opening interview of *Who Put the 'M' in Manchester?* since Morrissey is now present, as if a feudal lord receiving the expected praise from his subjects. The idea seems lifted from a spontaneous trope of gigs by The Fall in the 1990s, in which the microphone, wrested from or abandoned by singer Mark E. Smith, would be used by rowdy audience members sympathetic to the marginalization (rather than elevation) of the singer, announced with their now amplified cries of 'He is not appreciated!' For Goddard and Halligan (2010), Morrissey and Mark E. Smith effectively represent polar opposites in terms of cultural baggage, sentimentality, nostalgia for the 1970s North of England and so on, and how this relates to their audiences. The difference seems to be between wanting to be told of one's worth, and finding oneself told of one's worth, respectively.
4 This is akin then to the issue of peacock's tail, as discussed by Dutton (2010, 136–137).
5 Dutton also draws on Kant's perspective on dependent beauty; see Dutton (2010, 189).

CHAPTER FOURTEEN

We Made This Together: How *Awesome; I Fuckin' Shot That!* Foresaw Changes in the Live Concert Experience Brought about by Digital Technology and Social Media

Neil Fox

Put that shit away! – the contemporary situation

This chapter explores the practice of recording arena experiences through portable devices and sharing them online via social media platforms. Furthermore it suggests that the 2006 Beastie Boys concert film *Awesome: I Fuckin' Shot That* (Hörnblowér 2006), documenting a New York show by the band at Madison Square Gardens, explicitly recognizes the arena audience as participants. The film also discusses the role audiences can play in documenting an arena experience. The chapter analyses the practice of recording arena events from a contentious and contemporary starting point before discussing the practice as something participatory and alternative and involving creative and democratic elements of the capturing and sharing of everyday life. The chapter highlights how the film, referred to throughout as *Awesome*, contains these various elements and reflects different sides of the debate between audience and artist on a practice referred to throughout as the practice or this practice.

In a May 2014 interview with *Rolling Stone* magazine Jack White shared his opinion on audience members engaging with their phones at his concerts saying 'people can't clap anymore, because they've got a [. . .] texting thing in their [. . .] hand' before making the statement 'I let the crowd tell me what to do. There's no set list. [. . .] If they can't give me that energy back? Maybe I'm wasting my time' (Rolling Stone 2014).

The sentiment contained in Jack White's quote echoes that in other artists' responses to the practice of engaging with phones on the part of an audience. Artists such as She & Him, Yeah Yeah Yeahs and Savages have issued notices to fans entering arenas for concerts asking for mobile phones not to be used during the performances. For Yeah Yeah Yeahs:

PLEASE DO NOT WATCH THE
SHOW THROUGH A SCREEN ONYOUR
SMART DEVICE/CAMERA.
PUT THAT SHIT AWAY as a
courtesy to the person behind you
and to Nick, Karen and Brian.
MUCH LOVE AND MANY THANKS!YEAH YEAH YEAHS

This sign was displayed at a 2013 New York Webster Hall concert at which Yeah Yeah Yeahs issued a request to refrain from recording the show in various forms citing it as courteous to both other audience members and the band. A similar sign at a Savages show claimed that using phones prevented audiences from being immersed in the event and urged everyone to 'make the evening special, silence your phones'. She & Him directly referenced the practice when they asked that 'people not use their cell phones to take pictures and video, but instead enjoy the show they have put together in 3D' (White 2013). The issuing of these signs suggests clear beliefs from artists that the use of technology for recording and sharing the performance in the arena context is detrimental to that performance and the entirety of the audience's experience.

In a July 2014 review of a Jack White Hammersmith Apollo concert around the time of the Rolling Stone magazine interview pre-show actions imploring the audience to not use their phones were mentioned and commented upon:

Shortly before Jack White takes the Hammersmith Apollo stage, a member of his entourage has an announcement to make. What's being announced is the mobile phone 'ban' being imposed by White. He hates the presence of mobile phones. He wants his shows to be first-hand experiences, 'you had to be there' moments that are lived to the full [. . .] And whilst there was still a fair amount of that tomfoolery on show tonight, it has to be said that the majority complied with White in taking a stand against technology for the night [. . .] Besides, who would want to be viewing the most seismic of renditions of 'Steady, As She Goes' from behind a three-inch screen? (Hancock 2014)

The requests of these artists reflect the presumption that this practice is disruptive, an annoyance and poor etiquette. However, there are also contentious elements that present themselves in relation to these artists' responses to the practice. A common theme that emerges from these requests/demands is the sense of the artist deciding how a performance should be enjoyed within a particular setting. There is a clear desire to control the entirety of an event attended by, and this would seem pertinent, consumers who have bought the records and concert tickets that have enabled the performance of that music within this context to exist in the first place.

There is also the assumption that the experience should be experienced en masse and not individually, again disregarding the position of the audience member in a context that pertains to exist for the enjoyment of those who consume the opportunity to engage in that context. Around the time of Yeah Yeah Yeahs, She & Him and Savages issuing their notices a number of articles appeared online at various music websites that acknowledged this practice. The majority of opinion pieces and blogs discussed concert or gig etiquette citing this practice as poor etiquette. The overriding sentiment was that this practice impacted the experience and spectacle detrimentally as if the decision that an arena performance is communal and enjoyed the same way by everyone was a decision reached uniformly, democratically and not merely historically through technological contexts. There was also the sense due to changes in the technological contexts that the practice was a negative inevitability of the increased digital activity in the everyday lives of the audience members.

These negative stances by artists are further problematized by the artists using the same technologies and social platforms in seemingly hypocritical ways. For example, the Yeah Yeah Yeahs' Instagram feed features a plethora of photographs captured during arena shows that display the band backstage and also mid-performance. There are photographs of fans taken from the stage during the show and of the stage and performance from vantage points including 'in the crowd' or from the sound desk. Jenkins says 'the circulation of media content – across different media systems, competing media economies, and national borders – depends heavily on consumers' active participation' (Jenkins 2006, 03). Yeah Yeah Yeahs and Jack White's record company Third Man Records understand this and use Instagram and other social media platforms such as Vine, Tumblr and Twitter to post still image and video content to promote their work to fans/consumers yet expect the fans/consumers to be passive when in the live presence of the work and not actively post their own experiences of the work through still image and video content. Jenkins adds that:

> Media companies are giving out profoundly mixed signals because they can't decide what kind of relationships they want to have with this new kind of consumer. They want us to look at but *not* touch, buy but *not* use, media content. (Jenkins 2006, 142; his italics)

These mixed signals, it seems, are also being sent out by artists and record companies who want to use digital technologies and social media to communicate with audiences about their work but desire that audiences refrain from using technology and social platforms to communicate with each other about that work within the arena context.

In this context *Awesome* stands at odds with this artist stance of restricting individual experience in many significant ways. By handing responsibility for recording the show over to the audience it validates the role of the audience in the documentation of the event and simultaneously exposes the hidden paradoxes of the arena experience and a previous, assumed role of the audience. The question of how audience members should enjoy an arena experience is answered in *Awesome* in a variety of ways but all with the common theme of 'however you want'. At the start of the film a representative of the band is seen orienting the camera operators and saying:

> You can rock out. You can do whatever you want. Just keep shooting. If you're not looking I don't care [. . .] When the lights go down you press the magic red button. I know I'm speaking for the guys. This is special and cool [. . .] everyone being part of this.

The following edited amalgamation of the footage recorded by the fan camera operators, presented as the concert, fulfils that commitment whilst simultaneously ensuring a resulting commercial product is created.

There are repeated moments where one of the fan camera operators exerts those around him to 'get excited' exclaiming 'you're going to be on the DVD' but the surrounding audience members display a range of emotions that include a definite lack of excitement either at this declaration or indeed the show itself. They stand, maybe sway slightly, or drink and look disinterested in what is going on. In standard commercial releases of arena shows fans are never shown looking less than enthralled, hyperactive, deeply emotional or singing themselves hoarse. The idea that some audience members do not enjoy the show or segments of the show, or respond to it less than enthusiastically, or engage with anything that is not their favourite song or one of the 'hits' is a reality that exists. This reality exists alongside the endless ways that individual members can experience a show. A lack of movement, not singing along, head bowed etc. are not necessarily negative responses but simply the way individuals chose to enjoy and experience the event. This range of experiences is rarely considered on film. The inclusion of these moments in *Awesome* and others such as audience members visiting the toilets mid-song, talking to stewards while the band perform and accidentally (possibly deliberately) turning on the time function on one of the cameras further suggest the artist attempting to stick to their word of including whatever the fans shoot. Thus the artist is seeking to explicitly acknowledge more authentic (but never truly authentic) participation of the audience in the show.

Get excited: Participatory culture and the extension of everyday life

Tarrant describes *Awesome* as imagining that its participants are members of a participatory culture (Tarrant 2009, 163) and that the film, DVD extras and artwork show that the artists' decision to hand over the cameras to the fans is not intended to placate or counter existing practices of bootlegging but rather to embrace the essence of those practices. He claims that *Awesome* informs the viewer that the participants were participants all along through a representation of fan culture that is productive and pre-emptive rather than simply reactionary (Tarrant 2009, 156–157).

Jenkins says 'the term participatory culture contrasts with older notions of passive media spectatorship', notions this chapter has already mentioned as still being problematic within the arena experience context, and that:

> Rather than talking about media producers and consumers occupying separate roles, we might now see them as participants who interact with each other according to a new set of rules that none of us fully understands. (Jenkins 2006, 03)

Awesome celebrates this idea of participant interaction as Tarrant's previous quote suggests while also embracing the contradictions and lack of rules.

Jenkins extends his analysis to emphasize that fans are involved in the application of new technologies:

> Fans have always been early adapters of new media technologies [they are] the most active segment of the media audience, one that refuses to simply accept what they are given, but rather insists on the right to become full participants. (Jenkins 2006, 135)

The status of this practice is then elevated to something that might be termed creative, something that will be discussed in the next section. Tarrant describes camera movies – of which *Awesome* is an example – as 'participatory only in the narrow sense that they involve a filmmaker handing multiple cameras over to subjects who would otherwise be expected to play their role in front of the camera' (Tarrant 2009, 149). What he does not discuss is how by doing so *Awesome* questions what that role really is and by handing over the camera validates the reality of the role, something previously unrecognized in official arena film documentation. By focusing the film on the audience in equal proportion to the artist – through their practical participation as well as appearance within the film – *Awesome* brings the idea of an audience consisting of individuals to the fore and the performance and event becomes linked to their lives and personalities in a way that shifts the focus of the film away from merely being the presentation of the artist in a specific way. The fact that the event is part of an audience's everyday lives becomes more apparent than has previously been represented in arena films. This idea coupled with aforementioned inclusion of minimally responsive audience members, toilet visits etc. as well as a segment which sees the band waiting for a lift to take them up and down floors within the venue suggest a celebration of the banality of the experience similar for artist and audience where all are party to downs and lows as well as ups and highs. Atton says,

> We must attend to [. . .] banality [. . .] and its relations to the wider world [. . .] Morris (1988) had rightly criticized a tendency towards the banal in cultural studies [but] ignores its [etymological] occurrence in medieval to mean 'communal use' [. . .] we can recover that meaning [. . .] to refer positively to the productive use of the 'common people'. (Atton 2004, 7–8)

Awesome is an attempt at least to include the experience of the 'common people', however banal at times, within an official record of an arena show. This practice of recording a personal experience, banality included, is now part of the fabric of arena shows, for better or worse.

If the traditional, artist sanctioned and professionally recorded and edited arena film is the standard media practice of the form then it makes sense to consider the practice of individual audience members filming their own record of a performance as a radical media practice. Tarrant says that 'camera movies can certainly be seen as reactions against certain aspects of media production' (Tarrant 2009, 151) and Atton says that 'one of the defining strengths of radical media practices is the possibility they allow for audiences to become producers as a result of democratised media practices' (Atton 2004, 07). The decision by Beastie Boy Adam Yauch (1964–2012) as director (under the pseudonym Nathanial Hörnblowér) to ensure *Awesome* was created in the way it was suggests a reaction against the traditional form of the concert film. Taking this idea further, Atton says:

> On the one hand then, market-led technological and economic practices appear to restrict other decentralized, 'amateur' forms of production; on the other hand we can see how those very restraints may be renegotiated and how the commercial processes they were intended to facilitate may be replaced (or at least challenged) by social practices that re-activate audiences as producers. (Atton 2004, 07)

With *Awesome*, Beastie Boys not only challenge the aesthetic of the official artist produced and sanctioned arena document by bringing portable, personal technology into the arena space to act as the means of recording the performance but pose the question of an official record of the event by handing responsibility for the documenting of the performance over to those individuals who are charged with experiencing and 'enjoying' the performance. The existence of *Awesome* problematizes the idea that the concert film could be an authentic representation of an experience for everyone in attendance, or indeed anyone in attendance, in the way that the traditional, unchallenged concert film did by default. *Awesome* suggests that no single document or indeed experience is possible and engages with some of the potential pluralities of experience. Tarrant says that 'we should recognise [camera movies] as a targeted appeal to audiences who expect to be engaged in novel ways' (Tarrant 2009, 153). This practice could be seen as an evolution of this thinking and also an acknowledgement that certain elements of the audience prefer personal documentation of events to professional, artist, venue and also potentially broadcaster versions of arena events. The question of whether this validates the practice as good etiquette or acceptable practice is unanswered by this but it does suggest a rejection of official documents in favour of an individual response. Atton says:

> The cultural production of fans can generally be seen to constitute a 'semi-autonomous' field [. . .] its authors and creators are autonomous [. . .] They exhibit non-professionalised characteristics in their media activities: they will tend to have no formal education or training in media production [. . .] They will be largely self-taught and interested in producing [. . .] in order to participate in a [. . .] community of like-minded individuals. (Atton 2004, 142)

Semi-autonomy is present in *Awesome*. The fan camera operators are given free rein to record the show as they see fit, with no professional training or guidance proffered. The only guidance is essentially 'keep shooting', as declared by the representative handing out cameras before the show as part of the orientation. However, the results were then professionally edited and the footage manipulated. Special effects were added. Transitions and repetitions that are based on the rhythmic structure of the songs being performed are deployed to enhance the footage. As a result the question of how authentic the idea being presented of an 'authorized bootleg' (*Awesome; I Fuckin' Shot That!* 2006) and fan-documented performance actually is becomes pertinent again. Beastie Boys could easily be accused of using the gimmick of the fan recording for commercial gain. The presentation of a democratic representation is seemingly at odds with a very slick and careful manipulation of democratically sourced material. However, there are other contextual considerations that impact this paradox in positive ways. Tarrant says that despite these manipulations:

> The film is a highly visible example of a desire to hand the camera over and it is this quality, more than any other [. . .] this extreme 'camera visibility' that [means] the very question of who the subject of the documentary is becomes unstable. (Tarrant 2009, 156)

Around the release of the film in 2006 Yauch spoke of both a desire to 'collaborate with the audience' and capture a truer 'feeling in the room' as reasons for making the film in this way while simultaneously looking at a seating plan of Madison Square Garden to ensure an even spread of the camera operators within the venue (Rubenstein 2006). This combination of the creative and personal with the keenly commercial is at the heart of the problematic nature of *Awesome*. In a 2006 interview Yauch said:

> It's really a weird thing to be in a huge arena. What I really like about the movie is that the people shot it, so it's like the essence of hip-hop and punk rock. It's like these people made it; it's like we all made it, and that's what I like about the movie. [. . .] I kept wanting to see more about what was going on with the audience and that's why I thought it was so cool with them filming it. As a performer, I'm never allowed to see that. I don't have an insight into that world; I don't really see what they're up to or what their world is like while we're performing so that to me is a really cool thing to have that represented. (quoted in Rubenstein 2006)

Yauch's intentions for the film display a creative curiosity and urge for collaboration that belie the risks inherent in such an undertaking. On the DVD there is the option to witness the show through a simultaneous feed of all available cameras and one of the things learned is that apart from the fifty fan-operated cameras there were only two other cameras used. One is a roving backstage/on stage camera that follows the band and was linked to screens inside the Madison Square Garden venue. The other camera was static, fixed on the turntables used by Mix Master Mike who provides the majority of the musical backing to the group's vocals. Had the footage collected by fans been unusable the back up for the show was these two camera feeds. This is a risky investment in a film that would represent the first official film of the band performing and their largest hometown headline show in six years on a world tour promoting *To The 5 Boroughs* (2004), their emotional response to the 9/11 attack and its aftermath, and their first release since the acclaimed *Hello Nasty* in 1998. As Tarrant says:

> Although the participatory camera can be understood as a symbol of the democratisation of media production, it also represents a pointed appeal to audiences known to be responsive to the extra-textual provocations and invitations of the contemporary media producer. (Tarrant 2009, 150)

The elements being discussed suggest a desire by Yauch and the band to create a collaborative piece of work that showcases a more representative audience experience, tempered with an understanding of the commercial potential of something visually alternative to other concert films that also reflects the band's brand personality. There seems to be a desire to showcase and remind of their punk rock and hip-hop roots and by extension, retain a closer proximity to their audience physically and ideologically than other artists. The attraction is clear according to Tarrant who says 'participatory documentaries [. . .] revel in participatory culture's techno-spontaneity, and its anti-institutional, anti-authorial processes' (Tarrant 2009, 151).

Viewed in this light it is tempting to see *Awesome* as defining all arena concerts where the event is not recorded by fans to some degree as not participatory and ultimately passive, controlled experiences. He also highlights the paradoxes present within the motives of the creative forces behind camera movies. In the case of *Awesome* it is Yauch as director that 'stimulates and flatters the audience, while simultaneously ensuring the ongoing primacy of their own role in that process' (Tarrant 2009, 153), which highlights again some of the problematics and contradictions present within the film but also how it represents a natural progression for the practice discussed in this chapter. Contemporarily the audience can stimulate and flatter themselves as authors of their own experience technologically and socially. As Tarrant later asserts, this participatory practice leads to the fact that 'participants in the audience are valued because they belong to the same culture as the filmmaker' (Tarrant 2009, 154). Contemporarily the arena audience is the film-maker.

Pass the mic: Creating, documenting, sharing

The idea for filming *Awesome* as a camera movie came to Adam Yauch, the main creative force behind Beastie Boys, after he saw a bootleg clip online. The clip was from a Beastie Boys arena show earlier in the same world tour, for which the Madison Square Garden show would be the culmination. Yauch saw the opportunity to produce a series of recordings that documented the show from fans' perspectives and captured what he believed was a vital energy lacking from most traditional concert films (Rubenstein 2006). However, crucially, he was also aware of what creative elements would be required in addition to this footage to ensure both a degree of commercial potential and an engaging feature length audiovisual experience. Hence why throughout the film professional soundboard audio is used to accompany the footage and so much of the footage is manipulated with VFX and different editing styles and techniques. In essence, both the audience and the artist have the same basic tools at their disposal, cheap video recording devices and online platforms to share them through. However, the difference in what might be termed 'vision' of how to make the greatest impact with these technologies varies and suggests the gap that inherently exists between artist and audience. This attempt to narrow the gap between artist and audience is emblematic of Yauch's abiding punk rock ethos. As he said upon the film's release 'the kids made it, we all made it together' (Rubenstein 2006). However, although 'the kids' shot it, *Awesome* is only commercially viable and potentially interesting to both fans at large and non-fans through the direction of Yauch in the manipulation and presentation of a particular aesthetic.

Central to *Awesome* is the aesthetic of the content – handheld, shaky, fragmented, with poor sound, highly subjective, unedited and unmediated. It is the aesthetic of footage collected by Radiohead fans at a Roseland Ballroom show in 2011 that similarly saw the band donate soundboard recordings to a fan website that was editing the footage together to create an unofficial bootleg of the show in 2012 (Greene 2012). It is the aesthetic of footage collected against the artist's wishes by fans at the 2014 Jack White Hammersmith Apollo show mentioned at the outset. In the context of *Awesome* this aesthetic is present with professional sound recording from the show applied in the editing of the footage. However, despite professional manipulations for commercial reasons *Awesome* stands out as something truly creative, a film that highlights the potential for audience participation with the arena experience while simultaneously showcasing what is unique and visionary about the creativity employed by Yauch in the documenting of a specific arena performance and moment in his band's history.

Gauntlett describes the twentieth century as 'empathetically the era of "sit back and be told" media' (Gauntlett 2011, 09) and that this has since changed with the rise of DIY cultures, including punk and hip-hop cultural scenes, which Beastie Boys have experienced and represent(ed) to varying degrees at various times of their career. Gauntlett also claims that creativity is 'something that is felt, not something that needs external expert verification' (Gauntlett 2011, 79) which maintains the problematic nature of classifying the practice discussed in this chapter. It may also account for why this practice is frequently viewed as contentious by artists and audience members wishing for a different type of experience. Some audience members seek to be involved in documenting their own experience and sharing it. They will not sit back and be told how to experience an event and they will use the tools at their disposal. However, they may do so with very little if any objective context applied or deep mining of the creative possibilities of the devices they possess. Ultimately they are still consumers and still using creative tools as objects of consumption rather than creativity.

Conclusion

Atton states that 'a key feature of these [alternative] media is the erosion of the expert who is dependent on formal education and professionalization, to be replaced by the autodidact, informally skilled often through collective experimentation' (Atton 2002, 153). *Awesome* highlights the difference between the expert and the autodidact in this context and also suggests a greater and more subjective role for the autodidact presented by technological opportunities. Prior to *Awesome* concert films were sanctioned and overseen by artists and their record labels. They were both recorded and edited by professionals. They were lavish documents with multiple angles where footage was curated to ensure the artist was always displayed in appropriate, positive ways and that audiences were always seen to be anticipating or enjoying the performance.

Looking at the practice discussed in this chapter as autodidactic is to make explicit the question of the rights of the audience member as consumer to remove the expert from the experience and capture their own experience of an event. The relationship of an audience member to the footage they create and share is potentially more poignant, memorable and powerful despite its lack of 'professionalism' than an official concert film or DVD where the camera may never pick out their seat in the arena rafters. Traditional concert films feature close ups of the artists at work – singing, strumming etc. This privileged view is one unavailable to the majority of audience members due to their seating/standing position except via video screens within the venue. *Awesome* again stands out in this context through its almost complete lack of artist close ups due to unsympathetic camera positions. The contemporary practice that stems from the ideas contained within *Awesome* allows audience members to regain a proportion of control of their visual experience from the official film and venue screens. Tarrant says that 'if the audience is to be treated as more than a simple observer, and more than a cog in the promotional machine, they must be free to challenge the image of participation they are being sold' (Tarrant 2009, 164). This practice suggests that audiences are challenging the image of participation in the form that *Awesome* suggests is possible and desirable. Jenkins says:

The advent of new production tools and distribution channels have lowered barriers of entry into the marketplace of ideas. These shifts place resources [. . .] into the hands of everyday citizens [. . .] which were once the exclusive domain of the [. . .] mass media [. . .] Such practices blur the lines between producer and consumer, between consumers and citizens, between the commercial and the amateur and between education, activism, and entertainment, as groups with competing and contradictory motives [. . .] serve their own end. (Jenkins 2006, 293)

Awesome is almost a direct declaration of the need for this shift as well as a record of the moment of the shift. It prefigures the current commonplace contemporary practice discussed in this chapter and declares that arena experiences should be as much about the audience as the artist if not more so and that the event should be collaborative. The experience should be made together.

CHAPTER FIFTEEN

Framing Experience: Filming and the Excesses of Aesthetics

Erich Hertz

As the rise of ubiquitous personal filming of live music performances continues, the numbers of complaints from both sides of the stage accrete. If, at the end of the twentieth century, when some low-resolution cameras and microphones made their initial appearance on cell phones, concert patrons were routinely told by security or by signage to return their devices to their vehicles, concert-goers in the second decade of the twenty-first century find themselves awash in a sea of smartphones capturing every moment of a live performance in high definition. With T-Mobile claiming that 53 per cent of people attending concerts use their phones as cameras during performances, it is not just a general feeling of sitting in a particular section of the arena of the concert; it is an empirical fact of being surrounded by recording devices.[1] Even those people who are using recording devices farther from the stage are capturing images of dozens of other recording devices recording the same thing. This dramatic turn in the experience of a concert in the last decade or so has caused many disgruntled writers in various forums to make claims about the 'stupidity' of such an exercise: you'll never watch the video again, the sound is horrible and, something to which we will return, you are missing the experience of the show itself.[2] And it's not just that some members of the audience are expressing varying degrees of dissatisfaction with being surrounded by recording devices, it is also the performers who have expressed their grievances with varying levels of exasperation. The Yeah Yeah Yeahs posted notices at their 2013 concert that plainly stated: 'Please do not watch the show through a screen on your smart device/camera. Put that shit away as a courtesy to the person behind you and to Nick, Karen and Brian.'[3] While the band is clearly making an appeal to others to respect those around them who don't want to be surrounded by screens, it's also clearly an appeal to not have a device between the performer and the listener. As Johnny Marr would put it in an interview with the New Musical Express in 2013: 'I don't really mean to be unkind, but I think you should put your phone down because you're just being a dick.'[4]

The tension of this particular moment in history of going to concerts surrounded by personal screens endlessly filming is fascinating from several vectors, coming from both who is on the stage and those who are around it, whether they are recording or not. However, what I find most particularly worthy of attention here is the ways in which the arguments against recording a live show as a member of the audience has deep echoes with those familiar with arguments about the possibility of aesthetic experience from eighteenth-century concepts of the Sublime and how those ideas shaped concepts of aesthetic experience in Modernity. One finds in

FIGURE 15.1 Mass mediation: The audience film Miley Cyrus during the Bangerz tour.

various jags against filming a restaging of the same issues that animated critical theories about aesthetics in the mid-twentieth century. Those who are against experiencing the concert through their phone often point to missing out on the totality of experience. The 2013 Unsound Festival made an appeal to attendees. Under a headline that ran 'Unsound Festival Bans Photography, Filming on Cameras, Phones', it was revealed that the festival organizers made an appeal not just built on respecting the artists and other attendees, but also included an aesthetic judgement as well:

> Our aim is to encourage our audience to focus on being in the moment, and not distract others out of that moment. We want to question the automatic tendency to place photos and videos of concerts online, be it on social networks, music websites or video streaming platforms, to put some tiny glitch in the constant bombardment of images, today's main tool of communication. The ban will not be policed by security guards, this is going to be a community action – if you see someone next to you filming, ask them politely to stop.[5]

One thing that is quickly evident is that there is no official 'ban' in place (as the title of the piece implied); it was not enforced by anything but community policing and shame. More importantly, though, is the injunction to be 'in the moment', to allow yourself to be immersed and overcome by the communal experience of the aesthetic of the concert. As Bobby Caruso recently claimed on his blog at *The Huffington Post*, if you put your phone down, 'you will notice the little things'. More: 'You'll Be More Present. There's no easy way to explain this but there's something so much more magical about fully committing yourself to the show. You aren't on YouTube or listening to iTunes, this is a live performance. When you unplug, there's something almost spiritual about being fully immersed in what is transpiring around you.'[6] This language of 'full immersion' is exactly the kind of language that Kant nuanced, that Hegel historicized and that German Critical Theory unpacked and dismantled to reveal its politics. Caruso's admonition to commit oneself to the 'magic' of the show, to its 'almost spiritual' dimension takes the concert fully out of the dimension of what Kant would refer to as the comprehensible category of the Beautiful into the category of the Sublime where the aesthetic being experienced has too much surplus to be experienced as anything other than something beyond a categorical framework, as something 'magical'. Following and building upon this notion of encountering the concert as something Sublime provides a useful theoretical framework for thinking about one way to approach the compulsion to personally film live music events.

In the *Critique of Judgment*, Kant makes a useful distinction between the aesthetic category of the Beautiful and the Sublime. For Kant, something that is Beautiful has boundaries and can be framed within the context of something to be appreciated aesthetically; its apprehensibility is equal to and matches the idea of its sensuousness. The ability to 'take in the moment' of something Beautiful might escape pure reason, but is nonetheless something that can be given shape and can be bracketed off into a coherent aesthetic experience. The Sublime, in contrast, is an experience of nature or art that exceeds these boundaries. Kant famously discusses the experience of St Peter's Square in Rome as a space capable of producing both modes of aesthetic experience. While certain aspects of the spectacle of St Peter's could be recognized as Beautiful, other aspects must be qualified as Sublime because it contains an element that cannot be incorporated and categorized. This leads Kant to state:

> The feeling of the Sublime is, therefore, at once a feeling of displeasure, arising from the inadequacy of imagination in the aesthetic estimation of magnitude to attain, to its estimation by reason, and a simultaneously awakened pleasure, arising from the very judgment of the inadequacy of the greatest faculty of sense being in accord with ideas of reason, so far as the effort to attain to this is for us a law. (Kant 1964, 106)

The Sublime is a category that contains within it both the feelings of pleasure and displeasure: Beauty but also the terror of recognizing that it escapes us. In other words, the experience of the Sublime does not come without a cost, and that cost is knowing that something is lost in the process, the very 'losing oneself to the moment' is the very thing that ensures that not all of it can be categorized, recognized, taken in as something that is happening. And this is especially the case in the arena concerts where the sheer magnitude of concert-goers becomes another element of the Sublime experience. While smaller venues surely have their quota of filmers, the filming seems to go up much more than just a percentage of per capita in the arena concert. The overwhelming nature of the arena concert in the postmodern world has been transformed into a kind of anti-Bacchanalia in which the preservation of oneself against the ek-stasis of experience is to be guaranteed by cataloguing and maintaining individual experience against loss of self 'in the moment'.

Without travelling too far down a path of over-explaining a well-trod concept in the History of Ideas, we might already recognize that many of the pleasures of the concert are much like the experience of St Peter's Square as Kant describes. The sensory assault is simultaneously something we can isolate to different moments where we direct our vision and our hearing, but in those attempts to direct ourselves, we lose out on the experience of the moment in its totality. There is a terrible bargain in the works for having been lost in the 'magic', for having given oneself over to the 'spiritual' at the concert venue. The cost is that part of the comprehensible Beauty of the experience cannot be retained. We can already acknowledge an impulse here to try to frame that which cannot be framed. Is not the smartphone, until the latest technology surpasses it, the closest approximation of our own personal memory log? Even if users don't look at the recording again, there is still the essential sense of having blocked off the Sublime concert excesses and captured our aesthetic experience in a device that we can take with us. And this is important to register regardless of how horrible the sound is on the recording; what is fascinating is the compulsion to frame, have it and keep it, regardless of its fidelity to our own authentic experience. As Theodor Adorno argues in 'On the Fetish Character of Music and the Regression of Listening', it is the buying and owning of the experience that turns the aesthetic experience into a reified thing – that is, a thing that becomes a commodity rather than an artwork. Adorno first defines Marx's sense of the commodity and then applies it to the concert-goers of the mid-twentieth century:

> A commodity is therefore a mysterious thing, simply because in it the social character of men's labour appears to them as an objective character stamped upon the product of that labour; because the relation of the producers to the sum total of their own labour is presented to them as a social relation, existing not between themselves, but between the products of their labour.' This is the real secret of success. It is the mere reflection of what one pays in the market for the product. The consumer is really worshipping the money that he himself has paid for the ticket to the Toscanini concert. He has literally 'made' the success which he reifies and accepts as an objective criterion, without recognizing himself in it. But he has not 'made' it by liking the concert, but rather by buying the ticket. (Adorno 1991, 39)

Adorno makes the case that concert-goers are alienated from the labour of the creation of music to begin with. Music is something that is merely something to be sensuously experienced, to be 'lost in moment' with. More, the aesthetic experience becomes a commodity because it also reflects the cultural status and capital it takes to purchase the ticket. Adorno reasons that the act itself becomes a self-aggrandizing moment of acknowledging one's own capacity to exercise use of capital. It is not then, much further, to say that our purchase of smartphones, with their upfront costs and data plan rates, also allows us to exercise our capital in this same mode of reducing the aesthetic experience to a commodity. These 'experiences' belong to us all the more because we have paid for them. Having them and uploading them to services like YouTube allow us to announce that we have the capital to both have access to certain spaces where music is performed, and that we have the equipment necessary to make it something that we have, that we own.

However, this gets us further into the problem of the idea of an aesthetic experience in the modern world. If, on one level, the use of smartphones to commodify our experiences is already deeply problematic, then the idea of what would constitute a legitimate or valuable experience of a concert is the subterranean core of the problem. As thinkers like Adorno and Benjamin argued, Kant's theory of experience was de-historicized in dangerous ways. It was precisely the issue of what could be an authentic and valuable experience, in a world in which it seemed less and less likely that such a thing was possible, that led to certain thinkers like Adorno and Benjamin to argue against the neo-Kantians in the early twentieth century.[7] As Adorno later clarified in *Aesthetic Theory*: 'Kant's doctrine of the feeling of the sublime all the more describes an art that shudders inwardly by suspending itself in the name of an illusionless truth content, though without, as art, divesting itself of its semblance character. The enlightenment concept of nature contributed to the invasion of the sublime into art' (Adorno 1997, 196). While I maintain that thinking about the Sublime remains a useful term for thinking about the surplus of aesthetic experience, Adorno's criticism is that the category of the Sublime doesn't register any critical force because, by its very definition, it has no semblance, no representation, that can engage the individual in the world. In this aspect, he aligns himself with Benjamin's earlier work in his arguments with Neo-Kantians on a similar front and allows us to think more carefully about aesthetic experience.[8]

The capacity for experience in general and aesthetic experience in specific is one of the main facets of thinking about Modernity for Benjamin. Life in the twentieth century has become marked by a gulf between the experience of one's own life and the experience of how we fit into the totality of history. Like the soldiers that had returned from the First World War, people have experiences of what they personally lived through in the trenches, but that experience doesn't allow for any individual to experience how those moments connect to a social totality, to how their actions link up with the movement of History itself. In his work on experience, like his highly influential 'On Some Motifs in Baudelaire', Benjamin parses and differentiates two different kinds of experience in conversation with the Neo-Kantians of the 1920s and 1930s: *Erlebnis*, which is the kind of experience that is lived through as an individual and *Erfahrung*, which is a kind of experience which dislocates the individual from their own experience. As Martin Jay puts it: '*Erlebnis* was an honorific term for subjective, concrete, intuitive responses to the world that were prior to the constructed abstractions of science or the intellect [. . .] The immediate, passive, fragmented, isolated, and unintegrated inner experience of *Erlebnis* was, Benjamin argued, very different from the cumulative, totalizing accretion of transmittable wisdom, of epic truth, which was *Erfahrung*' (Jay 1998, 48–49). Benjamin draws out the etymological implications of these two different German words for experience. *Erlebnis* contains *Leben*, to live, while *Erfahrung* contains not only the sense of *fahren*, to travel, but also *Gefahr*, danger. This dangerous experience is the kind of experience that Benjamin tries to place a premium on for Modernity in the sense that it is the kind of experience most absent and atrophied in the modern world. Our overly mechanized and fragmented experience of *Erlebnis* mitigates the sense of apprehending the totalizing historical possibilities of *Erfahrung*. Benjamin sees possible glimpses of *Erfahrung* in Modern art works that attempt to shake us loose from clinging to our safer lived experience in the form of *Erlebnis*. In these terms, we might easily see the temptation to record, to bracket off and frame the concert is a way to reduce *Erfahrung* to *Erlebnis*.

In his essay 'On the Destruction of Experience', Giorgio Agamben picks up and draws out Benjamin's concerns about experience in the modern world. As Agamben notes: 'experience is now definitively something one can only undergo but never have. It is never accessible as a totality, it is never complete except in the infinite approximations of the total social process' (Agamben 2007, 38). For the very reasons that Benjamin had elaborated experience in the modern world as something that one can 'live through', but can never have in the sense of making the connection between individual experience and the social totality that the individual is isolated from. Agamben is careful to qualify that experiences do in fact happen: 'This does not mean that today there are no more experiences, but they are enacted outside the individual. And it is interesting that the individual merely observes them, with relief. From this point of view a visit to a museum or a place of touristic pilgrimage is particularly instructive. Standing face to face with one of the great wonders of the world [. . .], the overwhelming majority of people have no wish to experience it, preferring instead that the camera should' (Agamben 2007, 17). Agamben doesn't follow much further through on this idea of filming in place of experience itself on this essay from 1977, but his charge here is a provocative one. That is, with a sense of severance between the individual and social totality, the individual wishes to mark the break by having technology do the experiencing for them. For Agamben, this clearly is a negative marker, a wounded reflection, of our relationship to experience. Rather than find some way of negotiating the rift between the world and our capacity to experience it, we would rather that that rift be registered in a technological device. In that way, at least, something has the experience for us.[9]

More contemporary analyses of the phenomena of recording the concert have examined the subject more neutrally. Lisa Chouliarki, for example, notes that 'this mediated participation of ordinary people in public cultures is being hailed as blurring traditional boundaries between media producers and consumers, and leading to new forms of playful citizenship, critical discourse and cosmopolitan solidarity' (2010, 227). Steven Colburn argues, drawing on Bourdieu, that many filmers believe that their reasons for filming concerts are altruistic in the ways that Chouliarki enumerates, but in fact are couched in nefarious undertones of cultural capital. Much as Adorno had already adumbrated in his analysis of the attendees of certain classical music concerts, the filmers are keen not to just share, but to demonstrate their access to rarified and exclusive venues and occasions. What I find compelling in Colburn's study and draws us back to the notion of experience at the concert is the way that many people who view the films on YouTube were actually present at the very event that they might have attended themselves. As Colburn notes: 'My research suggests [. . .] that that in contrast to the claims of the numerous filmers, many of their viewers did attend the same concert in person. They were not using the videos to access the concert but instead as adjunct to their own memories' (2015, 64). While this stage of Colburn's argument bolsters his charge about not using the footage for altruistic, cosmopolitan reasons, I am more interested in the way that it returns us to the idea that the recording serves as 'adjunct' to memory. That is, not only do the filmers themselves admit that they get to have the experience again when they look at their own videos, they are also interested in seeing another version of that same experience in an attempt to bolster the re-experience.[10] In essence, it is like revisiting the site of the trauma of the inability to experience the concert as *Erfahrung*. Instead, we find ourselves seeking out others' shards of *Erlebnis* in order, possibly, to make whole our partial experience. This seeking of a montage of perspectives to create a greater whole was something that Benjamin argued positively for about cinema itself, as a rare opportunity for the experience of *Erfahrung*.[11] But we can quickly rejoin that whereas cinematic montage might be capable of the historical charge of *Erfahrung*, a compilation of moments of *Erlebnis* would only be a harsher reminder of what was lost.

Given Agamben's assertion that the camera has the experience for us in the face of living in a world in which experience doesn't seem to take place at a level where the experience would make sense in terms of the movement of History from which we feel alienated, the filming of the concert as a substitute for our own experience also provides us with hard data which makes it *feel* as though and approximates that we've come closer to an historical experience. The smartphone provides us not just with times of clip duration, but also with dates that clearly demarcate when the experience happened. The longing to collect mediated experiences merely reflects the attempt to salve this gash between ourselves and our capacity to experience. If the Kantian Sublime is always about a certain surplus that can never be categorized, and that surplus is always a reminder of our gap between ourselves and the world, then the smartphone becomes a device which helps us to frame and make sense of this excess especially when we are surrounded by throngs of people at an arena concert. When being 'lost in the moment' comes with the cost of the possibility of not have accurate memories, filming the show provides us with a shard of that experience – even if that shard is merely a marker of our having lost out on the immersion into the surplus of aesthetic experience and the ek-stasis of the Bacchanalian nature of the arena concert. The lure of hard 'historical' data to transform our *Erlebnis* into an approximation of *Erfahrung* is a seductive quality of filming at concerts and may ultimately be one of the most productive ways to think through the compulsion to film when we think about what is at stake in the moment of the aesthetic experience of the live music event.

Notes

1 See the results of T-Mobile poll and an engaging graphic of this historic shift by Sarah Nazim (2012).
2 A typical rant appeared by Rebecca Haithcoat in the *LA Weekly*, see Haithcoat (2014).
3 See Spin's coverage of the moment (*Spin* staff, 2013).
4 The video of the interview can be found on the *NME* website: http://www.nme.com/news/johnny-marr/71759 (accessed December 2014).
5 See Jenn Pelly's coverage for *Pitchfork,* see Pelly (2013).
6 See Caruso's blog at Caruso (2014).
7 In a mode of Marxist-driven analysis when one must 'always historicize', Robert Kaufman's essay 'Red Kant, or The Persistence of the Third *Critique* in Adorno and Jameson', is one of the strongest to take on and takes seriously the Kantian heritage of German Critical Theory. See Kaufman (2000).
8 George Hartley (2003) makes a compelling case for thinking about how the Sublime operates in more contemporary Marxist thinkers like Althusser and Jameson in his book *The Abyss of Representation: Marxism and the Postmodern Sublime.* These are two complex thinkers that it would be interesting to pursue in a significantly longer piece. Such a piece would also need to include Lyotard's deployment of the Sublime in his work.
9 Žižek makes a very similar argument about recording machines that watch television for us in *The Sublime Object of Ideology* (1989). Also see Rober Pfaller's elaboration of this in his *On the Pleasure Principle in Culture: Illusions without Owners* (2014).
10 This is the main thrust of Colburn's argument about how filmers return to YouTube as an 'adjunct to their memories' (2015, 64).
11 See Thomas Elsaesser's 'Between Erlebnis and Erfahrung: Cinema Experience with Benjamin' (2009). Also, Marian Bratu Hansen's book *Cinema and Experience: Siegfried Kracauer, Walter Benjamin, and Theodor Adorno* (2011) offers an excellent contextualization of Benjamin among his contemporaries.

PART FIVE

The Arena Experience

CHAPTER SIXTEEN

'Sing It with Me Now': Audience Participation in Arena Concerts

Nicola Spelman

As vital and esteemed sites of audience activity, arena concerts provide examples of a wide variety of participatory practices. Recent tours by global artists Beyoncé, Coldplay, Green Day, Metallica, Muse, Paramore and Taylor Swift demonstrate the acute propensity for singalong behaviour among audiences keen to contribute to an aural (and visual) spectacle that ostensibly unites performers and fans in ways only possible via the concert medium. For Cavicchi, 'how one participates in an event' as opposed to 'how one consumes a product' informs the very distinction between 'fandom and ordinary audience behaviour' (Cavicchi 1998, 89). While this highlights the importance placed by many on displays of active engagement, it is worth clarifying that the precise nature of such participation is neither fixed nor consistent across musical styles or even individual bands/artists operating in the same genre. Indeed, it is typically the inner structures of individual musical texts – and the extent to which they invite, and/or permit, expressive contributions from audiences – alongside the verbal and gestural actions of performers, that determine this. With the aim of augmenting existing research into participatory practice (see Dockwray 2005 and Fonarow 2006) my chapter begins by outlining some of its common forms in the contemporary arena concert before going on to suggest the possible motivations behind such, and their likely functions. Since levels of audience participation are often used to attest to the relative success of individual performances, I also problematize specific elements of it, considering how it has the potential to not only augment the arena spectacle, but also impose more one-dimensional and routine elements of performance practice.

Modes of musical participation

Both Fonarow and Dockwray have identified various modes of audience participation in line with the objectives of their respective investigations. For Fonarow, differing types of 'participatory spectatorship' are identified to demonstrate the correlation between spectatorial positioning and audience behaviour in British indie music (Fonarow 2006, 79–121) while Dockwray focuses her attention on the textual and performative characteristics responsible for facilitating audience participation in rock anthems (Dockwray 2005, 32–122). Both studies have admirably advanced our understanding of audience–performer relations; however, the scope remains to explore the broader range of participatory techniques employed by performers from divergent musical genres in large concert venues. Here it is possible to identify numerous modes of musical participation, some of which have become the routine means for generating a sense of expressive attachment between performer and audience, while others are less frequently employed, and some are only now emerging as a result of recent technological advancement. It is important to acknowledge that participation methods are continuously evolving, and that the modes identified below are not meant to constitute a finite list. They should be familiar to experienced arena concert attendees, and in order to display their constituent characteristics, a variety of artists has been chosen whose behaviours best illustrate such modes at work in the arena performance context.

Perhaps the most commonly cited participatory mode is the call and response exchange between performer and audience. When operating between discrete songs, it offers a diversion from the commonplace progression of musical events, momentarily interrupting the flow to permit the time and textural space necessary for the artist to direct imitative gestures from the crowd. Relevant to this, Dockwray notes, 'Firstly, there is a duality of constituents: the audience and performer. Secondly there is an inequality, demonstrated by the fact that most audiences face the performers on stage and respond to their direction and leadership' (Dockwray 2005, 112). Within this dynamic, performers produce a visible, objective sign of their power, and if they succeed in garnering a response from their audience, they have effectively 'won them over'. The audience participants become the subjects of the performer on-stage via the process of what social philosopher, Louis Althusser, termed 'interpellation' or 'hailing': 'the rituals of ideological recognition [. . .] guarantee for us that we are indeed concrete, individual, distinguishable and (naturally) irreplaceable subjects'

(Althusser 2001, 117). Interpellation invites a person to accept a particular subject position (in this case the collective identity of the participating fan); by implication it also suggests concurrence with the ideas and ideals of that collective group.[1]

Freddie Mercury's 1985 Live Aid performance provides one of the most notable and influential occurrences of this participatory mode in action. His opening 'Eh-oh' calls were imitated by a large portion of the 72,000 strong crowd with impressive accuracy; his gradual pitch ascent and ornamental embellishments suggesting a contest of sorts as the audience attempted to match his progressively intricate demonstrations of technical ability. Although the event took place in a multi-artist stadium setting, the example is nevertheless relevant here as the participatory methods and skills employed by Mercury were honed during the numerous arena concerts previously delivered by Queen as part of European and world tours such as The Game (1980) and The Works (1984). Queen's recorded performance at the Montreal Forum Montreal (November 1981) offers valuable insights in this regard: the participation section preceding the start of 'Dragon Attack' is relatively ambitious and includes one or two instances where the audience noticeably struggle to interpret Mercury's 'calls' in sufficient time to allow a suitably cohesive and rhythmatized 'response', so much so that Mercury has to instruct them to 'get with the beat' while employing exaggerated leg slapping and finger clicking gestures to underline it. Mercury's enactment of a quasi-conductor role is subsequently assisted by the addition of minimal bass and hi-hat, but the tactics used to initiate a sense of play and competition between caller and responder – augmented pitch, quickening rhythmic pace, marked physical gesturing – are the same as those witnessed in his later Live Aid performance.

As Susan Fast observes, 'the vocalizations that Mercury expects audience members to copy should, theoretically, be much too difficult for them; he pulls gestures out of a musical repertory that belongs to elite culture, which only a few should be "talented" enough to (re)produce, and yet manages to get a massive rock audience to succeed at the task' (Fast 2006, 146). By contrast, Paramore vocalist Hayley Williams employs simple, melodic statements seemingly drawn from the school playground as source materials for her participatory segments during The Self-Titled tour (2013). Beginning with a teasingly slow ascending glissando between the notes Bb and C, which the fans duly imitate, she progresses to descending 'wo-oh' gestures on the pitches Bb and G, increasing the rhythmic pace of the interchanges and eventually cutting the length of the statement to a staccato 'wo' while darting the microphone backwards and forwards, directing the responses until maximum speed is reached and the moment of climax marked by an upsurge of fans screaming their appreciation. There follows a brief tantalizing pause before she sounds a new call utilizing pitches reminiscent of the playground taunt 'na, na, na, na na': (Bb, G, C, Bb, G), which again the audience imitates, before plunging unexpectedly into the next song. While the melodic statements derive from the opposite end of the music repertory spectrum to that of Mercury's, their treatment as a means of evoking a sense of playfulness and frustrated energy is markedly similar.

An element of competitiveness often characterizes call and response participation. Iron Maiden's World Slavery tour saw Bruce Dickinson divide the audience in half to initiate a call and response contest of loudness between the two during 'Running free', while Green Day's Billie Joe Armstrong encourages fans to prove their stamina against previous participatory audiences, the 'hey' of his trademark 'hey-ohs' call being sustained by the responding crowd for as long as possible. Of course, examples of call and response participation devoid of simulated rivalry do exist: the opening to AC/DC's 'Whole Lotta Rosie' is arguably one of the most iconic instances of a guitar riff call followed by appreciative audience response 'Angus!'; and Opeth's Mikael Åkerfeldt utilizes the technique as part of a quasi-tutoring role in which he instructs the audience in the art of growl vocalizing (the response cues in this case are underlined by the house lights going up, informing the interpretation of audience members as active performers).

For the most part, call and response participation is initiated and controlled by the lead vocalist with minimal support from the other musicians on stage, unless, as with the aforementioned AC/DC example, it takes place within the rendition of a pre-existing song – a further notable example being the Beastie Boys' 'Time to Get Ill' where space is left following the vocal call, 'So what's the time?' for the audience to fervently shout 'it's time to get ill!' Other modes of participation are similarly reliant upon the lead vocalist establishing the boundaries within which individuals and/or defined groups of audience members can assume an audible performance role. The selection of a single member of the audience to sing down the lead vocal mic while in situ is typically integrated into the lead vocalist's walk-about, either along the front row of the audience or into more central positions via extending walkways. Beyoncé used the opening of 'Irreplaceable' for this purpose during her Mrs. Carter Show world tour (2013) cajoling the lucky individuals to sing the opening phrase 'To the left, to the left' in turn via conventional directives: 'I want to hear you sing it' (points mic in their face) 'Alright, you ready? Here we go' (points mic at another audience member) 'There you go' (exclamation of satisfaction; they were deserving of their moment in the spotlight).

Clearly the most privileged of these artist-initiated modes of participation, in terms of singularity and prominence, involves the selection of an individual to join the band on stage. Bruce Springsteen has frequently employed this device during his live performances of 'Waiting for a Sunny Day' often selecting a child from the crowd to sing a verse to the evident delight of those present, who applaud and whoop enthusiastically when it's over (partly due to the humorous undertone Springsteen imparts during such episodes). However, the ultimate opportunity for any audience member in terms of achieving an, albeit fleeting, appreciation of the star experience comes when they are invited to participate as an additional band member. In such instances their position is not merely that of vocal stand-in, a replacement for, or support to, the lead vocalist, but something far more inclusive. The large number of online postings, and viewings, of such instances attest to the appeal of this individualized mode of spectator participation, particularly when the privileged audience member ingratiates him or herself with the crowd by putting on a convincing performance. One of the best examples of this may be seen on amateur footage of Green Day's Phoenix concert which took place in the US Airways Center as part of the band's 21st Century Breakdown world tour (2009).[2] Armstrong's request for a guitarist and brief check on the volunteer's credentials: 'Key of C# major?' is followed by the invitation to 'Get your ass up here!' The chosen fan has clearly had prior performance experience; although the chords are not at all taxing, his demeanor on stage is remarkably idiomatic as he quickly assumes the same kinds of performance gestures exhibited by Armstrong while positioning himself in relation to the other band members in a way that appears to justify his purpose and place beyond that of simply 'volunteer fan'. He even concludes his moment of fame with a running stage dive (involving further audience participation as Armstrong conducts the crowd in a held 'woh' of anticipation).

A more ambitious version of 'fan plays along' occurred during Weezer's 2008 Hootenanny tour for the performance of two of their classic songs, as twenty to thirty audience members were invited to join in on their own instruments. A review of their Rosemont Allstate Arena concert concluded: 'Even with the randomness, the vast backing troupe added extra enthusiasm to "Island in the Sun" (complete with an impromptu oboe solo from one of the guests) and "Beverly Hills" (rounded out with a smoldering sax).'[3] The scale and 'jam night' character of such participation is normally confined to much smaller venues, and its obvious risk to the fluency and quality of a performance means it is unlikely to become anything more than a niche antic. A rather more feasible approach to large-scale, non-vocal participation is instead exemplified in the work of electro musician, Richie Hawtin, whose iPhone/iPod Touch application Plastikman SYNK allows audience members to interact with his performance by manipulating the placement of word samples and real-time generated rhythmic patterns via their mobile devices. As Hawtin explains, 'On a creative level, it's my attempt to play with the crowd, blurring the border between the audience and the performer [. . .] The app enables the audience to interact with me, playing samples back, taking visuals from the screen' (Pratt 2010). While Hawtin's participants tend to be located in pop-up arenas within larger festival settings, his approach, coupled with the fact that almost all mainstream artists now have their own dedicated apps, may well herald further developments in the use of interactive technologies for music participation purposes.

Currently, the most intricate modes of participation in arena concerts comprise vocal counterpoint, where separate melody lines coexist between audience and performer, or designated groups of audience members. Two common techniques are employed here, the first being the easier option of establishing a melodic phrase that the audience then maintains while the lead singer layers a second, distinct melody over the top. Coldplay's live performance of 'Viva La Vida' (2008) is one such example, as the audience and Chris Martin first articulate the four bar melismatic 'Woh-oh' melody in unison, after which the audience repeat it while Martin breaks away to superimpose the chorus melody, enhancing the sense of build prior to the song's subsequent point of closure. The second technique requires a higher level of organization and control as the lead vocalist designates individual phrases to specific portions of the audience. Ben Folds's live rendition of 'Not the Same' typically involves his direction of three sections of the audience, each one having been assigned a separate phrase, sung to 'aah'. Much of its success presumably relies on his ardent fans' prior knowledge of the song in question, as exemplified in live performances of 'Army' where, during the instrumental section, the audience divide in two, one side articulating the trumpet part and the other the saxophone part from the studio recording.

The aforementioned vocalizing of instrumental lines constitutes a further customary mode of participation, but in contrast to those previously discussed, it is ordinarily initiated by the audience members themselves. Doubling the melodic content of prominent guitar riffs and melodies is arguably the most prevalent practice. As Dockwray identifies, 'Vocalization of the riff is an attempt at finding a participatory element within the song beyond simply the lyrics' (Dockwray 2005, 59). Audience members often articulate the pitches to 'dah' as evidenced by the enthusiastic doublings of Muse's guitar lines during live performances of 'Knights of Cydonia' and 'Plug in Baby'. The rhythmic character of songs or specific instances of rhythmic emphasis can also be amplified through audience participation; the clapping gestures of Queen's 'Radio Ga Ga', Muse's 'Uprising' and the yelled 'woh!' of Springsteen's 'Born to Run' indicate the way in which the sound and view of collective participation have the potential to heighten one's awareness, and appreciation, of a song's emphatic qualities.

The most obvious mode of musical participation left to discuss can simply be termed 'singalong'. Longstanding artists will often assign individual sections of songs for audience members to sing the lead melody to (the first verse of Springsteen's 'Hungry Heart', for example) and occasionally this leads to a sustained rendition (as in Billy Joel's 'Piano Man'). Others appear to gauge the level of participation and spontaneously select sections in which to step away from the mic and bestow full vocal responsibility on the audience. Bruno Mars's 02 Dublin arena concert (2013) included such an occasion during the final chorus of 'When I Was Your Man'. Having traversed a number of tricky vocal extemporization passages, the willing crowd are allowed to assume precedence over the final chorus, a reward of sorts to both parties. During Green Day's 'Boulevard of Broken Dreams', Armstrong often sits down with his guitar on his lap, an act that visibly advocates the trust he has in his fans' ability to sustain the chorus melody without him. For some artists, however, singalong participation is determinedly incessant, regardless of the lead vocalist's proximity to the microphone. Audiences at arena concerts by My Chemical Romance and Taylor Swift, for example, rarely show signs of diminishing commitment towards singalong participation, as they synchronize with the object of their expressive involvement – the performing 'star' – throughout the duration of the concert.

Motivations and encouragement – why participate?

Audience members can be coaxed to engage in participatory musical practice but its widespread occurrence is dependent on their general inclination and readiness to partake in such behaviour. No amount of cajoling would work otherwise. Liking a particular song or artist, while for many an important prerequisite, is, on its own, insufficient explanation for why people singalong during live concerts, since, 'it need not be the case that attendance or participation also *expresses investment in a text* [. . .] Participation may reflect a desire to test or enjoy membership in the participatory audience' (Rubinkowski 2013).[4] There are, of course, many interconnected reasons, and these vary in relative importance and number from person to person. At a basic level, the audience desires a sense of connection and unity with the performer, and since the 'dynamic of performance is [. . .] predicated on the distinction between performers and spectators' (Auslander 2008, 65), active spectatorship via the act of vocal participation offers a means to achieve a modicum surface layer of unification. Simon Frith's observation concerning the link between listening and performing is relevant since it accounts for our natural preparedness for vocalizing: 'we listen by performing, by reproducing (even if only silently, tentatively) those muscular movements for ourselves, 'sympathizing with a singer by pushing the words up against the top of our mouths when she does' (Frith 1996, 191).

Numerous writers have commented on the way in which the arena concert experience is removed from everyday life, and how this sanctions a range of unconventional behaviours (Cavicchi 1998; Earl 2001)[5] including, presumably, loud singing and shouting in public. Yet, in some cases, singalong may be interpreted as merely an extension of 'playing' the pop star identity at home, especially when, as in the case of Taylor Swift, the karaoke aesthetic is a part of the training and ongoing experience of both fan and artist. Swift engaged in karaoke contests as a child, and reviews of her concerts often focus on their high levels of audience participation:

> For two hours on Friday, the Air Canada Centre in Toronto was transformed from a hockey rink into the biggest karaoke club in Canada [. . .] it was hard to shake the sense that most of the 15,000 fans in attendance were there to sing along with Swift [. . .] it was always there, a high girlish echo of everything Swift sang. Fan fervour doesn't come any louder than that. (Considine 2011)

Guest stars, the like of Carly Simon and Hayley Williams, often put in an appearance at her shows, and the two then collaborate vocally on one another's material (again displaying the practice of singalong). Sarah Barker bemoans the way in which girls' imitation of female performers has often been dismissed as '"inauthentic" behaviour, which copies already inauthentic pop music' (Barker 2013, 16–17). Her extensive fieldwork revealed how, 'girls would frequently break into song [. . .] in after-school care, in their homes and even over the phone [. . .] the ability to sing was a mark of distinction in the girls' peer group' (Barker 2013, 20). Thus the arena concert can function to facilitate the expression of a familiar practice, albeit in unfamiliar surroundings, that is essential to the girl's personification of the pop star identity.[6]

The saying 'Imitation is the sincerest form of flattery' implies a further motivation behind musical participation. The majority of modes outlined above rely on imitative processes/gestures, and the audience's willingness to engage in such activity may also be prompted by a straightforward desire to compliment the performer(s) in question. Artists such as Rihanna and Beyoncé often appear visibly overwhelmed and touched by their audience's ability to sing back their songs. Amateur footage of Beyoncé's 2012 residency show in Atlantic City[7] illustrates such an instance. During the song 'Love on Top', the penultimate chorus line, 'When I need you make everything stop', initiates a planned aural and physical 'freeze frame' moment for all on-stage performers, at which point the resulting space is instantly filled by the audience's singing of the subsequent line 'Finally you put my love on top'. The crowd continue to sing alone throughout the next section as Beyoncé stands in a relaxed pose, looking out over the crowd, shaking her head slightly while smiling and intermittently mouthing the words 'Oh my God'. Her 'natural' and 'appreciative' response is communicated via a large screen, meaning all participants can witness the emotive impact of their collective singing. One incentive for singing along is thus to permit such moments of reciprocal appreciation between performer and audience to occur. But such a premise requires audiences to understand that such possibilities are likely, and this underlines the importance of shared knowledge: 'Like languages, practices need to be learnt before they can be shared through contexts of social interaction' (Laughey 2006, 90). Here, the way in which music video 'acts as a form of participatory instruction to teach viewers how and when to participate' (Dockwray 2005, 98) is clearly relevant, as are the live concert recordings, reviews and comments of experienced audience participants, and the multitude of artist and band designated apps that together retell the narrative of audience participation to the uninitiated concert-goer.[8]

In his discussion of music audiences and performances, Dan Laughey advocates a 'Spectacle/Performance Paradigm' that 'considers spectacle and narcissism as processes in which diffused audience members play at being spectators *and* performers in multimedia contexts' (Laughey 2006, 87–88).[9] The act of musical participation in arena concerts can be viewed as being, in part, motivated by such play, since it is possible to spectate and perform simultaneously. The validity of this idea rests on dismissing the notion of the *passive* audience in favour of the *active* audience[10] that contributes to the formation of the performance as a whole. As Fast notes, 'Physical engagement with a performance, whether through singing, clapping or bodily movement, makes one feel invested because there is participation in the creation of the performance' (Fast 2006, 147). Susan Kattwinkel's observation that, within music theatre, 'Audience participation problematizes the line between spectator and performer, and occasionally breaches the line completely' (Kattwinkel 2003, xiv) seems equally pertinent to some of the musical participation examples previously outlined, although any rupture of this line seems to occur knowingly, by way of an act sanctioned by the artist as a means of playing with an audience/performer role reversal (see the individualization of the fan-performer in the earlier Green Day example). Nevertheless, how such participation fits into what Nico Carpentier refers to as 'a longer evolution of increased audience autonomy' (Carpentier 2011, 524) is interesting to consider. Technological developments enabling audiences to interact with their favoured artists in more intimate and informed ways perpetuate the desire for an ever greater sense of participatory connection. The creative promotional video devised for X box's 'Sing it with Lips' campaign[11] demonstrates how technological novelty might encourage an expectation for increased interaction. It allegedly involved the recording of 2,000 people in different locations singing along to Lily Allen's number one song, 'The Fear' (2008). The individual performance clips were then cleverly edited and compiled to suggest a synchronized 'singalong' with Allen before being assimilated into a moving mosaic image of her (the 'star' image being revealed as the sum of the separate fan 'parts'). In this instance, collective singalong, as a unifying factor, is attributed value through both the product itself (a karaoke game) and its effective promotion.

The past decade has seen a growth in singalong entertainment in general, with the production of karaoke DVDs such as *Let Me Entertain You: Karaoke Versions of Hits Made Famous by Robbie Williams* (2003) and singalong shows ranging from *Sing-Along Sound of Music* (2005 Hollywood Bowl) to *Singalong with the CBSO: Carmina Burana* (2014 Birmingham Symphony Hall). Even the very young are pressed to engage in such activity through products such as Disney's CD Karaoke Series: *Disney High School Musical Karaoke* (2006) and *Frozen* (2014). It is therefore possible that a concomitant increase in singalong activity has taken place in the arena concert site of live performance. While an investigation of such is beyond the scope of this study, a compatible observation clearly informed Guardian journalist Tony Naylor's 2008 music blog article, 'Has Crowd interaction Gone Too Far?'[12] (Naylor 2008). A host of other internet-based materials similarly underline the cultural significance of singalong participation and thereby promote the activity as a seemingly natural and anticipated element of concert spectatorship: internet polls invite us to vote for the 'best singalong concert' and websites dedicated to the instruction of how to 'get your audience to singalong' target fledgling performers.[13]

Arguably the most important forms of encouragement to participate occur within the arena concert itself. Video screens can be used to show, and also underline, lyrics in key participatory sections. During Muse's The 2nd Law world tour, synchronized lyrics appeared on multiple screens and were stretched horizontally to match, and thereby highlight, the sustained note durations and end points of rhyme, 'alive' and 'survive'. Lead singer Matthew Bellamy would turn and point up to them to reinforce the requisite vocalization. Artists sometimes re-position themselves on alternative stages to instigate interactive moments with the audience, and lighting effects are frequently used to accentuate response timings and heighten overall awareness of mass participation. Verbal appeals from performers often involve standard repertory: 'Everybody!'; 'Make some noise!' and are accompanied by a range of physical gestures – the most common being the lead mic held out to the crowd – that can articulate entry points, pitch ascents and descents, and desired increases in dynamic emphasis.[14] In relation to the placement of participation, Earl identifies, 'A definite cycle of heightened arousal followed by a process of winding down [. . .] with skilled stagecraft entailing multiple musical orgasms for the audience' (Earl 2001, 347). Within discrete songs, the prominence of the chorus section designates the most likely point of participation, although song structures are often adapted to permit additional call and response exchanges, false endings and extended outros. The manipulation of musical texture is often crucial to achieving the sense of 'heightened arousal' Earl refers to; in many instances, a move to sparse texture, or a total drop in accompanying sound sources, allows the participating audience to hear itself. In the Foo Fighters'

2011 Wembley Arena concert, the band cuts out during the performance of 'My Hero' to allow Dave Grohl the opportunity to taunt the audience into ever louder statements of the song's refrain. His final goad, 'Why are you gotta sing it fucking like that when Seattle can sing it ten times better? Let's hear that shit, ready? Let's go!' is followed by full band re-entry to generate an immediate boost in momentum and perceived energy level.

When evaluating the suitability of songs for participatory purposes, and indeed commercial appeal, 'singability' is often deemed significant.[15] Dockwray's detailed identification of the textual attributes of rock anthems is relevant here, as her findings appear more broadly relevant to the types of popular music involving audience participation in arena concerts: for example, pitch range not exceeding an octave; small intervallic leaps or step-wise movements; regular phrasing; short phrase lengths; melodic rhythm with a fairly slow to medium rate; avoidance of complex melismas and syncopation; familiar sequences of notes; and smooth, descending pitch contours (see Dockwray 2005, 32–51). Also significant are the lyrical themes and structures, since the most conspicuous instances of participation often occur when the lyrics, enlivened by the musical text, appear to unequivocally express a particular emotional state (as in Rage Against the Machine's infamous refrain 'Fuck you, I won't do what you tell me' and Queen's 'We are the champions'). Keith Salley's research into patterns of vocal articulation is also pertinent, since he claims that, 'alliteration facilitates memory and encourages participation [...] Songwriters may [...] write lines that create alliterative (and near alliterative) patterns because they are more engaging to sing' (Salley 2011, 429).

Important functions of musical participation

Participatory singing imparts a sense of solidarity because audience members can 'feel like they are creating and expressing common sentiment along with the performers and each other' (Kattwinkel 2003, x). The performer's use of emotive language to encourage active participation intensifies this impression. During Take That's 2006 Beautiful World Live performance of 'Patience', Gary Barlow exclaims, 'We've still got one chorus to go, are you still with us?' while Metallica's James Hetfield included the following words as part of a call and response segment in the band's 2012 performance of 'Enter Sandman' at Atlantic City: 'together at last . . . like a family . . . Metallica's family'. While the former example was perhaps intended to engender feelings of togetherness, an alternative, more cynical, reading is that such devices serve mainly to bolster the performer's ego; they want to feel the adoration and it empowers *them* rather than the audience, who are in effect being manipulated by the performer through their willingness to 'give themselves up to it'.

Singalong allows fans to actively express their fandom; not only their knowledge of songs and lyrics but what it means to them. At one point in the aforementioned Beautiful World tour, Take That ask their audience 'Who remembers the *Take That and Party* album?' (1992). What follows is a lengthy, unaccompanied, participation section where each band member takes a turn to sing a starting line before permitting the audience to take over and prove their recollection of the song in question (which they do with remarkable clarity and conviction).[16] As Nessim Watson makes clear, 'displayed [fan] knowledge' is 'one of the shared markers of community belonging' (Watson 1997, 108).

While audiences want to recognize songs performed live from the recordings they have listened to outside the arena concert, it is impossible for performances to replicate these exactly, and this is clearly not the intention of most artists, nor the desire of their fans:

> There's nothing worse, nothing that looks more self-satisfied and feels less rewarding, than going to watch some self-consciously cool guitar band rattle through their album, with barely a word of acknowledgement or a chord out of place. It's boring [. . .] It's like being at home, listening to the album, with none of the fringe benefits. (Naylor 2008)

Musical participation serves to enhance the perceived individual identity of each concert, and even mitigates against any potential disappointment in sound quality.[17] It contributes to the memorability of the live experience on account of the way in which audiences are actively engaged and thus 'immersed' in the arena spectacle. Participants are often encouraged to perceive themselves as 'performers', and passages of unaccompanied participation allow artists to acknowledge and commend their contribution. Rihanna's O2 Dublin concert in 2011 involved the crowd singing an extended section of 'Take a Bow' after which she claimed, 'That was honestly the most special thing any audience has ever done [. . .] That's why I love performing here because I always get a show right back from you guys.'

Most performer/audience interaction occurs in what Auslander, building on the work of Frith (1996), defines as the 'performance persona (the performer as social being)' meaning it is not done in '*character* (Frith's song personality)' (Auslander 2009, 305). The artist's techniques for encouraging live music participation, and the ensuing dialogue between them and their audiences, are a part of how performances of popular music are understood to involve the communication of 'genuine' emotion. Since most large concerts are carefully choreographed, singalong not only introduces a perceived element of spontaneity but also an opportunity for audience members to feel a heightened and more direct level of communication between them and the performer(s). However, there is a need for caution here, since 'what is spontaneous and what is rehearsed will almost certainly overlap' (Inglis

2006, xv), and most participatory sections instigated by performers are pre-planned and relatively predictable in form and structure, rendering spontaneity as merely illusory.[18]

Structural roles are also fulfilled as participatory segments build levels of excitement and anticipation during gaps between songs, and, in their more informal guise, help to build the expected climax of the encore. A sense of fulfilment is often felt at the ends of competitive call and response exchanges as the crescendo reaches a conclusion and both sides join in unison (as in the previously cited example of Iron Maiden's 'Running Free' and Beyoncé's knack of dividing the audience's sung response between the 'fellas' and the 'ladies': 'Come on ladies, show them how it's done'; before directing 'everyone' to 'sing it!'). Such instances also convey feelings of togetherness and shared experience. From the performer's perspective, musical participation, particularly that which appears to be instigated by the audience, functions as a gesture of affirmation and accomplishment (see previous reference to Althusser's interpellation), and individual spectator participation often serves as a marker of their distinction, since it is incredibly rare for the fan-performer to match the artist's level of vocal proficiency.

Potential adverse effects of participatory practice

Despite the numerous affirmative functions that audience participation fulfils, there is the possibility for a relatively small number of negative effects to occur. The first of these relates to the proclivity for continual singalong, which has the potential to result in a more one-dimensional concert experience. In some instances, the intensely scripted and choreographed nature of the arena show can provide the requisite peaks and troughs in energy level (see, e.g. Taylor Swift's Red tour 2013). However, in the case of some long-standing bands, songs that were previously characterized by contrasting exchanges between artist and crowd appear to have lost some of their inherent shape. Metallica's 'Seek and Destroy', for example, no longer exhibits the ritual call 'Searching' and response 'Seek and destroy', since audiences have begun to sing the refrain in its entirety, relegating James Hetfield's role to that of lead motivator: 'Louder! . . . Come on!' And there are also risks associated with the sectioning out of particular lyrics and the impact this has upon interpretations of the wider text. As Keith Negus observes in relation to Bob Dylan's work, 'singing along with choruses [. . .] is also one of the clearest examples of how the words of pop songs become detached from their semantic significance within the song's lyrical narrative or argument' (Negus 2007, 78–79).

While audience participation has the capacity to promote feelings of togetherness, it can also prove divisive. Newer, less ardent fans can feel excluded due to their lack of knowledge concerning lyrics, and sometimes a band's artistic progression can result in different demographics failing to unite in singalong passages. Charles Lin's review of Weezer's Hootenanny tour provides a relevant example: 'it seemed the audience was divided in two groups. Older fans [. . .] and younger fans [. . .] This proved cumbersome for singalongs as neither group was familiar with the other's Weezer repertoire' (Lin 2008). Paradoxically, clearly understood and reciprocated calls to participate can also prove problematic as their repetition becomes stale and predictable for devoted concert-goers. In online reviews, Green Day fans have occasionally commented negatively on their staged theatrics, specifically the 'Hey-oh' gestures and repeated shouts to 'Come on!' The danger here is that any sense of pretence will affect perceptions of spontaneity, but failing to engage in such ritual behaviour can also disappoint, meaning arena artists are forced to negotiate a fine line between delivering the expected and the unforeseen. While the discourse of audience participation is sometimes parodied over such matters (see, e.g. Tim Minchin's comedy song 'Hello'), it is interesting to note that audience musical participation of any kind is not listed in *Rolling Stone*'s '10 Most Annoying Concert Behaviours' (Greene 2013) which instead seeks to denounce noncommittal, distracted conduct such as checking emails and chatting to friends. Despite the aforementioned risks, for many concert-goers, the opportunity to partake in collective vocalization is a patent source of pleasure, and a marker of their commitment to the performer and the event itself. How it is instigated, managed and acknowledged by the artist enlightens, and predominantly enhances, audience perceptions of performer identity. Musical participation is consequently an essential consideration when evaluating the significance and appeal of the arena concert experience.

Notes

1　Kath Woodward usefully defines the process of interpellation as a 'process whereby people recognize themselves in a particular identity' (Woodward 2000, 19).

2　The footage may be accessed at https://www.youtube.com/watch?v=Bd_nv1TUQDY and is titled 'Green Day Pulls Me on Stage to Play Guitar for Jesus of Suburbia'. The accompanying text, 'I got picked and this is my story' indicates the extraordinary nature of his experience – despite being only 10 minutes in duration, it has been granted 'my story' prominence.

3　See full review by Andy Argyrakis at http://www.concertlivewire.com/weezer3.htm (accessed November 2014).

4 Leo Rubinkowski (2013). 'When You Know the Words to Sing . . . ': Sing-Along Exhibition and Participatory Audiences'. Conference paper for Cinema and Media Studies Conference, Chicago, 7 March 2013.

5 Cavicchi explains how, in a concert, 'people behave in ways that they would not outside the performance: [. . .] audience members clap and yell [. . .] all things which would be inappropriate in the context of everyday life' (Cavicchi 1998, 89) and for Peter Earl, 'A live concert allows opportunities for social behavior that may be precluded in a domestic setting.' (Earl 2001, 351).

6 Like many arena artists, Swift inserts spoken segments where she imparts her own lived experience with the aim of generating an emotional response from the audience that takes a variety of forms: clapping, hands held in the air, yells and, of course, sing along.

7 The footage was recorded at one of the Revel Presents: Beyoncé Live (2012) concerts (25–28 May) and is available at https://www.youtube.com/watch?v =RPB4wXtFM1Y&list=RDRPB4wXtFM1Y#t=11 (accessed January 2015). The accompanying online comments reveal the attractiveness of the artist's own demonstrations of appreciation: 'Singing to her with everyone was such a beautiful moment! The look on her face when no one stopped was priceless, she looked like she was in heaven.' 'You see how touched she was by the crowd. She keeps getting greater and greater.' 'She looks so happy that everyone actually knew the words.' (anonymous)

8 Fonarow's discussion of initiate concert-goers is relevant here since she claims 'most have well-defined expectations of what to do at a gig even before attending one. Many have been reading the weekly press for some time prior to their first gig, and they form clear expectations of what people do at gigs from reviews, photos, and videos' (Fonarow 2006, 95).

9 To explain why people engage in such processes, Laughey refers to Abercrombie and Longhurst's claim that, 'the aim of modern life is to see and be seen' (Abercrombie and Longhurst 1998, 81, quoted in Laughey 2008, 81).

10 For a brief outline of active/passive audience theory, see Carpentier (2011, 518–519).

11 The full video (directed by Caswell Coggins and produced by Phil Tidy) is available at https://vimeo.com/9728302 (accessed July 2014). Allen's fans were filmed in various UK locations via mobile studio booths.

12 Naylor's admission that, 'It can be hard work going to gigs – particularly when you have to do the singing' is also indicative of the pressure one may feel to engage in such activity. The article is available at http://www.theguardian.com/music/musicblog/2008/jul/14/crowdedoutcanyoukeepupwi (accessed August 2014).

13 See, for example, websites such as http://popwatch.ew.com/2010/06/09best-stadium-concert-sing-along-song/POLL and http://www.wikihow.com/Get-Your-Audience-to-Sing-Along (both accessed October 2013).

14 For a detailed analysis of gestural participation, see Dockwray (2011, 83–98).

15 Song-writer and performer, Callie Noakes, provides a useful artistic perspective: 'Initially my approach was dictated by large arena sized acts such as Blink-182, Coldplay, and The Killers. As a consequence, I was subconsciously guided down the path of easy to digest and regurgitate top lines. Subsequently my writing process became more calculated. For example,

lyrical themes, particularly the chorus hook, are always of a universal nature ("when the weight of the world is on your shoulders, light it up"). On a large capacity scale, it's imperative that everyone can identify and relate to the song's message. Furthermore, to encourage sing-back, the range of the top line is carefully considered' (Personal interview, 3 March 2015). Noakes is keyboard player and supporting vocalist for Eliza and the Bear. The band supported Paramore and Athlete in UK Arena concerts during 2013.

16 Taking place just one year after their reunion (The Ultimate tour) in 2006, this section of the concert provides what Earl, in his discussion of reunion concerts, refers to as 'a context for recapturing the past and reflecting on how far one has come since then' (Earl 2001, 352). In other words, music participation can be central to the act of reminiscence.

17 It is arguably the case that an inactive audience is more prone to judge, since they are more detached from the creation of the performance.

18 The existence of spontaneity is dubious because of the routine aspect of arena concert participation (a performer using the same prompts night after night at different venues to inaugurate the same crowd response).

CHAPTER SEVENTEEN

Performing Kylie: Looks Divine

Sunil Manghani

In the early 1990s the British stand-up comedian Jack Dee included in his repertoire a commentary on stadium concerts, which had seemingly reached their apogee with the 'earnest' performances of bands like U2 and Simple Minds, the global event of Live Aid in 1985 and the extravagant shows of iconic performers such as Michael Jackson, Madonna and Prince. With his characteristically deadpan and acerbic delivery, Jack Dee suggested if you wanted to hear your favourite band play you might consider avoiding the sweat and crush of the stadium. Instead, you would do well to put the CD cover at the end of the garden and simply turn up the stereo. There was not much difference he argued: you can still barely see what the performers look like, but at least the sound is of a better quality. Jack Dee appeared to strike a chord with his audience, and, coupled with the fact that expectations were changing with regards to music technology (and the new sounds this was producing), it is perhaps little surprise a shift was taking place from a stadium sound to that of the arena, allowing for a more choreographed and multimedia staging of music.

Kylie Minogue was one pop artist able to take advantage of the changing trends, though this only came to the fore after the re-launching of her career around the year 2000. Today, she is recognized as a major-selling artist, an icon of both the pop and fashion worlds. She has achieved record sales in excess of £70 million (over $1 billion US dollars), and received multiple awards over a period of nearly thirty years in the music industry. Yet, she is still regarded more for her commercial success than any critical acclaim. In an interview as recently as 2014, on BBC Radio 4's arts review programme,

Front Row (broadcast 19 March 2014) the presenter John Wilson offered something of a backhanded compliment as he introduced the star while she sat across from him in the studio. Making note of the release of her fifty-fifth pop single, he remarked: 'Whatever you may think of her qualities as a recording artist, Kylie's commercial resilience is undeniable.' John Wilson's remark was seemingly a thinly veiled criticism of the quality of Kylie Minogue's voice.

The intimacy and fidelity of the arena environment can place greater scrutiny upon a singer's voice, and as such it might seem a surprise that Kylie Minogue has proved to be not just a commercially successful recording artist but also a live performer too. Added to which, it has to be remembered that she stands little over 5 feet tall. If we thought it was difficult to see a band play at distance, how does a petite performer, with a vocal style of little acclaim, manage to command an audience of 10,000–20,000? The Leeds First Direct Arena in the UK, for example, boasts the claim of a maximum distance for a spectator from the stage of 68 metres, whereas a typical arena is more likely 95–130 metres away.[1] Were a member of audience to reach out their hand to frame the singer between finger and thumb, she would appear faraway indeed – as if plucking a fairy from a picture.

One explanation for Kylie Minogue's success as live performer is certainly the rapport she has with her audiences. We might think of Minogue as the perfect go-go dancer for her own shows. Yet, significantly, as will be noted, she does not move about the arena stage to a great extent. Rather, the staging, the costumes and the dancers are choreographed around her, as if to display her at the heart of a 'mass ornament' (Kracauer, 1995). As Siegfried Kracauer argued of the Tiller Girls of the 1920s, the figure is 'subject to its performers [. . . and] this does not lead to its being scrutinized by a more incisive gaze'. In fact, as he adds, 'nobody would notice the figure at all if the crowd of spectators, who have an aesthetic relation to the ornament and do not represent anyone, were not sitting in front of it' (Kracauer 1995, 77). In short, choreography is key to *defining* Minogue as a live performer. Of course, Minogue's petite body is very much a part of her 'unique selling point'; something to which she is astute. The cover of the photobook *Kylie* (1998), for example, has become an iconic image for the singer, showing a life-sized photograph of the singer's forearm and clenched fist (complete with a 'Kylie' wrist-band). It is this kind of 'citation' of her actual body-size that has been cleverly used in developing her image, which works to both authenticate the singer and 'mark her out' from the crowd. However, as will be explored in this chapter, it is arguably the concatenation of various *faces* of 'Kylie' that is of key importance. Until, that is, the stage performer departs, leaving the audience – in the harsh light of the emptying auditorium – only with her afterimage.

FIGURE 17.1 Manghani, 'Actual Size', 2014. (after *Kylie*, Farrow Designs/Booth-Clibborn Editions, 1999)

The theatre of pop

The grandeur of the rock concert arguably reached a peak in the late 1980s, with the extravagance of Michael Jackson's Bad tour jarring with the ethos and style of the Live Aid event. Stadium-filling acts were in danger of becoming mere parodies of themselves. A notable response to this dilemma came from two unlikely bedfellows. To critical acclaim U2 redefined themselves from righteous rock group to postmodern act, presenting *Zoo TV* (1992–1993), a highly complex, multimedia arena experience that was an ironic remediation of the band's own international star status. The band went from 'three chords and the truth' to a provocative and witty 'performance' of themselves. Bono, the lead vocalist, developed a series of 'drag act' personas and performed not just out towards the audience but equally back 'into' the vast video walls behind, upon which played a complex 'hypertext' of visual materials and effects (prefiguring the rise of the World Wide Web). Given this reinvention, it is perhaps not so out of place that some years later Bono would perform with Kylie Minogue during her Showgirl Homecoming tour, in 2006 (singing, of all things, 'Kids', the duet penned by Robbie Williams and Guy Chambers).

The significance of U2's new image for the development of a new 'theatre of pop' cannot be underestimated. The band's manager, Paul McGuiness, gives some sense of the changing context:

> Zoo TV was perceived worldwide as a new category of presentation. It was the dawn of video as a creative element rather than what we call i-mag, image magnification. We were being written about by architectural critics and art critics. [. . .] Psychologically, it took U2 into a very elite group that really only included Pink Floyd and The Rolling Stones . . . from then on audiences were not going to accept a band on a black box with a bit of steel and tarpaulin over their heads and a couple of big white sheets at the side of the stage with pictures. (Cited in U2, 2006, 238)

Concurrently, the Pet Shop Boys emerged as an unlikely live act (indeed they had been against touring for fear of diluting their studio-crafted sound). Nevertheless, having completed tours in Japan and the surrounding region, they took the decision to tour more extensively, working with various stage designers (including the maverick film-maker Derek Jarman), to translate their signature dry-wit for the large stage. Similarly eschewing mere 'image magnification', the Pet Shop Boys considered themselves at the heart of *creative productions* of theatrical pop, rather than simply 'going on tour'. As Chris Lowe remarks, 'we hadn't toured because we didn't see any reason for us to tour in a naturalistic way . . . [I]t was an attempt to get around that

FIGURE 17.2 Bono: 'I felt like I was in a musical or something . . . it was like a holiday from a rock band. It was brilliant.' (Still from *White Diamond: A Personal Portrait of Kylie Minogue* [William Baker, 2007])

by putting on a film multimedia show . . . We wanted to put on a theatrical event' (cited in Hoare and Heath 2006, 116). Technology is a key factor in the turn to the arena concert. Neil Tennant explains: 'the starting point for all of our tours has been the fact that the way we make music means you don't have to have the stage full of musicians, as we have computers playing live, so you could do whatever you wanted on stage' (cited in Hoare and Heath 2006, 116). The Pet Shop Boys' cover version of U2's 'Where the Streets Have No Name' adds a further knowing twist to this period of arena reinvention.

The deliberate play of the postmodern surface and challenging montage of historical sources and styles, evident with both U2 and the Pet Shop Boys, paved the way for a new aesthetic of wit and irony in the arena setting – echoed by many artists since. And, 'whatever we might thing of her qualities . . . ', Kylie Minogue has been one such artist able to fully embrace the medium of the arena. Surrounded by an intimate team of creatives, and with connections and influence in the world of fashion and design, she has co-produced a series of well-regarded arena performances. Her Money Can't Buy You Love concert to showcase the *Body Language*

(2003) album drew direct visual influence from Brigitte Bardot, with a signature outfit designed by Jean Paul Gaultier. The greatest hits tour, *Showgirl* (2005), referenced Art Deco, Las Vegas showgirls and the Folies-Bergère. While the *X* tour of 2008 offered a more futuristic look (combined with Japanese-influenced designs), with 'some of the spectacular back projections [upon a huge screen] . . . produced by The Mill, the London-based company who also work on the visual effects for *Doctor Who*' (Sheridan 2012, 259). The tour for the *Aphrodite* (2010) album was even more elaborate, drawing inspiration from the MGM musical *Ziegfeld Follies* (Vincente Minnelli et al. 1946) to produce a camp homage to Greek mythology.

Setting the tone

Kylie Minogue's particular stamp on the arena experience evolves a decade on from U2's *Zoo TV* of the early 1990s. Indeed, around this time Minogue is only just emerging from her teen-orientated image. The sleeve notes for a recording of one of her concerts in 1991 describes her as 'entering a new phase of her already highly successful career. Having become an international dance-pop star at a young age, with a high-energy, clean-cut image, the Kylie Minogue we encounter here has begun the transition into a mature, highly sexualised persona that would mark much of her work in the ensuing years' (Hodgeland 2011). It is true she begins to court a more sexualized image, and as part of which begins to experiment with fashion and styling. However, in retrospective, the 1991 concert belies an amateur approach. The staging and lighting is very limited, the singing poor, there are only a handful of dancers and the choreography is lacklustre. Minogue is frequently lost to the overall 'street dance' choreography. In effect, she is too animated, lost within the group of dancers. Overall, it is a performance that betrays the commercial incentive to get the artist out on the road to capitalize on chart success, rather than any determined effort to create a live experience.

Many thought Kylie Minogue would not make the transition from a successful 'manufactured' pop singer (as crafted by producers Stock, Aitken and Waterman at PWL) to a truly international recording artist. Her split with PWL and subsequent signing with the indie dance label deConstruction Records, in 1993, resulted in both commercial and creative failure. Throughout most of the 1990s Minogue stayed away from the stage, appearing only at one-off events. In 1998, however, she returned to live performance with a highly successful, but small-scale tour, Intimate and Live. The tour deliberately opted for small venues (typically of around 2,000 capacity) and originally was planned only within Australia, though demand was such that dates were also played in the UK. 'This was Kylie's tentative step back into the cosiness of the live lounge, far away from the massive arenas of old, but the concerts were responsible for revitalising her love of performing in front of a crowd' (Sheridan 2012, 147). Rumour had got around that Minogue would be performing her old Stock Aitken Waterman hits, which meant, according to Simon Sheridan, '[g]ay fans went into meltdown. As a result Kylie was obliged to tack on three dates at London's Shephard's Bush Empire nearly four weeks after the tour had concluded' (Sheridan 2012, 147–148). Whatever the truth of this remark, it is a reminder of the significance of Kylie Minogue's gay following; the live shows put together from this period onwards make explicit acknowledgement of the fact.

The Intimate and Live tour is significant for setting the tone for the later, large-scale international tours. While it was minimal in design and budget, with a small band, and just 'two beatific go-go boys dressed in cod-pieces and Stetsons', Kylie Minogue was able to assume her role as pop icon. She is seen to descend the stage on a flight of stairs, and to make a 'teasing silhouette . . . before silently appearing beneath the spotlight' (Sheridan 2012, 259). There were a series of costume changes which begin to reflect a more experimental, high-fashion consciousness, and most notably the show prefigures a growing sensibility for a *multimedia* experience. This was a point marked at the very start: 'As ticketholders entered the concert venues a gigantic pair of Kylie eyes surveyed them from a video screen, looking left to right, then up and down. The effect was deliberately unnerving' (Sheridan 2012, 148).

Body accoutrements

In 1999, Kylie Minogue signed to the Pet Shop Boys' record label, Parlophone (part of the large EMI Group). The first album for this label, *Light Years* (2000), proved both a turning point and saving of her career. Indeed, the first single, 'Spinning Around', with its Gloria Gaynor-like line, 'I found a new direction and it leads back to me', made for a perfect new start. However, it was arguably the video for the song that really re-launched Minogue's career. It shows her flirting and dancing in a hedonistic club: 'totally carefree, happy and shimmering with St Tropez fake tan – it was her bottom that fixated fans and journalists alike. [. . . T]he video's budget, reputedly £400,000, was dwarfed by a 50 pence pair of second-hand gold lamé hotpants which Kylie wore throughout' (Sheridan 2012, 163). Having 'spun things around' with the move to the new record label (and everything that the gold hotpants did for her stock), Minogue and her team seemed finally to hit upon the right creative approach to *perform* 'Kylie'. Off the back of the success of the *Light Years* album, Kylie Minogue embarked upon her first proper tour, On a Night like This (2001). Wholly different

FIGURE 17.3 Manghani, 'Transformed into something satisfying in themselves', 2014.

in scale than anything she had engaged in before, the tour was much more extravagant in its costumes and design, drawing on references from *South Pacific* (Joshua Logan, 1958), *Anchors Aweigh* (George Sidney, 1945) and American burlesque theatre. It also signalled a much more sexually provocative style:

> William Baker [as creative director] took advantage of every hardcore S & M gay porn cliché, with Kylie's nymphomaniac dancers dressed in Tom of Finland leathers, grinding their crotches and sweaty abdominals all over her petite female form. Kylie was the dominatrix in charge, strutting eroticism and enjoying every second of her descent into Frankie Goes to Hollywood territory. During 'Kids' she even sang the controversial Robbie Williams rap, sticking out her pert little bum during the risqué 'sodomy' lyric. (Sheridan 2012, 174)

The role Kylie Minogue is able to assume, to be 'in charge', is in part related to her growing reputation as a major artist. Parlophone took to marketing Kylie Minogue very effectively as simply 'Kylie', and this is reflected in the tour with this single name 'up in lights' as part of the stage design. However, the shift from Kylie Minogue to just Kylie is more than just a point of marketing and branding. It denotes a performance, and its various accoutrements. Compared with the early performances at the start of the 1990s, Kylie Minogue's movements upon the stage became far less energetic. She is set apart from her dancers, with greater emphasis upon pose and poise. The performance of 'Kylie' is less about inhabiting the stage, than inhabiting the *staging*.

As noted elsewhere, '[m]ore than anyone, Kylie Minogue knows she is *not* Kylie. In interview, she notes how she assumes a role: "I change characters when I do a photo shoot. It's kind of avoiding being me"' (cited in Manghani and McDonald 2013, 221). It is a very carefully *designed* and *edited* performance, which arguably only properly takes shape through the making of music videos. Kylie is a celluloid construction, fashioned of a singular (rhythmic) body, haute couture and experimental designs, and the collaging of various citations and reference points. During the On a Night Like This tour, Kylie Minogue debuted 'Can't Get You Out of My Head'. The song – which went on to be her biggest selling record, indeed a huge international hit – had been recorded only weeks before the tour, and was months away from being released (ahead of the new album *Fever*, released in October 2001). On stage she offered a somewhat low-key performance. There was no sense of what the song was going to become. Clearly, it had not gone through a full 'editorial process'. Again, in this case, it is the creation of 'Kylie' through music video that is significant.

For the video of 'Can't Get You Out of My Head' Kylie Minogue is shown driving through a futuristic landscape, towards a Ballardian cityscape. The various outfits in the video, not least a Grace Jones-inspired white hooded jumpsuit, with improbable plunging neckline (causing huge tabloid sensation), and a stylized robotic dance routine, helped make the song an anthem for 'Kylie'. In effect the video marks the completion of the creation of 'Kylie', which is then (literally) unveiled at the opening of her next tour, KylieFever (2002):

> Kylie set the scene by ascending from the stage floor, clad in beautiful silver robotic armour (reputed to have cost £40,000). Reminiscent of the android beauty from Fritz Lang's 1926 movie classic *Metropolis*, or a super-sexy female Cyberman, Kylie's outrageous costume was simply breathtaking. Named 'Kyborg', the figure remained motionless for a moment before the metal plates slowly began to peel off, revealing Kylie dressed in a crystal-sparkling Dolce & Gabbana miniskirt and bra. Kylie became a futuristic sorceress controlling the marionette movements of her dancers with a flick of her hand, lunge of a buttock or a thrust of an elbow. (Sheridan 2012, 192)

We might readily suggest the cybotic, compartmentalizing of the body reads off as a pure example of the male gaze, whereby the 'woman as object' is reified, in part, from fragmented close-ups. However in the context of the arena, and the physical distance and natural flow this creates, the arrival of the 'Kyborg' is not of the same order of the fetish created in videos such as for 'Spinning Around'. Away from the fast-editing of a music video, which in 'Spinning Around', for example, fetishistically *transforms* the gold hotpants into something satisfying in themselves, live performance makes for a different visual experience. Of course, it should be noted, the DVD recordings of such concerts edit *whole* performances into sequences and close-ups, which in turn leads to a form of fetishistic scopophila. Using stills from these recordings to illustrate this chapter no doubt further heightens the gaze, with the images fixed evermore outside of their original unfolding time. Nevertheless, in the arena, fetish wanes, or at least cannot so readily take hold. Instead we are overtaken by a sense of constructedness and distanciation.

In his book, *Iconology*, W.J.T Mitchell reflects upon the enigmatic line in Milton's *Paradise Lost*, in which Adam and Eve are described as 'In naked majesty seemed lords of all / And worthy seemed, for in their looks divine / The image of their glorious Maker shone.' As Mitchell points out, '[e]verything hinges on the equivocal function of the key word "looks", which may refer us to the outward appearance of Adam and Eve, [. . .] or to the less tangible sense of "looks" as the quality of their gazes' (Mitchell 1987, 35–36). In short, the lines allude to both a *material*

FIGURE 17.4 Kylie Minogue as the 'Kyborg'. (Still from *KylieFever2002: Live in Manchester* [William Baker and Alan Macdonald, 2002]).

sense of radiance (that fascinates onlookers) and *mental* reflection (as in possessing a certain 'outlook' upon or *of* the world). For Milton, this is a historically important 'scene of a struggle between iconoclastic distrust of the outward image and iconophilic fascination with its power' (Mitchell 1987, 36). But, equally, it is instructive of the *live* relational properties of the gaze. In the arena, watching Kylie Minogue live on stage – and most likely through the bodies of audience members in front – we are *faced* with quite a different 'Kylie'. In Deleuze's terms (considered further below), whereby the face equates with the close-up as a form of deterritorialization (Deleuze 1992, 96), Minogue's face *and* body parts become the many faces of 'Kylie' – we are taken elsewhere, with body parts as entities (as 'faces') in their own right. Furthermore, while Kylie might then 'look divine', providing an apparent pleasurable affect, equally, she is in possession of an 'outlook' that – lost to the spectacle of the stage – we likely imagine is one of pleasure: for *her* (we suspect) she too 'looks divine'. In 'looks divine', then, we can regard both a body that 'looks' to beholders as being divine (being of the 'encounter' – or set of encounters – associated with the face of an*other*); yet that also tells of a 'subject' in possession of their own point of 'view'.

FIGURE 17.5 The 'face' of Kylie Minogue emerges from the 'Kyborg'. (Still from *KylieFever2002: Live in Manchester* [William Baker and Alan Macdonald, 2002]).

Facing Kylie

The 'look' created by Kylie is carefully stage-managed. The musicians, the dancers, the blocking and the costumes are all carefully choreographed to form a single moving entity: everything, that is, except Kylie herself. It is necessary that she is both integral to the show, and yet somehow apart from it. Reference can be made to Cindy Sherman's *Untitled Film Stills* series (1977–1980), in which the one thing that never 'fits' is Sherman's own face. As Joan Copjec puts it, 'in the various diegetic spaces of this photographic series, the face of Sherman does not belong to them' (Copjec 2002, 76).

Copjec's account of Sherman's work goes against the dominant reading whereby 'it is always assumed that *the situation imprints itself*, however, ambiguously, *on the woman's face*. She is stamped by her setting' (Copjec 2002, 74). Settings, narratives, (theoretical) frameworks can too easily predominate, taking us away from what we literally see. In the case of Sherman's photographs, as Judith Williamson noted very early on, '[w]hat comes out of the imagined narratives is, specifically, femininity. It is not just a range of feminine expressions that are shown but the *process* of the 'feminine' as an effect, something acted upon' (Williamson 1983, 104). Despite the importance of such readings, it has been difficult to consider the 'look' of these photographs from alternative viewpoints, to allow for their own 'looks divine'. The *Untitled Film Stills* might be thought an exemplary teaching aid for the 'passivity of the feminine', as if to *illustrate* how 'in the culture evoked by the photographs woman is not allowed to become the "bearer of the look," but is condemned to be its object' (Copjec 2002, 67).

For Copjec, we need to look past the different 'characters' to see that one woman (Cindy Sherman) frequents each of the images. The point is not to suggest Sherman an 'essential' anchor. Rather, Copjec invokes a thesis about the 'self' as multiple, and here particularly to ascribe multiple *'appearings/ masqueradings'* to femininity (Copjec 2002, 74). She makes reference to Deleuze's account of the face/close-up in his analysis of cinema. Against the idea that the mise-en-scène, or historical context, comes to determine the meaning of facial expression, Copjec notes how Deleuze looks from the opposite direction: 'It is the very ambiguity of the facial expression that allows it to 'receive' or be appropriately juxtaposed to so many different scenes, scenes that do not exhaust its meaning' (Copjec 2002, 75).

Of course, for Deleuze (as suggested in the preceding section), what he means by 'face' is not simply the human face. His interest is in observing two concurrent poles. He gives the example of a clock face, which *intensively* marks time (pole one), but that equally is a 'receptive immobile surface' (pole two). In its 'looks divine', as it were, or as an 'affection-image' as Deleuze refers to it, the clock helps us think about the interval between whole and part, between *forms* (or common qualities) and independent *sensations* (or the affective 'potential' that passes between points). This is the interval of the face: 'Each time we discover these two poles in something – reflecting surface and intensive micro-movements – we can say that this thing has been treated as a face [visage]: it has been "envisaged" or rather "faceified" [visagéifiée], and in turn it stares at us [dévisage], it looks at us . . . even if it does not resemble a face' (Deleuze 1992, 88).

As Kylie is slowly and deliberately released from the Kyborg costume we are presented less with fetishized parts of her body, than with a series of 'faces', or close-ups – which stare out at us (albeit fleetingly) as newly fashioned spatiotemporal coordinates. As Bogue explains:

Rather than being a body part in a determinate spatio-temporal setting, or a marker of an identity, a role or a relation, the face in close-up is an autonomous object, an immobile surface with motor tendencies. Once removed from social codes and the commonsense coordinates of space and time, the face becomes an affection-image: an image expressing an affective quality or power. (Bogue 2003, 78)

Deleuze's account of 'faces' begins to suggest 'something' of the potential of thought-images in that, in themselves, these faces can be read as presenting philosophical concepts, or entities of meaning in their own right. He uses Charles Pierce's language of Firstness and Secondness (as different orders of meaning making), a differentiation between 'a quality as pure possibility or potential and a quality as actualized in a concrete situation' (Bogue 2003, 79).

Of course, the context of the arena is not a particularly 'concrete' situation, but a temporarily fashioned setting or imaginary space, not too dissimilar to cinematic space. And, within this 'space', just as Sherman's images are a consideration of their own medium, Kylie's performance (in its 'looks divine') cannot help but be about its own medium – about pop, citation and glamour; about appearances as pure possibility and/or a fiction about their own fiction. As Copjec suggests in the case of Sherman, she remains 'immersed in the world of appearances. But where film theorists condemned this theoretical and cinematic conflation of the woman with the image, the *Untitled Film Stills* does not' (Copjec 2002, 77). Copjec, then, seeks to place these works outside of the argument that they are indicative of a gendered gaze; a gaze that seeks to display women merely for erotic ends. Similarly, Kylie's live performances are an immersion in a world of appearances. Of course, in this case they are surely more about pleasure than critique. Nonetheless, in looking out to her audience, rather than simply being looked upon, Kylie's performance is as much about *us*, as it is about her.

Periscopic

The preceding account of the 'face' of Kylie perhaps only holds in relation to the *archive* of live performances, that is, to her *recorded* image. The fact Deleuze's account is borne of an analysis of cinema arguably relates to deterritorialization as needing mediation, to transcribe outside of the frame: Deleuze is emphatic that the close-up 'does *not* tear away its object from a set of which it would form part' (Deleuze 1992, 95). Yet, seemingly, the only way this can occur is to have a medium such as celluloid or paint to achieve both abstraction and flow: a means by which a singular entity, or 'face', can appear as being in its own right (though assuming some form of symbiosis of medium and object). Crucially, however, Deleuze's account of the close-up – as not simply set apart, but rather 'deterritorisalized' from the whole – leads him to explicitly deny comparison with the partial object of psychoanalysis. Copjec, however, suggests otherwise, since she argues the psychoanalytic notion of the partial object 'does not pretend to be a part of some whole, but is instead a part that replaces a whole' (Copjec 2002, 75). Understood this way, Copjec is able to bring the 'face' to accord with Lacan's gaze, reintroducing a problematic of loss or desire (the desire perhaps for replacement with the 'live' bodies of the performance and audience). It is a move that allows us to consider a certain deterritorization of desire between *live* bodies (within the nexus of the gaze). Here, then, we step out of the filmic space into that of the arena.

For Copjec, when faced with an object, we are confronted by 'Freud's thesis that love, any love, is always and fundamentally narcissistic . . . that *what we love in the object is ourselves*' (Copjec 2002, 79). To this, she adds Lacan's claim that when in love 'there are not two ones, but a One and an Other, or One plus a', from which she explains, 'we must understand the One to be not the lover, but the beloved object' (Copjec 2002, 80). Again, in this sense, we can argue, when watching Kylie perform live, she is not the compartmentalized and fetishized body we typically see from her circulated, mediated image. Rather, it is the audience member who is 'in pieces', for the lover is (using Lacan's terminology of displacement and desire) 'locatable only in the object a'. As Copjec puts it, regarding Cindy Sherman, 'genuine love is never selfless – nor, for that matter, is sublimation' (Copjec 2002, 80).

Copjec's account helps turn the tables on where we truly take the arena performance to lie. Of course, we are likely too distracted to remember ourselves in this act of love. Or, equally perhaps, we might consider ourselves too well versed in issues of mediation and representation to be drawn into any such narcissistic 'net'. Walter Benjamin long since noted how '[t]he camera that presents the performance of the film actor to the public need not respect the performance as an integral whole', and clearly in trying to write about the arena performance it is always tempting to pick upon the recorded image, whereby we unwittingly examine the performer as if 'subjected to a series of optical tests' (Benjamin 1992, 222). Of course, even in the arena we can still identify a complex of 'optical tests'. The live performer needs to negotiate both a live audience and deliver their part alongside a film-image, which plays out simultaneously to the audience across video screens – and increasingly now as part of the illuminated stage itself. Kylie Minogue's X tour (2008), for example, utilized sophisticated interplays of dance, music and video-work, which included visualizations screened across the stage floor; seemingly out of view for many in the audience, but no doubt impacting on the performances given by those on stage (and highly effective in the recorded DVD version).

However, within the contemporary arena setting there is another optical test at play. It is a test placed upon the individual audience member as they grapple with their mobile phone to capture the experience. It is an optical test that brings home the need identified by Copjec to locate ourselves in the One on stage, as if to become attuned to many 'faces' looking out at us. This compulsion to *take* photos comes of our own lack of face. It does not matter about the quality of the image. This is simply an action, a form of periscopic viewing: we seek to make sense of what is beyond us, to gain access over the heads of others; like a periscope we use the mobile phone to gain an advantage on those around us. Yet, without realizing it, the attempt to overcome or get around the condition that prevents our direct line-of-sight is ultimately about observing or at least locating *ourselves*. Mitchell describes this action as 'drawing desire':

> This becomes clearer if we reflect on the double meaning of *drawing* as an act of tracing or inscribing lines, on the one hand, and an act of pulling, dragging, or attracting, on the other . . . 'Drawing Desire,' then, is meant not to just suggest the depiction of a scene or figure that stands for desire, but also to indicate the way that drawing itself, the dragging or pulling of the drawing instrument, is the performance of desire. Drawing draws on us. (Mitchell 2005, 59)

As someone intimately engaged with the practice of drawing, it happens that John Berger's descriptions of drawing echo Mitchell's remarks very closely. The act of drawing he suggests is to understand that '[a]ny fixed contour is in nature arbitrary and impermanent. What is on one side of it tries to shift it by pushing or pulling' (Berger 2011, 113). Of course, there are important distinctions to be made between the 'optical tests' of photographing and drawing. The holding up of a mobile phone to record a performer on the stage is arguably a habitual, even lazy gesture. To commit pencil to paper in the setting of the arena involves a rather less steady mode of looking, which ultimately is an observation of the fragile nature of one's own ocular and bodily site of observation. A distinction emerges perhaps between sign and substance: 'The lines of a sign are uniform and regular: the lines of a drawing are harassed and tense. Somebody making a sign repeats an habitual gesture. Somebody making a drawing is alone in the infinitely extensive' (Berger 2011, 113).

Nevertheless, regardless of its mode, the optical test of the arena is short-lived. Before we know it the show is over, the harsh lights of the auditorium making plain the futility of our former periscopic vision. The music is gone. We are left only with blurred pictures upon our phone and a swirl of mental imagery. These become what Victor Burgin terms 'sequence-images' (Burgin 2004, 14–28). They are not static, fixed images, nor are they sequenced in any narrative sense; rather a 'concatenation of images raises itself, as if in *bas relief*, above the instantly fading, then forgotten, desultory thoughts and impressions passing through [one's] mind' (Burgin 2004, 21). Yet the sequence-image is no delusion: 'It is a *fact* – a transitory state of percepts of a 'present moment' seized in their association with past affects and meanings' (Burgin 2004, 21).

Jack Dee was no doubt correct. We might as well stay home and listen to the album, at least regards the auditory experience. Yet, still we seek out the sequence-image that an arena can provide. It is 'neither image nor image sequence . . . [i]ndeed it may be doubted whether it can ever be fully

FIGURE 17.6 Periscopic: Getting around the condition that prevents our direct line-of-sight is ultimately about observing ourselves. Kylie Minogue's *Kiss Me Once Tour*, O2 Arena, London, 30 September 2014. Photo: Manghani.

'What's on one side of contour has got its tongue in the mouth of what's on the other side. And vice versa. The challenge of drawing is to show this, to make visible on the paper or drawing surface not only discrete, recognizable things, but also to show how the extensive is one substance' (Berger 2011, 113).

FIGURE 17.7 Manghani, 'Live Drawings', 2014. Drawings from Kylie Minogue's Kiss Me Once tour, O2 Arena, London, 30 September 2014.

FIGURE 17.8a Kylie Minogue's Anti-Tour, Manchester Academy, 2 April 2012.
Photo: Manghani.

FIGURE 17.8b Kylie Minogue's Anti-Tour, Manchester Academy, 2 April 2012.
Photo: Manghani.

a *theoretical* object, at least so long as theory remains an affair of language' (Burgin 2004, 27). Our only recourse is constantly to *make* the sequence-images that make up who we think we are. We flock to the arena for the chance to 'perform' memories of having-been-there, which in turn conjoin to create newly 'recovered' memories, new confluences of having seen a star such as Kylie, whatever she may look like, indeed regardless of what she may look like, but rather for how she makes us look.

Note

1   See FAQs on the First Direct Arena website: http://www.firstdirectarena.com/ venue-information/frequently-asked-questions/ (accessed January 2015).

FIGURE 17.9 *Remembered Performance?* Kylie Minogue's Anti-Tour, Manchester Academy, 2 April 2012. Photo: Manghani.

CHAPTER EIGHTEEN

Intimacy in Public

Jos Mulder

Sounding out the arena

It is not uncommon in the humanities to fall back on ancient Greece for inspiration in academic writing. Arenas (although Roman rather than Greek), theatres, circuses and stadiums are well established both in the literature and the landscape of the classics. Even though the subject of this book bears little resemblance to the Greek theatrical tradition, or a Roman spectacle, some comparison is warranted. One such similarity is the size of the audiences; an important difference is the distance between audience members and the stage, not in terms of metres but in hearing the sounds produced on stage. This chapter is aimed at disentangling the complex web of sound and distance, both physical and social. The combination of contemporary arenas as entertainment venue and electronically amplification highlights the uncoupling between sound level and physical distance. For the duration of a concert social etiquette and personal preferences for proximity are suspended while the unique distance encoding of the human voice is extend into the hyperreal.

The Roman arena allowed for an auditory experience in the best tradition of bread and games.[1] The anticipation of violent entertainments would have translated into yelling and cheering fuelled by a combination of excitement, horror and empathy. A crowd of thousands would have created a noisy accompaniment to races and fights. The sounds emanating from the arena would have been of blows and yells, roaring animals or gladiators. Any speech sounds more modest than yelling or screaming would have probably gone unheard to all but those closest to the action. The thumbs up or down tradition that decided on a fighter's faith might bear witness to this (Corbeill 1997).

Notwithstanding the phenomenal reputation of speech acoustics in the classic theatre and amphitheatre, in a congregation of 10,000–15,000, people would have had to be spectacularly quiet in order to understand the actors' voices. Some forms of acoustic amplification may have been used and the synchronous choir sections would have reinforced transmission of the choruses, but even when optimized for intelligibility addressing a large outdoors theatre would have been a challenge. The audience behaviour would, perhaps, have been similar to the late romantic concert tradition where silent audiences are expected to undergo music in subdued or contemplative concentration. The sheer size of the classical venues made the theatrical presentations very formal; the bulk of the audience was seated relatively distant from the performers on stage. And although there was no 'fourth wall' in the shape of a proscenium, audience discipline would have been firmly established by the need for reduced background noise. To illustrate the issue: a pre-electronic amplification adaptation of a Shakespeare play in a stadium where intelligibility was failing can be found in Coppelia Kahn's (2000) paper *Caliban at the Stadium*. The paper describes how the size of the former Lewisohn stadium in New York, which was in fact an 8,000-seat amphitheatre, stopped the audience from grasping more than ten out of a hundred words. A millennium and a half or so later, in Shakespeare's much smaller Globe theatre audiences habitually participated by heckling and cheering, which required and perhaps created a certain informal intimacy. An informality that was, as far as we can tell, lacking or simply unattainable in Epidaurus or other ancient theatres.

Such informality can easily be identified in pop and rock arena concerts to the point where a mass spectacle actually becomes an intimate experience. Steve Mithen (2006, 156) in his book *The Singing Neanderthals* refers to the exceptional situation in which strangers enter our intimate space, as common at large pop concerts:

> We all have an unconsciously intimate body space around us, which we only allow our family and closest friends to enter. Should a stranger enter that space, we experience the physiological responses of increased heart rate, adrenalin pouring into the bloodstream, and the tightening of muscles, all of which are preparations for a potential 'fight or flight' situation.

This intimacy is not simply because patrons stand shoulder to shoulder in each other's personal space, it resonates in the sonic experience of the musical efforts on stage. Elizabeth Wollman (2006, 271) writes in her book about rock musicals: 'successful live rock performances are designed to cultivate a sense of intimacy, even in the largest venues'. Rock music in a theatre, with an audience on plush, does not easily trigger the same response as a rock concert with dancing or standing room only. Some would think Wollman's remark puzzling, since the sheer volume of sound amplification excludes rock concerts from being intimate. But the sounds that are blasted at the audience are in fact of an intimate nature: the intimacy of the close microphone. In the words of Alan Durant (1984, 196) the acronym PA for public address gets a whole new meaning that is 'unmediated by conventions of representation'. Electronic amplification makes possible the seemingly contradictory of vocal intimacy and the public in 'Public Address', which provides, Durant continues: 'the basis of rock's oratory and proposed social alternative'. An arena concert audience is allowed to overhear an intimate message to a chronic absentee.

Electronic amplification is not limited to pop and rock concerts, these days for instance performances of Indian classical music are generally amplified. While often even the suggestion of amplifying Western classical music meets with resentment, by musicians in particular, Indian performers often insist on performing their traditional musics electronically amplified (Potter and Sorrel 2012, 181). According to Amanda Weidman (2006, 126) this is in part due to the enhanced intimacy the use of sound technology suggests. She cites a patron at an amplified Indian classical music concert: 'It seemed like we were overhearing a conversation in which a devotee spoke intimately to her God.' Referring to Simon Frith (1996, 187) Weidman describes the ability of a microphone to project intimacy to a vast audience as one of its 'most prominent effects'. Earlier in her book (2006, 91) Weidman remarks: 'That same mic[rophone] that could convert a lion's roar into a sweet lamb's voice reserved, mysteriously, the power to convert it back, with a difference, at any moment.' (Here referring to the occasional mishap of amplification: ear-piercing feedback.)

The Greek theatres helped shape Greek drama just as much as the churches of the reformation shaped Bach's music.[2] Popular music was born not necessarily in a particular venue but in radio and recording studios. It had to find appropriate venues, breaking from the traditions and the rationality of the classical concert hall, affirming the rebellious underscore of rock music in the 1950s. In his debunking of traditional academic approaches to music Christopher Small (1998, 26) argues that classical concert halls are built on the assumption that: 'music is a system of one-way communication', and it comes as no surprise that amplified music in an overly reverberant room is a recipe for sonic disaster. Amplification allowed many places to be turned into venues, whether acoustically appropriate or not and it was only towards the end of the twentieth century that purpose built venues have become more common.[3] Sound amplification together with the arena and the stadium as music venues left their own marks on, what David Byrne (2012, 25) describes as: 'Arena rock . . . rousing stately anthems', music made as (in Byrne's words) soundtrack to a gathering, providing a whole different social cadre for musical experience.

Edward Hall's social distance

Hall (1966), in his book *The Hidden Dimension* introduced the study of social distance (or proxemics), inspired by observations of animal behaviour. Animals exhibit what is called a 'flight-or-fight' distance: if approached it may choose to run away, and if you come too close it may react by attacking. According to Hall (1966, 120) this is how for instance a lion tamer operates with the rather dangerous animals, playing at the fringe of the two reactions:

> The hypothesis behind the proxemic classification system is this: it is in the nature of animals, including man, to exhibit behaviour, which we call territoriality. In so doing they use the senses to distinguish between one space or distance and another.

Social proximity is multimodal, a concept which is well demonstrated by the behaviour of male frogs. These amphibians adapt the loudness of their quacking to the proximity of a rival frog, in order to attract females or repel other males. That proximity is measured by disturbances in the water surface caused by the quacking of a rival. The difference in time between sound waves travelling in air and in water, sensed by different modalities, allows the frogs to 'sound out' the proximity of a rival (Halfwerk et al. 2014). In the human world, Hall identifies four zones of spatial social interrelations: the intimate, the personal, the social and the public. The zones are found in speech sound; a whisper is intimate ('for reasons of intimacy or conspiracy' in Hall's words), but also in smell (if we are too close to a co-worker we may be troubled by garlic breath, smelly feet or armpits). Or we may be close enough to touch someone, opening a whole range of communicative devices, with strict social implications. The workings of the proxemics change over time (we take a very different stance towards body smells when compared to the days before daily showers and teeth brushing) and can differ culturally. Hall compares informal voice usage across different cultures: Arabs speak louder than Americans but the upper class Brits and Japanese speak more softly. In France (to the tourist) everyone seems to be kissing everyone always even when newly introduced, to the astonishment of Brits, Germans or Australians (Hall 1966, 123; Van Leeuwen 1999, 24).[4]

In recording, broadcasting or amplification the 'sonic social distance' is a consequence of microphone distance (and type selection), and technically a matter of both timbre and level.[5] The recorded scream of a rock singer can be played back at a bearable level in one's headphones; a whisper can be amplified to a deafening sound.[6] The close microphone's whisper has a boost in the low frequencies enhancing the intimacy; the piercing treble of a scream suggests a distance; with increasing distances to cover our voice becomes higher and sharper. With the aid of synthesized reverberation close microphone sounds can be made to sound 'far-way', while still retaining the timbral parameters of the intimate.[7]

In the days before the advance of electroacoustic technologies (telephone and later radio and electronic recording) this relation between voice level and social distance could not be overcome. Voice level would signify actual relationships, along the lines described by Hall. The electronic transductions by microphones and loudspeakers have changed this and their ubiquity has redefined sonic experience. Examples that are often mentioned in this context are the crooning singing style (Crosby, Sinatra) and Roosevelt's 'fireside chats' which were intended to convey an intimacy between the President and citizens listening to the radio; in contrast with the affected, projected radio (and cinematic) voices of the 1930s and 1940s (Ryfe 1999). There was a lot of objection to the promiscuity promised in the seductive voice of the boy crooners, as described by Allison McCracken (1999) and much earlier in Rudolph Arnheim's *Radio* (1936). After the turbulent early days of crooning Frank Sinatra was the first to 'seem comfortable with the *sexual* subtext of the microphone's intimacy', as observed by Roy Hemming (1992, 120). He continues: 'Sinewy and blatantly sexual, boyishly brooding in down-tempo numbers, Sinatra's style seemed as radically erotic in its day as Elvis Presley's air-humping would fifteen years later.' Hemming ends his argument by quoting a psychologist from the 1940s (unreferenced): 'Sinatra was doing "a sort of emotional striptease in which he lays bare his soul."'

Public and the private in the mix

In a chapter about sonic perspective Theo van Leeuwen (1999, 24) argues that in the case of recording and amplification 'social distance' becomes an independent semiotic parameter. When there is no technological interference: 'Soft and loud are most crucially associated with distance' (1999, 133); when we record (or amplify) someone's voice with a microphone the social distance is maintained; a whisper is still a whisper, a scream a scream, even though the level may be completely different. Intimacy can be suggested even at the highest amplification levels, and as such becomes detached from musical dynamics. This mixing of and the tension between the public and private paved the way for: 'the production of other kinds of meaning with vocal style', Van Leeuwen adds. The mixing of public and private appears to be an important sociological element of music. Philip Tagg writes in *Music's Meanings* (2013, 1):

Music also oscillates between private and public because musical experiences that seem intensely intimate and personal are often performed publicly or diffused globally.

This comes to the fore equally in the silent classical concert tradition and in the arena concert. In a concert hall, private silent listening (presumable) is enjoyed in a very public place supported by a number of unwritten rules. At a rock or pop concert the private experience of one's favourite music is enjoyed very publicly again with some implicit rules. Such rules may change with music style, for instance we don't expect a mosh-pit at a Celine Dion concert. The social and experiential importance of the tension, between the public and the private, is emphasized by Tagg (2013, 2) and likened to sexuality:

> Deep fissures can arise between how we see ourselves as sexual beings in private and how we respond to displays of sexuality in the media, just as our intensely personal musical experiences seem to be at the opposite end of the notional spectrum to all the technical, economic and sociocultural factors without which much of the music that so deeply moves us could not exist.

The inability of music consumers to overcome the tension between the two poles and a dual consciousness as a result is a central thesis in Tagg's book. This tension and the challenges of positioning oneself in a public environment have become increasingly clear in the different social media: people posting very intimate details on a network that has many different levels of public accessibility.[8] In recorded music social distance has become a parameter of play (although in many popular musics the intimacy of the close microphone appears to be the de facto standard). At concerts where the physical distance between performers and spectators adds an additional layer, the relevance of these social distance characteristics is further emphasized and sometimes explored creatively. For instance, in theatrical sound design, for dramatic effect a very soft whisper may be amplified to the extreme, creating a theatrical experience that borrows from the cinematic.

The arena space

Electronic music composer and scholar Denis Smalley (2007, 41) applies Hall's theory in an article that discusses space in terms of acousmatic music, based on Henri Lefebvre's work in *The Production of Space* that treats space as a social morphology and as such: 'bound up with function and structure'. Smalley argues that: 'performed space is gesturally rooted':

In performed space in instrumental music we can identify mixtures of Hall's four zones at work, producing three spaces – gestural, ensemble, and arena space; gestural space is nested in ensemble space, and ensemble space is in turn nested within arena space.

The arena space according to Smalley describes a range of possible venues for musical performance, while the ensemble space is the: 'personal and social space among performers'. Gestural space emerges from the intimacy of performer and instrument: 'Sounding body and performance gesture are physically indissolubly linked in intimate space'; more intimate for a violinist or a flautist than for a pianist or a percussionist operating in a more personal space: two can play a marimba or a piano. The idea of perceiving a gestural intimacy in play can equally be observed in popular musics, the success of air-guitar playing – and competitions – being a great example. Ethnomusicologist Weidman (2006, 126) in her analysis of the use of amplification in Indian classical music remarks that the microphone also narrows the physical space of a performer. In order to realize the desired intimacy the microphone must be kept close, the microphone functions: 'as a ballast for a singer or violinist, limiting the distance he or she can move'. As such the microphone also informs a performer's gestural space. Queen's Freddie Mercury and many pop and rock vocalists explore and craft a choreography involving a microphone and, no lesser, its humble stand. Obviously this changes when singers resort to a head-worn 'Madonna' microphone that keeps the transducer very close while freeing a singers' hands and arms.

The complex of nested spaces can be mediated by technologies such as amplification and the use of large video screens, creating what Smalley (2007, 43) presents as: 'mediatised performed space'. Smalley distinguishes between the use of amplification within the arena space: 'so that an extrovert and gesturally extravagant, or a more introvert and gesturally discrete, performance can thereby hope to achieve more acceptable impact or intimacy', and even larger venues:

> With popular or rock music concerts or open-air musical events, where relative distance between gestural space and further boundaries of the arena can be so extended that aural and visual contact are lost, the video image is able to zoom in on the intimate and personal spaces of performance, thereby transporting a mediatised intimacy to the remote perceiver.

Technologies, Smalley continues, can cure the deficiencies of performance spaces that have become too large to fulfil their 'primary communicative function'.

Large video screens displaying close ups of performing band members are a common element of the arena show. Their significance can be observed in a comparable application at classical music concerts as related by Emily Dolan (2013, 1). The Philadelphia Orchestra has positioned small remote-controlled cameras among the performers when in concert. Selected imagery is projected on large screens and as such the 'cameras can take the audience inside the orchestra'. Miami's new concert hall the New World Center, designed by Frank Gehry, has five screens integrated into the auditorium to allow exactly this type of visual extension of the concert experience. Dolan (2013, 2) cites music critic and author Alex Ross who described his experience of the New World Center as: 'not just a technological forward leap but the emergence of a new genre'. The visuals have a profound influence on how we experience the orchestral balance as the camera direction chooses to zoom in and emphasize an instrument playing a crucial melody line or solo, Dolan analyses: 'New technological forms of mediation, perhaps ironically, serve to make the orchestra more vivid, more immediate, rendering details more palpable.' The same trend that enhances classical performance with video projection is found in a recent concert of Sydney's symphony orchestra. As part of a relatively novel tradition of using the Sydney Opera House's iconic sails as a projection canvas, close-up images of musicians and instruments from inside the auditorium are brought out in the open, this time entirely disconnected from the audible performance inside.[9]

The transduction of social distance is something we have accustomed ourselves to after the genesis of electronic media, as described by Emily Thompson (2002) in *The Soundscape of Modernity*. Amplified sound simply complies; we have come to expect the same sound quality, with a similar effect on social distances as heard on radio and TV. The consequence for electronically amplified sound is the necessity of a detached sound, drowning out the acoustic source. It is the amplified, intimate, direct, transduced sound we want to hear, not the acoustic, distant sound with all its spatial information that has become, in popular music aesthetics, nothing but noise.[10] A final example from Sydney: at a Bon Jovi concert I attended at the football stadium the rockers relocated for a few songs to a semi-circular catwalk extending into the audience. Playing acoustic instruments (acoustic guitars, cajón and accordion) an 'unplugged' setting was created, amplified with microphones so the 65,000 people could hear. The distance between performers and audience was bridged in two ways, literally by leaving the stage to be closer to the fans and musically by playing acoustic instruments, as if in a local bar.[11]

Recording or performance?

Simon Frith (2002, 286) has suggested that rock music is, rather than a performance art, essentially a recorded music, constructed in the studio. Theodore Gracyk (1996, 74) goes a step further: 'In rock music the musical instruments are almost always several steps removed from the audience.' In the case of recorded music this is clear, for example in playback technology, recording medium, mastering and editing, pitch and timing correction, mixing, multi-track recording and microphone selection. Not that this is unique to rock and pop, classical music nowadays is recorded on multiple tracks and in several takes, the recording is 'produced' in editing, mixing and mastering, long after the musicians and conductor went home. Gracyk (196, 74) argues: 'In live performance, speakers deliver a combination of amplified and electronic sounds. We almost never hear "original" sounds; when the electricity fails the music stops.' Authors such as Jonathan Sterne (2006) and Paul Théberge (2001, 3) have argued against discussing sound media in terms of copy and original.[12] But Gracyk adds a relevant observation to his argument: human voices and acoustic instruments are several (modifying) steps away from the audience by (in concord with Van Leeuwen's ideas) microphone selection and mixing/filtering: 'shaping the sound in response to the auditorium's acoustics'. The distance created by the technologies causes Gracyk to conclude that rock music is essentially not a performing art: 'recording is the most characteristic medium of rock'.[13] However, from a perspective of proxemics this created distance is a salient feature of the transduction processes in use both in music recording and electronic amplification. For a rock or pop band these 'transduction effects' are essential whether in the studio or live: electric guitars need amplifiers and the singing voice needs an amplified, close microphone.

As much as the idea that loud pop concerts can be intimate strikes some as a contradiction in terms, a similar particularity can be observed in headphone music. As explored by Michael Bull (2004, 177) the headphone toting individual metaphorically colonizes space: 'Mobile privatization is about the desire for proximity, for a mediated presence that shrinks space into something manageable and inhabitable', and 'Through the power of sound the world becomes intimate, known, and possessed' (2004, 181).

Conclusion

Different configurations of musical and other entertainment presentations with regard to spatial acoustics, sound technologies and audience behaviour can be observed, both historically and in contemporary practices. The blend of public and private elements that can be identified in the arena concert experience helps identifying, if not defining some of its salient features. For a few hours people allow or even welcome strangers – the public – in their immediate private space and appear to enjoy it. The fascinating ability of sound transduction by microphones and loudspeakers to alter the social distance encoded in sound, whether recorded, broadcast or amplified, plays an important role in this mix. Sound level and distance are disconnected from each other and from vocal and musical instrument timbre, making it possible to suggest intimacy in a public place (more often than the other way around). These uncouplings allow for an oscillation between the public and the private, which can be found in all performance arts but brought to extremes in the concert arena. Loudness, sweaty armpits and poking elbows are part of the experience. For the duration of the concert the audience's attention is undivided, intimate and immersed as if between lovers.

Notes

1 The word arena refers to the sand that covered the fighting pit.
2 See for instance Bagenal and Wood (1931, 368) *Planning for Good Acoustics* or Michael Forsyth (1985, 9).
3 See Robert Kronenburg's discussion of music venues in the introduction to his book *Live Architecture* (2012).
4 When meeting expatriate friends in Australia I am puzzled whether or not I should be kissing the French guy, and generally end up embarrassed regardless.
5 For voice use in particular the close microphone is ubiquitous, microphones at greater distance of sound sources are common in classical music recording.
6 Scarlett Johansson's performance in Spike Jonze's movie *Her* (2013) comes to mind, acting out sexual tension through her voice alone
7 Relevant discussions of the use and meaning of potentials of the addition of echoes and reverberation to recordings and live performances can be found in Peter Doyle's (2005) *Echo and Reverb* and Barry Blesser and Linda-Ruth Salter's (2006) *Spaces Speak*.
8 Typically, Adorno (1991 [1938]) in his *Of the Fetish* underlines the tension by suggesting that there is no simple public–private binary by referring to the public and the unprivate.
9 On 4 February 2015, the Sydney Symphony Orchestra's performance of 'Greatest Hits from Vienna' was projected onto the sails of the Sydney Opera House. During the 2011 performance of what was dubbed the 'YouTube Symphony Orchestra', similar footage was projected inside the venue, and simultaneously on the iconic building's exterior.
10 This is one of the great contradictions of pop music performance, the need for loud energetic drums and guitar amplifiers versus the desire for low levels on stage sound with minimal interference with the PA loudspeakers addressing the audience.
11 Sydney Football Stadium, 17 December 2010. The example also shows that the term unplugged is not synonymous with unamplified.
12 In that article Sterne makes the case that: 'The recording process didn't capture a "live" performance. If anything, the performance was designed to capture the recording.'
13 Antoine Hennion (1997, 428) suggests the opposite: 'Unlike classical music, which seeks to give primary significance to the music itself, rock's core element is the stage. Records, television, radios, posters all refer to the stage as their gold standard.'

CHAPTER NINETEEN

Beyoncé's Celebrity Feminism and Performances of Female Empowerment in the Arena Concert

Kirsty Fairclough-Isaacs

'This perfect, godly woman'

I had known that I was going to see her for months, but nothing could have prepared me for the real thing. When she rose out of the stage with all the smoke and her silhouette appeared, the real her, there in front of my eyes for the first time, I screamed and cried whilst simultaneously trying to rock out to 'Run the World (Girls)'. I couldn't believe she was really there it didn't seem real, this perfect, godly woman in the same vicinity as me, singing my favourite songs note perfect. I don't think I actually stopped crying the whole way through but it was undoubtedly one of the best nights of my life, it's been 2 years and I've not forgotten a second of it. The end was pretty overwhelming, I couldn't believe it was over, I had to be calmed down by my sisters but looking back, it was perfect. It is an overwhelming experience being in the same room as your idol, someone you see as completely flawless![1]

These are the words of a nineteen-year-old woman in response to witnessing R&B/pop singer Beyoncé live for the first time. The fervour with which she speaks of seeing Beyoncé on stage seems, for her, indicative of something akin to a religious experience. For Helena, the image of Beyoncé as the epitome of womanhood, and as an aspirational figure is evident. The use of such effusive descriptions as 'perfect', 'godly' and 'flawless' are not unusual within Beyoncé's devoted fan base, the 'Bey Hive', known for its obsessive devotion. But such descriptions are not solely reserved for fans. Beyoncé's live performances are widely renowned as some of the most impressive that popular music has ever witnessed.

This chapter will examine Beyoncé and her 2013–2014 arena concert tour, The Mrs Carter Show, to explore the ways in which she employs the tropes of what appear to be female empowerment and celebrity feminism in order to maintain and develop her position in popular music and pop culture more widely. It will consider attempts to promote her status as celebrity feminist through her arena concerts and will assess how Beyoncé calls on her fans to use her music and imagery to engage with a rather simplistic notion of female empowerment.

Beyoncé Knowles-Carter is a multi-platinum and Grammy Award winning artist who is often hailed as one of the best, if not the best, performers of her generation by cultural commentators and fellow artists associated with 'high brow' publications such as *The New Yorker, The Guardian* and *Time* magazine (Rosen 2013; Llewyn-Smith 2009; Luhrmann 2013 respectively). Such is the magnitude of praise that Beyoncé, the singer, gives way to Beyoncé, 'the event', for Luhrmann, since 'no one has that voice, no one moves the way she moves, no one can hold an audience the way she does . . . [w]hen Beyoncé does an album, when Beyoncé sings a song, when Beyoncé does anything, it's an event, and it's broadly influential. Right now, she is the heir-apparent diva of the USA – the reigning national voice' (Luhrmann 2013). *Time* has listed her in lists of the 100 most influential people, and placed her on their cover, and her sales (both albums and concert tickets) match such acclaim.[2]

In December 2013 Beyoncé released the innovative 'visual album', *Beyoncé*, consisting of fourteen tracks and seventeen videos, without any pre-publicity and then only through using social media as the means of promotion once the album had been released solely on iTunes. Its initial sales neared one million 'copies' within the first three days. This strategy, around the album itself, was immediately considered to be a game-changer by the music industry which has long relied on the system of releasing singles and their accompanying music videos systematically, prior to the trumpeted release of a full album. The themes of the record were intimate, even dark at times, and so signalled a shift in tone from previous releases. The album examined a greater sense of agency by the singer, and contained what appears to be an engagement with feminist themes.

From these comments alone, it is noticeable that standard methodological approaches to popular music will not encompass Beyoncé's oeuvre in a satisfactory way. In the post-CD age, in which the arena concert emerges as a kind of new materiality in terms of 'possessing' music (to have been at the gig, as evidenced via social media, rather than 'merely' to possess the album), an expanded frame of reference is required. And this frame of reference is one that crucially, as I shall argue in relation to feminism, ushers the body back into the terrain of analysis. Recent critical writing on music and performance (Auslander 2004, 2008, 2009; Inglis 2006; Cook 2012)[3] has called for greater attention to be paid to the physical, gestural and social dimensions of musical performance, and for the treatment of the performance as a musical text. The cross-disciplinary debates engendered by this desire to develop an approach that fundamentally acknowledges visual and musical elements are signalled in Cook's rhetorical question of 'How might we put the music back into performance analysis?'(2012, 192). In this regard, Simon Frith's influential work on the interpretation of performance as a social process (1996, 205) has contributed important models for the disentangling of the many layers of expression that comprise song performance (to include sounds, gender, race, sexuality, lyrics, vocal styles, performativity and technology). Auslander (2004, 2009) has extended Frith's work to construct the analytic framework of 'person-persona-character' in order to analyse the singer's enactment of song meanings: his work focuses critical attention upon the singer's body as the site of visual and narrative communication, but does not incorporate aspects of musical content and structure. These advances in critical thought are lent a further urgency, and effectively stress tested, by the enormity of the arena concert, both in terms of the forensic close-up presentation of the singer and his or her body (relayed via giant video screens, captured innumerable times on mobile phones and cameras), and the cumulative millions in attendance.

Beyoncé and the live concert experience

In recent years a number of female R&B/pop performers have utilized tenets of female empowerment, with vague links to feminist ideas, as part of their brand and as incorporated into performances, as with Alicia Keys, Lady Gaga, Pink and Nicki Minaj. Beyoncé's engagement, however, was considerably more pronounced. That oscillation between spectacle and intimacy which appears to be the foundation of a successful arena concert, as combined with themes of empowerment, has become part of the expected package for many star female artists in performance. This is in part attributable to the visibility of feminist themes in popular culture since the 1990s, especially the emergence of Third Wave feminism and its propensity to utilize mainstream culture as a way of advancing the cause of female emancipation.

Audiences now expect their stars to reveal something personal on stage as well as entertain them. The lineage of this expectation is bound up with three elements: a gossip and scandal-fuelled, and paparazzi-driven, celebrity culture where the private has become the public; the development of technologies that encourages individuals to share every moment of their lives via the digital realm; and the development of Reality Television in the late 1990s, where the public and the private collided and were packaged as entertainment. These developments, now embedded in popular music cultures, invariably mean that the arena concert is indeed the arena in which they are played out. The illusion of intimacy and the pursuit of 'truth' that characterize the negotiation of the celebrity image are central to the socio-political role of the celebrity in contemporary times, as embodied in that which Marshall terms 'the celebrity sign' (1997). Social media is morphing celebrity culture in dramatic ways, particularly in terms of the ways in which audiences relate to celebrity images, how celebrities are 'produced' and how celebrity is actually practised. Gossip websites, fan sites and blogs provide a plethora of new locations for the circulation and creation of celebrity, moving between and blending user-generated content and the mainstream media. And this much more fragmented media landscape has created a shift in traditional understandings of celebrity management, from a highly controlled model to one in which celebrities actively address and interact with fans with seemingly less control and censure from their management. Contemporary celebrity is a performative practice that shifts and reformulates itself. This practice involves the ongoing maintenance of a performed intimacy, authenticity and access, and the creation of the construction of a persona that is consumable, and ongoing fan management. The presentation of a seemingly authentic, intimate image of the self, creating the illusion of access and lending the impression of uncensored glimpses into the lives of celebrities, is often at the heart of these developments. There is, of course, no way to determine the authenticity of any celebrity practice for those outside the immediate circle. And this uncertainty, paradoxically, appeals to some audiences, who enjoy the game playing intrinsic to gossip consumption, as Gamson (1994) argues.

Beyoncé took her first steps into social networking relatively late in comparison to many celebrities. Her first tweet, in April 2012, was an invitation to fans to visit her new website and Tumblr account. The account presented both staged and candid imagery documenting her life as wife, mother and global R&B/pop star. Her marriage to rap icon Jay-Z (Shawn Carter) is presented throughout in family photographs that often appear authentic and natural. Earlier in 2012, Beyoncé and Jay-Z had pre-empted the launch of Beyoncé's revamped online brand with the Tumblr account, dedicated to the birth of their daughter Blue-Ivy Carter. Tumblr is a micro-blogging platform and social networking website which allows users to post multimedia and other content to a short-form blog. Users can follow other user's blogs as well as make their blogs private. Both Beyoncé and Jay-Z had been perceived as rather 'traditional' celebrities up until this point, with little direct involvement in social networking as a mechanism through which they sought to maintain control of their dual brand. And, unlike many other celebrities, the two have fiercely protected their privacy, never publicly discussed their relationship and as evidenced in stories such as reportedly renting the entire floor of the hospital where their daughter was born to avoid paparazzi. Beyoncé's refusal to engage in the discourse surrounding her life, outside of her career, had made her a rather unique figure in a market over-saturated with discussions about celebrities' private lives. Indeed, information regarding Beyoncé and Jay-Z as a couple is scant (and so, in media terms, of heightened value), and carefully controlled in its dissemination. The occasional seemingly actual glimpse, then, is all the more shocking.[4]

Neal Gabler suggests that celebrities have a power over consumers and audiences because of the spell that their 'narratives' provide:

[N]o matter how well a celebrity sings, dances, acts or engages the consumer in some other way, a celebrity only retains his or her status only so long as he or she is living out an interesting narrative, or at least one that the media finds interesting. The size of the celebrity is in direct proportion to the novelty and excitement of the narrative. (Gabler 2009)

Yet Beyoncé's image has been safe, palatable and largely inoffensive. The most controversial aspects of her image were firstly her marriage to Jay-Z (who once courted controversy) and, secondly, her pregnancy.[5] Potentially, the narrative lacks novelty. And one could question the need for a narrative, as generated via personal images on social media, in the first place for such a successful duo. But projecting authenticity holds out the promise of validating the 'realness' of an otherwise untouchable or distant, and so indeed 'godly', person. Firstly, and perhaps most crucially, it is this sense of authenticity that makes Beyoncé's website (www.beyoncé.com) interesting for visitors. The website is not, of course, a gossip or fan site; it belongs to her, and she is configured as its author/creator, and so the sense of authenticity (i.e. it is authentically Beyoncé) is persuasive. Images of husband, sister and close friends, who appear in natural shots, evidence this, as well as being part of the fabric of celebrity social media. The intimacy engendered by celebrities on Twitter typically provides the glimpse into the inner life that their fans crave, as well as validating the authorship of the Twitter account. This is all the more important in that Twitter is generally a site where personal disclosure and intimacy are normative (as argued by Marwick and Boyd 2010), even to the point of intemperate outbursts, and so access, intimacy and affiliation are deemed valueless if an account is fake or written by an assistant. And Tumblr is near-dumb: little or no text is offered or required, to 'explain' the images. The viewer is freer to surmise and project. In these respects, something of the post-racial 'everyman', pan-ethnic brand of Beyoncé can be understood: meaning is not imposed. And those images posted that might be described as unflattering (where Beyoncé looks unkempt at times) suggest an access to the 'real' Beyoncé, and so counter the 'real' as presented by the unauthorized or semi-authorized outlets (tabloids, gossip magazines, paparazzi photos). What is not shown is the labour involved in maintaining such a discretely controlled brand.

The link between Beyoncé's live performances and fan engagement with ideas of intimacy and empowerment is acutely evident in her arena shows. Beyoncé's live concerts have been widely praised in the media due to their seamless execution and ground-breaking production values, their blending of the spectacular and the intimate and her ability to sing and dance simultaneously. At the time of writing, six concert tours have occurred during her solo career (four of which have been worldwide, and two of which have been collaborative). Her debut solo tour began in 2003, while Beyoncé was on hiatus from Destiny's Child, with the Dangerously in Love Tour, which was based primarily in the UK. Her first major solo world tour, The Beyoncé Experience, took place in 2007, in the wake of the disbanding of Destiny's Child in 2005. In 2008, after the release of a third studio album, *I Am . . . Sasha Fierce,* Beyoncé embarked on her next world tour, the I Am . . . World Tour. While all of these tours were commercial successes, none were more so than The Mrs. Carter Show World Tour which, according to Billboard, reportedly grossed US $229,727,960 after 132 dates. This made The Mrs. Carter Show World Tour the highest grossing female and solo tour of 2013, and one of the highest grossing tours of the decade. Performances of numerous songs from the tour were broadcast and promotional behind-the-scenes footage was released. The tour was initially criticized, to various degrees, for its name, as it was widely considered that Beyoncé was disavowing her status as a self-proclaimed independent woman by wanting to be known as simply Jay-Z's wife (see, e.g. Swash 2013).

The Mrs. Carter Show was loosely based on a royal theme, with Beyoncé emulating a variety of queens through the costume and stage design. The production design, by LeRoy Bennett (the designer of Beyoncé's half-time Superbowl show in 2013) consisted of a concept that was based around a giant wall of light, which was given the moniker 'The Wall of Inferno'. This lighting wall consisted of over 400 strobe lights and was designed to complement the choreography and essentially assisted the dancers and Beyoncé, who were to be thrown into relief against the background. A main stage and a 'b' stage, to which Beyoncé travelled via a flying rig, were deployed; the second stage allowed her to become physically closer to her audience. The set list from the 2013 leg of the tour consisted of twenty-five songs drawn from Beyoncé's four studio albums. During the 2014 leg of the tour many of the previously performed songs were dropped and eight new songs, from the fifth and self-titled studio album (of 2013), were added to the set list. This partial reworking of the event encouraged fans to attend for a second time.

Beyoncé and celebrity feminism

Despite the widespread criticism of the name, the Mrs. Carter Show World Tour also marked the apparent debut of Beyoncé as the self-proclaimed feminist. Musically speaking, Beyoncé's engagement with feminism, or issues aligned with feminism, predates this moment. Although she did not publicly identify as 'feminist' until 2014, songs from her former band Destiny's Child back catalogue, such as 'Independent Woman Pt. 1' (2000), present a basic, if perhaps naïve and post-feminist, 'girl power'-inspired feminism. And on Beyoncé's second solo album, *B'Day* (2006), an album that is essentially concerned with the politics of romantic, sexual, emotional and economic labour, there is a vague feminist thread that runs throughout, as articulating Beyoncé's control over, and the ownership of, her work and body. Furthermore, this album marks the introduction of her all-female band, the Sugar Mamas, which she formed in order to inspire young girls to learn to play musical instruments, since she lacked such role models in her own childhood. The 2013 *Beyoncé* album, however, marked a full and public 'coming out' as a feminist. The album incorporates a sample of lauded Nigerian novelist Chimamanda Ngozi Adichie's Ted-X speech 'We Should All Be Feminists' in the song '***Flawless'.[6] Additionally, Beyoncé published an essay, 'Gender Equality is a Myth!', for the Shriver Report website.[7] The album therefore serves as a catalytic moment in her oeuvre, now framing the old themes of bodily and monetary control in an explicitly feminist way. That a mainstream R&B/pop artist with a global reach should proclaim themselves a feminist in such an unapologetic manner was particularly noteworthy given that many female pop artists, including Katy Perry and Kelly Clarkson, have actively avoided being labelled as feminists in recent years. Yet Beyoncé's declaration appeared to propel other celebrities to acknowledge their own shifting positions in respect to the 'f-word', to the point that 'celebrity feminism' became a recurring feature of US/UK celebrity culture, snowballing to become a sustained and ongoing flashpoint of the cross-media celebrity landscape. Others 'came out' too, and this could be seen, in 2014, in declarations both carefully orchestrated to garner high-profile publicity, to those that were more responsive to unforeseen events or reactive to what was fast becoming a celebrity zeitgeist. Hollywood A-list actress Jennifer Lawrence's response to the online publication of her stolen nude photos (as part of the so-called 'fappening') saw her publicly take up an ostensibly feminist stance. In an interview with *Vanity Fair* in October, Lawrence denounced the leak as a 'sex crime' (quoted in Kashner 2014, 136). Singer Taylor Swift declared a revision of her position on feminism: she had misunderstood the term as a teenager and has since adopted the fundamental ideas of feminism (see Hoby 2014). And actress Emma Watson made her debut as a high-profile celebrity feminist through her status as a United Nations Goodwill Ambassador, and her endorsement of the #HeforShe Twitter campaign to encourage men to consider gender equality as their issue. In these cases, highly visible public personas, in articulating political positions broadly consistent with feminism, capitalize on their celebrity to promote the feminist cause. For many liberal commentators, this in itself is sufficient.

On the other hand, Beyoncé's identification as feminist, prompting a predictably huge reaction on social media, particularly via Twitter, resulted in a more mixed picture. Many criticized her for a perceived double standard: the familiar arguments of dressing provocatively, and selling her body/image as a brand for consumption, while spouting pseudo-feminist ideas. Singer Annie Lennox claimed that Beyoncé's use of the word represented 'feminist lite' (quoted in Azzopardi 2014) and bell hooks described Beyoncé as a 'terrorist', who potentially harms African-American girls' sense of identity with her sexualized performance, and that this is effectively an assault on feminism see (Sieczkowski 2014).

Both sets of positions illustrate that celebrity feminism has become a lightening conductor for these debates. Discursive struggles over the meanings of feminism are now, and perhaps more than ever, largely staged in and through media culture. And, given that celebrity interventions into ongoing debates over feminism have recently intensified, scholars of celebrity (the relatively new academic field of 'Celebrity Studies') are seeking to come to terms with the ideological and cultural implications and coordinates of these debates as played out in public, and across social media platforms. Lennox's statement seems to reflect an unease that was very clear on social media, with the conflation of a (possibly post-feminist) sense of empowerment through sexuality as blended into feminist politics. This is more evident in Lennox's subsequent elaboration; she places Beyoncé on a spectrum of feminism, with Beyoncé as representative of the tokenistic end (rather than feminists working at grassroots levels, at the other end) (Leight 2014).

What Lennox misses, however, is that it is the public persona of Beyoncé that is being identified as feminist. Previously, Beyoncé chose to perform her more sexually adventurous routines as her alter-ego, 'Sasha Fierce', and such masking is surely indicative of the continuing regulation of black female sexuality, as Durham (2012) argues. This fictional alter-ego had effectively served to separate and free Beyoncé, to an extent, from a history of the restricting image of the hypersexualized black woman. After all, the feminist discourse identified here is one of white privilege (Lennox,

Watson and even Lena Dunham). Thereafter, Beyoncé's juxtaposition of her sensually and sexually suggestively dancing body with Ngozi Adichie's words ('We teach girls that they cannot be sexual beings in the way that boys are') can be read as a negotiation of that marginalization. In this respect, there is a reclaiming of the black female body and sexuality. Arguably, this juxtaposition of voices and dance moves serves to advance the image of Beyoncé, from self-sexualizing pop star to female sexual agent, from a consumer image to an image of autonomy. And this progressive impulse is played out across, and galvanizes and harnesses the power of, and affiliations around, social media. If it was not for the aspirations to authenticity, despite my questioning of their good faith and constructed nature above, such an impulse would be negligible.

The limitation is perhaps more usefully considered, looking to debates surrounding Third Wave feminism, in respect to the presentation of a non-transgressive, and squarely mainstream, version of empowerment and feminism. It is at this juncture that the importance of Beyoncé's unparalleled ability to engage a live audience returns as a key element in this analysis. Celebrity feminism, in this respect, is not a matter of platitude but performance. The body itself reverberates with empowerment and autonomy: the reclamations, mentioned above, are witnessed live by those in the arenas.

Grown woman: Beyoncé and embodied empowerment

The touring arena concert provides an opportunity for audiences who may be located in suburban or rural areas, and with little ability to experience an international R&B/pop star, to finally connect, 'live', with the object of their affections. As with Helena above, and cases discussed elsewhere in the current volume, this can be an overwhelming, and even traumatic, experience.

To some extent Beyoncé could be affectionately described as an Old School diva, in terms of her performance, in such spaces. Her shows do not use social media interaction or live feeds to the audience (as with Roger Waters and Miley Cyrus respectively, as discussed in the current volume). The show relies on high production values in terms of staging, lighting and sound quality, constructing a multi-faceted spectacle that privileges the collision of the public presentation of her high-octane performances and the intimate representations of her personal life, as presented via social media, which are projected onto a giant video wall. What the audience is offered is a carefully constructed image that invites them to now become part of her world, in this moment, and to revel in her talent, and to share in the effusive and exuberant celebration of womanhood that Beyoncé would seem to encapsulate. The physical gestures that she delivers while performing are cues for the audience to participate: they are needed to create or complete the show. At the same time, the show is one that remains connected to the Beyoncé of social media, and to the sense of Beyoncé as global superstar.

The textual layers of the concert, and her interpretation of a given song within a physical setting, is mediated by both the concert staging and the films that are played throughout. If the arena concert evidences the superstardom of its protagonist (as Edgar argues in the current volume), this is balanced by the intimacy of the encounter with the protagonist: the promise of some intimate 'face time' with the superstar. In this respect, the usual tropes are deployed (between-song banter, observations on the audience), but the social media construction of the 'real' Beyoncé is also called upon. Short films present images from her Tumblr and 'private' life, presenting her as vulnerable and sensitive (in the midst of the enormity of her performance and presence) and possessing, as the synthesis of this dialectic, the qualities that she sees as being universal to the human experience.

Beyoncé collides large-scale demonstrative presentations of her music with intimate representations of female empowerment in such a way that she manages to ostensibly feminize the arena space. Or, from another perspective, that she capitalizes on the effective 'feminization' of the arena space: in terms of the gender balance of the audiences on the Mrs. Carter World Tour, it is clear that from analysis of images, and through my experiences of two of the shows, her audience is predominantly female. The mode of communication, then, is female-to-female – an aspiration of feminist reclaiming or remaking of public spaces during the 1970s and one which, as Halligan has argued (2013a), has re-emerged in recent years around ideas of performance, interaction and Third Wave feminism.

The arena space during a Beyoncé show is also feminized in terms of its thematic content: female-to-female and on 'female' matters. Many of the songs performed possess lyrical content that is designed to appeal to women, following the lineage of her early songwriting with Destiny's Child. Songs such as 'Grown Woman' and 'Single Ladies (Put a Ring On It)' (2008) could be said to engage with issues of growth, freedom, confidence, maturity and sexuality that are female-specific. But the platitudinal and anthemic nature of the songs ('I'm a grown woman / I can do whatever I want'; 'I got gloss on my lips / a man on my hips'; 'All the single ladies / now put your hands up'), wreathed in spectacular lighting and dance routines, ostensibly present a kind of female party atmosphere in which Beyoncé, as emcee, encourages her audience to celebrate their own girl- and womanhood. In this respect, the songs hold more in common with the blatant feminism of brash 1990s Riot Grrrl music than the nuanced explorations of female subjectivity found in many 1970s female singer-songwriters. The experience of attending a Beyoncé arena concert is memorable because it is such an assault on the senses. One contends with the mix of extremely high production values (in terms of glitzy short films) that meld into the song performances to produce a brilliant but often confusing effect, lighting that contains a multitude of strobes that are utilized almost continually, hysteria from the audience and Beyoncé's actual presence, which is a curious mix of uber-professionalism, sincerity and compassion.

Beyoncé's mastery of the communication of musical content through her body is perhaps one of the key reasons that she is so comfortable, and successful, in an arena space. She embodies the music in a visceral way, and so connects with her audiences in a non-intellectualized way in respect to imminent female empowerment. Crudely put, she *is* female empowerment – or one strain of it at least, contestations acknowledged. Through her live performances, Beyoncé appears to promote a shiny, depthless feminism that mass audiences can embrace. However, when thinking through the complicated nexus of feminism and celebrity, it is important not to simply re-inscribe those familiar critiques that presume this relationship to be inherently negative for feminist politics. Instead, 'feminist celebrity studies' needs to attend to how feminism and celebrity cultures necessarily intersect in ways that may be at once productive and unproductive, both with constraints and possibilities.

Notes

1 Beyoncé fan interviewee Helena Fox, speaking in 2015. During March 2015 a number of face-to-face interviews were conducted for a larger and ongoing research project on Beyoncé.

2 See http://www.billboard.com/biz/articles/news/touring/6069972/beyonce-wraps-world-tour-in-europe-with-411m-in-ticket-sales (accessed April 2015). The Recording Industry Association of America acknowledged that through sixty-four gold and platinum certifications, she was the decade's top-selling artist (see https://www.riaa.com).

3 My thanks to Philip Auslander for his time at the University of Salford, as a Visiting Fellow in Performance, in respect of my thinking about this chapter.

4 The most notable example to date was seemingly a family altercation; see http://hollywoodlife.com/2014/05/12/solange-attacks-jay-z-video-punch-kick-beyonce-elevator-fight/ (accessed April 2015).

5 The rumour was widely discussed on social media that Beyoncé was not actually pregnant, and her child was born to a surrogate. This was later subtly addressed via careful imagery posted on her Tumblr site.

6 The sample is: 'We teach girls that they cannot be sexual beings in the way that boys are. Feminist: the person who believes in the social, political and economic equality of the sexes.'

7 See http://shriverreport.org/gender-equality-is-a-myth-beyonce/ (accessed February 2015).

CHAPTER TWENTY

Intimate Live Girls

Benjamin Halligan

Intimate with Miley

That essential experience, or even just ambience, of intimacy, is endangered in the transition to arena concerts.[1] As the concert is, as it were, 'supersized' – in terms of audience members, and of the spectacle that is expected by those amassed fans, and the business and consumer environment that services the event – such intimate moments, which presuppose smaller scales, are seemingly rendered unobtainable. Even just one comment beyond just the generic 'Hey [insert host city name]!' on the part of the performer can go some way to personalizing, and so redeeming, the spectacle that is being consumed by reminding those present that they are all living in this particular moment, and so share feelings about the weather, or local sports results, or understand where an observational quip is coming from. The missteps and resulting corpsing of Kylie Minogue's dancers during the X tour, and her comments directed at audience members related to members of her band, or spying t-shirts and posters from previous tours in the audience and commenting accordingly, or taking song requests and delivering a few bars unaccompanied, added just such a human element to an otherwise slickly predesigned, pre-cued and so pre-ordained and impersonal, spectacle.[2] On the other hand, Katy Perry's inter-song comments about 'going through crap' ('feel[ing] alone in the situation – he's not texting back, you understand, right? There's light at the end of the tunnel if you put one foot in front of another'), trying locally produced pies and then downing much of a pint of beer (the remainder handed to an audience member to finish), sounded scripted, even rehearsed, and so raised suspicion, while her shilling for an underperforming Hollywood film of the moment, and general product placement, was just contemptibly opportunistic.

Without such redemption, and with the spectacle itself as the entirety of the show, a sense of disconnection occurs: the experience becomes that of the star parachuted in, to perform and talk here, on this night, much as in any other arena, and as on the nights before and the nights to come, with choreography and cues delivered as rehearsed. And where lip-synching is also deployed, or partially deployed (as with Britney Spears, but also Katy Perry), problematic ontological questions arise in the audience, who can feel themselves as passive consumers of mass-produced product rather than engaged spectators of, and even participants in, a one-off and human moment. Or, even worse, to find themselves unwittingly cast as paying extras in some further promotional filming for the singer, with photocopied notices of assumed binding legal import ('by attending this concert [. . .] be aware that you may be filmed [. . .] agree to the inclusion of your image [. . .]' etc) pasted up on entrance doors. So Perry, along with Keane and Lady Gaga, included segments of quieter and more intimate music, often acoustic, often with the singer playing an instrument with the huddled group of musicians, and the songs perhaps introduced as having personal meaning, and so shared now with the audience, or reflecting a difficult time in the band's past and so on. Or, as in the case of Alicia Keys, offloading the band for a stretch while she played and sang alone in sympathetic and intimate lighting. Perry even articulates the problem: 'there are 12,000 people here but it's so weird: sometimes I feel like I'm singing to five . . . We have a special bond, don't you think?'

More arrestingly, Peter Gabriel began his Back to Front concert by ambling on stage, unannounced and with no dip in the house lights – so that it was only the whoops and clapping prompted by startled audience recognition that marked the start of the evening – in order to apologetically talk about a still incomplete new song, which he then nevertheless delivers solo, accompanying himself on a piano. Others simply perform, or intimate, an assumed intimacy: Kylie signalled her home life (stripping and taking a bubble bath on stage, while singing 'I Should Be So Lucky') during the Kiss Me Once tour, while Britney signalled her party life (selecting a male from the audience who was then tied to a car on stage, whereupon she pole danced for him in sparkly hot-pants), for the Femme Fatale tour.

Intimacy has the potential to cut through the spectacle, which is the achievement of a team of often anonymous collaborators, and restore communication with the individual star: to put the show, and even the business, to one side in order to speak as if in a one-on-one moment. That moment looks to be, and indeed sometimes seems to be, authentic. For Barker and Taylor, MTV Unplugged is presented as just such an essential mitigation as 'the quest for authenticity in popular music' has been waylaid by spectacle: this broadcast series of 'stripped down' and live concerts, often acoustic and with the studio audience in very close proximity to the performers, 'was conceived as a response to the public perception that the contemporary music scene was obsessed with image rather than content [. . . as . . .] people want to see artists in "real" conditions' (Barker and Taylor 2007, 5). Kylie Minogue's entire 2012 Anti Tour was structured around this aspiration, but now with long-forgotten B-sides rather than international hits in the setlist, performed by a small band, with a minimal set, and plenty of between-song reminiscences.[3] And, ultimately, the balance between spectacle and intimacy is one that needs to be struck in terms of covering the full spectrum of experiences of exposure to contemporary pop: a fan may well later recall both the moment of high spectacle (say, the grand entrance of Girls Aloud, with each mounted on ten foot high letters spelling the band's name, moving through the air above the arena audience via guy ropes), and the moment at which one of the Girls recalled nervously first auditioning on that same stage years before achieving fame, with equal fondness. Both denote the evening in its ebb and flow of spectacular and intimate elements.

Intimacy, additionally, is the very currency of contemporary popular stardom: the minimum expectation is that the private becomes the public, and that art and life are played out equally in the public eye – even to the extent that the two become inextricably entwined. The arena concert film *Hannah Montana and Miley Cyrus: Best of Both Worlds* (Bruce Hendricks, 2008) begins backstage, cinéma-vérité, with vocal exercises for Miley and attendant make-up artist. And innumerable television talent show competitions chart and co-opt the emotional journey and often troubled back stories of the competing singers as they rehearse and prepare, as narratives which then contextualize the performance's success or failure.

All this seems to be a radical reversal of old models of popular music stardom, where one variant of the myth of celebrity concerned those unheralded or largely unseen, only to be belatedly (even posthumously) discovered and acclaimed, and so seem to appear from nowhere, and retain their mysterious and impenetrable persona, even to the point of collaborating in outright falsification. This earlier sense of the star as fundamentally unknowable is found in *'Round Midnight* (Bertrand Tavernier, 1986), in which the poky French jazz clubs in which the exiled saxophonist is seen to perform give way, in the film's final seconds, to a posthumous tribute concert in front of a massed audience. And it is found too in the concert documentary *Ziggy Stardust and the Spiders from Mars* (D. A. Pennebaker, 1973), in which the 'real' David Bowie, although ever present, seems an absent presence throughout – obscured by make-up, performance persona and self-conscious quipping backstage. And even films that promised to document intimacy once tended to circumnavigate the matter: the buffers of the comedy turns of the Beatles in *A Hard Day's Night* (Richard Lester, 1964), or Abba as, tantalizingly, just beyond the reach of the camera crew, and journalist pack, of *ABBA: The Movie* (Lasse Hallström, 1977) and the use of stand-ins rather than stars – partially (the impromptu punk group Terry and the Idiots in *D.O.A.: A Rite of Passage*, Lech Kowalski, 1980) or wholly (the Barbie doll cast of *Superstar: The Karen Carpenter Story*, Todd Haynes, 1987).

At this time, such aesthetic or structural strategies may have been in operation not only to simply shield stars from the curious, in relation to matters of sexual and narcotic preferences, or mental health issues, but also to maintain the illusion of men of the people, and so 'one of us', despite the enviable lifestyles of the rock aristocracy.

In contrast, by the point of the melding of pop with Reality Television, the music seems secondary to the persona, amplifying the trope of 'famous-for-being-famous', and a full media spectrum domination of the private and the personal occurs: distress and intoxication in public, leaked sex tapes and even, as the persona wrestles back ownership of this narrative, the sober and tearful public confession.[4] That component of 'reality' itself becomes an aesthetic vernacular. *Hannah Montana and Miley Cyrus: Best of Both Worlds* and *Ziggy Stardust and the Spiders from Mars* start in completely identical ways: a few candid documentary seconds of star and entourage in a scruffy green room, not yet dressed-up or fully made-up, and preparing to perform. But whereas Pennebaker sought to document a cultural phenomenon (and with its attendant 'shock of the new': Bowie's comment 'Well, you're just a girl – what do you know about make-up?' carries a payload of subversion), Hendricks seems to simply recreate or restage such a moment. And whereas Bowie seems stressed, disorientated and maybe even hallucinating, and the air around him is thick with cigarette smoke, Cyrus seems mid-work out, loving life and thrilled by the actualité of herself being such a successful entertainer. Reality, in this latter sense, is not only an aesthetic vernacular, but a proviso that works to announce the healthy and conservative cultural nature of the entertainment to come – at least, in respect to Cyrus in 2008.

'Intimate', however, is also a style of music, and in this respect it is possible to trace the development of an ambience – and a gendered ambience at that. Larger venue concerts in the 1970s were often a matter of a kind of enormity of performance: the larger-than-life, in theatrical terms (Genesis and Elton John, for example), and in maximal, sonic terms (The Who, Queen, Led Zeppelin and their heavy/hair metal disciples) or even a blend of the two. The grand piano laboriously, and ridiculously, shifted onto the stage, and then directly off again, for the sake of a few dozen bars of playing during a Guns 'n Roses gig, is therefore best considered as a theatrical prop rather than musical necessity. This maximal grouping, in particular, can be read in terms of presenting a direct correlation between masculinity, musical prowess and the 'alpha male' mastery and dominance of the space of performance. The music and performance expanded to meet and match the size of the venue. But the necessity of the introduction of enormous video screens in order to allow ever-expanding audiences to actually see what they had come to see, also marked the point at which the idea of intimacy could be regenerated. And what then occurs, in terms of young girl pop, which is the concern of this chapter, first prompts a retrospective note of what could be taken as a parallel and mostly marginalized music history – one of intimacy rather than pomp, and of immediate personal space rather than domination of the space of performance. It is possible to chart a certain trajectory in this regard, from 1970s female singer-songwriters (themselves and their guitar or piano, often imagined in close surroundings, bare feet as if comfy at home, performing as if just for you), and a latter generation of female pop: Tiffany performing for teen crowds in shopping malls, and Debbie Gibson on her bed in her bedroom.[5] These are their places, not public spaces: the viewer is invited into the 16- or 17-year-old's bedroom, listens to their 'telling secrets' and enters the revelry with them: 'Only in my dreams / as real as it may seem / it was only in my dreams'. The private then becomes an element of the performance, which seems to be circumscribed within the immediate sphere. There is an echo of this in arena concerts, in the tendency to confession: Minogue on her breast cancer, Alicia Keys talking about, and playing, the formative R&B music from her childhood, Tom Chaplin on the troubles he had caused for his group, Keane, Morrissey on feeling slighted by Manchester City Council, Lady Gaga imparting life lessons and often a tendency, as with Lady Gaga, for female artists to start weeping during such moments. The problem, for historians of popular music, is that the intimate, at the juncture at which Gibson and Tiffany can be found, often gives way to trivial and banal romantic concerns. The individuality of the 1970s female singer-songwriters seems to find a surer path, for writers such as Raphael (1996), Whiteley (2000) and O'Brien (2012), through female-fronted punk and post-punk groups, and their belated refrains in gobbier female pop stars of the 1980s, and Riot Grrrl. The latter's manifesto was clear on such romantic matters: the danger of pop conformism as one of 'assimilating someone else's (boy) standards', waylaying the need to 'create our own moanings' (Anon, 1991). Joni Mitchell is a 'significant force' for Whiteley (2000, 92) through her articulation of a female subjectivity as formed, and coloured and nuanced, by the at times successful and at times disastrous chasing after desires. Mitchell's narrative is confessional and disarming, and locked into wider societal questions and struggles (especially during the 1970s) of wants understood and freedoms gained, self-determination and self-realization and the belated 'modernization' of woman. This subjectivity is certainly a much more satisfactory terrain for exploration than that of the bluntly exuberant and sloganeering performance of desire, of 'what I really, really want' (for Whiteley's later discussion of the 'imperatives of commercial success' of The Spice Girls).

If Gibson is used as emblematic here, to the exclusion of previous and entirely comparable girl pop stars, it is in part because her brief moment in the spotlight coincided with a general transition in MTV towards the predictable, bland and safe. MTV seemed to shift from a parasitical model of absorption of extant popular musics to a eugenic model of effective incubation and promotion of their own.

The music texts themselves evidence their own strategies of intimacy, which are often manifest in the ways in which they retain and even showcase vocal tics or unusual annunciations, as understood to be particular to the singer. Gibson's feisty and even at times strained vibrato on 'Only In My Dreams' works in such a way: it seems almost too showy, pushes too hard on a voice not fully formed and so is very much indicative of the 'real' presence of the singer. Vocal character is often imparted in the way in which the singing clearly sounds as if it emanates from the singer as she smiles. For a singer as distinguished as Amerie, a similar effect of presence is achieved through a seemingly anarchic disregard for the structure of the song: during 'Gotta Work' (in the album version, from *Because I Love It*, 2007) the lyrics of the verse crash into and then across (to the point of almost three bars) the chorus, as if too much needs to be said, and too urgently, to cut the discourse in deference to the chorus. The inclusion of extraneous, personal material (such as Taylor Swift's giggle, after the lyric 'I go on too many dates', for the 2014 single 'Shake It Off', but there is a laugh on 'Gotta Work' as well), can be read in just such a way too. In these instances, the intimation is often towards vulnerability or exposure (too much emotion, or simply sharing a joke with the listener) on the part of the singer.[6]

In this regeneration of the close encounter is a kind of contrarian movement: at the point at which the increasing size of mass entertainment prompts the creation of technology to further enable that reach, the technology in turn allows for this bignesses's very obverse – the fruition of a mise-en-scène of intimacy, of smallness and of confidences, allowing for a feminization of space, even the vast space of the arena. And this mise-en-scène, now, speaks of and to the very origins of young girl pop: no longer the mass-release of an album, singles climbing in the one national chart, trailed appearances on must-watch broadcast television programmes. Rather, the grassroots selling of the pop star, via individual downloads, or YouTube views, takes the product straight to the bedroom, and private spaces – and perhaps with an entrée endorsed by familiars: emailed MP3s, or via the Facebook 'likes' of friends, or friends' friends or via Spotify's Artificial Intelligence-mimicking algorithm declaring that a certain piece of music is to your taste. In this way, the intrusion of the new song occurs on the individual's terms, and into that intimate sphere of being, 'wired up', 'in the zone': headphones on while computing, isolated mentally and aurally from the outside world.

One promo video for Cyrus's 'Wrecking Ball' (2013) is perfectly calibrated in these respects: the official released version is pretty much entirely contained within a box. There is no narrative that needs to break the oblong framing, or requires much expansion for the viewer to 'get' the concept. The promo fits exactly and neatly into that reduced space that the eye scans in the Facebook embed. Its concept is immediately graspable: Miley Cyrus, in ever-further states of undress, sits atop a wrecking ball that smashes into a wall of concrete slabs, or is seen with walls smashing behind her, all intercut with a medium close-up head shot. And, of course, despite the nudity, in this strategy is a not quite NSFW ('not suitable for work') peepshow: it's 'not not' – that is, it is safe for titillation at work. The promo seems tailor-made for YouTube and social media dissemination, and so functions as akin to snatches of intimacy available via user-generated image content on Facebook.

And, just as this version of the promo video trades on the intimacy of nudity, there's a complimentary 'director's cut' version in which Miley looks now straight into the camera and delivers the song in a pained, emotion-filled way: tears and nasal mucus stream down her face, her tongue and teeth show excessive spittle. This latter version concludes with the video's director in the frame, with Miley, and indeed both videos are 'signed', on-screen, by their director: celebrity photographer Terry Richardson.

This is the access afforded by intimacy. The use of Richardson here, and in more general terms the inspiration from Terry Richardson that seemed to be in Miley's post-*Hannah Montana* work and persona, functioned to reinvent the star.[7] Post-Hannah Miley is 'ugly' (in the sense of gurning, un-girly, even aspiring to the grotesque), self-consciously edgy (achieved with nudity or state of undress that flirt with the pornographic or paedophilic; and drug paraphernalia), a presence lacking in sentimentality, and presented as a commercial prospect via Warholian tropes: a sheen and glamour, and often the subject as pinned down, or backed-up against a wall, or enclosed within a small space, for forensic examination (as with Warhol's *Screen Tests*, 1964–1966). Richardson's images – controversial in themselves, and for some redolent of a working method that has been met with accusations of sexual assault – talk directly to notions of self-authenticating presentation, not least in terms of Richardson's own deracinated image appearing in so many of his photos. The 2004 exhibition (at the Deitch Projects gallery in SoHo, New York) and collection, *Terryworld*, anticipates the intimate performance of the sexualized self, for social and private media: for 'chatroulette' via self-taken, sometimes mid-intercourse, shots; reportage 'camwhore' snapshots of a certain party atmosphere; and, perhaps in its 'selfie' and Snapchat manifestations, in the illicit, individualized come-on or invitation.[8] For much of *Terryworld*, the use of underage-looking models seems in dialogue with an underage-looking sexualization of the popular culture – the ground on which most of Miley's critics assemble. Is popular culture, and girl pop culture, then, just the cleaned-up version of this? Or is this the degeneration inevitable in the direction (or just the imagined underside) of girl pop culture? Or does Richardson just shoot the status quo: that the condition of tweens is in itself sexual, and that this is what teddy bears and lollies, and so on, are actually now all about? Or are these images merely outriders to an emergent genre: the social media selfie as evidence of wild times, and a way of self-documenting (as the photoblogger Merlin Bronques puts it for his 2006 collection), last night's party.

What is arresting in Richardson's images is that, unlike the typical 'good girl gone bad' narrative of contemporary pop culture, where 'papped' photos evidence the decline and fall of former Disney pop princesses into the Spring Break/'Girls Gone Wild' excesses of 'raunch culture' (as identified by Levy,

2006), Richardson's photographs actually are the 'going bad'. The straitened aesthetic, often flatly (or even flash) lit and so lacking in depth, simply underlines the straight reportage of the image, or evidences the event: her, back to the bare wall, actually 'misbehaving'; her, on her bed, fully adopting a pornographic pose for the camera (as if a photo from a cheap 1970s porn mag); her, eroding her media respectability, partially or fully nude. In this respect, these enclosed spaces favoured by Richardson seem a kind of laboratory for intimacy: the camera lens as microscope, and the photoshoot designed as a provocation to the model to go ever further, and then an index of just how much further. And in these straitened circumstances, the tongue becomes all important: as used for an infantile gesture of facial distortion, or an invitation for or mimicking of (or just actual) fellatio – edging towards the moderately extreme, silly pose adopted for mid-party or nightclubbing photos for social media. In Richardson's work, the tongue is a kind of chute to the plughole of the post-ejaculatory moment – the face wet with liquids, as with Miley's tears and mucus and spittle.

Terryworld was published a decade before the *Bangerz* album and related tour (2013; 79 public concerts, February–October 2014), and Richardson's vision took some time to be considered palatable for, and to some extent filter into, fashion media. *Bangerz* mined this seam (as well as many other seams, and modish memes) to find its own character, and the tour was advertised and merchandised with a Richardson image: Miley pressed up against her own reflection, a homage of the auto-homo-erotic narcissus of Jean Marais in Jean Cocteau's *Orphée* (1950), albeit with added tongue. Part of the use of Richardson comes in the sense of the invention of an identity through the killing of innocence, and the innocent that is killed is the virginal Disney alter-ego, Hannah Montana, to allow the emergence of an urban/indy pop girl, Miley Cyrus. The CD album of *Bangerz* even comes with stickers for iPhone customization, including a marijuana leaf, an amended Acid House smiley face and a topless Miley covering her breasts. The tour, on the back of a much-discussed 'twerking' incident at the 2013 MTV Video Music Awards show,[9] included simulated masturbation (including with outsized foam 'hands') and group sex (consciously 'edgy': interracial, including a person of restricted growth, who was also in the dance troupe), with an 'explicit' version of the tour programme containing endless images of Miley miming fellatio. And, as with the scrap-book aesthetic of the *Bangerz* inlay, and the projection design of the Bangerz concerts (which often looked as if created by a hyperactive teenage designer, cramming everything possible into a freeware-generated animation, including then passé memes of singing cats for 'We Can't Stop'), the new look, and persona, was one of happy amateurism.[10] Thus there was something terribly karaoke-like about Miley's renditions of The Smith's 'There's a Light That Never Goes Out', The Beatles's 'Lucy in the Sky With Diamonds' (as a duet with Wayne Coyne, fumbled first time, unsatisfactory for Cyrus the second time, and so played three times in a row, with apologies to the small segment of the audience able to see that particular stage, since this was for outside broadcast) and Dolly Parton's 'Jolene' (which was so ineptly played that at one point the song seemed in danger of grinding to a halt before its conclusion).[11] But, at the same time, the intention itself was enough: not only in terms of actually singing (rather than lip-synching), but in terms of achieving a sense of a spontaneous event, and of those gathered sharing in one seemingly off-script (or, at least, counter-expectations) moment. This was the art in the age of digital reproduction, to paraphrase Benjamin's 1936 essay: the auratic presence of actual and unmistakeable Miley. Put in a much cruder way, Miley's spitting of water over the front rows of the audience – to see how far she could project the water, she said, and trying to out-spit her previous personal best – works in a similar fashion: to cut through the hype of the event, the starriness of the persona and the engulfing mediascape of the arena concert, for a 'real' and human moment, of being there, with Miley. It is a matter of actually achieving intimacy rather than just intimating the liveness of her actual presence: to be intimate rather than to intimate her closeness. (Prince's inane version of this was to ban, and have that ban swingeingly enforced, the use of any camera device on the grounds that it distracted from the music). In terms of the pop star herself, in respect to appearances in the global nexus of arenas, such liveness cannot just be a matter of Barker and Taylor's 'quest for authenticity' (2007, 5).[12] Liveness is also a matter of mitigating the hyperreal or digital realms in which the pop star mostly exits: of finally offering the referent of the endlessly digitally reproduced image. This moment suggests a reversal of the old maxim that you should never meet your heroes: the heroes have to be met, in order to have their heroism actually validated, along with the validation of the esteem in which the fan holds them.

In this respect, a sense of a biological presence, rather than digital presence or avatar, is all-important. When this is achieved via the routines of sexual arousal (in the feigned orgy, in her feigned masturbation and in the fetish-like outfits she wears), so that the intimate is equated with the private, the connection seems clear and would prompt a turn to theorizations of striptease and burlesque. (Or, diagnostically, psychoanalysis: public masturbation held as a very typical sign of mental disorder.) But the materialization of sexuality in this manner is writ large, across towering video screens: this is not the strip club with its private booths and private dances, but a cultural event with the scope and space of a football match. And the spotlight that follows our star as he or she walks the promenade, and so seems to walk on the crowd, as Christ seemed to walk on water, is suggestive of the divine light, often a golden beam from heaven, that illuminates the deity as he walks in the fallen world, across centuries of Western painting. The materialization of sexuality in the arena may be said to work in just such a manner as the materialization of the infant Christ's genitals in Renaissance art, for the unbelievers: genitalia as the final proof of the absolute presence of the biological (rather than digital, or ghost-like vision) human figure.[13] Christ has walked among us – even if, as with the arena experience, only to be seen and heard from a distance (as with the Sermon on the Mount); and Miley has walked among us – as apparent in the fleshiness that she displays, and integrates into the performance, and as part of the whole spectacle.[14] Steinberg's 'plausible theological grounds for the genital reference' (1996, 3) need not be much updated: the deity-like superstar is now manifest in her presence, along with gathered disciplines, and to answer Doubting Thomases ('can she actually sing?', 'is she just hype?') and the Pharisees of the commentariat ('this isn't good music', 'this isn't a good role model') alike.

Richardson's tongues function in such a way too: a muscle movement that, unlike a facial expression, illustrates desire and intent, and a sensual reaching out into the world for experience and sensation. Miley's tongue is similarly cast: a star of the show. Compare this to John Pasche's famous 'tongue and lips' Rolling Stones logo: more of a distillation of the essence of the vulgarity of the band, minimalism in the manner of Samuel Beckett's *Not I* ('Stage in darkness but for MOUTH, upstage audience right, about eight feet above stage level', Beckett [1973] 2014, 13), than the Richardson/ Miley appropriation of the blunt semiotics of porn. In fact, the show begins with Miley sliding down the enormous tongue that protrudes from the backdrop image of her face. But Miley's tongue and Richardson's tongues are only a fraction of the matter in terms of the Bangerz tour.

Snogging with tongues

After a tribute to her newly deceased dog, Floyd, of 'Can't Be Tamed' (a towering inflatable statue of Floyd is wheeled on and off stage), Miley introduces a rendition of 'Adore You' by exhorting audience members to 'make out' once the 'kiss cam' is on them, and being 'sluttier than America' (the previous continent for the Bangerz tour). The images from the 'kiss cam' are projected behind her as she sings. Roving cameras in the audience, with feeds on video screens, are far from unusual – allowing for cut-away shots of audience members, now incorporated into the spectacle. During a sort of rave-themed interregnum during Perry's show, with Perry and her troupe dancing freely on stage, the instruction 'Dance' appears on the video screens, with shots of compliant audience members and groups doing just that (with the biggest cheers from the audience reserved for dancing dads). In this, Perry adopts a DJ/conductor role: instructions to be followed, with her example offered. But the loop is uncertain: do the dancing audience members perform for her, or – with respect to their fleeting inclusion in the show – for others: this audience? or the future audience for a commercial transmission or release of this show? Many of them, once they become conscious of the broadcast of their images, begin to take photos of themselves on the big screen, capturing the capturing.

During the first few minutes of the kiss cam feeds, it was mostly young girls 'snogging' each other, egged on by their friends (the audience seemed to consist of many parties of young girls) – demonstrably with tongues, but not

FIGURE 20.1 The live 'kiss cam' feed during 'Adore You': Miley Cyrus Bangerz tour, Manchester Arena, 2014.

always in a way which is typically read as bi- or homosexual, but more just a youthful affectation, and often adopting 'selfie'-like poses.[15] But as men, this time seemingly partners, were also picked up and broadcast, and kissed deeply and with gusto, enormous, arena-shaking cheers broke out from the whooping audience. Such a celebration of difference, in an area that is not typically read as given over to gatherings of that class (the British middle) who have attempted to annex the righteousness of liberal mindedness, was striking.

Months later, Peter Gabriel ended his Back to Front concert with the 1980 single 'Biko', introduced ('for those young people around the world, [who currently] are fighting oppression and injustice'; 'as always: what happens now is up to you'), and performed, in an appropriately serious and unshowy manner (as Gabriel has done over the decades with this song), and with an image of the murdered anti-apartheid activist projected behind the stage as the song ended.[16] The outro's chanting, as orchestrated by Gabriel, included the audience, on its feet, returning the raised fist salute of, in this context, solidarity with the historic struggles of the African National Congress. Gabriel finally twisted the microphone around to catch and amplify that chanting, and discretely left the stage as the music played on. This twisting and exit perfectly dramatizes Gabriel's position of 'what happens now is up to you'. The Back to Front tour itself seemed to reproduce the aesthetics and technology of state surveillance and state intimidation: blindingly bright white mobile search lights, moving threateningly onto the audience, and at times the singer himself, whose fearful image (sometimes in close-up, sometimes as thermal imaging) was projected onto the back screen. In this context, the concluding dynamic of 'Biko' was a resounding retort, and a moment of inclusivity (and education) for the audience, in the continuum of the narrative of the fight for democratic representation. And yet, the moment was, ultimately, gestural. Miley's stratagem, on the other hand, was affective. And while few would now argue against the spirit of Gabriel's position of 'Biko' (and the comparison engendered by the line of argument here, comparing tributes to the late Floyd and the late Steve Biko, seems in terrible bad taste), Miley's position remains vexed. Such a 'promotion' of homosexuality to this predominantly young audience would have been, under British law, technically illegal only some ten and a half years before.[17] And, even in the heart of Western metropolitan centres, same-sex / 'alt-sex' relationships continue to meet with discrimination, both in terms of queer-bashing on the street, and in terms of public and private sector discrimination and marginalization in the institutions of state and its proxies.

The recognition in the audience would have seemed to have been that the kissing couples were both living in the moment, on Miley's guidance, and heightening and amplifying that moment for themselves and all others, and laughing in the face of sexual mores, discretions, taboos and prohibitions. Such a dynamic is familiar to activists: the affective example set by Occupy events, the freedoms of what Bey (2003) identifies as the 'Temporary

Autonomous Zone', which are often also sensual too and position pleasure as a weapon of political opposition. Miley's own hyper-sexualization, in and through the show, figures as a centrifugal force in these matters – shamanically spurring on this skanky, sensual solidarity. And 'Adore You', in its stately pace (especially in terms of its opening position on the *Bangerz* album), use of strings, and seeming narrative of increasing desperation on the part of the singer/character as her stalker-ish adoration (and fantasies of marriage, and divine guidance) are not fully returned by the object of her affection, obliterates the ADD-like power pop of the Hannah Montana persona. Miley's voice is siren-like, in the sense of singing up and above and echoing across the music – perhaps inviting the entranced into this 'danger zone' of confession, and acting unconditionally on impulse. This is the mood in which Miley's then covering of 'There is a Light That Never Goes Out' seems entirely appropriate: that other great anthem of unrequited longing.

If the stepping up to such an alternative to that embodied by the Disney pop princess of Hannah Montana had been achieved via an immersion in Richardson's aesthetic, then the implementation – via an engulfing of the arena event with a sense of shared intimacy and actual intimacy – was Miley's, and Hannah's, own. The television series and Hannah Montana film, and *Hannah Montana and Miley Cyrus: Best of Both Worlds*, illustrate that the protagonist, across her different personae, is an arena figure from the outset: the first arena star at the point of her origin, and whose musical beginnings began by her performing live as the fictional Montana, before the 'Hannah Montana' series had first aired.[18] But the negotiation of such a star status remains on the grounds of intimacy: the dialectic of the lyrics of 'Best of Both Worlds' (also the theme song for the series) is entirely correct. The schizophrenic balance of the thesis of Tennessee 'small town girl' versus the antithesis of international pop star ('in some ways you're just like all your friends / but on stage you're a star'; 'chill it out, take it slow / then you rock out the show', 'living two lives is a little weird / but school's cool 'cos nobody knows' and so on) results in synthesis in Miley Cyrus. And the synthesis is one in which small town intimacy is retained even in the persona of superstardom (and, for the television series, the intimate and everyday of the settings were juxtaposed with the Montana persona as a superstar, for comedic effect – now at home, arguing with her brother, being ignored by boys, the indignities of her father's unhip behaviour, etc). In this way, and on these grounds of small town girl and international superstar, Cyrus reinvents the culture of the arena show, propelling it into an as-yet unknown future.

Being more closely linked

Such great claims were also once made for the open-air music festival, as gatherings which seemed to be 'a rehearsal for the time when basic amenities as we know them have broken down, perhaps through the running out of natural resources, perhaps through revolution and social eruption, perhaps through nuclear war' (quoted in Sandford and Reid 1974, 5). In this way

> There are many among those who use festivals who believe . . . that this is the way that much of Britain may one day be; that the life style provided and lived at pop festivals may be an indication of the way that society itself may be moving. Future social structures are seen as being more closely linked to the soil, to be more concerned with sharing . . . to contain more tribal togetherness than now. (Sandford and Reid 1974, 119)

Such idealism is difficult to take at face value, or only wishfully and fitfully translated into squatting and Green movements and activism, and the history of music festivals itself and, later, raves. But, pace Hardt and Negri (2005), the multitudinal coming together of singularities, and new forms of immaterial labour that arise within that shift, partially confirm the contention of the 'many among those who use festivals' that the lineaments of new forms of living and togetherness, and communication, can be detected.[19] Sandford and Reid's 'tomorrow's people' still seem to emerge from such cultural spheres.

So how does the arena concert, in general, compute in relation to updating this 1970s imaginary, with the iPhone entry to the live social media hinterland of the arena event as replacing LSD or MDMA as the essential gateway to fully embracing the experience? Arguments could be made from a number of positions (and are made in the current volume): the arena concert as the model of interactive yet atomized communication; intimacy as mediated exclusively through social media, and so achieved in bad faith; a virtual 'being there' (at the behest of generating photos for Facebook and Instagram) as holding more ontological weight than an actual proximity. In the context of the Bangerz tour the sharing, and tribal togetherness, seems to have been edged towards, affectively. So what, then, is the equivalent to the soil, and the mud, to which we are now 'being more closely linked' through this? Seemingly, to return to the technological achievements of the arena concert and Hardt and Negri's terminology, vibrations in the digital 'communicative ether' (Hardt, Negri 2000, 360; see also 346–347): the sharing occurs not just with those in the festival field or the music hall or arena itself, but with those, and maybe those who know those, as all connected via social media.

The worth of what is communicated, whether it is then considered as viral advertising and/or, for the fan, self-validation through evidencing that auratic moment (when the fan shared the space and moment with the star: the being there), is a matter of debate. (And where one aspect of that debate is that relaying live images of Beyoncé to friends via social media is no kind of communication at all, but the sorry condition of excommunication;

see Galloway, Thacker and Wark 2014.) But it is in this context that the ideas of intimacy, and the feminization of the space, where the spectacle around the central female performer is expanded beyond the confines of the arena, and out into the ether, is truly played out. In this, irrespective of, say, the actual saliva of Miley mingling with the bottled water and then spat out onto fans, comes the virtual construction and dissemination of Miley, and with performance and intimacy as facets of this construction, and this construction as founded on the event of the arena concert, and its myriad images simultaneously and permanently showcased and archived on social media. The arena concert is the central transmitter for, and optic of, this transformation: the spectacle of the intimate, and the intimate as spectacular.

Notes

1 This chapter was first given as the conference paper 'Skanky Shamanism' at the AHRC-funded symposium Carnivalising Pop: Music Festival Cultures (13 June 2014, University of Salford); my grateful acknowledgement for the feedback from colleagues at that event, particularly Gina Arnold, and to the symposium's convenor, George McKay. Unless otherwise noted, the following tours are referred to in the text, in relation to concerts given in the Manchester Arena: Alicia Keys, As I Am tour (9 July 2008); Kylie Minogue, KylieX2008, aka X tour (18 July 2008), Aphrodite: Les Folies tour (1 April 2011), Kiss Me Once tour (26 September 2014); Lady Gaga, the Monster Ball tour (3 June 2010); Britney Spears, Femme Fatale tour (7 November 2011); Keane, Under the Iron Sea tour (2 March 2007), Strangeland tour (29 November 2012); Guns 'n Roses, Up Close and Personal tour (29 May 2012); Morrissey (28 July 2012), Girls Aloud, Ten: The Hits tour (5 March 2013); Peter Gabriel, Back To Front tour (25 October 2013); Miley Cyrus, Bangerz tour (14 May 2014); Prince, Hit and Run tour (17 May 2014); Katy Perry, The Prismatic World Tour (20 May 2014).

2 Thus the author's vintage pink roses Hartford shirt (visible from his position on front row) briefly preoccupied Kylie during the 2008 concert, resulting in an outstretched arm, a pointed figure and the individual instruction to 'make some noise!'

3 Minogue, Anti Tour (2 April 2012, Manchester Academy). My thanks to Sunil Manghani for his observations during and after the show.

4 These strains, as apparent in the public persona of Farrah Abraham (from reality show star, to her 2012 album My Teenage Dream Ended, to leaked sex tapes) illustrate the endurance and expansiveness of the model of girl pop culture. For further information, see my discussions of the confessional mode of female performance and activism, in the context of Third Wave feminism (Halligan 2013a; Halligan forthcoming).

5 Footage of the former is incorporated into the music video for Tiffany's 'I Think We're Alone Now' (1987); the latter refers to the promo music videos

for Gibson's 'Only In My Dreams' (1987) and 'Out of the Blue' (1988), from the album *Out of the Blue* of 1987. On the question of young female pop singers as seen in their bedrooms, as precariously between 'the classic schoolgirl fantasy image' and hard sell 'paedopop' (Whitely 2005, 58, 59), see Whitely (2005, 22–23).

6 A fuller analysis of sonic strategies of intimacy, which are entirely commonplace in pop music, is beyond the scope of this chapter.

7 The 'Hannah Montana' television series ran from 2006 to 2011. The public transition to 'adult' star occurred across 2010/2011. Some missteps along the way are apparent, where Miley seems to have been granted an insufficient modicum of non-sexualized maturity, as with the films *Hannah Montana: The Movie* (Peter Chelsom, 2009), *LOL* (Lisa Azuelos, 2010, released 2012) and *So Undercover* (Tom Vaughan, 2011), in which she seems cosmically bored.

8 The anticipation seems to be a matter of a slight projection into the future, into the then-coming rise of social media; "Everyone has taken these pictures of themselves and posted them on the internet,' Mr Richardson said. 'I'm just putting them out there on a gallery wall" (Trebay 2004).

9 At this point, 'twerking' (formerly known as grinding) was seen as the nadir of 'raunch culture': a shameless and public display of 'girls gone wild'. Writing in 1999, Tiqqun anticipated twerking in respect to their developing of a post-feminist theory akin to Deleuze and Guattari's 'body without organs': 'The young girl considers her ass a sufficient foundation for her sentiment of incommunicable singularity' (2012, 51).

10 Diane Martel was the Creative Director of the Bangerz tour.

11 The former for several gigs during the Bangerz tour, the latter two in Manchester. The broadcast was for the 2014 Billboard Music Awards, held at the MGM Grand Garden Arena.

12 Indeed, the matter of such intimate concerts is surely undermined by their being recorded for broadcast and commercial release: this intimacy is a matter of style or even affectation rather than exclusively experiential. Alicia Key's Manchester Cathedral concert of 24 September 2014, for 'MTV Crashes Manchester', required a relatively small (and screened) crowd, effectively as part of the set design, while the performance itself remained 'big' and rehearsed, even in this context (including down to the matching outfits of the band members). The effect of being at the front for this concert was little different from Keys at a distance, in an arena, some four years earlier.

13 This argument draws on Steinberg's (1996) reading of the figure of Christ in Renaissance art, but in popular music history terms there is a substantial body of work that posits the singer as Christ- or guru-like, the concert as religious ritual and so forth. In addition, actual young pop star displays of vaginas, accidental or otherwise, was seemingly de rigueur at one point, as Schwartz notes (2011), and thereafter was seemingly the subject of hacking for the so-called Fappening of 2013. Steinberg is reluctant to assemble an incarnational/theological reading derived from the displays of Christ's genitalia (see Steinberg 1996, 238–239) but allows John W. O'Malley, S. J., to do so in relation to Steinberg's original, 1983 text: 'This God [. . .] is unveiled, revealed, in these scenes as truly and fully man' (O'Malley, quoted in Steinberg 1996, 215).

14 In this respect, achieving a close encounter with the pop star, in the enormous space of the arena, becomes all-important for the audience, and a major concern of those working on arena tours. Most artists will use a catwalk and walkways for this reason, in respect of ground and lower-level audiences. Miley, Kylie, Katy and, as noted, Girls Aloud, take to the air to cater for the rest of the audience: flying over the stadium audience or, in Kylie's case, riding on the back of a flying dancer dressed as an angel while singing a cover of The Eurythmic's 'There Must Be an Angel (Playing with My Heart)' (1985) for the Aphrodite tour.

15 For girl-on-girl snogging as a rite of passage rather than matter of sexual identity, see Sanghani (2014). The subject itself was celebrated in Perry's best-selling single, 'I Kissed a Girl', in 2008.

16 On the problematic political radicalism of Gabriel's song, which Easlea claims as 'instrumental in challenging apartheid' as well as the sine qua non of Gabriel's recording career (2013, 10), see Drewett (2012, 99–112) and Byerly (2012, 113–130), and elsewhere in this current volume. A performance of this song, for this tour, is included the film/DVD *Back to Front: Peter Gabriel Live in London* (Hamish Hamilton, 2014). The design of this tour is discussed elsewhere in the current volume.

17 Assuming that the local council would have ultimately licensed the venue on the condition of avoiding illegal activities, which would have then included a prohibition against anything understood to 'intentionally promote homosexuality', as per the Section 28 amendment of the Local Government Act 1986, with the inclusion of section 2a. Text available at http://www.legislation.gov.uk/ukpga/1986/10/section/2A (accessed December 2014).

18 For Cyrus's own reflection on the event, see Cyrus and Liftin (2010, 65–67). The fictional Miley Stewart plays the fictional Hannah Montana, both actually played by Miley Cyrus, who then reverts to this variant of her birth name (which was Destiny Hope, rather than 'Miley', Cyrus) once Montana is retired, which she then has legally adopted, describing her birth certificate as 'defunct' (Cyrus and Liftin 2010, 64). There are plenty of indications that the question of identify is not a psychologically settled state of affairs; during the live concert, Cyrus talked on at length, and in a self-obsessed way, about her public persona, often inaudibly and with only the repeated mantra of her own stage name, said in full each time, as discernible. And, reflecting on her use of the kiss cam during an interview on the *Bangerz* tour DVD (Diane Martel and Russell Thomas, 2015), and the way in which the kiss cam reveals the problems for her audience members suffering from being 'a normal person' when in fact they are 'different', Cyrus claims, messianically, 'I think the universe puts this kind of responsibility to certain people that they know can handle it, and I think I'm strong enough to handle it, and some of those people maybe aren't, and that's why I'm kind of a leader in giving them that little push.' Despite the distance between such sentiments and the above-noted tendency towards the trivial and banal concerns of young girl pop, many of the interviews, including one which involves the recitation of the beginnings of a feminist pop manifesto, are conducted in a hotel bedroom and bed, with Miley in her underwear.

19 On questions of the imagining of immaterial labour in popular culture, see Goddard, Halligan (2012). For a multitude-inflected reading of post-1968 music subcultures, see Mueller (2014).

BIBLIOGRAPHY

Adorno, Theodor. 1997. *Aesthetic Theory*. Minneapolis: University of Minnesota Press.

Adorno, Theodor. 1991. 'On the Fetish Character in Music and the Regression of Listening'. In *The Culture Industry: Selected Essays on Mass Culture*, edited by J. M. Bernstein, 29–60. London and New York: Routledge.

Agamben, Giorgio. 2007. *Infancy and History: On the Destruction of Experience*. London and New York: Verso.

Aguilera, Thomas. 2013. 'Configurations of Squats in Paris and the Ile-de-France Region'. In *Squatting in Europe: Radical Spaces, Urban Struggles*, edited by Squatting Europe Kollective, 209–231. New York: Minor Compositions/ Autonomedia.

Althusser, Louis. 2001. *Lenin and Philosophy and Other Essays*. Translated by Ben Brewster. New York: Monthly Review.

Amis, Martin. 1984. *Money: A Suicide Note*. London: Jonathan Cape.

Anon. 1966. 'Is Beatlemania Dead?' *Time*, 2 September, 38–39.

Anon. 1991. 'Riot Grrrl Manifesto'. *Bikini Kill Zine* 2. Available at: http://one-warart.org/riot_grrrl_manifesto.htm (accessed January 2015).

Anon. 2008. 'Shea It Ain't So! Promoter of The Beatles Dissed'. *New York Daily News*, 22 July. Available at: http://www.nydailynews.com/entertainment/gossip/shea-ain-promoter-beatles-concerts-dissed-article-1.349111 (accessed March 2015).

Antos, Jason. 2007. *Shea Stadium*. Mount Pleasant: Arcadia Publishing.

Argyrakis, Andy. 2008. 'Geek Rock Anthems Overpower Newer Alt-Pop Offerings'. Concertlivewire.com. Available at http://www.concertlivewire.com/weezer3.htm (accessed November 2014).

Armental, Maria. 2014. 'Live Nation Profit Falls as Attendance Drops'. Market Watch, 31 July. Available at: http://www.marketwatch.com/story/live-nation-profit-falls-as-attendance-drops-2014–07–31 (accessed November 2014).

Arnheim, Rudolf. 1971. *Radio*. Translated by Margaret Ludwig and Herbert Read. New York: Arno Press and *The New York Times*.

Atton, Chris. 2002. *Alternative Media*. London: Sage Publications.

Atton, Chris. 2004. *An Alternative Internet*. Edinburgh: Edinburgh University Press.

Auslander, Philip. 2004. 'Performance Analysis and Popular Music: A Manifesto'. *Contemporary Theatre Review*, 14 (1): 1–13.

Auslander, Philip. 2006a. 'Music as Performance: Living in an Immaterial World'. *Theatre Survey*, 47 (2): 261–269.

Auslander, Philip. 2006b. *Performing Glam Rock: Gender and Theatricality in Popular Music*. Ann Arbor: University of Michigan Press.

Auslander, Philip. 2008. *Liveness: Performance in a Mediatized Culture*. London and New York: Routledge.

Auslander, Philip. 2009. 'Musical Persona: The Physical Performance of Popular Music'. In *The Ashgate Research Companion to Popular Musicology*, edited by Derek B. Scott, 303–315. Farnham: Ashgate.

Azzopardi, Chris. 2014. 'Q&a: Annie Lennox on Her Legacy, Why Beyonce Is 'Feminist Lite''. *PrideSource*. 25 September. Available at: http://www.pridesource.com/article.html?article=68228 (accessed March 2015).

Badman, Keith. 2001. *The Beatles Off the Record 2: The Dream Is Over*. London: Omnibus Press.

Bagenal, Hope and Alex Wood. 1931. *Planning for Good Acoustics*. London: Methuen.

Baker, Sarah. 2013. 'Teenybop and the Extraordinary Particularities of Mainstream Practice'. In *Redefining Mainstream Popular Music*, edited by Sarah Baker, Andy Bennett and Jodie Taylor, 14–24. London: Routledge.

Bakhtin, Mikhail. 1984. *Problems of Dostoevsky's Poetics*. Translated by Caryl Emerson. Minneapolis: University of Minnesota Press.

Barker, Hugh and Yuval Taylor. 2007. *Faking It: The Quest for Authenticity in Popular Music*. New York and London: W. W. Norton.

Baudrillard, Jean. 1994. *Simulacra and Simulation*. Translated by Shelia Faria Glaser. Chicago: University of Chicago Press.

Baugh, Christopher. 2005. *Theatre, Performance and Technology: The Development of Scenography in the Twentieth Century*. Basingstoke: Palgrave Macmillan.

The Beatles [George Harrison, John Lennon, Paul McCartney, Ringo Starr]. 2000. *The Beatles Anthology*. San Francisco: Chronicle Books.

Becker, Howard S. 1982. *Art Worlds*. Berkeley and Los Angeles: University of California Press.

Beckett, Samuel. 2014. *Not I / Footfalls / Rockaby*. London: Faber and Faber.

Benjamin, Walter. 1936. 'The Work of Art in the Age of Mechanical Reproduction'. Available at: https://www.marxists.org/reference/subject/philosophy/works/ge/benjamin.htm (accessed January 2015).

Benjamin, Walter. 1992. *Illuminations*. Translated by Harry Zohn. London: HarperCollins.

Benjamin, Walter. 1997. *Charles Baudelaire: A Lyric Poet in the Era of High Capitalism*. Translated by Henry Zohn. London: Verso.

Benjamin, Walter. 2006. 'On Some Motifs in Baudelaire'. In *Walter Benjamin: Selected Writings: Vol. 4 1938–1940*, edited by Howard Eiland and Michael W. Jennings, 313–355. Cambridge, MA and London: Belknap Press of Harvard University Press.

Berger, John. 2011. *Bento's Sketchbook*. London: Verso.

Berglund, Nina. 2013. 'Nobel Concert Hunts for New Sponsors'. *News in English*, 11 December. Available at: http://www.newsinenglish.no/2013/12/11/nobel-concert-hunts-for-new-sponsors/ (accessed April 2015).

Berman, Gary. 2008. *We're Going to See the Beatles: An Oral History of Beatlemania as Told by Fans Who Were There*. Santa Monica, CA: Santa Monica Press.

Bey, Hakim. 2003 [1985]. *T.A.Z. The Temporary Autonomous Zone, Ontological Anarchy, Poetic Terrorism*. New York: Autonomedia.

Black, Harry. 2002. *Canada and the Nobel Prize: Biographies, Portraits and Fascinating Facts*. Ontario: Pembroke Publishers.

Blackadder, Neil. 2003. *Performing Opposition: Modern Theater and the Scandalized Audience*. Westport, CT and London: Praegar.

Blesser, Barry and Linda-Ruth Salter. 2006. *Spaces Speak, Are You Listening?: Experiencing Aural Architecture*. Cambridge, MA: MIT Press.

Bogue, Ronald. 2003. *Deleuze on Cinema*. New York: Routledge.

Bramwell, Tony. 2005. *Magical Mystery Tours*. New York: Thomas Dunne Books.

Brennan, Matt and Emma Webster. 2011. 'Why Concert Promoters Matter'. *Scottish Music Review*, 2 (1): 1–25.

Bronques, Merlin. 2006. *Lastnightsparty*. New York: Image/Harry N. Abrams.

Bull, Michael. 2004. 'Thinking about Sound, Proximity and Distance in Western Experience'. In *Hearing Cultures: Essays on Sound, Listening and Modernity*, edited by Veit Erlmann, 173–190. New York: Berg Publishers.

Burgess, Anthony, Daniel Angeli and Jean-Paul Dousset. 1980. *Private Pictures*. London: Jonathan Cape.

Burgin, Victor. 2004. *The Remembered Film*. London: Reaktion Books.

Byerly, Ingrid Bianca. 2012. 'Music Markers as Catalysts in Social Revolutions: The Case of Gabriel's "Biko"'. In *Peter Gabriel, From Genesis to Growing Up*, edited by Michael Drewett, Sarah Hill and Kimi Kärki, 113–130. Surrey: Ashgate.

Byrne, David. 2012. *How Music Works*. Edinburgh: Canongate Books.

Carlin, Paul. 2009. *Paul McCartney: A Life*. New York: Touchstone.

Carpentier, Nico. 2011. 'Contextualising Author-Audience Convergences'. *Cultural Studies* 25 (4–5) (September 15): 517–533.

Caruso, Bobby. 2014. 'Millennials, Put Your Phone Down at Concerts'. *Huffington Post*, 2 December. Available at: http://www.huffingtonpost.com/bobby-caruso/millennials-put-your-phone-down_b_6256276.html (accessed December 2014).

Cash, Rosanne. 2010. *Composed: A Memoir*. New York: Viking.

Cavicchi, Daniel. 1998. *Tramps Like Us: Music and Meaning Among Springsteen Fans*. Oxford: Oxford University Press.

Chaney, Edward. 2006. 'Egypt in England and America: The Cultural Memorials of Religion, Royalty and Revolution'. In *Sites of Exchange: European Crossroads and Faultlines*, edited by Maurizio Ascari and Adriana Corrado, 39–74. Amsterdam, New York: Rodopi.

Charles, Paul. 2004. *The Complete Guide to Playing Live*. London: Omnibus.

Charlesworth, Chris. 1975. 'The Who: Stafford Bingley Hall, Stafford, Oct 3 & 4, 1975. Part Two – The First Night'. *Melody Maker*. 5 October. Available at: http://justbackdated.blogspot.co.uk/2014/06/the-who-bingley-hall-stafford-october-3_9.html (accessed January 2015).

Chouliarki, Lisa. 2010. 'Self-Mediation: New Media and Citizenship'. *Critical Discourse Studies*, 7 (4): 227–232.

Clarke, Alfred. 1966. '2000 Beatles Fans Storm Box Office Here'. *New York Times*, 1 May, 80.

Cleave, Maureen. 1966. 'Old Beatles – A Study in Paradox'. *New York Times*, 3 July, 118–121.

Colburn, Steven. 2015. 'Filming Concerts for YouTube: Seeking Recognition in the Pursuit of Cultural Capital'. *Popular Music and Society*, 38 (1): 59–72.

Competition Commission. 2010a. 'Appendices and Glossary'. In *Ticketmaster and Live Nation: A Report on the Completed Merger between Ticketmaster Entertainment, Inc. and Live Nation, Inc.* London: Competition Commission.

Competition Commission. 2010b. 'Full Text of Report'. In *Ticketmaster and Live Nation: A Report on the Completed Merger between Ticketmaster Entertainment, Inc. and Live Nation, Inc.* London: Competition Commission.

Connell, John and Chris Gibson. 2003. *Sound Tracks: Popular Music, Identity and Place.* London: Routledge.

Considine, J. D. 2011. 'An Upbeat Singalong with Taylor Swift'. *The Globe and Mail*, 17 July. Available at: http://www.theglobeandmail.com/arts/music/an-upbeat-singalong-with-taylor-swift/article629425/ (accessed August 2014).

Cook, Nicholas. 2012. 'Music as Performance'. In *The Cultural Study of Music: A Critical Introduction*, edited by Martin Clayton, Trevor Herbert and Richard Middleton, 184–194. New York: Routledge.

Cooke, Chris. 2013. 'Live Nation Charged Over Fatal Stage Collapse at Radiohead Gig'. *CMU: Complete Music Update*, 10 June. Available at: http://www.completemusicupdate.com/article/live-nation-charged-over-fatal-stage-collapse-at-radiohead-gig (accessed April 2015)

Cooper, Gary. 2004. 'Interview: Christian Heil, Founder of L-ACOUSTICS, France – the Father of Modern Line Array Speaker Systems'. *Audio Pro International*, November. Available at: http://www.garycooper.biz/articles/interviews0411–1.html (accessed March 2015).

Copjec, Joan. 2002. *Imagine There's No Woman: Ethics and Sublimation.* Cambridge, MA: MIT Press.

Corbeill, Anthony. 1997. 'Thumbs in Ancient Rome: "Pollex" as Index'. *Memoirs of the American Academy in Rome*, 42: 1–21.

Couldry, Nick. 2003. *Media Rituals: A Critical Approach.* London: Routledge.

Couldry, Nick and Andreas Hepp. 2010. 'Introduction: Media Events in Globalized Media Cultures'. In *Media Events in a Global Age*, edited by Nick Couldry, Andreas Hepp and Friedrich Krotz, 1–20. London: Routledge.

CSO (Central Statistics Office). 2013. 'Population 1901–2011'. Central Statistics Office, 27 March. Available at: http://www.cso.ie/Quicktables/GetQuickTables.aspx?FileName=CNA13.asp&TableName=Population+1901+-+2011&StatisticalProduct=DB_CN (accessed March 2015)

Cunningham, Mark. 1999. *Live & Kicking: The Rock Concert Industry in the Nineties.* London: MPG Books/Sanctuary Publishing.

Cyrus, Miley with Hilary Liftin. 2010. *Miley Cyrus: Miles to Go.* Bath: Parragon.

Dant, Tim. 2012. *Television and the Moral Imaginary: Society through the Small Screen.* Basingstoke: Palgrave Macmillan.

Dardo, Mauro. 2004. *Nobel Laureates and Twentieth-Century Physics.* Cambridge: Cambridge University Press.

Dayan, Daniel and Elihu Katz. 1996. *Media Events: The Live Broadcasting of History.* Cambridge, MA: Harvard University Press.

Dayan, Daniel. 2010. 'Beyond Media Events: Disenchantment, Derailment, Distruption'. In *Media Events in a Global Age*, edited by Nick Couldry, Andreas Hepp and Friedrich Krotz, 23–31. London: Routledge.

Debord, Guy. 1990 [1988]. *Comments on the Society of the Spectacle*. Translated by Malcolm Imrie. London: Verso.

Debord, Guy. 1995 [1967]. *The Society of the Spectacle*. Translated by Donald Nicholson-Smith. New York: Zone Books.

Deleuze, Gilles. 1992. *Cinema 1: The Movement Image*. Translated by Hugh Tomlinson and Barbara Habberjam. London: Continuum, 1992.

Di Benedetto, Stephen. 2007. 'Guiding Somatic Responses within Performative Structures: Contemporary Live Art and Sensorial Perception'. In *The Senses in Performance*, edited by Sally Banes and Ande Lepeke, 124–137. New York, London: Routledge.

Dillon, Brian. 2012. 'Ugly Feelings'. In *Damien Hirst*, edited by Ann Gallagher, 21–37. London: Tate Publishing.

Dockwray, Ruth. 2005. 'Deconstructing the Rock Anthem: Textual Form, Participation and Collectivity'. Unpublished PhD thesis, University of Liverpool.

Dolan, Emily I. 2013. *The Orchestral Revolution: Haydn and the Technologies of Timbre*. Cambridge: Cambridge University Press.

Doyle, Peter. 2005. *Echo and Reverb: Fabricating Space in Popular Music, 1900–1960*. Middletown, CT: Wesleyan University Press.

Dredge, Stuart. 2014. 'Global Music Sales Fell in 2013 Despite Strong Growth for Streaming Services'. *The Guardian*, 18 March. Available at: http://www.theguardian.com/technology/2014/mar/18/music-sales-ifpi-2013-spotify-streaming (accessed April 2015).

Drewett, Michael. 2012. 'The Eyes of the World Are Watching Now: The Political Effectiveness of "Biko" by Peter Gabriel'. In *Peter Gabriel, From Genesis to Growing Up*, edited by Michael Drewett, Sarah Hill and Kimi Kärki, 99–112. Surrey: Ashgate.

Duffett, Mark. 2003a. 'False Faith or False Comparison: A Critique of the Religious Interpretation of Elvis Fan Culture'. *Popular Music and Society*, 26 (4): 513–522.

Duffett, Mark. 2003b. 'Imagined Memories: Webcasting as 'Live' Technology and the Case of Little Big Gig'. *Information, Communication & Society*, 6 (3): 307–325.

Duffett, Mark. 2014a. 'Celebrity: The Return of the Repressed in Fan Studies?' In *The Ashgate Research Companion to Fan Cultures*, edited by Linda Duits, Koos Zwaan and Stijn Reijnders, 163–180. Farnham: Ashgate.

Duffett, Mark. 2014b. 'Introduction'. In *Popular Music Fandom: Identities, Roles and Practices*, edited by Mark Duffett. New York: Routledge, 1–15.

Durant, Alan. 1984. *Conditions of Music*. New York: State University of New York Press.

Durham, Aisha. 2012. 'Check on It'. *Feminist Media Studies*, 12 (1): 35–49.

Durkheim, Emile. 2008 [1912]. *The Elementary Forms of Religious Life*. Oxford: Oxford University Press.

Dutton, Denis. 2010. *The Art Instinct: Beauty, Pleasure and Human Evolution*. Oxford: Oxford University Press.

Earl, Peter E. 2001. 'Simon's Travel Theorem and the Demand for Live Music'. *Journal of Economic Psychology* 22: 335–358.

Easlea, Daryl. 2013. *Without Frontiers: The Life and Music of Peter Gabriel.* London: Omnibus Press.

Edmondson, Jacqueline. 2010. *John Lennon: A Biography.* Santa Barbara: Greenwood Press.

Edwards, Anne. 1997. *Streisand.* London: Orion Books.

Ehrenreich, Barbara. 2006. *Dancing in the Streets.* New York: Metropolitan Books.

Elsaesser, Thomas. 2009. 'Between *Erlebnis* and *Erfahrung*: Cinema Experience with Benjamin'. *Paragraph,* 32 (3): 292–312.

Etheridge, Melissa. 2010. 'Introduction by Melissa Etheridge'. In *Rock & Roll Jihad: A Muslim Rock Star's Revolution*, by Salman Ahmad, 1–4. New York: Free Press.

Farber, Manny. 1998. *Negative Space: Manny Farber on the Movies.* New York: Da Capo Press.

Farren, Mick. 1977. 'Pink Floyd: Eyeless in the Galaxy'. *New Musical Express,* 26 March. Reproduced at: http://www.rocksbackpages.com/Library/Article/pink-floyd-eyeless-in-the-galaxy (accessed March 2015).

Fast, Susan. 2006. 'Popular Music Performance and Cultural Memory. Queen: Live Aid, Wembley Stadium, London, July 13, 1985'. In *Performance and Popular Music: History, Place and Time*, edited by Ian Inglis, 138–154. Aldershot: Ashgate.

Ferguson, James. 2013. 'Manchester Arena Signs Deal with Phones4U', Manchester Evening News, 31 July. Available at: http://www.manchester-eveningnews.co.uk/business/business-news/manchester-arena-signs-deal-phones-5385660, accessed 21/11/2014 (accessed April 2015).

Fitch, Vernon. 1997. *The Pink Floyd Encyclopaedia.* Burlington, Ontario: Collector's Guide Publishing.

Fitch, Vernon. 2001. *Pink Floyd. The Press Reports 1966–1983.* Burlington, Ontario: Collector's Guide Publishing.

Fonarow, Wendy. 2006. *Empire of Dirt: The Aesthetics and Rituals of British Indie Music.* Connecticut: Wesleyan University Press.

Forsyth, Michael. 1985. *Buildings for Music: The Architect, the Musician, and the Listener from the Seventeenth Century to the Present Day.* Cambridge: Cambridge University Press.

Franceschet, Antonio. 2009. 'Four Cosmopolitan Projects: The International Criminal Court in Context'. In *Governance, Order, and the International Criminal Court: Between Realpolitik and a Cosmopolitan Court*, edited by Steven C. Roach, 179–204. Oxford: Oxford University Press.

Frith, Simon. 1982. '1967: The Year It All Came Together'. *The History of Rock Volume 1*, edited by Ashley Brown, 2–17. London: Orbis Publishing.

Frith, Simon. 1996. *Performing Rites: On the Value of Popular Music.* Oxford and New York: Oxford University Press.

Frith, Simon. 2002. 'Look! Hear! The Uneasy Relationship of Music and Television'. *Popular Music,* 21 (3) (October): 277–290.

Frith, Simon. 2010. 'Analysing Live Music in the UK: Findings One Year into a Three-Year Research Project'. *IASPM@Journal,* 1 (1): 1–3.

Frith, Simon. 2012. 'Live Music 101 #1 – The Materialist Approach to Live Music'. *Live Music Exchange*, 2 July. Available at: http://livemusicexchange. org/blog/live-music-101–1-the-materialist-approach-to-live-music-simon-frith (accessed March 2015)

Frith, Simon, Matt Brennan, Martin Cloonan and Emma Webster. 2013. *The History of Live Music in Britain, Volume I: 1950–1967: From Dance Hall to the 100 Club.* Aldershot: Ashgate.

Gabler, Neal. 2009. 'Tiger-Stalking: In Defence of Our Tabloid Culture'. *Newsweek*, 11 December. Available at: http://www.newsweek.com/tiger-stalking-defense-our-tabloid-culture-75577 (accessed April 2015).

Galloway, Alexander, Eugene Thacker and McKenzie Wark. 2014. *Excommunication: Three Inquiries in Media and Mediation.* London: University of Chicago Press.

Gamson, Joshua. 1994. *Claims to Fame: Celebrity in Contemporary America.* Berkeley: University of California Press.

Gauntlett, David. 2011. *Making Is Connecting: The Social Meaning of Creativity, from DIY and Knitting to YouTube and Web 2.0.* Cambridge: Polity Press.

Goddard, Michael and Benjamin Hallgan. 2010. *Mark E. Smith and The Fall: Art, Music and Politics.* Surrey: Ashgate.

Goddard, Michael and Benjamin Halligan. 2012. 'Cinema, the Post-Fordist Worker, and Immaterial Labour: From Post-Hollywood to the European Art Film'. *Framework* 53, (1) (Spring): 172–189.

Goddard, Michael, Benjamin Halligan and Nicola Spelman. 2013. *Reverberations: Noise and Contemporary Music.* New York: Bloomsbury.

Goldman, Vivien. 1978. 'Bob Dylan: [*sic*] Earl's Court London'. *Sounds.* 24 June. Available at: http://www.rocksbackpages.com/Library/Article/bob-dylan-earls-court-london (accessed January 2015).

Goodrich, Lawrence and Ruth Walker. 2010. *Cultural Studies: An Introduction to Global Awareness.* Sudbury: Jones & Bartlett Publishers.

Goodwin, Andrew. 1990. 'Sample and Hold: Pop Music in the Digital Age of Reproducing'. In *On Record: Rock, Pop, and the Written Word*, edited by Simon Frith and Andrew Goodwin, 258–273. London: Routledge.

Gracyk, Theodore. 1996. *Rhythm and Noise: An Aesthetics of Rock.* Durham, NC: Duke University Press.

Greene, Andy. 2012. 'Radiohead Teams with Fans to Create Concert Video for Charity,' *Rolling Stone*, 30 November. Available at: http://www.rollingstone. com/music/news/radiohead-teams-with-fans-to-create-concert-video-for-charity-20121130 (accessed March 2015).

Greene, Andy. 2013. '10 Most Annoying Concert Behaviours'. *Rolling Stone*, 14 January. Available at: http://www.rollingstone.com/music/news/the-10-most-annoying-concert-behaviors-20130114 (accessed August 2014).

Guralnick, Peter and Ernst Jorgensen. 1999. *Elvis Day by Day.* New York: Ballantine.

Haithcoat, Rebecca. 2014. 'Hey, Moron! Why Are You Recording Concerts on Your IPhone?' *LA Weekly*, 21 February. Available at: http://www.laweekly. com/music/hey-moron-why-are-you-recording-concerts-on-your-iphone-2408718 (accessed December 2014).

Halfwerk, Wouter, Rachel A. Page, Ryan C. Taylor, Preston S. Wilson and Michael J. Ryan. 2014. 'Crossmodal Comparisons of Signal Components Allow for Relative-Distance Assessment'. *Current Biology*, 24 (15) (August 4): 1751–1755.

Hall, Edward T. 1966. *The Hidden Dimension*. New York: Doubleday.

Halligan, Benjamin. 2009. 'Please Ensure That Your Mobile Phone Is Switched Off Theatre Etiquette in an Age of Outsourcing'. *Studies in Theatre and Performance*, 29 (2): 193–197.

Halligan, Benjamin. 2013a. '"({})": Raunch Culture, Third Wave Feminism and *The Vagina Monologues*'. *Theory and Event*, 17:1.

Halligan, Benjamin. 2013b. 'Shoegaze as the Third Wave: Affective Psychedelic Noise, 1965–1991'. In *Resonances: Noise and Contemporary Music*, edited by Michael Goddard, Benjamin Halligan and Nicola Spelman, 37–63. New York and London: Bloomsbury.

Halligan, Benjamin. Forthcoming. '"My Uterus Doesn't Expel Rape Sperm": SlutWalk and the Activist Legacy of the Suffragettes'. In *The Suffragette Legacy*, edited by Camilla Rostvik and Louise Sutherland. London: Cambridge Scholars Press (in press).

Hancock, Tom. 2014. 'Jack White – Hammersmith Apollo, London 03/07/14'. *The Line Of Best Fit*, 7 July. Available at: http://www.thelineofbestfit.com/reviews/live-reviews/jack-white-brixton-academy-london-04–07–14 (accessed March 2015).

Hansen, Miriam Bratu. 2011. *Cinema and Experience: Siegfried Kracauer, Walter Benjamin, and Theodor Adorno*. Oakland: University of California Press.

Hardt, Michael and Antonio Negri. 2000. *Empire*. London: Harvard University Press.

Hardt, Michael and Antonio Negri. 2005. *Multitude: War and Democracy in the Age of Empire*. London: Hamish Hamilton.

Harrison, Olivia. 2002. *George Harrison*. New York: Simon & Schuster.

Hartig, Terry and Henk Staats. 2006. 'The Need for Psychological Restoration as a Determinant of Environmental Preferences'. *Journal of Environmental Psychology*, 26: 215–226.

Hartley, George. 2003. *The Abyss of Representation: Marxism and the Postmodern Sublime*. Durham, NC and London: Duke University Press.

Hartwell, Clare, Matthew Hyde and Nikolaus Pevsner. 2004. *Buildings of England: Lancashire: Manchester and the South-East*. London: Yale University Press.

Heffermehl, Fredrik S. 2010. *The Nobel Peace Prize: What Nobel Really Wanted*. Santa Barbara: Praeger.

Hegarty, Paul and Martin Halliwell. 2011. *Beyond the Before: Progressive Rock Since the 1960s*. London and New York: Bloomsbury.

Hemming, Roy. 1992. *Discovering Great Singers of Classic Pop: A New Listener's Guide to the Sounds and Lives of the Top Performers*. London: HarperCollins.

Hennion, Antoine. 1997. 'Baroque and Rock: Music, Mediators and Musical Taste'. *Poetics*, 24 (6): 415–435.

Herkman, Juha. 2012. 'Introduction: Intermediality as a Theory and Methodology'. In *Intermediality and Media Change*, edited by Juha Herkman, Taisto Hujanen and Paavo Oinonen, 10–27. Tampere: Tampere University Press.

Hewison, Robert. 2014. *Cultural Capital: The Rise and Fall of Creative Britain*. London: Verso.

Himmelfarb, Gertrude. 2002. 'The Illusions of Cosmopolitanism'. In *For Love of Country?*, edited by Martha C. Nussbaum, 72–77. Boston: Beacon Press.

Hoare, Philip and Chris Heath. 2006. *Pet Shop Boys Catalogue*. London: Thames & Hudson.

Hoby, Hermione. 2014. 'Taylor Swift: "Sexy? Not on My Radar"'. 23 August. Available at: http://www.theguardian.com/music/2014/aug/23/taylor-swift-shake-it-off (accessed March 2015).

Hodgeland, William. 2011. Sleeve notes for *Kylie Minogue: Live in Dublin*, 1991. DVD: IMC Music.

Holding, Eric. 2000. *Mark Fisher: Staged Architecture*. Architectural Monographs No 52. Chichester: Wiley-Academy.

Holm-Hudson, Kevin. 2008. *Genesis and 'The Lamb Lies Down on Broadway'*. Surrey: Ashgate.

Hoskyns, Barney. 2012. *Trampled under Foot: The Power and Excess of Led Zeppelin*. London: Faber and Faber.

Huck, Janet. 1997. 'Up against the Wall'. In *Pink Floyd: Through the Eyes of . . . the Band, Its Fans, Friends and Foes*, edited by Bruno MacDonald, 118–129. New York: Da Capo Press.

IMG Media. 2013. 'Nobel Peace Prize Concert 2012 Media Report'. Nobel Peace Prize Concert AS. http://www.nobelpeaceprizeconcert.org/wp-content/uploads/2012/11/NPPCMediaReport2012_lowres-copy.pdf (accessed March 2015).

Inglis, Ian. 2006. *Performance and Popular Music: History, Place and Time*. Hampshire and Burlington: Ashgate.

Insider Media. 2013. 'Falling Attendances Hit Profits at Manchester Arena Operator SMG', 9 September. Available at: http://www.insidermedia.com/insider/north-west/98014-falling-attendances-hit-profits-manchester-arena-operator-smg/ (accessed November 2014).

Jackson, John. 2005. *We All Want to Change the World: The Life of John Lennon*. London: Haus Publishing.

Jannarone, Kimberley. 2009. 'Audience, Mass, Crowd: Theatres of Cruelty in Interwar Europe'. *Theatre Journal*, 61 (2): 191–211.

Jay, Martin. 1998. *Cultural Semantics*. Amherst: University of Massachusetts Press.

Jenkins, Henry. 2006. *Convergence Culture: Where Old and New Media Collide*. New York: New York University Press.

Johnson, Paul. 2006 [1964] 'The Menace of Beatlism'. In *Read the Beatles*, edited by June Skinner Sawyers, 51–55. London: Penguin.

Jones, Cliff. 1996. *Echoes: The Stories behind Every Pink Floyd Song*. London: Omnibus Press.

Jones, Lucy. 2013. '"PUT THAT SHIT AWAY" – Should Smartphones Be Banned At Gigs?'. NME, 9 April. Available at: http://www.nme.com/blogs/nme-blogs/put-that-shit-away-should-smartphones-be-banned-at-gigs (accessed March 2015).

Julien, Olivier. 2009. *Sgt. Pepper and The Beatles: It Was 40 Years Ago Today*. Farnham: Ashgate.

Kahn, Coppelia. 2000. 'Caliban at the Stadium: Shakespeare and the Making of Americans'. *The Massachusetts Review*, 41 (2) (Summer): 256–284.

Kaldor, Mary. 2011. 'Social Movements, NGOs and Networks'. In *Global Activism Reader*, edited by Luc Reydams, 3–22. New York: Continuum.

Kane, Larry. 2003. *Ticket to Ride*. New York: Penguin.

Kant, Immanuel. 1964. *Critique of Judgement*. Oxford: Clarendon Press.

Kant, Immanuel. 1993. *Critique of Pure Reason*. London: Everyman, 1993.

Kanter, Rosabeth Moss. 1995. *World Class: Thriving Locally in the Global Economy*. New York: Simon & Shuster.

Kaplan, Rachel. 1993. 'The Role of Nature in the Context of the Workplace'. *Landscape and Urban Planning*, 26: 193–201.

Kärki, Kimi, 2005. '"Matter of Fact It's All Dark": Audiovisual Stadium Rock Aesthetics in Pink Floyd's *The Dark Side of the Moon* Tour, 1973'. In *'Speak to Me': The Legacy of Pink Floyd's The Dark Side of the Moon*, edited by Russell Reising, 27–42. Burlington, VT: Ashgate.

Kärki, Kimi. 2010. 'Turning the Axis: The Stage Performance Design Collaboration between Peter Gabriel and Robert Lepage'. In *Peter Gabriel From Genesis to Growing Up*, edited by Michael Drewett, Sarah Hill and Kimi Kärki, 225–240. Aldershot: Ashgate.

Kärki, Kimi. 2014. *Rakennettu areenatähteys: Rock-konsertti globalisoituvana media-aspektaakkelina 1965–2013*. Turku: Turun yliopiston julkaisuja Sarja C, osa 397.

Kashner, Sam. 2014. 'Both Huntress and Prey'. *Vanity Fair*, November, 130–137, 183.

Kattwinkel, Susan. 2003. *Audience Participation: Essays on Inclusion in Performance*. Westport, CT: Praeger.

Kaufman, Robert. 2000. 'Red Kant, or The Persistence of the Third *Critique* in Adorno and Jameson'. *Critical Inquiry*, 26 (4): 682–724.

Kellner, Douglas. 2003. *Media Spectacle*. New York: Routledge.

Kellner, Douglas. 2010. 'Media Spectacle and Media Events: Some Critical Reflections'. In *Media Events in a Global Age*, edited by Nick Couldry, Andreas Hepp and Friedrich Krotz, 76–91. Abingdon: Routledge.

Kendall, Gavin, Ian Woodward and Zlatko Skrbis. 2009. *The Sociology of Cosmopolitanism: Globalization, Identity, Culture and Government*. Basingstoke: Palgrave Macmillan.

Kent, Nick. 1973. 'Aladdin Distress'. *New Musical Express*, 19 May. Available at: http://www.5years.com/ad.htm (accessed November 2014).

Kershaw, Andy. 2005. 'Bob Dylan: How I Found the Man Who Shouted "Judas!"' *The Independent*, 23 September. Available at: http://www.independent.co.uk/arts-entertainment/music/features/bob-dylan-how-i-found-the-man-who-shouted-judas-314340.html (accessed April 2015).

Kracauer, Siegfried. 1995. *The Mass Ornament: Weimar Essays*. Edited by Thomas Y. Levin. Cambridge, MA: Harvard University Press.

Kronenburg, Robert H. 2007. *Flexible: Architecture that Responds to Change*. Lawrence King: London.

Kronenburg, Robert H. 2011. 'Typological Trends in Contemporary Popular Music Performance Venues'. *Arts Marketing: An International Journal*, 1 (2): 136–144.

Kronenburg, Robert H. 2012. *Live Architecture: Venues, Stages and Arenas for Popular Music*. London and New York: Routledge.

Kronenburg, Robert H. 2014a. *Architecture in Motion: The History and Development of Portable Building*. London: Routledge.

Kronenburg, Robert H. 2014b. 'Safe and Sound: Audience Experience in New Venues for Popular Music Performance'. In *Coughing and Clapping: Investigating Audience Experience*, edited by Karen Burland and Stephanie Pitts, 35–52. Farnham: Ashgate.

Krupskaya, Nadezhda. 1970 [1930/1932]. *Memories of Lenin*. Translated by Martin Laughey, Dan. 2006. *Music and Youth Culture*. Edinburgh: Edinburgh University Press. Lawrence, London: Panther.

Lahusen, Christian. 2001. 'Mobilizing for International Solidarity: Mega-Events and Moral Crusades'. In *Political Altruism?: Solidarity Movements in International Perspective*, edited by Marco Giugni and Florence Passy, 177–195. Lanham: Rowman & Littlefield.

Larsson, Goran. 2011. 'The Return of Ziryab: Yusuf Islam on Music'. In *Religion and Popular Music in Europe: New Expressions of Sacred and Secular Identity*, edited by Thomas Bossius, Andreas Hager and Keith Kahn-Harris, 82–104. London: I. B. Taurus.

Leight, Elias. 2014. 'Annie Lennox: "Twerking Is Not Feminism"'. *Billboard*, 21 October. Available at: http://www.billboard.com/articles/news/6289251/annie-lennox-twerking-not-feminism (accessed March 2015).

Levy, Ariel. 2006. *Female Chauvinist Pigs: Women and the Rise of Raunch Culture*. London: Simon & Schuster.

Lewis, Dave. 2006. *Led Zeppelin: Concert File*. London: Omnibus.

Lewisohn, Mark. 1986. *The Beatles Live!* New York: Henry Holt.

Lewisohn, Mark. 1992. *The Complete Beatles Chronicle*. New York: Harmony.

Lewisohn, Mark. 2014. *Tune In*. New York: Crown Archetype.

Lin, Charles. 2008. 'Weezer Does What They Want to Do'. *The Tech*, 26 September. Available at: http://tech.mit.edu/V128/N42/weezer.html (accessed January 2015).

Llewyn-Smith, Caspar. 2009. 'Beyoncé – Artist of the Decade'. *The Guardian*, 29 November. Available at: http://www.theguardian.com/music/2009/nov/29/beyonce-artist-of-the-decade (accessed March 2015).

Lofthus, Kai R. 2000. 'Nobel Concert Goes Pop: Show Straddles Artistic and Commercial Goals'. *Billboard*, 30 December, 24.

Luhrmann, Baz. 2013. 'Beyoncé – The 2013 Time 100'. *Time*, 18 April. Available at: http://time100.time.com/2013/04/18/time-100/slide/beyonce/ (accessed March 2015).

Lull, James. 2007. *Culture-on-Demand: Communication in a Crisis World*. Malden: Blackwell.

MacAloon, John J. 1984. 'Olympic Games and the Theory of the Spectacle in Modern Societies'. In *Rite, Drama, Festival, Spectacle: Rehearsals Toward a Theory of Cultural Performance*, edited by John J. MacAloon, 1–15. Philadelphia: Institute for the Study of Human Issues.

Macan, Edward. 2006. *Endless Enigma: A Musical Biography of Emerson, Lake and Palmer*. Chicago, IL: Open Court.

Macan, Edward. 1997. *Rocking the Classics: English Progressive Rock and the Counterculture*. Oxford and New York: Oxford University Press.

Macek III, J. C. 2012. 'The Cinematic Experience of Roger Waters' "The Wall Live"'. *PopMatters*. Available at: http://www.popmatters.com/column/162226-the-cinematic-experience-of-roger-waters-the-wall-live (accessed May 2014).

Mackie, John. 2007. 'One Night with You and Elvis Fled'. *Vancouver Sun*, 18 August. Available at: http://www.canada.com/vancouversun/news/westcoast-news/story.html?id=3b772880–6761–4f22-aeb3–7fc475a6cb3c&k=84620 (accessed March 2015).

Makowski, Pete. 1975. 'Led Zeppelin: Earls Court'. *Sounds*, 24 May. Available at: http://www.rocksbackpages.com/Library/Article/led-zeppelin-earls-court-london (accessed January 2015).

Manghani, Sunil and Keith McDonald. 2013. 'Desperately Seeking Kylie! Critical Reflections on William Baker's *White Diamond*'. In *The Music Documentary: Acid Rock to Electropop*, edited by Robert Edgar, Kirsty Fairclough-Isaacs and Benjamin Halligan, 219–234. London: Routledge.

Marshall, P. David. 1997. *Celebrity and Power: Fame in Contemporary Culture*. Minneapolis: University of Minnesota Press.

Martin, Geoff and Erin Steuter. 2010. *Pop Culture Goes to War: Enlisting and Resisting Militarism in the War on Terror*. Lanham: Rowman & Littlefield.

Marwick, Alice E. and Danah Boyd. 2010. 'I Tweet Honestly, I Tweet Passionately: Twitter Users, Context Collapse, and the Imagined Audience'. *New Media and Society* 13 (1): 10–20.

McBain, Sophie. 2013. 'J Lo Joins Beyonce and Mariah Carey in Lineup of Dictator Divas'. *The New Statesman*, 22 July. Available at: http://www.news-tatesman.com/business/2013/07/j-lo-joins-beyonce-and-maria-carey-lineup-dictator-divas (accessed April 2015).

McCracken, Allison. 1999. 'God's Gift to Us Girls: Crooning, Gender, and the Re-Creation of American Popular Song, 1928–1933'. *American Music*, 17 (4): 365–395.

McCulloch, Janelle. 2010. *Design in Black & White*. Mulgrave: Images Publishing Group.

McGinn, Matt. 2010. *Roadie: My Life on the Road with Coldplay*. London: Portico.

McKay, George. 2015. *The Pop Festival: History, Music, Media and Culture*. New York and London: Bloomsbury.

Metz, Christian. *Film Language*. Translated by Michael Taylor. New York: Oxford University Press, 1974.

Miles, Barry. 1998. *Paul McCartney: Many Years From Now*. London: Vintage Books.

Millard, André. 2012. *Beatlemania: Technology, Business and Teen Culture in Cold War America*. Baltimore, MD: Johns Hopkins University Press.

Mitchell, W. J. T. 1987. *Iconology*. Chicago: University of Chicago Press.

Mitchell, W. J. T. 2005. *What Do Pictures Want? The Lives and Loves of Images*. Chicago: University of Chicago Press.

Mithen, Steven J. 2006. *The Singing Neanderthals: The Origin of Music, Language, Mind and Body*. London: Phoenix.

Montero, Barbara. 2006. 'Proprioception as an Aesthetic Sense'. *The Journal of Aesthetics and Art Criticism*, 64 (2): 231–242.

Montgomery, Paul. 1966. 'Beatles Bring Shea to a Wild Pitch of Hysteria'. *New York Times*, 24 August, 40.

Moodie, Clemmie. 2013. 'Coldplay Play Millions as They Splash Out on Freebies for Fans at Their Gigs'. *The Mirror*, 14 December. Available at: http://www.

mirror.co.uk/3am/celebrity-news/coldplay-millions-wristbands-perks-fans-2924664 (accessed March 2015).

Moreton, Cole. 2010. 'Backstage with Roger Waters as He Prepares for The Wall Spectacular $60 Million Live Show'. *Daily Mail*, 7 November. Available at: http://www.dailymail.co.uk/home/moslive/article-1327045/Roger-Waters-Backstage-prepares-The-Wall-live-show.html?ito=feeds-newsxml (accessed March 2015).

Morrissey. 2013. *Autobiography*. London: Penguin.

Mueller, Charles. 2014. 'Were British Subcultures the Beginning of Multitude?' In *Countercultures and Popular Music*, edited by Sheila Whiteley and Jedediah Sklower, 65–78. Surrey: Ashgate.

Nancy, Jean-Luc. 2000. *Being Singular Plural*. Translated by Robert Richardson and Anne O'Byrne. Stanford: Stanford University Press.

Naylor, Tony. 2008. 'Has Crowd Interaction Gone Too Far?' *The Guardian*, 14 July. Available at: http://www.theguardian.com/music/musicblog/2008/jul/14/crowdedoutcanyoukeepupwi (accessed August 2014).

Nazim, Sarah. 2012. 'The T-Mobile Camera Phone Chart Looks at the Increased Usage of Cellphones'. *Trendhunter*, 20 August. Available at: http://www.trend-hunter.com/trends/tmobile-camera-phone-chart (accessed December 2014).

Negri, Antonio. 2013. *The Winter Is Over: Writings on Transformation Denied, 1989–1995*. Edited by Giuseppe Caccia, translated by Isabella Bertoletti, James Cascaito and Andrea Casson. Los Angeles: Semiotext(e).

Negus, Keith. 2007. 'Living, Breathing Songs: Singing along with Bob Dylan'. *Oral Tradition*, 22 (1): 71–83.

Neill, Andy and Matt Kent. 2007. *Anyway, Anyhow, Anywhere: The Complete Chronicle of The Who, 1958–1978*. London: Virgin Books.

Nolan, David. 2006. *I Swear I Was There: The Gig That Changed the World*. London: Independent Music Press.

Northcutt, William. 2006. 'The Spectacle of Alienation: Death, Loss and the Crowd in *Sgt. Pepper's Lonely Hearts Club Band*'. In *Reading The Beatles: Cultural Studies, Literary Criticism and the Fab Four*, edited by Kenneth Womack and Todd F. Davis, 1290146. Albany: State University of New York Press.

O'Brien, Lucy. 2012 [2002]. *She Bop: The Definitive History of Women in Popular Music*. London: Jawbone.

O'Grady, Alice. 2013. 'Interrupting Flow: Researching Play, Performance and Immersion in Festival Scenes'. *Dancecult: Journal of Electronic Dance Music Culture*, 5 (1): 18–38. Available at: https://dj.dancecult.net/index.php/dance-cult/article/view/353 (accessed September 2014).

ONS (Office for National Statistics). 2013. 'Population Estimates for UK, England and Wales, Scotland and Northern Ireland, Mid-2011 and Mid-2012'. Available at: http://www.ons.gov.uk/ons/rel/pop-estimate/population-esti-mates-for-uk–england-and-wales–scotland-and-northern-ireland/mid-2011-and-mid-2012/index.html (accessed March 2015).

Pelly, Jenn. 2013. 'Unsound Festival Bans Photography, Filming on Cameras, Phones'. *Pitchfork*, 29 August. Available at: http://pitchfork.com/news/52093-unsound-festival-bans-photography-filming-on-cameras-phones/ (accessed December 2014).

Pfaller, Robert. 2014. *On the Pleasure Principle in Culture: Illusions without Owners*. London and New York: Verso.

Pine, Joseph and James H. Gilmore. 1999. *The Experience Economy*. Boston, MA: Harvard Business School Press.

Pleasants, Henry. 1974. *The Great American Popular Singers*. London: Victor Gollancz.

Pollard, Alexandra. 2015. 'The Boss of Reading and Leeds Festivals Say Women Are Not Marginalised. So Why Are So Few on His Bill?' *The Guardian*, 25 February. Available at: http://www.theguardian.com/music/musicblog/2015/feb/25/reading-leeds-festivals-why-so-few-women-on-bill (accessed April 2015).

Pollstar. 2013. *Year End Worldwide Ticket Sales Top 200 Arena Venues*. Available at: http://sprint_center.s3.amazonaws.com/doc/2013YearEndWorld wideTicketSalesTop200ArenaVenues.pdf (accessed January 2015).

Potter, John and Neil Sorrell. 2012. *A History of Singing*. Cambridge: Cambridge University Press.

Pratt, Tim. 2010. '5 Questions with Richie Hawtin, a.k.a. Plastikman, Legendary Techno Artist'. *Detroit Free Press*, 26 May. Available at: http://archive.freep.com/article/20100527/ENT04/5270316/5-questions-Richie-Hawtin-k-Plastikman-legendary-techno-artist (accessed April 2015).

Prendergast, Monica. 2010. 'Theatre Audience Education or How to See a Play: Toward a Curriculum Theory for Spectatorship in the Performing Arts'. *Youth Theatre Journal*, 18 (1): 45–54.

Pryke, D. W. 2005. *The Legacy of John Lennon in the Words of the Fans Who Love Him*. Newcastle: Exposure Publishing.

Pyhtilä, Marko. 2005. *Kansainväliset situationistit – spektaakkelin kritiikki*. Helsinki: Like.

Raphael, Amy. 1996. *Never Mind the Bollocks: Women Rewrite Rock*. London: Virago.

Reising, Russell. 2005. 'On the Waxing and Waning: A Brief History of *Dark Side of the Moon*'. In *'Speak to Me': The Legacy of Pink Floyd's The Dark Side of the Moon*, edited by Russell Reising, 15–26. Burlington, VT: Ashgate.

Richards, Chris. 2010. 'Give Peace a Dance'. *The Washington Post*, 13 December. Available at: http://www.washingtonpost.com/wp-dyn/content/article/2010/12/12/AR2010121203764.html (accessed March 2015).

Richards, Keith and James Fox. 2010. *Life*. London: Weidenfield & Nicholson.

Richardson, John and Claudia Gorbman. 2013. 'Introduction'. In *The Oxford Handbook of New Audiovisual Aesthetics*, edited by John Richardson, Claudia Corbman and Carol Vernallis, 3–35. Oxford: Oxford University Press.

Richardson, Terry. 2012 [2004]. *Terryworld*. Köln: Taschen.

Rolling Stone. 2014. 'Jack White's Private World: Inside Rolling Stone's New Issue'. Rolling Stone, 21 May. Available at: http://www.rollingstone.com/music/news/jack-whites-private-world-inside-rolling-stones-new-issue-20140521 (accessed March 2015).

Rose, Phil. 1998. *Which One's Pink? An Analysis of the Concept Albums by Roger Waters & Pink Floyd*. Burlington, Ontario: Collector's Guide Publishing.

Rosen, Jody. 2013. 'Her Highness'. *The New Yorker*, 20 February. Available at: http://www.newyorker.com/culture/culture-desk/her-highness (accessed March 2015).

Rowe, David and Deborah Stephenson. 2006. 'Sydney 2000: Sociality and Spatiality in Global Media Events'. In *National Identity and Global Sporting Events: Culture, Politics, and Spectacle in the Olympics and the Football World Cup*, edited by Alan Tomlinson and Christopher Young, 197–214. Albany: State University of New York Press.

Rowley, Kay. 1991. *Pop World Concerts*. Wayland: Hove.

Rubenstein, Raeanne. 2006. 'Awesome: I . . . Interviewed the Beastie Boys'. *Dish Magazine*. Available at: http://dishmag.com/issue54/music/1765/awesome-i-interviewed-the-beastie-boys-/ (accessed April 2015).

Ryfe, D. M. 1999. 'Franklin Roosevelt and the Fireside Chats'. *Journal of Communication*, 49 (4): 80–103.

Rys, Richard. 2009. 'The Full Spectrum: An Oral History'. *Philadelphia*, 24 June. Available at: http://www.phillymag.com/articles/the-full-spectrum/?all=1 (accessed November 2014).

Salley, Keith. 2011. 'On the Interaction of Alliteration with Rhythm and Metre in Popular Music'. In *Popular Music*, 30 (3): 409–432.

Sandford, Jeremy and Ron Reid. 1974. *Tomorrow's People*. London: Jerome Publishing.

Sanghani, Radhika. 2014. 'Teenage Girls: "Kissing Our Female Friends? It's Just a Rite of Passage"'. *The Daily Telegraph*, 29 October. Available at: http://www.telegraph.co.uk/women/womens-life/11192904/Keira-Knightly-is-right-say-teenage-girls-Kissing-our-female-friends-is-just-a-rite-of-passage.html (accessed December 2014).

Schaffner, Nicholas. 1992. *Saucerful of Secrets: The Pink Floyd Odyssey*. London: Delta.

Schonberg, Harold. 1965. 'What Attracts More People that the Beatles? Beethoven!' *New York Times*, 22 August, X11.

Schumach, Murray. 1965a. 'Fans Put on Show to Rival Beatles'. *New York Times*, 15 August, 82.

Schumach, Murray. 1965b. 'Shreiks of 55,000 Accompany Beatles'. *New York Times*, 16 August, 29 and 49.

Schumach, Murray. 1965c. 'Teen-Agers (Mostly Female) and Police Greet Beatles'. *New York Times*, 14 August, 11.

Schwartz, Margaret. 2011. 'The Horror of Something to See: Celebrity "Vaginas" as Prostheses'. In *In The Limelight and Under the Microscope: Forms and Functions of Female Celebrity*, edited by Su Holmes and Diane Negra, 224–241. London: Continuum.

Schwensen, Dave. 2014. *The Beatles at Shea Stadium*. Cleveland, OH: North Shore Publishing.

Sedgwick, Nick. 2000a. 'David Gilmour'. In *Is There Anybody Out There? The Wall Live Pink Floyd 1980–81*. CD booklet one, 7–8. European Union: EMI Records.

Sedgwick, Nick. 2000b. 'Roger Waters'. In *Is There Anybody Out There? The Wall Live Pink Floyd 1980–81*. CD booklet one. 5–6. European Union: EMI Records.

Shelton, Robert. 1965. 'The Beatles Will Make the Scene Here Again, but the Scene Has Changed'. *New York Times*, 11 August, 40.

Shelton, Robert. 1966. 'Rolling Stones Gather Avid Fans'. *New York Times*, 4 July, 11.

Sheridan, Simon. 2012. *The Complete Kylie*. London: Titan Books.

Sieczkowski, Cavan. 2014. 'Feminist Activist Says Beyonce Is Partly "Anti-Feminist" and "Terrorist".' *The Huffington Post*, 5 September. Available at: http://www.huffingtonpost.com/2014/05/09/beyonce-anti-feminist_n_5295891.html (accessed March 2015).

Small, Christopher. 1998. *Musicking: The Meanings of Performing and Listening*. Hanover and London: University Press of New England.

Smalley, Denis. 2007. 'Space-Form and the Acousmatic Image'. *Organised Sound*, 12: 35–58.

Smith, Peter. 2013. 'Ladies and Gentlemen: The Rolling Stones in Concert'. In *The Rolling Stones: Sociological Perspectives*, edited by Helmut Staubmann, 201–222. Lexington, MA: Lexington Books.

Southall, Brian. 2012. *Bob Dylan Treasures*. London: Carlton Books.

Spin Staff. 2013. 'Yeah Yeah Yeahs Post Amazing 'No Cameras' Sign Outside Show'. *Spin*, 8 April. Available at: http://www.spin.com/articles/yeah-yeah-yeahs-karen-o-sign-no-cameras-smart-device-live-shows/ (accessed December 2014).

Stark, Steven D. 2005. *Meet The Beatles*. New York: HarperCollins.

Steinberg, Leo. 1996 [1983]. *The Sexuality of Christ in Renaissance Art and in Modern Oblivion*. London: University of Chicago Press.

Sterne, Jonathan. 2003. *The Audible Past: Cultural Origins of Sound Reproduction*. Durham, NC: Duke University Press.

Sterne, Jonathan. 2006. 'The Death and Life of Digital Audio'. *Interdisciplinary Science Reviews*, 31 (4): 338–348.

Sullivan, William C., Frances E. Kuo and Stephen DePooter. 2004. 'The Fruit of Urban Nature: Vital Neighborhood Spaces'. *Environment & Behavior*, 36 (5): 678–700.

Svenonius, Ian F. 2012. *Supernatural Strategies for Making a Rock 'n' Roll Group*. New York: Akashic Books.

Swash, Rosie. 2013. 'Why Is Beyoncé Calling Herself Mrs Carter?' *The Guardian*, 5 February. Available at: http://www.theguardian.com/lifeandstyle/the-womens-blog-with-jane-martinson/2013/feb/05/beyonce-calling-herself-mrs-carter (accessed April 2015).

Tagg, Philip. 2013. *Music's Meanings: A Modern Musicology for Non-Musos*. New York and Huddersfield: Mass Media Music Scholars' Press.

Tarrant, Patrick. 2009. 'Camera Movies: Awesome, I Fuckin' Shot Them!' *Journal of Media Practice*, 10: 149–165.

Taylor, P. 2010. 'The Arena Put Manchester on Top of the World'. *Manchester Evening News*, 13 July. Formerly available at: http://menmedia.co.uk/manchestereveningnews/life_and_style/s/1301523_the_arena_put_manchester_on_top_of_the_world (accessed January 2013, since removed).

Théberge, Paul. 2001. 'Plugged In'. In *The Cambridge Companion to Pop and Rock*, edited by Simon Frith, Will Straw and John Street. Cambridge: Cambridge University Press.

Thompson, Dave. 2002. *To Major Tom: The Bowie Letters*. London: Sanctuary.

Thompson, Emily Ann. 2002. *The Soundscape of Modernity: Architectural Acoustics and the Culture of Listening in America, 1900–1933*. Cambridge, MA: MIT Press.

Till, Rupert. 2010. *Pop Cults: Religion and Popular Music*. New York: Continuum.

Tiqqun. 2012 [1999]. *Preliminary Materials For a Theory of the Young-Girl*. Los Angeles: MIT/Semiotext(e).

Torres, Louis. 2010. 'What Makes Art Art? Does Denis Dutton Know?' *Aristos*, April. Available at: http://www.aristos.org/aris-10/dutton.htm (accessed April 2015).

Total Production International. 2013. 'Nobel Peace Prize Concert'. February. Available at: http://www.tpimagazine.com/production-profiles/1826710/nobel_peace_prize_concert.html (accessed January 2015).

Townshend, Pete. 2012. *Who I Am*. London: Harper Collins.

Trebay, Guy. 2004. 'Fashion Diary; What Fashion Owes to XXX'. *New York Times*, 12 September. Available via: http://query.nytimes.com/gst/fullpage.html?res=9C01EED81530F931A2575AC0A9629C8B63 (accessed November 2014).

Trendell, Andrew. 2013. 'Norwegians Furious at Morrissey Playing Nobel Peace Prize'. *Gigwise*, 29 November. Available at: http://www.gigwise.com/news/86552/norwegians-furious-at-morrissey-playing-nobel-peace-prize (accessed January 2015).

Turino, Thomas. 2000. *Nationalists, Cosmopolitans, and Popular Music in Zimbabwe*. Chicago: University of Chicago Press.

Turino, Thomas. 2008. *Music as Social Life: The Politics of Participation*. Chicago: University of Chicago Press.

U2, 2006. *U2 by U2*. London: Harpercollins.

Ulrich, Roger S. 1984. 'View through a Window May Influence Recovery from Surgery'. *Science*, 224: 420–421.

Van den Dungen, Peter. 2001. 'What Makes the Nobel Peace Prize Unique?' *Peace & Change*, 26 (4): 510–524.

Van Leeuwen, Theo. 1999. *Speech, Music, Sound*. Hampshire: Macmillan.

Vincent, Alice. 2014. 'Where Are All the Women Headlining Music Festivals?' *The Telegraph*, 8 August. Available at: http://www.telegraph.co.uk/culture/music/music-festivals/11016441/Where-are-all-the-women-headlining-music-festivals.html (accessed April 2015).

Vogel, Michael D. 2012. 'Led Zeppelin – Celebration Day'. *Revved Magazine*, 16 October. Available at: http://revvedmagazine.com/category/music-reviews/concerts-movies-theatre/led-zeppelin-concerts-movies-theatre/ (accessed November 2014).

Wainwright, Oliver. 2013. 'Leeds Arena: Giant Mint Helmet or Technicolour Dreamboat?' *The Guardian*, 5 April 2013. Available at: http://www.theguardian.com/artanddesign/architecture-design-blog/2013/apr/25/leeds-arena-architecture-bling-budget (accessed March 2015).

Waksman, Steve. 2007. 'Grand Funk Live! Staging Rock in the Age of the Arena'. In *Listen Again: A Momentary History of Pop Music*, edited by Eric Weisbard, 157–171. Durham, NC: Duke University Press.

Walters, Paul and Raj Razaq. 2004. 'Sponsorship, Funding and Strategic Function: Carling Festival and V Festival'. In *Festival and Events Management: An International Arts and Culture Perspective*, edited by Ian

Yeoman, Martin Robertson, Jane Ali-Knight, Siobhan Drummond and Una McMahon-Beattie, 358–371. Oxford: Elsevier.

Watson, Nessim. 1997. 'Why We Argue about Virtual Community: A Case of the Phish.Net Fan Community'. In *Virtual Culture: Identity and Communication in Cybersociety*, edited by Steven G. Jones, 102–132. London: Sage.

Watts, Lewis and Eric C. Porter. 2013. *New Orleans Suite: Music and Culture in Transition*. Berkeley: University of California Press.

Watts, Michael. 2000. 'Bob Dylan'. In *Rock 'n' Roll People: The Pioneers of Pop in their Own Words*, edited by David Sandison, 8–23. London: Octopus.

Webster, Emma. 2011. 'Promoting Live Music in Britain: A Behind-the-Scenes Ethnography'. Unpublished PhD thesis, University of Glasgow.

Weidman, Amanda. J. 2006. *Singing the Classical, Voicing the Modern: The Postcolonial Politics of Music in South India*. Durham and London: Duke University Press.

White, Nicholas. 2013. 'Concert Etiquette – Has Cell Phone Use Gone Too Far?' *Rukkus.com*, 18 September. Available at: http://rukkus.com/blog/concert-etiquette/ (accessed March 2015).

Whiteley, Sheila. 2005. *Too Much Too Young: Popular Music, Age and Gender*. London: Routledge.

Whiteley, Sheila. 2000. *Women and Popular Music: Sexuality, Identity and Subjectivity*. London: Routledge.

Wiener, Jon. 1990. *Come Together: John Lennon in His Time*. Champaign, IL: University of Illinois.

Wiener, Jon. 1999. *Gimme Some Truth*. Berkeley: University of California Press.

Williamson, Judith. 1983. 'Images of "Woman" – the Photographs of Cindy Sherman'. *Screen*, 24 (6) (November-December): 102–116.

Winn, John. 2009. *That Magic Feeling: The Beatles' Recorded Legacy – Volume 2, 1966–70*. New York: Random House.

Wollman, Elizabeth L. 2006. *The Theater Will Rock: A History of the Rock Musical, from Hair to Hedwig*. Michigan: University of Michigan Press.

Woodward, Kath. 2000. 'Questions of Identity'. In *Questioning Identity: Gender, Class, Nation*, edited by Kath Woodward, 5–42. London: The Open University.

Womack, Kenneth. 2009. *The Cambridge Companion to the Beatles*. Cambridge: Cambridge University Press.

Wurtzler, Steve. 1992. 'She Sang Live, but the Microphone was Turned Off: The Live, the Recorded, and the Subject of Representation'. In *Sound Theory Sound Practice*, edited by Rick Altman. New York and London: Routledge.

Zepf Siegfried. 2008. 'Pop Concerts – a Symbol and an Instrumentalization of Inexpressible Experiences?' *Psychoanalysis, Culture & Society* 13: 279–298.

Žižek, Slavoj. 2009. *The Parallax View*. London and Cambridge, MA: MIT Press.

Žižek, Slavoj. 1989. *The Sublime Object of Ideology*. London and New York: Verso.

Zweig, Ferdynand. 1961. *The Worker in an Affluent Society: Family Life and Industry*. London: Heinemann.

INDEX